Lecture Notes in Economics and Mathematical Systems

516

Springer
Berlin
Heidelberg
New York
Barcelona
Hong Kong
London
Mailand
Paris
Tokyo

Bernd Schmid

Pricing Credit Linked Financial Instruments

Theory and Empirical Evidence

Springer

Author

Bernd Schmid
Head of Credit Analytics
Risklab Germany
Arabellastrasse 4
81925 Munich, Germany

Cataloging-in-Publication data applied for

Die Deutsche Bibliothek - CIP-Einheitsaufnahme

Schmid, Bernd:
Pricing credit linked financial instruments : theory and empirical evidence / Bernd Schmid. - Berlin ; Heidelberg ; New York ; Barcelona ; Hong Kong ; London ; Mailand ; Paris ; Tokyo : Springer, 2002
(Lecture notes in economics and mathematical systems ; Vol. 516)
ISBN 3-540-43195-0

ISSN 0075-8450
ISBN 3-540-43195-0 Springer-Verlag Berlin Heidelberg New York

Springer-Verlag Berlin Heidelberg New York
a member of BertelsmannSpringer Science+Business Media GmbH

http://www.springer.de

Typesetting: Camera ready by author
Cover design: Erich Kirchner, Heidelberg

Printed on acid-free paper SPIN: 10866084 55/3142/du 5 4 3 2 1 0

Was man zu verstehen gelernt hat,

fürchtet man nicht mehr.

- Marie Curie -

Acknowledgements

This monograph is based on my PhD thesis (Schmid 2001a), which I wrote under the supervision of Prof. Dr. Wolfgang Schmid at the Europe University Viadrina, Frankfurt (Oder). It is a great pleasure to thank him for his support throughout my PhD studies.

I am grateful to Prof. Dr. Rudi Zagst who created the ideal environment for productive research at RiskLab GmbH, Munich, and provided always valuable feedback.

Further thanks go to Dr. Rüdiger Kiesel for the invitation to London University where I could present parts of my research in seminars at Birkbeck College and Imperial College.

I would also like to thank the participants at the various conferences for their questions, comments and suggestions.

I express my thanks to my colleagues Anna Kalemanova, Reinhold Hafner, and Jan Kehrbaum for many discussions on credit risk subjects.

Last but not least I want to thank Uli Göser for endless patience, encouragement, and support, my family and especially my sister Wendy for being there at all times.

Financial support from HVB Asset Management GmbH, Munich, is gratefully acknowledged.

Stuttgart, November 2001 *Bernd Schmid*

Contents

1. Introduction

"Securities yielding high interest are like thin twigs, very weak from a capital-safety point of view if taken singly, but most surprisingly strong if taken as a bundle, and tied together with the largest possible number of differing external influences."
- British Investment Registry & Stock Exchange, 1904 -

1.1 Motivation

Although lending money is one of the oldest banking activities at all, credit evaluation and pricing is still not fully understood. There are many difficulties in assessing the impact of credit risk on prices in the bond and loan market. Two key problems are the data limitations and the model validation.

In general, credit risk is the risk of reductions in market value due to changes in the credit quality of a debtor such as an issuer of a corporate bond. It can be measured as the component of a debt instrument's yield that reflects the expected value of the risk of a possible default or downgrade. This so called credit risk premium is usually expressed in basis points. More precisely, according to the Dictionary of Financial Risk Management (Gastineau 1996), credit risk is

1. Exposure to loss as a result of default on a swap debt, or other counterparty instrument.
2. Exposure to loss as a result of a decline in market value stemming from a credit downgrade of an issuer or counterparty. Such credit risk may be reduced by credit screening before a transaction is effected or by instrument provisions that attempt to offset the effect of a default or require increased payments in the event of a credit downgrade.
3. A component of return variability resulting from the possibility of an event of default.
4. A change in the market's perception of the probability of an event of default, which affected the spread between two rates or reference indexes.

Although credit risk and default risk are quite often used interchangeably, in a more rigorous view, default risk is understood to be the risk that a debtor will be unable or unwilling to make timely payments of interest or principal. These definitions force several questions on us:

- What does it make important to consider these types of risk ?
- Why have credit risk modelling and credit risk management issues received renewed attention only recently ?

The last few years have seen dramatic developments in the credit markets with the declining of the traditional loan markets and the development of new markets. Corporate defaults have increased tremendously but haven't stopped investors from investing in risky sectors such as high-yield markets. In addition, banks have come up with new products to manage credit risks such as credit derivatives and asset backed securities. At the same time regulators have started changing their view on the credit markets and discussing their capital rules. More than a little this discussion has been driven by academics and practitioners who both have been developing new models for credit risk measurement and management that satisfy regulatory rules on the one hand and the needs for internal credit risk models on the other hand.

Regulatory Issues. There are growing regulatory pressures on the credit markets. Regulators wish to ensure that firms have enough capital to cover the risks that they run, so that, if they fail, there are sufficient funds to meet creditors' claims. Therefore, regulators set up capital rules which define the amount of capital a firm must have in order to enter a given position (the so called minimum capital requirements which are calculated based on a standardized approach). Roughly speaking, the amount necessary to put up against a possible loss depends on how risky the entered position is. As the valuation of credit risk still poses significant problems, the question raises, when, if at all, should regulators recognize banks' internal models for credit risk ? More than a decade has passed since the Basel Committee on Banking Supervision introduced its 1988 Capital Accord[1]. The business of banking, risk management practices, supervisory approaches, and financial markets each have undergone significant transformation since then. As a result, in June 1999 the Committee released a proposal to replace the 1988 Accord with a more risk-sensitive framework. The Committee presented an even more concrete proposal[2] in February 2001 and expects the final version of the new Accord to be published by the end of 2001. This version is supposed to be implemented in 2005. A range of risk-sensitive options for addressing credit risk is contained in the new Accord. Depending on the specific bank's

[1] For details on the 1988 Capital Accord see the webpage of the Bank for International Settlements (www.bis.org) and Ong (1999), chapter 1.

[2] For details on the new Capital Accord see the following publications of the Bank for International Settlements: *A New Capital Adequacy Framework* (1999), *Update on Work on a New Capital Adequacy Framework* (1999), *Best Practices for Credit Risk Disclosure* (2000), *Overview of the New Basel Capital Accord* (2001), *The New Basel Capital Accord* (2001), *The Standardised Approach to Credit Risk* (2001), *The Internal Ratings-Based Approach* (2001).

supervisory standards, it is allowed to choose out of at least three different approaches to credit risk measurement: The "standardized approach", where exposures to various types of counterparties will be assigned risk weights based on assessments by external credit assessment institutions. The "foundation internal ratings-based approach", where banks, meeting robust supervisory standards, will use their own assessments of default probabilities associated with their obligors. Finally an "advanced internal ratings-based approach", where banks, meeting more rigorous supervisory standards, will be allowed to estimate several risk factors internally. So banks should start improving their risk management capabilities today to be prepared for 2005 when they will be allowed to use the more risk-sensitive methodologies. At the same time academics must continuously develop further and better methods for estimating credit risk factors such as default probabilities.

Internal Credit Risk Models. Almost every day, new analytic tools to measure and manage credit risk are created. The most famous ones are KMV's[3] Portfolio Manager™ (see, e.g., Kealhofer (1998)), the Risk Metrics Group's CreditMetrics® and CreditManager™ (see, e.g., *CreditMetrics - Technical Document* (1997)), Credit Suisse Financial Products' CreditRisk+ (see, e.g., *CreditRisk+ A Credit Risk Management Framework* (1997)), and McKinsey & Company's Credit Portfolio View (see, e.g., Wilson (1997a), Wilson (1997b), Wilson (1997c), Wilson (1997d)). These models allow the user to measure and quantify credit risk at both, the portfolio and contributory level. KMV follows Merton's insight (see, e.g., Merton (1974)) and considers equity to be a call option on the value of a company's business, following the logic that a company defaults when its business value drops below its obligations. A borrower's default probability (i.e. the probability that a specific given credit's rating will change to default until the end of a specified time period) then depends on the amount by which assets exceed liabilities, and the volatility of these assets. CreditMetrics® is a Merton-based model, too. It seeks to assess the returns on a portfolio of assets by analyzing the probabilistic behavior of the individual assets, coupled with their mutual correlations. It does this by using a matrix of transition probabilities (i.e. the probabilities that a specific given credit's rating will change to another specific rating until the end of a specified time period), calculating the expected change in market value for each possible rating's transition including default, and combining these individual value distributions via the correlations between the credits (as approximations of the correlations between relevant equities), to generate a loss distribution for the portfolio as a whole. CreditMetrics® has its roots in portfolio theory and is an attempt to mark credit to market. The model looks to the far more liquid bond market and the largely bond-driven credit derivatives market, where extensive data is available on ratings and price movements and instruments are actively traded. CreditRisk+ is based

[3] San Francisco based software company specialized in developing credit risk management software.

on insurance industry models of event risk. It doesn't make any estimates of how defaults are correlated. It rather considers the average default rates associated with each notch of a credit rating scheme (either a rating agency scheme or an internal score) and the volatilities of those rates. By doing so, it constructs a continuous, rather than a discrete, distribution of default risk probabilities. When mixed with the exposure profile of the instruments under consideration, it yields a loss distribution and associated risk capital estimates. CreditRisk+ is a modified version of the methodology the Credit Suisse Group has used to set loan loss provisions since December 1996. It has therefore evolved as a way to assess risk capital requirements in a data-poor environment where most assets are held to maturity and the only credit event that really counts is whether the lender gets repaid at maturity. In contrast to all other models it avoids the need for Monte Carlo simulation and therefore is much faster. The McKinsey model differs from the others in two additional important respects: First, it focuses more on the impact of macroeconomic variables on credit portfolios than other portfolio models do. Therefore it explicitly links credit default and credit migration behavior to the economic drivers. Second, the model is designed to be applied to all customer segments and product types, including liquid loans and bonds, illiquid middle market and small business portfolios as well as retail portfolios such as mortgages or credit cards. Munich based RiskLab GmbH has created a new credit risk portfolio model only recently, called Credit View. It combines the strength of the three other models and is especially designed for loan portfolios.

To summarize, CreditMetrics® is a bottom-up model as each borrower's default is modeled individually with a microeconomic causal model of default. CreditRisk+ is a top-down model of sub-portfolio default rates, making no assumptions with regard to causality. Credit Portfolio View is a bottom-up model based on a macroeconomic causal model of sub-portfolio default rates. For a detailed overview and a comparison of these models see, e.g., Schmid (1997), Schmid (1998a), and Schmid (1998c). In addition, Gordy (1998) shows that, despite differences on the surface, CreditMetrics® and CreditRisk+ have similar underlying mathematical structures. Koyluoglu & Hickman (1998) examine the four credit risk portfolio models by placing them within a single general framework and demonstrating that they are only little different in theory and results, provided that the input parameters are somehow harmonized. Crouhy & Mark (1998) compare the models for a benchmark portfolio. It appears that the Credit Value at Risk numbers according to the various models fall in a narrow range, with a ratio of 1.5 between the highest and the lowest values. Keenan & Sobehart (2000) discuss how to validate credit risk models based on robust and easy to implement model performance measures. These measures analyze the cumulative accuracy to predict defaults and the level of uncertainty in the risk scores produced by the tested models. Lopez & Saidenberg (1998) use a panel data approach to evaluate credit risk models based on cross-sectional simulation.

For calculating the minimum capital requirements based on the new Capital Accord and for using internal credit risk models, financial institutions need mathematical models that are capable of describing the underlying credit risk factors through time, pricing financial instruments with regard to credit risk, and explaining how these instruments behave in a portfolio context.

1.2 Objectives, Structure, and Summary

During the last years we saw many theoretical developments in the field of credit risk research. Not surprisingly, most of this research concentrated on the pricing of corporate and sovereign defaultable bonds as the basic building blocks of credit risk pricing. But many of these models failed in describing real world phenomena such as credit spreads realistically. This work presents a new hybrid term structure model which can be used for estimating default probabilities, pricing defaultable bonds and other securities subject to default risk. We show that it combines many of the strengths of previous models and avoids many of their weaknesses, and, most important, that it is capable of explaining market prices such as corporate or sovereign bond prices realistically. Our model can be used as a new and more sophisticated basis for credit risk portfolio models that satisfy the rules of regulators and the internal needs of financial institutions.

In order to build a model for credit risk pricing it is essential to identify the credit risk components and the factors that determine credit risk. Therefore, we show in section 2 that default risk can mainly be characterized by default probabilities, i.e. the probabilities that an obligor defaults on its obligations, and recovery rates, i.e. the proportion of value still delivered in case of a default. The literature on modelling default probabilities evolves around three main approaches. The historical method, mainly applied by rating agencies, determines default probabilities by counting defaults that actually happened in the past. The asset based method[4] relates default to the value of the underlying assets of a firm. All models in this framework are extensions of the work of Merton (1974), which has been the cornerstone of corporate debt pricing. Merton assumes that default occurs when the value of the firm's assets is less then the value of the debt at expiry. Extensions of this approach have been developed among others by Black & Cox (1976), Geske (1977), Ho & Singer (1982), Kim, Ramaswamy & Sundaresan (1992), Shimko, Tejima & Deventer (1993), Longstaff & Schwartz (1995b), Zhou (1997), and Vasicek (1997). The intensity based method (or sometimes called reduced-form model) relates default time to the stopping time of some exogenously specified hazard rate process. This approach has been applied among others by

[4] The asset based method is sometimes called firm value method, Merton-based method, or structural approach.

Artzner & Delbaen (1992), Madan & Unal (1994), Jarrow & Turnbull (1995), Jarrow, Lando & Turnbull (1997), Duffie & Singleton (1997), Lando (1998), and Schönbucher (2000). In sections 2.3.2, 2.3.3, and 2.3.4 we review the three approaches, add some new interpretations, and summarize their advantages and disadvantages. Section 2.3.5 shows that one shouldn't only rely on theoretical models but always should consider the view and opinion of experts as well. In section 2.4 we give an overview of possible ways to model recovery rates.

Asset based and intensity based methods can't only be applied for modelling default probabilities but also for pricing defaultable debt. A recent trend tries to combine both approaches to more powerful models, that are as flexible as intensity based models and explain the causality of default as well as asset based models. Examples are the models of Madan & Unal (1998) who assume that the stochastic hazard rate is a linear function of the default-free short rate and the logarithm of the value of the firm's assets, and Jarrow & Turnbull (1998) who choose the stochastic hazard rate to be a linear function of some index and the default-free short rate. Both models have the problem that their hazard rate processes can admit negative values with positive probability. Cathcart & El-Jahel (1998) use the asset based framework, but assume that default is triggered when a signalling process hits some threshold. Duffie & Lando (1997) model a default hazard rate that is based on an unobservable firm value process. Hence, they cover the problem of the uncertainty of the current level of the assets of the firm. The three-factor defaultable term structure model which we develop in section 3.2 is a completely new hybrid model. We directly model the short rate credit spread and assume that it depends on some uncertainty index, which describes the uncertainty of the obligor. The larger the value of the uncertainty index the worse the quality of the debtor is. In addition, we assume that the non-defaultable short rate process follows a mean reverting Hull-White process or a mean-reverting square root process with time-dependent mean reversion level. As such our model is an extension of the non-defaultable bond pricing models of Hull & White (1990) and Cox, Ingersoll & Ross (1985) to defaultable bond pricing. The non-defaultable short rate, the short rate credit spread and the uncertainty index are defined by a three-dimensional stochastic differential equation (SDE). We show that this SDE admits a unique weak solution by applying and generalizing results of Ikeda & Watanabe (1989a). This three-dimensional approach where we consider market and credit risk at the same time, serves as a basis for the application of advanced methods for credit risk management. In the past, financial institutions have disaggregated the various risks (see figure 1.1) generated by their businesses and treated each one separately. However, for reasons like the linkages between the markets, this approach need to be replaced by an integrated risk management which allows comparison of risk levels across business and product units. In particular, as credit risk is one of the key risks, financial institutions need to be able to

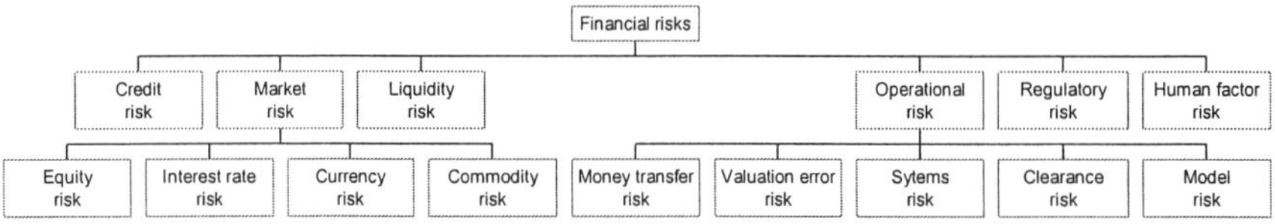

Fig. 1.1. Key risks of financial institutions.

provide an accurate and consistent measurement of credit risk. Our hybrid model can serve as a basis for a stochastic approach to an integrated market and credit risk management.

By using no-arbitrage arguments we apply the model to the pricing of various securities subject to default risk: The counterparty to a contract may not be able or willing to make timely interest rate payments or repay its debt at maturity. This increases the risk of the investor which must be compensated by reducing the price of the security contract. Our model determines a fair value for such a defaultable security and compares its price to the value of an otherwise identical non-defaultable security. In section 3.3 we determine closed form pricing formulas for defaultable zero coupon bonds and various other types of fixed and floating rate debt such as defaultable floating rate notes and defaultable interest rate swaps. In addition, we show that the theoretical credit spreads generated by our model are consistent with the empirical findings of Sarig & Warga (1989) and Jones, Mason & Rosenfeld (1984). Especially, we demonstrate that the term structure of credit spreads implied by our model can be upward sloping, downward sloping, hump shaped or flat. And in contrast to many other models we are even able to generate short term credit spreads that are clearly different from zero.

In section 3.4 we develop closed form solutions for the pricing of various credit derivatives by pricing them relative to observed bond prices within our three-factor model framework. Although there are a lot of articles that have been written on the pricing of defaultable bonds and derivatives with embedded credit risk, there are only a few articles on the direct pricing of credit derivatives. Das (1995) basically shows that in an asset based framework credit options are the expected forward values of put options on defaultable bonds with a credit level adjusted exercise price. Longstaff & Schwartz (1995a) develop a pricing formula for credit spread options in a setting where the logarithm of the credit spread and the non-defaultable short rate follow Vasicek processes. Das & Tufano (1996) apply their model, which is an extension to stochastic recovery rates of the model of Jarrow et al. (1997), to the pricing of credit-sensitive notes. Das (1997) summarizes the pricing of credit derivatives in various credit risk models (e.g., the models of Jarrow et al. (1997), and Das & Tufano (1996)). All models are presented in a simplified discrete fashion.

Duffie (1998a) uses simple no-arbitrage arguments to determine approximate prices for default swaps. Hull & White (2000) provide a methodology for valuing credit default swaps when the payoff is contingent on default by a single reference entity and there is no counterparty default risk. Schönbucher (2000) develops various pricing formulas for credit derivatives in the intensity based framework. Our work is different from all other articles in that we apply partial differential equation techniques to the pricing of credit derivatives.

In section 3.5 we construct a four dimensional lattice (for the dimensions time, non-defaultable short rate r, short rate credit spread s, and uncertainty index u) to be able to price defaultable contingent claims and credit derivatives that don't allow for closed form solutions, e.g., because of callability features or because they are American. In contrast to the trees proposed by Chen (1996), Amin (1995), or Boyle (1988) the branching as well as the probabilities don´t change with a changing drift, which makes the lattice more efficient, especially under risk management purposes. The probabilities for each node in the four dimensional lattice are simply given by the product of the one dimensional processes. We close this section by giving an explicit numerical example for the pricing of credit spread options.

In section 3.6 we close the gap between our theoretical model and its possible applications in practice by demonstrating various methods how to calibrate the model to observed data and how to estimate the model parameters. This is an important add-on to other research in the credit risk field which is often only restricted to developing new models without applying them to the real world. Actually, the ultimate success or failure in implementing pricing formulas is directly related to the ability to collect the necessary information for determining good model parameter values. Therefore, we suggest two different ways how meaningful values for the parameters of the three stochastic processes r, s, and u can be found. The first one is the method of least squared minimization. Basically, we compare market prices and theoretical prices at one specific point in time and calculate the implied parameters by minimizing the sum of the squared deviations of the market from the theoretical prices. The second one is the Kalman filter method that estimates parameter values by looking at time series of market values of bonds. By applying a method developed by Nelson & Siegel (1987) we estimate daily zero curves from a time series of daily German, Italian, and Greek Government bond prices. The application of Kalman filtering methods in the estimation of term structure models using time-series data has been analyzed (among others) by Chen & Scott (1995), Geyer & Pichler (1996) and Babbs & Nowman (1999). Up to our knowledge we are the first ones to apply this method to defaultable term structure models, especially to our model. Based on the parameter estimations we apply a lot of different in-sample and out-of-sample tests such as a model explanatory power test suggested by Titman & Torous (1989) and find that our model is able to explain observed market data such as

Greek and Italian credit spreads to German Government bonds very well. Especially, we can produce more encouraging results than empirical studies of other credit risk models (see, e.g., Düllmann & Windfuhr (2000) for an empirical investigation of intensity based methods).

Based on our three-factor defaultable term structure model, in section 3.7 we develop a framework for the optimal allocation of assets out of a universe of sovereign bonds with different time to maturity and quality of the issuer. Our methodology can also be applied to other asset classes like corporate bonds. We estimate the model parameters by applying Kalman filtering methods as described in section 3.6. Based on these estimates we apply Monte Carlo simulation techniques to simulate the prices for a given set of bonds for a future time horizon. For each future time step and for each given portfolio composition these scenarios yield distributions of future cash flows and portfolio values. We show how the portfolio composition can be optimized by maximizing the expected final value or return of the portfolio under given constraints like a minimum cash flow per period to cover the liabilities of a company and a maximum tolerated risk. To visualize our methodology we present a case study for a portfolio consisting of German, Italian, and Greek sovereign bonds.

To summarize, this work contributes to the efforts of academics and practitioners to explain credit markets, price default related instruments such as defaultable fixed and floating rate debt, credit derivatives, and other securities with embedded credit risk, and develop a profound credit risk management. Models are developed to value instruments whose prices are default dependent within a consistent framework, to detect relative value, to mark to market positions, to risk manage positions and to price new structures which are not (yet) traded. We describe the whole process, from the specification of the stochastic processes to the estimation of the parameters and calibration to market data.

Finally, a brief note with respect to some of the terminology. In this work, risky refers to credit risk and not to market risk. Riskless means free of credit risk. Default free is a synonym to riskless or risk free. Default and bankruptcy are used as synonyms.

2. Modelling Credit Risk

"Prediction is very difficult, especially of the future."
- Niels Bohr -

"Credit risk management is being transformed by the use of quantitative portfolio models. These models can depend on parameters that are difficult to quantify, and that change over time."
- Demchak (2000) -

2.1 Introduction

Usually investors must be willing to take risks for their investments. Therefore, they should be adequately compensated. But what is a fair premium for risk compensation ? To answer this question it is essential to determine the key sources of risk. As we are concerned with credit risk, this section is devoted to the identification of credit risk factors. We show the current practice of credit risk factor modelling and present these methodologies within a rigorous mathematical framework.

2.2 Definition and Elements of Credit Risk

Credit risk consists of two components, default risk and spread risk. Default risk is the risk that a debtor will be unable or unwilling to make timely payments of interest or principal, i.e. that a debtor defaults on its contractual payment obligations. The default time is defined as the date of announcement of failure to deliver. Spread risk is the risk of reductions in market value due to changes in the credit quality of a debtor. The event of default has two underlying risk components, one associated with the timing of the event ("arrival risk") and the other with its magnitude ("magnitude risk"). Hence, for modelling credit risk, we have to consider the following risk elements:

- Default probabilities: The probability that the debtor will default on its contractual obligations to repay its debt.

- Recovery rates: The proportion of value still delivered after the default has happened. The default magnitude is the proportion of value not delivered.
- Transition probabilities: The probability that the quality of a debtor will improve or deteriorate. The process of changing the creditworthiness is called credit migration.

2.2.1 Basic Mathematical Setup

For modelling purposes we fix a terminal time horizon $T^* \in \mathbb{R}$ and let $\left(\Omega, \mathcal{F}, (\mathcal{F}_t)_{0\leq t\leq T^*}, \mathbf{P}\right)$ be a filtered probability space[1] where $\mathbf{P}$ is some subjective probability measure. We assume that $\mathcal{F}_0$ is trivial, i.e. $\mathcal{F}_0 = \{\emptyset, \Omega\}$, that $\mathcal{F}_{T^*} = \mathcal{F}$ and that the filtration $\mathbf{F} = (\mathcal{F}_t)_{0\leq t\leq T^*}$ satisfies the usual conditions[2]. The filtration $\mathbf{F}$ represents the arrival of information over time. Recovery rates, transition and default probabilities are modelled in this fixed probability space.

Because there are some specific classes of stochastic processes[3] that play an essential part in the theory of credit risk modelling we give some technical definitions first:

Definition 2.2.1.

1. *A stochastic process M on a filtered probability space $\left(\Omega, \mathcal{F}, (\mathcal{F}_t)_{t\geq 0}, \mathbf{P}\right)$ is called a martingale with respect to a filtration $(\mathcal{F}_t)_{t\geq 0}$ and with respect to $\mathbf{P}$ if*
   - *M_t is $\mathcal{F}_t$−measurable for all $t \geq 0$,*
   - *$E^{\mathbf{P}}(|M_t|) < \infty$ for all $t \geq 0$,*
   - *$E^{\mathbf{P}}(M_s | \mathcal{F}_t) = M_t$ for all $s \geq t \geq 0$.*
2. *$\mathcal{M}$ is the class of all uniformly integrable martingales, i.e. of all martingales M such that the family of random variables $(M_t)_{t\geq 0}$ is uniformly integrable.*

---

[1] Jacod & Shiryaev (1987), p. 2: A stochastic basis or a filtered probability space is a probability space $(\Omega, \mathcal{F}, \mathbf{P})$ equipped with a filtration $\mathbf{F} = (\mathcal{F}_t)_{t\geq 0}$; here filtration means an increasing and right-continuous family of sub-σ-fields of $\mathcal{F}$.

[2] Jacod & Shiryaev (1987), p.2: The stochastic basis $\left(\Omega, \mathcal{F}, (\mathcal{F}_t)_{t\geq 0}, \mathbf{P}\right)$ is called complete, or equivalently is said to satisfy the usual conditions if the σ-field $\mathcal{F}$ is $\mathbf{P}$−complete and if every $\mathcal{F}_t$ contains all $\mathbf{P}$−null sets of $\mathcal{F}$. It is always possible to complete a given stochastic basis.

[3] Jacod & Shiryaev (1987), p. 3: A stochastic process (or, an E-valued process) is a family $X = \{X_t\}_{t\geq 0}$ of mappings from Ω into some set E endowed with a σ−algebra $\mathcal{E}$ defined on a probability space $(\Omega, \mathcal{F}, \mathbf{P})$. Unless otherwise stated, E will be $\mathbb{R}^d$ for some $d \in \mathbb{N}$. We shall say indifferently: the stochastic process X, or $\{X_t\}_{t\geq 0}$, or $\{X(t)\}_{t\geq 0}$.

3. *A local martingale is a process that belongs to the localized class* $\mathcal{M}_{loc}$ *constructed from* $\mathcal{M}$. *A process* M *belongs to the localized class* $\mathcal{M}_{loc}$ *if and only if there exists an increasing sequence* $(T_n)_{n\in\mathbf{N}}$ *of stopping times*[4] *such that* $\lim_{n\to\infty} T_n = \infty$ *a.s. and that each stopped process*[5] $M_{T_n\wedge t}$ *belongs to* $\mathcal{M}$.
4. $\mathcal{L}$ *denotes the set of all local martingales* M *such that* $M_0 = 0$.
5. *We denote by* $\mathcal{V}$ *the set of all real-valued processes* A *that are right continuous with existing left limits,* $\mathcal{F}_t$*-adapted*[6]*, with* $A_0 = 0$*, and each path* $t \rightsquigarrow A_t(\omega)$ *is of finite variation*[7].
6. *A semimartingale is a process* X *of the form* $X = X_0 + M + A$ *where* X_0 *is finite-valued and* $\mathcal{F}_0-$*measurable, where* $M \in \mathcal{L}$*, and where* $A \in \mathcal{V}$.

Definition 2.2.2.
A Brownian motion is a real-valued, continuous stochastic process $\{X(t)\}_{t\geq 0}$, *with independent and stationary increments. In other words:*

- *continuity:* **P** *a.s. the map* $s \longmapsto X_s(\omega)$ *is continuous.*
- *independent increments: for all* $s \leq t$, $X_t - X_s$ *is independent of* $\mathcal{F}_s = \sigma(X_u, u \leq s)$, *i.e. the* $\sigma-$*algebra generated by* $\{X_u, u \leq s\}$.
- *stationary increments: if* $s \leq t$, $X_t - X_s$ *and* $X_{t-s} - X_0$ *have the same probability law.*

Remark 2.2.1.

1. If $\{X(t)\}_{t\geq 0}$ is a Brownian motion, then $X_t - X_0$ is a normal random variable with mean rt and variance $\sigma^2 t$, where r and σ are constant real numbers. For a proof consult the book by Gihman & Skorohod (1980).
2. A Brownian motion is standard if $X_0 = 0$ **P** a.s., $E[X_t] = 0$, $E\left[X_t^2\right] = t$.
3. A standard Brownian motion is a martigale.

---

[4] Lamberton & Lapeyre (1996), p. 30: τ is a stopping time with respect to the filtration $\mathbf{F} = (\mathcal{F}_t)_{t\geq 0}$ if τ is a random variable in $\mathbf{R}^+ \cup \{+\infty\}$, such that for any $t \geq 0 : \{\tau \leq t\} \in \mathcal{F}_t$.

[5] Jacod & Shiryaev (1987), p. 3: If X is a process and if T is a mapping: $\Omega \to \mathbf{R}^+ \cup \{+\infty\}$, we define the process stopped at time T by $X_{T\wedge t}$.

[6] Jacod & Shiryaev (1987), p. 3: An $E-$valued stochastic process X endowed with a $\sigma-$algebra $\mathcal{E}$ is adapted to the filtration $\mathbf{F}$ (or equivalently is $\mathcal{F}_t-$adapted), if for all t, X_t is $\mathcal{F}_t$-$\mathcal{E}-$measurable.

[7] Jacod & Shiryaev (1987), p. 28: The stochastic process X is of finite variation if almost all of the paths of X are of finite variation on each finite interval $[0, t]$, $t \geq 0$. The variation process $VAR(X)$ (sometimes denoted by $|X|$) of X is defined by

$$VAR(X)_t(\omega) = |X|_t = \lim_{n\to\infty} \sum_{1\leq k\leq n} \left|X_{tk/n}(\omega) - X_{t(k-1)/n}(\omega)\right|.$$

If X is of finite variation, then $VAR(X)_t(\omega) = |X|_t < \infty$.

2.3 Modelling Transition and Default Probabilities

The distributions of defaults and transitions play the central role in the modelling, measuring, hedging and managing of credit risk. They are an appropriate way of expressing arrival risk. Probably the oldest approach to estimating default and transition probabilities is the historical method that focuses on counting historical defaults and rating transitions. Because this method is very static, newer statistical approaches try to link these historical probabilities to external variables which can better explain the probability changes through time. Most of these econometric methods try to measure the probability that a debtor will be bankrupt in a certain period, given all information about the past default and transition behavior and current market conditions. Firm value or asset based methods implicitly model default or transition probabilities by assuming that default or rating changes are triggered, if the firm value hits some default or rating boundary. Intensity based methods specify an exogenous bankruptcy process which is calibrated to fit market data.

2.3.1 Basic Mathematical Definitions

Definition 2.3.1.
For each $0 \leq T \leq T^*$ *we let* $\{p^s(t,T)\}_{0 \leq t \leq T}$ $\left(\{p^d(t,T)\}_{0 \leq t \leq T}\right)$ *denote an* $\mathcal{F}_t$*-adapted stochastic process where* $p^s(t,T)$ $\left(p^d(t,T)\right)$ *is the conditional probability at time t, given all available information at that time, of survival to (default by) time* T*. Obviously,* $\forall\, t, T$*:* $p^d(t,T) = 1 - p^s(t,T)$*. In addition, we denote the probability of surviving to time* T*, given survival to time* t*, by* $p^s(T|t)$*.*

Based on these definitions we can introduce the concept of forward default probabilities:

Definition 2.3.2.
The forward default probability is defined as the probability of default by time T*, given survival to time* t*, and denoted by* $p^d(T|t)$ *(obviously,* $\forall\, t$*,* T*:* $p^d(T|t) = 1 - p^s(T|t)$*).*

We want to emphasize that $p^d(T|t)$ and $p^s(T|t)$ are only conditioned on survival up to time t, whereas $p^d(t,T)$ and $p^s(t,T)$ are conditioned on all information available at time t.

2.3.2 The Historical Method

Rating the quality of corporate, municipal, and sovereign debtors and providing transition and default[8] probabilities as well as recovery rates for creditors are the key businesses of rating agencies[9]. The four biggest US agencies are Moody's Investors Service (Moody's), Standard & Poor's (S&P), Fitch IBCA and Duff & Phelps. The interpretation of the letter ratings assigned are summarized in table 2.1. The rating agencies distinguish between issue and issuer credit ratings. Standard & Poor's gives the following issue and issuer credit rating definitions:

> "Standard & Poor's *Issue* Credit Rating is a current opinion of the creditworthiness of an obligor with respect to a specific financial obligation, a specific class of financial obligations, or a specific financial program. It takes into consideration the creditworthiness of guarantors, insurers, or other forms of credit enhancement on the obligation and takes into account the currency in which the obligation is denominated. [...] Issue Credit Ratings are based on current information furnished by the obligors or obtained by Standard & Poor's from other sources it considers reliable. Standard & Poor's does not perform an audit in connection with any credit rating and may, on occasion, rely on unaudited financial information. Credit ratings may be changed, suspended, or withdrawn as a result of changes in, or unavailability of, such information, or based on other circumstances. Issue Credit Ratings can be either long term or short-term. Short-term ratings are generally assigned to those obligations considered short-term in the relevant market. In the U.S., for example, that means obligations with an original maturity of no more than 365 days - including commercial paper. Short-term ratings are also used to indicate the creditworthiness of an obligor with respect to put features on long term obligations. The result is a dual rating, in which the short-term rating addresses the put feature, in addition to the usual long term rating. Medium-term notes are assigned long term ratings."[10]
>
> "Standard & Poor's *Issuer* Credit Rating is a current opinion of an obligor's overall financial capacity (its creditworthiness) to pay its financial obligations. This opinion focuses on the obligor's capacity and willingness to meet its financial commitments as they come due.

---

[8] According to Caouette, Altman & Narayanan (1998), page 194, for rating agencies "defaults are defined as bond issues that have missed a payment of interest, filed for bankruptcy, or announced a distressed-creditor restructuring".

[9] Rating agencies are providers of timely, objective credit analysis and information. Usually they operate without government mandate and are independent of any investment banking firm or similar organization.

[10] Standard & Poor's, (*Ratings Performance 1996: Stability & Transition* 1997), page 56.

It does not apply to any specific financial obligation, as it does not take into account the nature of and provisions of the obligation, its standing in bankruptcy or liquidation, statutory preferences, or the legality and enforceability of the obligation. In addition, it does not take into account the creditworthiness of the guarantors, insurers, or other forms of credit enhancement on the obligation. [...] Counterparty Credit Ratings, ratings assigned under the Corporate Credit Rating Service (formerly called the Credit Assessment Service) and Sovereign Credit Ratings are all forms of Issuer Credit Ratings. Issuer Credit Ratings are based on current information furnished by obligors or obtained by Standard & Poor's from other sources it considers reliable. Standard & Poor's does not perform an audit in connection with any credit rating and may, on occasion, rely on unaudited financial information. Credit ratings may be changed, suspended, or withdrawn as a result of changes in, or unavailability of, such information, or based on other circumstances. Issue Credit Ratings can be either long term or short-term. Short-Term Issuer Credit Ratings reflect the obligor's creditworthiness over a short-term time horizon"[11]

After issuance and the assignment of the initial issuer or issuance rating, regularly (periodically and based on market events) each rating agency checks and - if necessary - adjusts its issued rating. If there is a tendency observable, that may affect the rating of a debtor, in case of Moody's the debtor is set on the Rating Review List, in case of Standard & Poor's the obligor is set on the Credit Watch List. The growing number of rating agencies on the one hand and the increasing number of rated obligors on the other hand - while in 1960 Moody's had rated only 912 debtors, in 1997 the number had already grown up to 3841 - proves their increasing importance.

The default studies of the rating agencies summarize the default experience of issuers of public debt by comparing historical ratings of defaulting issuers with ratings of public issuers that did not default. They determine default rates based on all bonds of a given rating class, regardless of their age. The bond issuers are the basic units of account. The most important concepts are marginal and cumulative historical default and survival rates.

Definition 2.3.3.

1. *The historical marginal year t default (survival) rate $d_R(t)$ $(s_R(t) = 1 - d_R(t))$ based on the time frame $[Y_0, Y_1]$, $Y_0 \leq Y_1 - t$, in the past, is the average issuer-weighted default (survival) rate for an R-rated issuer in its $t-$th year as experienced between the years Y_0 and Y_1. Formally,*

[11] Standard & Poor's,(*Ratings Performance 1996: Stability & Transition* 1997), page 57.

Table 2.1. Long-term senior debt rating symbols.

Investment-grade ratings		
S&P	Moody's	Interpretation
AAA	Aaa	Highest quality, extremely strong
AA+	Aa1	High quality
AA	Aa2	
AA-	Aa3	
A+	A1	Strong payment capacity
A	A2	
A-	A3	
BBB+	Baa1	Adequate payment capacity
BBB	Baa2	
BBB-	Baa3	

Speculative-grade ratings		
S&P	Moody's	Interpretation
BB+	Ba1	Likely to fulfill obligations ongoing uncertainty
BB	Ba2	
BB-	Ba3	
B+	B1	High risk obligations
B	B2	
B-	B3	
CCC+	Caa1	Current vulnerability to default
CCC	Caa2	
CCC-	Caa3	
CC		
C	Ca	In bankruptcy or default, or other marked shortcoming
D		

Source: Caouette et al. (1998).

$$d_R(t) = \frac{\sum_{Y=Y_0}^{Y_1} M_R^Y(t)}{\sum_{Y=Y_0}^{Y_1} N_R^Y(t)},$$

where $N_R^Y(t)$ is the number of issuers with rating R at the start of year Y that have not defaulted until the beginning of year $Y+t-1$ and $M_R^Y(t)$ is the number of issuers rated R at the start of year Y and defaulted in the $t-$th year, i.e. during year $Y+t-1$.

2. *The historical cumulative $t-$year default (survival) rate $cd_R(t)$ $(cs_R(t) = 1 - cd_R(t))$ based on time frame $[Y_0, Y_1]$, $Y_0 \le Y_1 - t$, is the probability that an R-rated issuer will default (not default) within t years. Formally,*

$$cs_R(t) = \prod_{i=1}^{t} (1 - d_R(i)) \text{ and } cd_R(t) = 1 - cs_R(t).$$

3. *For each rating R we define the historical $t-$year transition rate to rating $\check{R}$, $tr_{R,\check{R}}(t)$, based on the time frame $[Y_0, Y_1]$, $Y_0 \le Y_1 - t$, as the average*

Table 2.2. S&P's one-year transition and default rates (based on the time frame [1980,2000]).

	Rating at year end (%)							
Initial Rating	**AAA**	**AA**	**A**	**BBB**	**BB**	**B**	**CCC**	**D**
AAA	93.66	5.83	0.40	0.09	0.03	0.00	0.00	0.00
AA	0.66	91.72	6.94	0.49	0.06	0.09	0.02	0.01
A	0.07	2.25	91.76	5.18	0.49	0.20	0.01	0.04
BBB	0.03	0.26	4.83	89.24	4.44	0.81	0.16	0.24
BB	0.03	0.06	0.44	6.66	83.23	7.46	1.05	1.08
B	0.00	0.10	0.32	0.46	5.72	83.62	3.84	5.94
CCC	0.15	0.00	0.29	0.88	1.91	10.28	61.23	25.26

Source: Standard & Poor's (*Ratings Performance 2000: Default, Transition, Recovery, and Spreads* 2001).

rate for an R-rated issuer to be rated $\check{R}$ at the end of its t−th year as experienced between the years Y_0 and Y_1. Formally,

$$tr_{R,\check{R}}(t) = \frac{\sum_{Y=Y_0}^{Y_1} M_{R,\check{R}}^{Y}(t)}{\sum_{Y=Y_0}^{Y_1} N_{R,\check{R}}^{Y}(t)},$$

where $N_{R,\check{R}}^{Y}(t)$ is the number of issuers with rating R at the start of year Y and $M_{R,\check{R}}^{Y}(t)$ is the number of issuers rated R at the beginning of year Y and rated $\check{R}$ at the end of the t−th year, i.e. at the end of year $Y+t-1$.

Remark 2.3.1.
The historical marginal year 1 default rate $d_R(1)$ based on the time frame $[Y_0, Y_1]$, $Y_0 \leq Y_1 - 1$, and the historical cumulative 1−year default rate $cd_R(1)$ based on the same time frame are obviously the same. For simplification we call both the one-year default rate based on the time frame $[Y_0, Y_1]$, $Y_0 \leq Y_1 - 1$. If we are not interested in the specific time frame $[Y_0, Y_1]$ we just say one-year default rate.

As an example, table 2.2 shows the historical one-year transition and default rates for the S&P ratings AAA, AA,,...,CCC based on the time frame [1980, 2000] (see *Ratings Performance 2000: Default, Transition, Recovery, and Spreads* (2001)). Such a table is called transition matrix.

Apart from the regularly published data of the rating agencies (e.g., Standard & Poor's yearly publications "Ratings Performance: Transition and Stability" and Moody's yearly special reports "Corporate Bond Defaults and Default Rates") there are a lot of academic empirical studies on historical default and transition probabilities for different financial instruments. The most detailed default statistics available are those for corporate bonds stratified by bond ratings. The statistics currently available for loans are less comprehensive. A summary of this academic work is given, e.g., by Caouette et al. (1998), chapters 15 and 16, by Carty & Lieberman (1998), and by Carty (1998).

The historical method has a lot of shortcomings:

- The default and transition rates can only be applied to firms with a known current rating. Where a firm is not rated, its financial data must be used to calculate key accounting ratios (usually those used by rating agencies). These ratios can then be compared with the corresponding median figures for rated firms. Based on such comparisons equivalent ratings and corresponding default probabilities can be assigned to the firms.
- Using historical default rate estimates as approximations for future default rates neglects default rate volatility, especially at low rating levels, and the correlation to the business cycle. Actual transition and default probabilities are very dynamic and can vary depending on general economic conditions. Hence, the historical observations may not reflect the current credit environment. The *CCC* one-year default rate curve of figure 2.1, e.g., shows the recessions of the years 1982, at the end of the 80's/beginning 90's and 1995. The standard deviations of the B and *CCC* curves are 2.78% and 10.84%, respectively.
- A number of studies performed by rating agencies and academics have documented not only the volatility of default rates but the dependence of ratings transition matrices on the industry of the obligor, the time since the issuance of the specific financial instrument and the stage of the business cycle. Prominent among these are Lucas & Lonski (1992), Altman & Kao (1992a), Altman & Kao (1992b), Carty & Fons (1993), Altman (1997), and Carty (1997). Nickell, Perraudin & Varotto (1998) show that there are significant differences in the transition matrices of banks and industrials, US and non-US obligors, business cycle peaks and troughs. Cross-country differences are especially important for highly-rated obligors, but appear to be less important for non investment-grade issuers. Business cycle effects are especially important for low ratings.
- Despite the large number of observations, some measurements have low statistical significance.
- The rating of a debtor is a too rough estimate of its actual quality. Within a rating class there are great variations in default rates. Especially in the high-yield debt market, stability provided by a broad categorization scheme is an illusion.
- Rating Agencies used to be too slow to change their ratings. Hence, the historical average probability of staying in the same rating class overestimates the true figure.

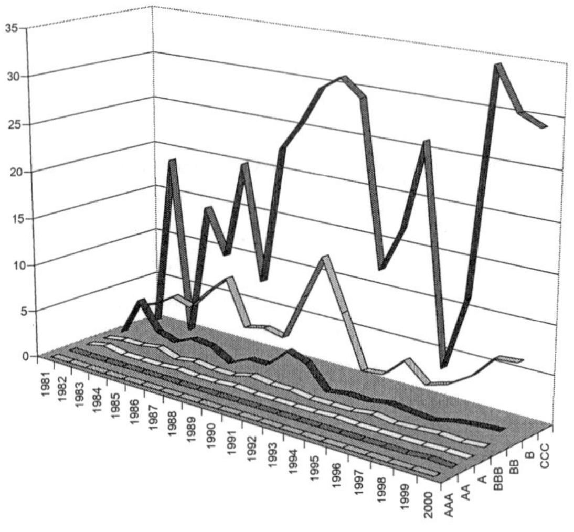

Fig. 2.1. S&P one-year default rates (%) by rating class based on the time frame [1980, 2000]. Source: Standard & Poor's (*Ratings Performance 2000: Default, Transition, Recovery, and Spreads* 2001).

- The differences between mean and median default rates within a rating class shows that the historical average default probability overestimates the true default probability.
- If rating agencies overestimate probabilities of staying in the same rating class and default probabilities, they must underestimate at least some of the transition probabilities to the other credit states.

At the moment, there are no different transition matrices for different countries published by the rating agencies. It is assumed that the same matrix can be applied to all of them. But the business cycle can vary quite substantially over different countries. Especially for emerging markets, the primarily US-based historical observations are inappropriate and there is only little reliable historical emerging market based data available. There have been only few actual defaults in these regions.

Conclusion 2.3.1
The ratings from rating agencies appear to be a too broad categorization method. Hence, one shouldn't only rely on historical default and transition rates but use alternative methods as well.

2.3.3 The Asset Based Method

The asset based approach[12] for modelling default probabilities goes back to the initial proposal of Merton (1974), where he assumes that a firm is only financed by equity and one type of zero coupon debt with promised terminal constant payoff $X > 0$ at maturity time T. The firm is able to redeem its debt if the total market value of its assets $V(T)$ at time T is worth more than the amount X owed to the creditor. Otherwise the obligor defaults on its obligation. Because this approach explicitly models the firm's capital structure, it is sometimes called structural approach. By the given assumptions, the $\mathbf{F}$−adapted stochastic process $\{p^d(t,T)\}_{0\leq t\leq T}$ in the filtered probability space $(\Omega, \mathcal{F}, \mathbf{F}, \mathbf{P})$, which describes the conditional default probability until time T, given all information available at time t, is implicitly defined by

$$p^d(t,T) = \mathbf{P}(N(T) < 0|\mathcal{F}_t) \;\; \forall\, 0 \leq t \leq T,$$

where $N(T) = V(T) - X$. If the dynamics of the firm value under the probability measure $\mathbf{P}$ are specified as the $\mathbf{F}$−adapted stochastic process $\{V(t)\}_{0\leq t\leq T^*}$ with

$$\frac{dV(t)}{V(t)} = \mu_V dt + \sigma_V dW_V(t), \;\; 0 \leq t \leq T,$$

where μ_V is the unknown instantaneous expected rate of return on the firm per unit of time, σ_V is the constant volatility parameter, and W_V is a standardized Brownian motion, easy calculations yield

$$p^d(t,T) = \Phi\left(\frac{\ln\left(\frac{X}{V(t)}\right) - \left(\mu_V - \frac{1}{2}\sigma_V^2\right)(T-t)}{\sigma_V\sqrt{T-t}}\right), \;\; 0 \leq t \leq T,$$

where Φ denotes the operator of the standard normal distribution. Because the instantaneous default probability of a healthy firm is zero under a continuous firm value process, Zhou (1997) models the evolution of the firm value as a jump-diffusion process. Formally,

$$\frac{dV(t)}{V(t)} = (\mu_V - \lambda_V\nu_V)\,dt + \sigma_V dW_V(t) + (\Pi_V - 1)\,dU_V(t), \;\; 0 \leq t \leq T, \quad (2.1)$$

where λ_V and ν_V are constants, $\Pi_V > 0$ is the i.i.d. log-normal distributed jump amplitude, such that $\ln(\Pi_V) \sim N(\pi_\Pi, \sigma_\Pi)$ for some constant $\sigma_\Pi > 0$ and $\pi_\Pi = \nu_V + 1$, U_V is a Poisson process[13] with intensity parameter λ_V,

[12] Equivalently firm value, Merton-based or structural approach

[13] Ross (1996), p.59: A stochastic process $\{X(t)\}_{t\geq 0}$ is said to be a counting process if $X(t)$ represents the total number of events that have occurred up to time t. Hence, a counting process must satisfy: $X(t) \geq 0$, $X(t)$ is integer valued, and

and $dW_V(t)$, $dU_V(t)$ and Π_V are mutually independent for all $0 \leq t \leq T$. N denotes the normal distribution. Because the process V is a semimartingale (for a proof see, e.g., Protter (1992), pages 47-48) we apply the semimartingale version of Itô's lemma[14] to equation (2.1) and get

$$d\ln(V(t)) = \left(\mu_V - \frac{1}{2}\sigma_V^2 - \lambda_V \nu_V\right) dt + \sigma_V dW_V(t) + \ln(\Pi_V)\, dU_V(t).$$

Hence, the conditional default probability for $0 \leq t \leq T$ is given by[15]

$$\begin{aligned} p^d(t,T) &= \mathbf{P}(V(T) \leq X | V(t)) \\ &= \mathbf{P}(\ln(V(T)) \leq \ln(X) | V(t)). \end{aligned}$$

Let $U_V(t,T)$ be the total number of jumps from time t to time T. Then we have

$$\begin{aligned} &\ln(V(T)) | (V(t), U_V(t,T) = i) \\ &\sim N\left(\ln(V(t)) + \left(\mu_V - \frac{1}{2}\sigma_V^2 - \lambda_V\nu_V\right)(T-t) + i\pi_\Pi, \sigma_V^2(T-t) + i\cdot\sigma_\Pi^2\right), \end{aligned}$$

and

$$\begin{aligned} p^d(t,T) = \sum_{i=0}^{\infty} & \frac{\exp(-\lambda_V(T-t))(\lambda_V(T-t))^i}{i!} \\ & \cdot \Phi\left(\frac{\ln\left(\frac{X}{V(t)}\right) - \left(\mu_V - \frac{1}{2}\sigma_V^2 - \lambda_V\nu_V\right)(T-t) - i\mu_\Pi}{\sqrt{\sigma_V^2(T-t) + i\cdot\sigma_\Pi^2}}\right). \end{aligned}$$

if $s < t$, $X(t) - X(s)$ equals the number of events that have occurred in the interval $(s,t]$.

A counting process $\{X(t)\}_{t\geq 0}$ is said to be a Poisson process with intensity λ, $\lambda > 0$, if $X(0) = 0$, the process has independent increments, and the number of events in any interval of length t is Poisson distributed with mean λt.

[14] Protter (1992), p.71: Let X be a semimartingale and let f be a twice continously differentiable real function. Then $f(X)$ is again a semimartingale , and the following formula holds:

$$\begin{aligned} f(X_t) - f(X_0) = &\int_{0+}^{t} f'(X_{s-})\, dX_s + \frac{1}{2}\int_{0+}^{t} f''(X_{s-})\, d[X,X]_s^c \\ &+ \sum_{0<s\leq t} \{f(X_s) - f(X_{s-}) - f'(X_{s-})\,\Delta X_s\}, \end{aligned}$$

where $[X,X]^c$ denotes the path by path continuous part of $[X,X]$ and $\Delta X_s = X_s - X_{s-}$. The quadratic variation of X is defined as

$$[X]_t = [X,X]_t = X_t^2 - 2\int_0^t X_{u-}dX_u, \ \forall\, t \geq 0.$$

[15] For a detailed proof see the paper by Zhou (1997), page 26.

First passage time models generalize the traditional asset based model, such that a default can occur not only at maturity of the debt contract but at any point of time, and assume that bankruptcy occurs if the firm value $V(t)$ hits a specified possibly stochastic boundary $X(t)$ such as the current value of the firm's liabilities. Let T^d represent the time when a default occurs the first time.

Definition 2.3.4.
For $\mathbf{F}-$*adapted firm value and boundary processes* $V(t)$ *and* $X(t)$ *we define the* $\mathbf{F}-$*adapted net firm value process* $\{N(t)\}_{0\leq t\leq T^*}$ *by*

$$N(t) = V(t) - X(t), \ 0 \leq t \leq T^*.$$

The first passage time or hitting time for $V(t)$ *to hit* $X(t)$ *is*

$$T^d = \inf\{0 \leq t \leq T^* | N(t) \leq 0\}.$$

Except for some very special processes, explicit solutions for first passage times are not known[16]. In this case the conditional default probability

$$p^d(t,T) = \mathbf{P}\left(T^d \leq T | \mathcal{F}_t\right), \ 0 \leq t \leq T,$$

can be determined by Monte Carlo simulation.
Asset based and first-passage time models have some shortcomings:

- Analyzing corporate-level data issuer by issuer is impractical to empirically study a structural model.
- Complicated balance sheets cannot be captured easily by structural models, e.g., there may be too many classes of claims on the assets of the firm that have to be priced.
- Different accounting standards in different countries complicate the whole process.
- Default can be determined by factors other than assets and liabilities (for example, default could occur for reasons of illiquidity, or, as it is sometimes the case with sovereign debt, for general economic and political considerations).
- Often it is difficult to define a meaningful firm value process, e.g., in case of sovereign debt.
- To generate realistic levels of default probabilities (especially short term default probabilities) one has to extend the basic Merton approach in many ways, hence, work with a complicated model. For example, if we model the firm value process only with a continuous diffusion the probability of a firm to default in the next instant is zero. Hence, firms would never default unexpectedly.

[16] For a survey of the first passage time problem see Abrahams (1986).

2.3.4 The Intensity Based Method

Intensity based methods take an approach completely different from asset based methods. They define the event of default as a stopping time T^d with respect to the filtration $\mathbf{F}$ with an exogenously given probability distribution. One may associate with the stopping time T^d the first jump time of the point or counting process[17] $\{A(t)\}_{0 \leq t \leq T^*}$ defined by $A(t) = \sum_{n \geq 1} 1_{\{T_n \leq t\}}$. The sequence T_n is a sequence of jump times with T_n defined as the time of occurrence of the nth jump. If we define $H(t)$ as the process $A(t)$ stopped at time T^d, then $H(t)$ can be interpreted as the default indicator function which equals 0 before default and 1 if default has already occurred, i.e. $H(t) = 1_{\{T^d \leq t\}}$. The default indicator function will play an essential part in our concept of modelling defaultable term structures which we develop in section 3.2. Now we are able to introduce the concept of stochastic intensity like, e.g., in Brémaud (1981), page 27:

Definition 2.3.5.
Let $\{A_t\}_{t \geq 0}$ be a point process adapted to some filtration $\mathbf{F}$, and let λ_t be a nonnegative $\mathcal{F}_t$-progressive[18] process such that for all $t \geq 0$

$$\int_0^t \lambda_s ds < \infty \; \mathbf{P} - a.s.$$

If for all nonnegative $\mathcal{F}_t$-predictable[19] processes C_t, the equality

[17] Brémaud (1981), pp.18-19: A realization of a point process over $[0, \infty)$ can be described by a sequence $(T_n)_{n \in \mathrm{N}}$ in $[0, \infty]$ such that $T_0 = 0$, $T_n < \infty \Longrightarrow T_n < T_{n+1}$. This realization is, by definition, called nonexplosive iff $T_\infty = \lim_{n \to \infty} T_n = \infty$. To each realization T_n corresponds a counting function A_t defined by

$$A_t = \begin{cases} n & , \text{ if } t \in [T_n, T_{n+1}), \; n \geq 0, \\ +\infty & , \text{ if } t \geq T_\infty. \end{cases}$$

If the above T_n are random variables defined on some probability space $(\Omega, \mathcal{F}, \mathbf{P})$, the sequence $(T_n)_{n \in \mathrm{N}}$ is called a point process. The associated counting process A_t is also called a point process, by abuse of notation. Moreover, if the condition $E^{\mathbf{P}}[A_t] < \infty$, $t \geq 0$, holds, the point process A_t is said to be integrable.

[18] Brémaud (1981), p. 288: Let $\mathbf{F} = (\mathcal{F}_t)_{t \geq 0}$ be a filtration defined on the probability space $(\Omega, \mathcal{F}, \mathbf{P})$. An E-valued process X endowed with a σ-algebra $\mathcal{E}$ is said to be $\mathcal{F}_t$-progressive (or $\mathcal{F}_t$-progressively measurable) iff for all $t \geq 0$ the mapping $(t, \omega) \to X_t(\omega)$ from $[0, t] \times \Omega \to E$ is $(\mathcal{B}([0,t]) \otimes \mathcal{F}_t) - \mathcal{E}-$ measurable.

[19] Brémaud (1981), p. 8: Let $\mathbf{F} = (\mathcal{F}_t)_{t \geq 0}$ be a filtration defined on the probability space $(\Omega, \mathcal{F}, \mathbf{P})$, and define $\mathcal{P}(\mathcal{F}_t)$ to be the σ-field over $(0, \infty) \times \Omega$ generated by the rectangles of the form

$$(s, t] \times A; \; 0 \leq s \leq t, \; A \in \mathcal{F}_s.$$

$\mathcal{P}(\mathcal{F}_t)$ is called the $\mathcal{F}_t$-predictable σ-field over $(0, \infty) \times \Omega$. A real-valued process X such that X_0 is $\mathcal{F}_0$-measurable and the mapping $(t, \omega) \to X_t(\omega)$ defined from $(0, \infty) \times \Omega$ into $\mathbf{R}$ is $\mathcal{P}(\mathcal{F}_t)$-measurable is said to be $\mathcal{F}_t$-predictable.

$$E^{\mathbf{P}}\left[\int_0^{\infty} C_s dA_s\right] = E^{\mathbf{P}}\left[\int_0^{\infty} C_s \lambda_s ds\right]$$

is verified, then we say: A_t *admits the* $(\mathbf{P},\mathcal{F}_t)-$*intensity* λ_t.

Remark 2.3.2.
A stochastic integral is defined with respect to a specific class of integrators (for possible choices such as right-continuous, square integrable martingales[20] see, e.g., Karatzas (1988), page 131). This integrator class defines which type of stochastic processes (e.g., $\mathcal{F}_t-$progressive processes or only the smaller class of $\mathcal{F}_t-$predictable processes) can be used as integrands of the stochastic integral (for details see, e.g., Karatzas (1988), page 131, and Protter (1992), pages 48-49). E.g., if the stochastic integral is defined for semimartingale integrators one can use $\mathcal{F}_t-$predictable integrands.

To be able to give an intuitive interpretation of the notion of intensity (in a setting where we want to model the arrival of default) we need to mention some properties of stochastic intensities:

Theorem 2.3.1 (Integration Theorem).
If A_t *admits the* $(\mathbf{P},\mathcal{F}_t)-$*intensity* λ_t, *then* A_t *is nonexplosive and*

1. $M_t = A_t - \int_0^t \lambda_s ds$ *is an* $\mathcal{F}_t-$*local martingale. We call* A_t *local compensated jump martingale.*
2. *If* X *is an* $\mathcal{F}_t-$*predictable process such that* $E^{\mathbf{P}}\left[\int_0^t |X_s| \lambda_s ds\right] < \infty$, $t \geq 0$, *then* $\int_0^t X_s dM_s$ *is an* $\mathcal{F}_t-$*martingale.*
3. *If* X *is an* $\mathcal{F}_t-$*predictable process such that* $\int_0^t |X_s| \lambda_s ds < \infty$, $\mathbf{P}-a.s.$, $t \geq 0$, *then* $\int_0^t X_s dM_s$ *is an* $\mathcal{F}_t-$*local martingale.*

Proof.
Brémaud (1981), page 27.

Theorem 2.3.2 (Martingale Characterization of Intensity).
Let A_t *be a nonexplosive point process adapted to* $\mathcal{F}_t$, *and suppose that for some nonnegative* $\mathcal{F}_t-$*progressive process* λ_t *and for all* $n \geq 1$, $A_{t\wedge T_n} - \int_0^{t\wedge T_n} \lambda_s ds$ *is a* $(\mathbf{P},\mathcal{F}_t)-$*martingale. Then* λ_t *is the* $(\mathbf{P},\mathcal{F}_t)-$*intensity of* A_t.

Proof.
Brémaud (1981), page 28.

If the intensity is constrained to be predictable, it is essentially unique:

[20] Karatzas & Shreve (1988), p.30: A martingale is called square integrable if $E^{\mathbf{P}}\left(X_t^2\right) < \infty$ for all $t \geq 0$.

Theorem 2.3.3 (Uniqueness of Predictable Intensities).
Let A_t be a point process adapted to the filtration $\mathbf{F}$, and let λ_t and $\widetilde{\lambda}_t$ be two $(\mathbf{P},\mathcal{F}_t)$ −intensities of A_t which are $\mathcal{F}_t$−predictable. Then $\lambda_t(\omega) = \widetilde{\lambda}_t(\omega)$ $\mathbf{P}(d\omega)\, dA_t(\omega) - a.e.$

Proof.
Brémaud (1981), page 31.

Also, one can always find such a predictable version of the intensity:

Theorem 2.3.4 (Existence of Predictable Versions of the Intensity).
Let A_t be a point process with an $(\mathbf{P},\mathcal{F}_t)$ −intensity λ_t. Then one can find an $(\mathbf{P},\mathcal{F}_t)$ −intensity $\widetilde{\lambda}_t$ that is $\mathcal{F}_t$−predictable.

Proof.
Brémaud (1981), page 31.

To show how default probabilities can be modelled using intensities we make the following assumption.

Assumption 2.3.1
The default indicator function H_t admits a $(\mathbf{P},\mathcal{F}_t)$ −intensity λ_t.

Thus, $M_{t\wedge T^d}(t) = H(t) - \int_0^{T^d\wedge t} \lambda_s ds = H(t) - \int_0^t \lambda_s 1_{\{s\leq T^d\}} ds$ is an $\mathcal{F}_t$−local martingale and λ_t is a nonnegative $\mathcal{F}_t$−progressive process with $\int_0^t \lambda_s ds < \infty$ $\mathbf{P} - a.s.$ for all $t \geq 0$. Hence, the conditional expectation $E^{\mathbf{P}}[H(t+\varepsilon) - H(t)|\mathcal{F}_t]$, $\varepsilon > 0$, is given by

$$\begin{aligned} & E^{\mathbf{P}}[H(t+\varepsilon) - H(t)|\mathcal{F}_t] \qquad (2.2) \\ &= E^{\mathbf{P}}[M_{t\wedge T^d}(t+\varepsilon) - M_{t\wedge T^d}(t)|\mathcal{F}_t] + E^{\mathbf{P}}\left[\int_t^{t+\varepsilon} \lambda_s 1_{\{s\leq T^d\}} ds|\mathcal{F}_t\right] \\ &= M_{t\wedge T^d}(t) - M_{t\wedge T^d}(t) + E^{\mathbf{P}}\left[\int_t^{t+\varepsilon} \lambda_s 1_{\{s\leq T^d\}} ds|\mathcal{F}_t\right] \\ &= E^{\mathbf{P}}\left[\int_t^{t+\varepsilon} \lambda_s 1_{\{s\leq T^d\}} ds|\mathcal{F}_t\right] \end{aligned}$$

and by application of the Lebesgue averaging theorem and the Lebesgue dominated convergence theorem, successively, in case of a right-continuous intensity λ_t, we get

$$\begin{aligned} & \lim_{\varepsilon\to 0} \frac{E^{\mathbf{P}}[H(t+\varepsilon) - H(t)|\mathcal{F}_t]}{\varepsilon} \\ &= \lim_{\varepsilon\to 0} \frac{E^{\mathbf{P}}\left[\int_t^{t+\varepsilon} \lambda_s 1_{\{s\leq T^d\}} ds|\mathcal{F}_t\right]}{\varepsilon} \\ &= \lambda_t 1_{\{t\leq T^d\}} \ \mathbf{P} - a.s. \end{aligned}$$

On the other hand,

$$\begin{aligned}
&E^{\mathbf{P}}\left[H\left(t+\varepsilon\right)-H\left(t\right)|\mathcal{F}_t\right] \\
&=0\cdot\mathbf{P}\left(T^d\leq t|\mathcal{F}_t\right)+1\cdot\mathbf{P}\left(t<T^d\leq t+\varepsilon|\mathcal{F}_t\right)+0\cdot\mathbf{P}\left(T^d>t+\varepsilon|\mathcal{F}_t\right) \\
&=p^d\left(t,t+\varepsilon\right)
\end{aligned}$$

and

$$\lim_{\varepsilon\to 0}\frac{E^{\mathbf{P}}\left[H\left(t+\varepsilon\right)-H\left(t\right)|\mathcal{F}_t\right]}{\varepsilon}=\lim_{\varepsilon\to 0}\frac{p^d\left(t,t+\varepsilon\right)}{\varepsilon}.$$

Hence,

$$\lambda_t 1_{\{t\leq T^d\}}=\lim_{\varepsilon\to 0}\frac{p^d\left(t,t+\varepsilon\right)}{\varepsilon},$$

i.e. given all information available at time t, the intensity λ_t can be interpreted as the arrival rate of default at time t.

Conclusion 2.3.2
The probability of default over the next infinitesimal time interval of length $\varepsilon>0$ is approximately $\lambda_t\cdot\varepsilon$. This interpretation links the notion of intensity to the problem of estimating default probabilities. Sometimes λ_t is called the intensity of T^d.

In addition, using equation (2.2), we have found the following result:

Proposition 2.3.1.
$p^d\left(t,T\right)$, $t<T$, is given by

$$p^d\left(t,T\right)=E^{\mathbf{P}}\left[\int_t^T\lambda_s 1_{\{s\leq T^d\}}ds|\mathcal{F}_t\right].$$

This proposition gives us a general relationship between the conditional probability of default $p^d\left(t,T\right)$ and the intensity process λ. Imposing some strict assumptions on the intensity process λ, Madan & Unal (1994) show that the probability of default can be related to a discount factor in which discounting is done at the intensity λ. Hence, a striking similarity to default-free interest rate modelling is found. Duffie (1998c) shows the same result under more general assumptions:

Proposition 2.3.2.
Suppose T^d is a stopping time with a bounded intensity process[21] λ. Fixing some time $T>0$, let

$$Y\left(t\right)=E^{\mathbf{P}}\left[\exp\left(-\int_t^T\lambda_s ds\right)|\mathcal{F}_t\right],\quad t\leq T.$$

[21] The assumption that λ is bounded can be replaced by some integrability conditions. For details see Duffie (1998c), p.5.

If the jump $\Delta Y\left(T^d\right) = Y\left(T^d\right) - Y\left(T^d-\right)$ *is zero almost surely, then*

$$p^d\left(t,T\right) = 1 - Y\left(t\right),\ t < T^d.$$

Proof.
See Duffie (1998c), pages 4-5.

Remark 2.3.3.
Given any predictable nonnegative process λ such that $\int_0^t \lambda_s ds < \infty\ \mathbf{P} - a.s.$ for all $t \geq 0$, and defining the stopping time T^d by

$$T^d = \inf\left\{t \geq 0 : \int_0^t \lambda_s ds = \Lambda\right\},$$

where Λ is an exponentially distributed random variable with mean 1, independent of Y defined in proposition 2.3.2, then λ is the intensity of T^d and $\Delta Y\left(\tau\right) = 0$ a.s.[22] Such a model is called a Cox process or doubly stochastic Poisson process model.

Conclusion 2.3.3
As soon as we have specified the intensity process λ, *the conditional default and survival probabilities are given by proposition 2.3.2.*

Example 2.3.1.
Analytically tractable choices of λ :

1. **Constant intensity models:** $\lambda\left(t\right) = \lambda$ if $0 \leq t < T^d$ and 0 otherwise, where $\lambda > 0$ is some constant. Under this assumption $p^s\left(t,T\right) = e^{-\lambda(T-t)}$ and $p^d\left(t,T\right) = 1 - e^{-\lambda(T-t)}$. Hence, the time to default is exponentially distributed. We are in the situation, where we associate with the arrival of default the first event of a Poisson arrival process, at some constant mean arrival rate λ.
2. **Affine jump diffusion intensity models:** $\lambda\left(t\right)$ is an affine function of the factors X, i.e. $\lambda\left(t\right) = l_0\left(t\right) + l_1\left(t\right) \cdot X\left(t\right)$ for bounded continuous functions l_0 and l_1 on $[0,\infty)$, where X is a strong $n-$dimensional Markov process[23] valued in $\mathbb{R}^n$ uniquely solving the stochastic differential equation

[22] For details see, e.g., Lando (1994), Lando (1996), Lando (1998), Duffie (1998c).
[23] The intuitive meaning of the Markov property is that the future behaviour of the process X after t depends only on the value X_t and is not influenced by the history of the process before t. Mathematically speaking, an $\mathcal{F}_t-$adapted process X satisfies the Markov property if, for any bounded Borel function f and for any s and t such that $s \leq t$, we have $E^{\mathbf{P}}\left[f\left(X_t\right)|\mathcal{F}_s\right] = E^{\mathbf{P}}\left[f\left(X_t\right)|X_s\right]$. Roughly, the strong Markov property states that a relation of the previous form continues to hold if the time s is replaced by a stopping time τ. Mathematically speaking, an $\mathcal{F}_t-$adapted process X satisfies the strong Markov property if, for any bounded Borel function f and for any stopping time τ with respect to the filtration$\{\mathcal{F}_t\}_{t\geq 0}$, $\tau < \infty$ a.s., we have $E^{\mathbf{P}}\left[f\left(X_t\right)|\mathcal{F}_\tau\right] = E^{\mathbf{P}}\left[f\left(X_t\right)|X_\tau\right]$. For further details see, e.g., Lamberton & Lapeyre (1996), pp. 54 ff., Oksendal (1998), pp. 107 ff., and Brémaud (1981), pp. 290 ff.

$$dX_t = \mu(X_t, t)\,dt + \sigma(X_t, t)\,dW_t + dZ_t.$$

W is an $\mathbf{F}$–adapted n–dimensional standard Brownian motion in $\mathbb{R}^n$, $\mu : D \rightarrow \mathbb{R}^n$, $\sigma : D \rightarrow \mathbb{R}^{n \times n}$, $D \subset \mathbb{R}^n \times [0, \infty)$, Z is a pure jump process whose jump-counting process A_t admits a stochastic intensity $\gamma : D \rightarrow [0, \infty)$ depending on X with a jump-size distribution ν only depending on t and for each t, $\{x : (x,t) \in D\}$ containing an open subset of $\mathbb{R}^n$. Then, under certain restrictions on the parameters of the process X and a specific choice of D the conditional survival probabilities are of the form

$$p^s(t,T) = e^{\alpha(t,s)+\beta(t,s)\cdot X(t)},$$

where $\alpha(t,s) \in \mathbb{R}$ and $\beta(t,s) \in \mathbb{R}^n$ are coefficients, depending on t and s that are given explicitly. Each model with survival probabilities of this form is called affine. The theory can be found in papers of Duffie & Kan (1996), Duffie, Pan & Singleton (1998), and Dai & Singleton (1998). All parameters of λ may be inferred from market data. Therefore, one can use methods similar to those described in section 3.6. Examples for empirical studies and parameter estimation of intensity based models include those of Duffee (1996a), and Düllmann & Windfuhr (2000).

Although intensity based methods are very flexible, nevertheless they have several shortcomings:

- The intensity process is purely exogenously specified.
- There is no link between the causes of default (e.g., low asset values) and the default event.
- "Default is never expected".

2.3.5 Adjusted Default Probabilities

The previous sections describe the determination of default probabilities by using stochastic models. Young & Bhagat (2000) from Goldman Sachs argue that

> "in certain circumstances, the purely stochastic approach overlooks valuable credit information".

Hence, the quantitative approach should always be linked to and be based on a strong fundamental credit analysis. This can be done by making mathematical models use and take advantage of the experience of credit analysts. They usually have a very good objective and intuitive feeling on how counterparties are going to perform on their contracts. One possibility to close this gap between quantitative modelling and fundamental analysis is the concept of default probability adjustment. Basically, for each counterparty the credit analyst adjusts the values of the default probabilities over time which were derived implicitly from public traded debt by using a quantitative method or from rating agencies. So the unique characteristics of the counterparties can be taken into consideration. These adjustments should be done such that they stay within a target range of the original default probabilities and take into account events that can have an impact on the default probabilities' term structure such as changes in regulatory obligations, changes in the stability of the industry, contract expirations or debt maturities.

2.4 Modelling Recovery Rates

In the real world payoffs of defaulted securities are usually greater than zero. The recovery rate (given default), denoted by w, is defined as the extent to which the value of an obligation can be recovered once the obligor has defaulted, i.e. the recovery rate is a measure for the expected fractional recovery in case of default and as such takes any value in the interval $[0, 1]$. If the defaultable security under consideration lives during the time interval $[t, T]$, $0 \leq t < T \leq T^*$, we allow for the occurrence of default at any time in the interval $[t, T]$. The loss rate (given default), denoted by l, is defined as $1 - w$. There are different concepts of expressing and modelling recovery rates:

- **Fractional recovery of par:** it is assumed that there is compensation in terms of cash (invested in the non-defaultable money market account[24]), and the recovery rate is expressed as a fraction of par. The model has been applied, e.g., by Duffie (1998b).
- **Fractional recovery of market value:** it is assumed that there is compensation in terms of equivalent defaultable bonds, which have not defaulted yet, i.e. the recovery rate is expressed as a fraction of the market value of the defaulted bond just prior to default. By equivalent we mean bonds with the same maturity, quality and face value. This model was mainly developed by Duffie & Singleton (1997) and applied, e.g., by Schönbucher (2000).
- **Fractional recovery of a default-free but otherwise equivalent bond (equivalent recovery model):** it is assumed that there is compensation in terms of (the value of) non-defaultable bonds, i.e. at the time of default T^d a defaultable bond has the payoff of w equivalent non-defaultable bonds. By equivalent we mean bonds with the same maturity and face value. Several authors have proposed this model, e.g., Jarrow & Turnbull (1995), and Madan & Unal (1998).

Different recovery models can be transformed into each other. The value of the defaultable security at default is only expressed using different numéraires.

[24] See, e.g., definition 3.2.1.

Recovery rates are really hard to estimate because all the cash flows subsequent to a default should be discounted back to the time of default. Obviously, this cash flow information is usually not available. Most of the firms in financial distress are not liquidated but restructured. It is dependent on the type (loan or bond) and seniority of the risky asset, the rating of the issuer before default and the collateral guaranteed by the asset. Nevertheless, there are some empirical studies on recovery rates. Altman & Eberhart (1994) examine recovery rates on defaulted debt by seniority at the default date. Altman & Kishore (1996) and Altman & Kishore (1997) show weighted average recovery rates on defaulted debt by seniority, industry and original rating from 1978 until 1996. They find an average recovery rate on a sample of over 750 defaulting bond issues of 40.11%. Carty & Lieberman (1998) find that the average bond recovery rate for the period 1970-1995 is 41.25% with a high standard deviation of 26.55%. Carty & Lieberman (1996) assessed the recovery rate on a small sample of senior unsecured defaulted bank loans and found it to be on average about 71%. Asarnow & Edwards (1995) analyzed defaulted loans of Citibank from 1970 until 1993 and found an average recovery rate of 65%.

3. Pricing Credit Linked Financial Instruments

"All models are wrong, but some are useful."
- George E. Box -

"The grand aim of all science is to cover the greatest number of empirical facts by logical deduction from the smallest number of hypotheses or axioms."
- Albert Einstein -

3.1 Introduction

3.1.1 Defaultable Bond Markets

Credit risk is one of the oldest forms of risk in the financial markets, and still revolutionary changes and developments are taking place in the credit markets today. To emphasize the growing importance of this market segment and its risks which shouldn't be ignored, we first give a brief overview of the latest credit market and credit risk developments.

Corporate Defaults. Corporate default risk[1] can't be neglected: in the mid-1980's, there was a huge number of defaults on bank loans and corporate bonds in the United States, and in the early-1990's about 10% of the junk bonds defaulted. Now, in the end-1990's and beginning-2000's, according to Standard & Poor's, corporate defaults are running at their highest level ever and are still on the rise[2]. In 1999 and 2000 S&P registered defaults by 101 and 117 rated or formerly rated companies, which is equivalent to a default ratio of 2.06% and 2.27%, on a total of US$ 37.8 billion and US$ 42.3 billion of debt, respectively. These were the highest one year overall default ratios since 1991, and in US$ values the highest values ever. The median corporate

[1] For a detailed definition of corporate default see appendix A.

[2] For all information based on S&P data see *Ratings Performance 1996: Stability & Transition* (1997), *Ratings Performance 1997: Stability & Transition* (1998), *Ratings Performance 1998: Stability & Transition* (1999), *Ratings Performance 1999: Stability & Transition* (2000), and *Ratings Performance 2000: Default, Transition, Recovery, and Spreads* (2001).

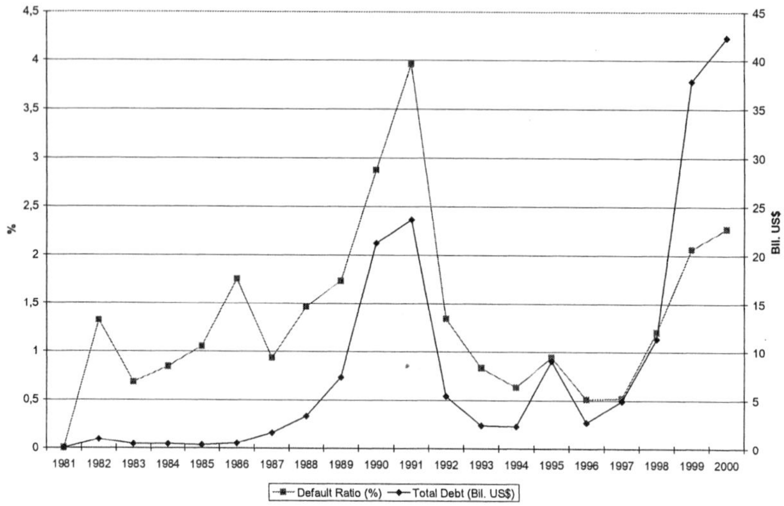

Fig. 3.1. S&P corporate default ratios and total corporate debt in default, 1981 – 1999. Source: (*Ratings Performance 2000: Default, Transition, Recovery, and Spreads* 2001).

rating assigned by S&P was "A"[3] in 1981, "A-" in 1991 and "BBB" by year-end 1999. In 1999, downgrades exceeded upgrades almost three to one, and the number of newly rated obligors with a speculative-grade rating[4] outnumbered those with an investment-grade rating[5]. This fact pushed the speculative-grade component from 36% in 1999 to 37.5% in 2000. According to Moody's Investors Services (Moody's)[6], 1999 147 corporate and sovereign issuers defaulted on US$ 44.6 billion of debt, which is more than double as much as in 1998. During 1999, there were four downgrades of corporate ratings for every upgrade.

Sovereign Defaults. Default risk is not only concentrated on corporate issuers. Although sovereign nations have the right to print money to repay their debts, for political and economical reasons, such as inflationary pressures or social welfare costs, they can decide not to do so. Sovereign obligors have come to the international financial markets in ever greater numbers. This expansion of credit is for example supported by the joint BIS (Bank

[3] For the definition of letter ratings see, e.g., section 2.

[4] Rating of "BB+" or lower by S&P and "Ba1" or lower by Moody's. For more details see, e.g., section 2.

[5] A rating of "BBB-" or higher by S&P or a rating higher than "Ba1" by Moody's.

[6] See *Historical Default Rates of Corporate Bond Issuers, 1920-1999* (2000a).

for International Settlements) - IMF (International Monetary Fund) - OECD (Organization for Economic Co-Operation and Development) - World Bank statistics on external debt[7]. While in the mid-1970's we heard Walter Wriston, a former Chairman of Citibank, say "Countries don't go bankrupt", the crises of the 1980's and 1990's in Russia, Asia and Latinamerica taught us better. Past sovereign defaults[8] were caused by such a different variety of factors as, e.g., wars, lax fiscal and monetary policies, or external economic shocks. For example, on September 3rd, 1999, repackaged bonds based on Ecuadorian Brady bonds[9] jointly issued by Dresdner Bank / J.P. Morgan and Merrill Lynch / Credit Suisse First Boston, respectively, defaulted with zero recovery.Ecuador was the first country not to pay its interest rates on Brady bonds ever: in August 1999, Ecuador defaulted on about US$ 6 billion in Brady bonds. In addition, in October 1999 the government defaulted on about US$ 500 million in Eurobonds. This decision followed a serious deterioration in the country's economic conditions:

- Ecuador was hit by "El Niño" which caused a damage to nearly 20% of GDP (Gross Domestic Product).
- Decline in prices of Ecuador's two largest export commodities.
- Increase in the cost of external finance.
- Deeply stressed banking system.
- Internal political uncertainties.

Given these political and economic circumstances, despite the risk of partly loosing access to the international capital markets - after all, at the end of 1998 Brady bonds represented nearly 40% of external liabilities - servicing the country's debt became impossible. Ecuador was the only new sovereign defaulting during 1999. Defaults by other sovereigns had originated earlier. Some of the most serious defaults are those of the Russian Federation, Indonesia, Ukraine, Mongolia, Pakistan and former Yugoslavia. Looking back in history, according to figure 3.3 the sovereign default rate started rising in the end 1970's. The Latin American debt crises in 1982 accelerated and pushed this trend further peaking in 1990 with Brazil's default on US$ 62 billion of debt. At the same time more and more sovereigns from other regions like Eastern Europe became involved. More conservative economic policy-making in the

[7] Can be downloaded from http://www.bis.org/publ/index.html.

[8] For a detailed definition of sovereign default see appendix A.

[9] A program established in 1990 to restructure the heavy debt burdens of emerging markets countries. Named after U.S. Treasury Secretary Nicholas Brady, it uses multilateral agencies such as the International Monetary Fund and the World Bank to provide funding. Under the program, a country's outstanding debt is converted to new long-term fixed-rate and/or floating-rate bonds whose principal is backed by U.S. Treasury bonds. Debtor nations are responsible for long-term interest payments. Bradys or Brady-style issues have been set up for Mexico, Venezuela, Brazil, Argentina, Panama, Philippines, Poland, Bulgaria, Morocco, Nigeria and Russia. Some of those nations are in the process of eliminating much of that form of debt.

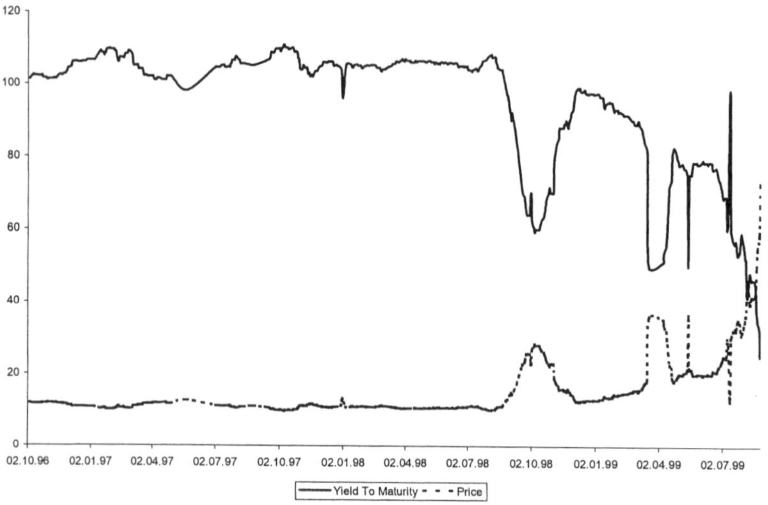

Fig. 3.2. Dresdner Bank's Synthetic Ecuador Bond LTD 12.25% 02/10/03 DEM - yields to maturity and prices. Source: Bloomberg.

last decade changed this trend and made default ratios decrease constantly. In spite of the fact that defaults by sovereign governments again declined in 1999 to 28 from 32 in 1998, on a total value of about US$ 102 billion of debt, the default rate in the sovereign sector is expected to increase over the next years. Sovereigns like Indonesia, Romania, Russia, and the Ukraine are facing strong economic and political pressures which makes them most delicate to default. In addition, an increasing number of speculative-grade ratings has been assigned since 1991 (see figure 3.4), which supports this opinion.

Credit Losses from Derivatives[10]**.** Debt instruments are not the only financial instruments with embedded credit risk. For example, all kinds of derivative contracts are subject to counterparty default risk, especially if they are not exchange traded[11]. Over-the-counter (OTC) derivatives[12] usu-

[10] A derivative is a financial contract whose value is derived from the performance of assets, interest rates, currency exchange rates, or indexes. Derivative transactions include a wide assortment of financial contracts including structured debt obligations and deposits, swaps, futures, options, caps, floors, collars, forwards and various combinations thereof.

[11] Exchange traded derivative contracts are standardized derivative contracts that are transacted on an organized exchange and that usually have margin requirements.

[12] Over-the-counter derivative contracts are privately negotiated derivative contracts that are transacted off organized exchanges.

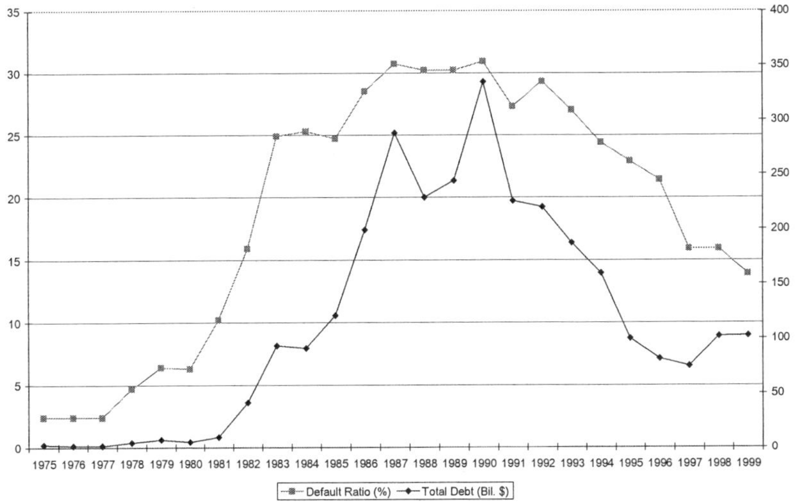

Fig. 3.3. S&P sovereign default ratios and sovereign debt in default, 1975-1999. Source: (*Ratings Performance 1999: Stability & Transition* 2000).

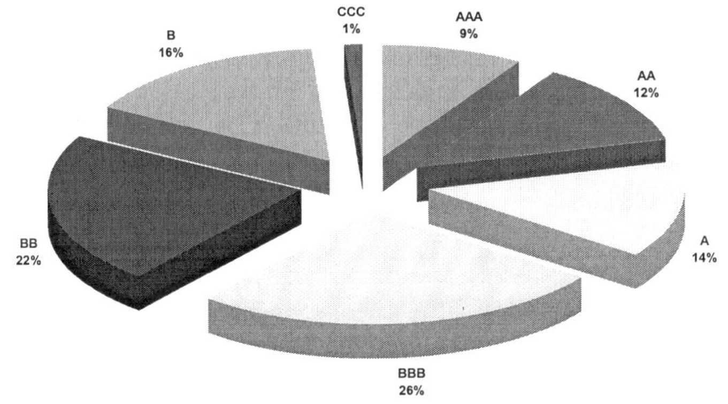

Fig. 3.4. New sovereign ratings, 01/91–11/99. Source: (*Ratings Performance 1999: Stability & Transition* 2000).

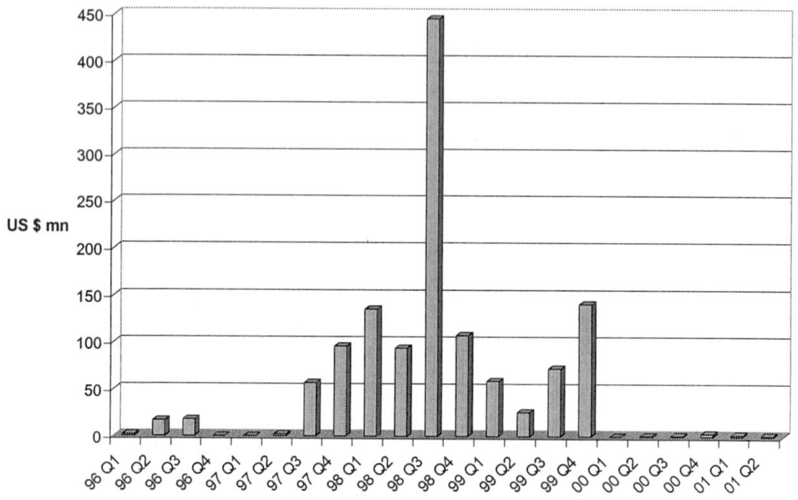

Fig. 3.5. Quarterly charge-offs (credit losses) from derivatives of all US commercial banks with derivatives. Source: Call report of the Office of the Comptroler, 2nd Quarter 2001.

ally don't have any kind of guarantees and, in many cases, are unsecured and without any collateral posted. In a study of financial reports, Basin (1996) finds out that not only highly rated firms serve as derivative counterparties. Quite the reverse is true. A significant part of the counterparties are speculative-grade companies. Figure 3.5 shows the quarterly credit losses from derivatives of all US commercial banks with derivatives. It seems evident that especially OTC derivatives should be priced with regard to credit risk. This is usually a more complex task than in the case of pricing debt such as fixed rate bonds since the payoff from derivatives is stochastic.

Appetite for Risk. Despite the increasing number of corporate defaults (and predicted sovereign defaults) there is a constantly growing number of investors willing to take this risk. One reason are the historically low nominal interest rates around the world that make many investors seek higher yields by taking more credit risk. Such a great appetite for risk has attracted large numbers of companies to the bond markets, especially many issuers of high-yield[13] and emerging market[14] bonds from very risky industries and countries.

[13] High-yield bonds are speculative-grade rated. Technically they are referred to as non-investment grade credits.

[14] Broadly defined, an emerging market is a country making an effort to change and improve its economy with the goal of raising its performance to that of

Often these companies are brand-new, poorly capitalized and new in business. Granted high-yield debt has existed for decades - but whereas junk bonds used to come from formerly higher rated firms whose quality had declined for reasons like economic recessions, today, issuing junk bonds is a quite natural strategy for firms which don't have access to other forms of credit. Routinely they sell their debt in the capital markets and very often can't pay the interest on it. According to Caouette et al. (1998), in 1997, the high-yield public bond issuance was US$ 120 billion, and new leverage loan volume reached US$ 197 billion. A report from Moody's (*Historical Default Rates of Corporate Bond Issuers, 1920-1999* 2000b) notes that such a surge in low-rated, first-time issuers that entered the market in late 1997 and 1998 was a key factor in pushing the default rate to a new high. This group of issuers contributed 40% of 1999's rated bond defaults. S&P reports (*Ratings Performance 1999: Stability & Transition* 2000) that out of the 101 companies, that defaulted in 1999, 92 were originally rated speculative-grade. 77% of these companies were first rated after the year 1994. 60% of 1999's defaults were not related to worse economic conditions caused by last years' Asian and Russian crises.

Growth of the Corporate Bond Market. Credit markets have undergone a dramatic change over the past few years. The growth rates of traditional loan products have stagnated relative to other corporate financing markets[15]. Although the European corporate bond market is still small in relation to the US market, according to McLeish (2000) it has grown rapidly over the past years. And this gap between the European and US bond market is expected to narrow more over time. Some of the main reasons are the following:

- Migration away from bank loans and similar products towards the fixed-rate bond market due to pressure from stockholders to generate higher returns[16].
- Explosion in the European Mergers & Acquisitions activities (partially) funded by bond issuance.
- Growth in pension and mutual fund assets as a demand driver.
- Existing institutional assets are shifted out of government bonds into corporate bonds due to the low European yield environment.

the world's more advanced nations. The World Bank classifies economies with a Gross National Product per capita of US$ 9656 and above as high-income countries. Antoine W. van Agtmael, an employee of the World Bank's International Finance Corporation, is credited with coining the term "emerging markets" in 1981. But the concept of investing in less developed countries with potential for economic expansion has been a part of individual and institutional investment strategies since the 19th century.

15 See, e.g., Wilson (1998), page 220.

16 See, e.g., exhibit 2 on page 222 in Wilson (1998) which shows the dramatically falling margins which banks earn from the traditional loan product.

- The European monetary union replaced the segmentation of the European corporate bond market into national markets by one Euro-zone market. This increased competition and liquidity[17].

In euro, outstanding industrial bonds expanded by 115% in 1998 and by 271% in 1999, outstanding financial bonds by 83% in 1998 and by 29% in 1999. In sterling, outstanding industrial bonds expanded by 25% in 1998 and by 44% in 1999, outstanding financial bonds by 16% in 1998 and by 13% in 1999[18]. And Neil McLeish from Morgan Stanley Dean Witter explains (McLeish 2000):

> "Although we do not expect the same percentage rates of growth for euro and sterling industrial bonds to be maintained going forward, we do expect solid growth in the overall size of these markets, which over time should converge with the US in terms of size. Our view is based on several factors that support both increased supply of and demand for European industrial bonds."

Credit Derivatives and Asset-Backed Securities. Traditionally, exposure to credit risk was managed by trading in the underlying asset itself. Over the last years innovative products like credit derivatives have been developed for transferring, replicating and hedging credit risk[19]. Even more complicated products are structured finance transactions (SPs), such as collateralized bond obligations (CBOs), collateralized loan obligations (CLOs), collateralized mortgage obligations (CMOs) and other asset-backed securities (ABSs). The key idea behind these instruments is to pool assets and transfer specific aspects of their overall credit risk to new investors and/or guarantors. According to J. P. Morgan (*Structured Products/ ABS Market Monthly* 1999), global SP/ABS supply from January 1999 through August 1999 rose by 24% versus the similar period in 1998 up to a record level of over US$ 333 billion. US$ public ABS issuance was close to US$ 150 billion, the European structured products market surpassed US$ 55 billion and the Japanese ABS market reached a volume of about US$ 13 billion. Compared to the corresponding 1998 period this was an increase of 25%, 50% and 230%, respectively.

3.1.2 Pricing Defaultable Bonds - Literature Review

Investors willing to invest in defaultable bonds should be compensated for the risk they take. But what is a fair risk premium ? There have been basically three approaches to this problem so far.

---

[17] European monetary union didn't affect only the corporate bond markets by making investors comparing credit risk over the entire Euro-zone, but rather made credit risk play the key role in the pricing of European government bonds.

[18] See McLeish (2000).

[19] For details see section 3.4.

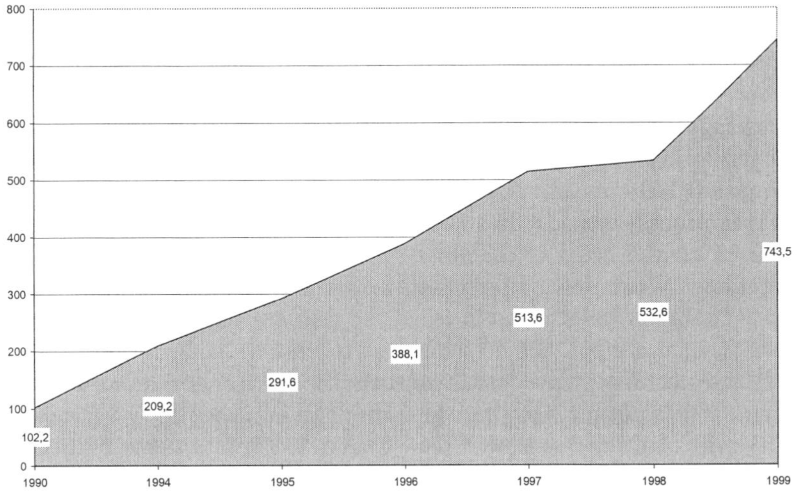

Fig. 3.6. Asset-backed securities outstanding 1990, 1994 – 1999 (in US$ billions). Source: The Bond Market Association.

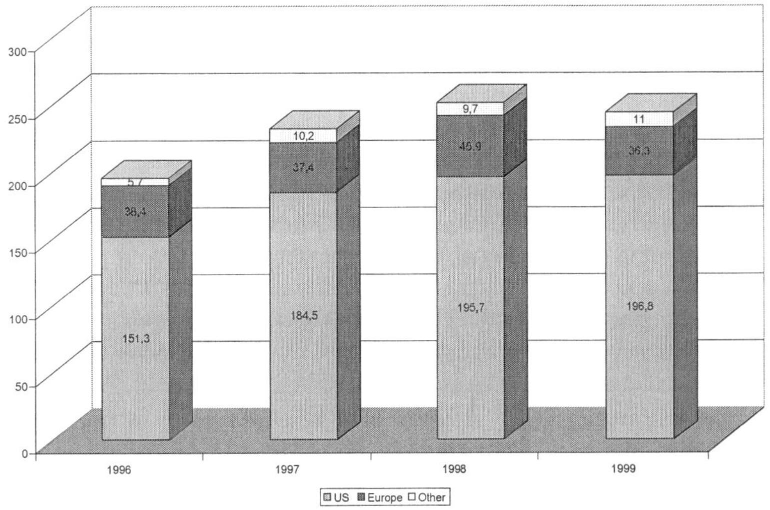

Fig. 3.7. Global ABS issuance, 1996 – 1999 (in US$ billions). Source: The Bond Market Association, Thomson Financial Securities Data and Capital Data.

Traditional methods for pricing defaultable bonds use historical default probabilities (see, e.g., section 2.3.2) to determine the expected loss on the specific bond. The price is then determined such that it compensates the investor for this expected loss under the empirical probability measure, i.e. there is no risk premium. One example for this approach is the research of Fons (1994).

The pricing of defaultable bonds in the asset based setting goes back to the initial proposal of Merton (1974), where he assumes that the dynamics for the value of the assets of a firm across time can be described by a diffusion-type stochastic process and the defaultable security can be regarded as a contingent claim on the value of the assets of the firm. Apart from the standard assumptions of continuous time no-arbitrage models[20] there are many shortcomings of this model: the liabilities of the firm are supposed to consist only of a single class of debt, the debt has a zero coupon, bankruptcy is triggered only at the maturity of the debt, bankruptcy is costless and interest rates are assumed to be constant over time. In addition, it is assumed that the absolute priority rule[21] is always enforced. But Franks & Torous (1994) find that the strict absolute priority rule was violated in 78% of the bankruptcies they considered. Thus, the assumptions of the Merton model are highly stylized versions of reality. As Kim et al. (1992), Kim, Ramaswamy & Sundaresan (Autumn 1993), and Jones et al. (1984) point out in their papers, Merton's model doesn't generate the levels of yield spreads which can be observed in the market. Rather they show that this model is unable to generate yield spreads in excess of 120 basis points whereas over the 1926-1986 period, the yield spreads of AAA-rated corporates ranged from 15 to 215 basis points. This inability to account for the magnitude of yield spreads was the motivation for a huge number of papers written during the last two decades to generalize Merton's risky debt pricing model: Black & Cox (1976) incorporate classes of senior and junior debt, safety covenants, dividends, and restrictions on cash distributions to shareholders, Geske (1977) considers coupon bonds by using a compound options approach and provides a formula for subordinate debt within this compound option framework, Ho & Singer (1982) allow for different maturities of debt and examine the effect of alternative bond indenture provisions such as financing restriction of the firm, priority rules and payment schedules. Leland (1994) extends the model further to incorporate bankruptcy costs and taxes which makes it possible to work with optimal capital structure. Because the empirical literature shows that credit spread curves can be flat or even downward sloping, that short-term debt often doesn't have zero credit spreads, and that sudden drops in the value of firms are possible, Mason & Bhattacharya (1981) consider a pure jump

[20] No taxes and transaction costs, perfectly divisible assets, no borrowing-lending spread, continuous costless trading and short-selling, equal access to information for all investors.

[21] If the strict priority rule is enforced, in case of bankruptcy, bondholders are paid off as good as possible while shareholders receive nothing.

process, and Zhou (1997) incorporates a jump diffusion for the underlying asset value. Brennan & Schwartz (1980) and Cox, Ingersoll & Ross (1980) introduce stochastic interest rates. Shimko et al. (1993) allow for stochastic non-defaultable short rates as in Vasicek (1997) with interest rates that follow a mean-reverting process with constant volatility. Kim et al. (1992) and Kim et al. (Autumn 1993) use a Cox-Ingersoll-Ross type model for the stochastic non-defaultable short rates. In addition, they study the role of call features in corporate and treasury bonds and find that the call feature is relatively more valuable in treasury than it is in corporate issues. Longstaff & Schwartz (1995b) develop a model similar to Shimko et al. (1993) except for the bankruptcy procedure. While in most papers using option pricing frameworks bankruptcy is triggered at the moment when the value of the firm reaches the value of the debt, they model default as the time when the value of the debt reaches some constant threshold value X which serves as a distress boundary, i.e. the default time T^d can then be expressed formally as $T^d = \inf\{t \geq 0 : V(t) \leq X\}$, the first passage time for $V(t)$ (the value of the firm's assets at time t) to cross the lower bound X. If the value of the assets breaches this level, default is triggered, some form of restructuring occurs and the remaining assets of the firm are allocated among the firm's claimants. Implicit in this formulation is the assumption that once this level is reached, default occurs on all outstanding liabilities at the same time. Thus, contrary to Merton's model, default can occur prior to maturity. Nielsen, Saà-Requejo & Santa-Clara (1993), Briys & de Varenne (1997) and Saá-Requejo & Santa-Clara (1997) allow for stochastic default boundaries and deviation from the absolute priority rule. Cathcart & El-Jahel (1998) exchange the firm value process by a so called signaling process. A signaling process can capture some effects like liquidity better than a firm value process. Briys & de Varenne (1997) assure that the payment to bondholders is not greater than the firm value upon default, and whenever the firm is "threshold-solvent", it is able to repay the face value of the bond. Because of the complexities of all these extensions, often a closed-form solution can't be obtained any more and numerical procedures must be used. Although the structural approach is conceptually important, gathering and analyzing corporate balance sheet data issuer by issuer is impractical. Complicated balance sheets can't be captured by the structural approach, anyway. And default is usually determined by much more factors than assets and liabilities.

Despite the immense efforts devoted to generalize Merton's methodology, all of these structural models have only limited success in explaining the behavior of prices of debt instruments and credit spreads. This has led to attempts to use models that make more direct assumptions about the default process. These alternative approaches, called reduced-form models, don't consider the relation between default and asset value in an explicit way but model default as a stopping time of some given hazard rate process, i.e. the default process is specified exogenously. This achieves two effects. The first is that the model can be applied to situations where the underlying asset value is not observable. Secondly, the default time is unpredictable and therefore the behavior of credit spreads for short maturities can be captured more realistically. In addition, the approach is very tractable and flexible to fit the observed credit spreads. Many papers have appeared recently that follow this approach. Some of the most important ones are the following:

- Jarrow & Turnbull (1995) present a model where the bankruptcy process is compared to a spot exchange rate process. Default is driven by a Poisson process with constant intensity parameter[22] and a given payoff at default.
- In Lando (1994), Lando (1996), and Lando (1998) default is driven by Cox processes, which can be thought of as Poisson processes with random intensity parameters.
- Duffie & Singleton (1997) and Duffie & Singleton (1998) show that valuation under the risk-adjusted probability measure can be executed by discounting the non-defaultable payoff on the debt by a discount rate that is adjusted for the parameters of the default process.
- Schönbucher (1996) presents a generalization in a Heath-Jarrow-Morton framework[23] that allows for restructuring of defaulted debt and multiple defaults.

Despite of all the attractive properties of the reduced-form models, their main draw-back is the missing link between firm value and corporate default. Finally, it should be mentioned, that Duffie & Lando (1997) show that there is a close connection between structural and reduced-form models.

Our work presents a middle ground between structural and reduced-form models to combine the strengths of both approaches and end up with a model that can be empirically validated.

3.1.3 A New Model For Pricing Defaultable Bonds

In the following, we develop a model for pricing defaultable debt that is capable of reflecting real world phenomena realistically. Before we actually introduce the model, we make some heuristic observations to motivate the theory. Throughout the following sections we examine and extend these considerations further:

- Since defaults actually happen, a bond pricing model must be able to deal with default events: For example, in August 1999 Ecuador defaulted on interest rate payments of Brady bonds with a total amount of about US$ 6 billions. In October 1999 there was a second default of US$ 500 millions. Figure 3.8 shows the yields to maturity and S&P ratings of an Ecuadorian sovereign bond that was downgraded to the rating D in September 1999.

[22] For a definition see section 2.

[23] For an introduction to the Heath-Jarrow-Morton framework see, e.g., Heath, Jarrow & Morton (1992).

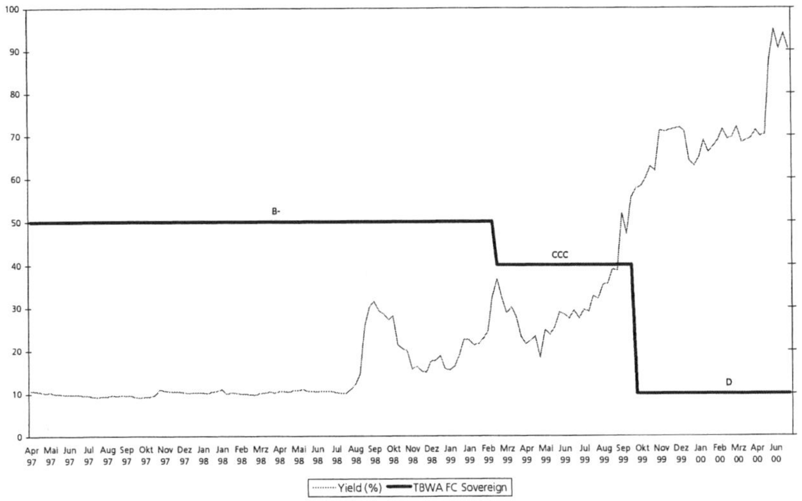

Fig. 3.8. Yields to maturity (in %) and Thomson Bankwatch Fitch IBCA (TBWA FC) ratings of the Ecuadorian sovereign bond BEEC 11.25% 25/04/2002 DEM from April 1997 until June 2000. Source: Reuters Information Services.

- Rating agencies can't check the ratings on a daily basis or even continuously. Ratings of rating agencies can only be described by discrete time processes. But the quality of an obligor usually changes according to a continuous time process (see, e.g., figure 3.8). Thus, the quality or the distance to default of an obligor should be observed continuously.
- Very often the quality of obligors shows mean reversion properties. In case of a downgrade the management of a firm usually takes actions to improve the quality again. Figure 3.9 shows this phenomenon for the firm Hertz. The mean reversion level of the rating of Hertz is A- and A3 for S&P's and Moody's rating, respectively.
- Many models for pricing defaultable zero coupon bonds don't allow for positive short term credit spreads: As time to maturity tends to zero the model credit spreads tend to zero, too. Obviously, these models are far away from describing reality. In figure 3.10 we show observed corporate credit spreads for different maturities. Even bonds with a rating of A and time to maturity of seven days can have credit spreads which are higher than 500 basis points. Hence, a model must be capable of generating high credit spreads even for short term debt.
- Yields and credit spreads usually depend on the quality of the obligor. The better the quality the smaller the yields (compare to figure 3.11). The time series of the yields show high correlations between the rating classes A and

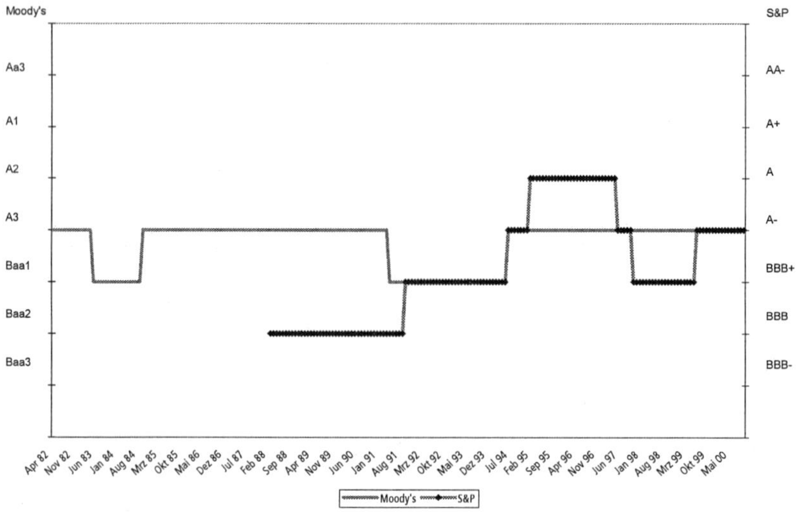

Fig. 3.9. History of the Moody's and S&P ratings of Hertz from April 1982 until August 2000. Source: Reuters Information Services.

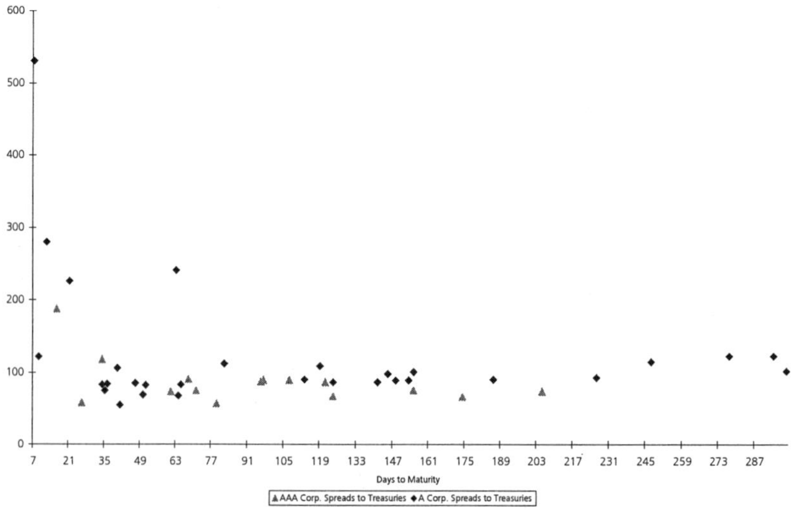

Fig. 3.10. Credit spreads of corporate bonds with S&P ratings of AAA and A for different maturities (in basis points). Source: Reuters Information Services.

Fig. 3.11. 1 year USA Euro $ bonds indices for the ratings A and AAA (yields in %). Source: Bloomberg.

AAA. Gains and losses are - at least to some extend - caused by changes in the quality of the obligor.
- Credit spread processes often show mean reversion properties. See, e.g., figure 3.12.
- Non-defaultable interest rates are usually mean reverting. See, e.g., figure 3.13.

In the following section we develop a three-factor defaultable term structure model for the pricing of a wide range of risky debt contracts and derivatives. It combines structural and reduced-form models. One of the factors that determine the credit spread is the so called uncertainty index which can be understood as an aggregation of all information on the quality of the firm currently available: The greater the value of the uncertainty process the lower the quality of the firm. A similar idea to this uncertainty process was first introduced by Cathcart & El-Jahel (1998) in form of a so called signaling process. In their model default is explicitly driven by the signaling process which is assumed to follow a diffusion process. The second underlying process is the non-defaultable short rate which is assumed to follow a mean reverting square root process. Our model differs from Cathcart and El-Jahel in several ways: First, we assume the underlying non-defaultable short rate to follow either a mean reverting Hull-White process or a mean-reverting square root process with time-dependent mean reversion level. The uncertainty or

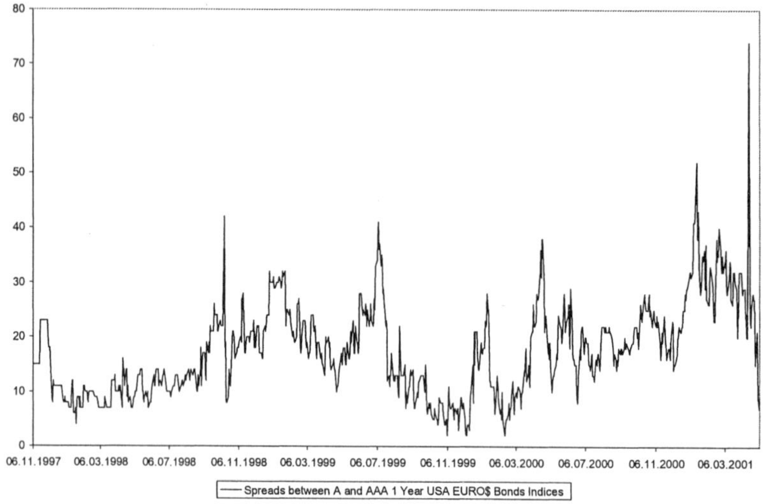

Fig. 3.12. 1 year credit spreads between A and AAA Euro $ bonds indices (in basis points). Source: Bloomberg.

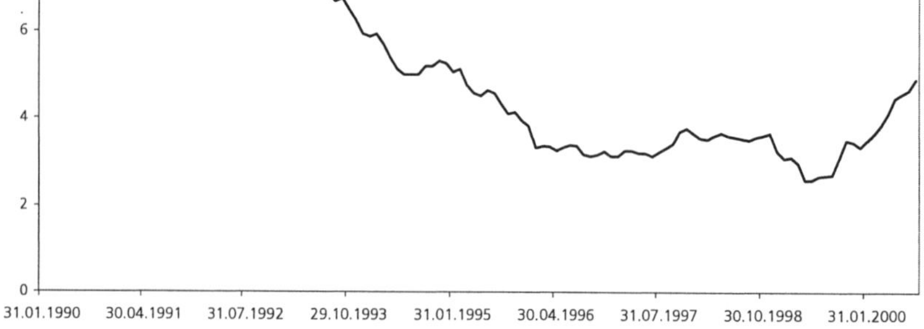

Fig. 3.13. 3-Months LIBOR from 1990 until 2000 (in %). Source: Bloomberg.

signaling process is assumed to follow a mean reverting square root process. We start our considerations in the "real world" instead of the "risk-adjusted world" and use Girsanov's theorem for the change of measure. Finally, in addition to the non-defaultable short rate and the uncertainty index, we directly model the short rate spread process: we assume that the spread between a defaultable and a non-defaultable bond is considerably driven by the uncertainty index but that there may be additional factors which influence the level of the spreads: at least the contractual provisions, liquidity and the premium demanded in the market for similar instruments have a great impact on credit spreads; we can easily relate credit spreads to business cycles by replacing the uncertainty index by some index of macroeconomic variables without any change of our theoretical framework.

Our approach seems to be reasonable in that credit spreads provide useful observable information on data upon which pricing models can be based. In addition, the model can be fitted directly to match the actual process followed by interest rate credit spreads. The analytical solution obtained for defaultable bonds can be implemented easily in practice, as all the variables and parameters can be implied from market data.

3.2 The Three-Factor Model

3.2.1 The Basic Setup

We want to develop a relative pricing theory based on the no-arbitrage assumption to determine fair values for defaultable securities and credit derivatives. As usual, we assume that markets are frictionless and perfectly competitive, that trading takes place continuously, that there are no taxes, transaction costs, or informational asymmetries, and that investors act as price takers. We fix a terminal time horizon T^*. Uncertainty in the financial market is modelled by a complete probability space $(\Omega, \mathcal{F}, \mathbf{P})$ and a filtration $\mathbf{F} = (\mathcal{F}_t)_{0 \leq t \leq T^*}$ of the three-dimensional standard Brownian motion $W(t)' = (W_r(t), W_s(t), W_u(t))$ (v' denotes the transpose of a vector v) satisfying the usual conditions (i.e. $\mathcal{F}_0$ is trivial and contains all the $\mathbf{P}-$null sets of $\mathcal{F}$ and the filtration $\mathbf{F}$ is right continuous). In addition, we assume $\mathcal{F}_{T^*} = \mathcal{F}$. The filtration $\mathbf{F}$ represents the arrival of information over time. We will assume throughout that the price of a security at time t is zero if all dividend payments after time t are zero. All prices are taken to be ex-dividend. All processes are defined on the probability space $(\Omega, \mathcal{F}, \mathbf{P})$. Furthermore, we make the following assumptions:

Assumption 3.2.1
The dynamics of the non-defaultable short rate are given by the following stochastic differential equation (SDE):

$$dr(t) = [\theta_r(t) - a_r r(t)]\,dt + \sigma_r r(t)^{\beta}\,dW_r(t), \ 0 \le t \le T^*, \tag{3.1}$$

where a_r, $\sigma_r > 0$ are positive constants, $\beta = 0$ or $\frac{1}{2}$, and θ_r is a non–negative valued deterministic function.

This specification implies that the current rate $r(t)$ is pulled towards $\frac{\theta_r(t)}{a_r}$ with a speed of adjustment a_r, and if $\beta = \frac{1}{2}$ the instantaneous variance of the change in the rate is proportional to its level.

Assumption 3.2.2
The development of the uncertainty index is given by the following stochastic differential equation:

$$du(t) = [\theta_u - a_u u(t)]\,dt + \sigma_u \sqrt{u(t)}dW_u(t), \ 0 \le t \le T^*, \tag{3.2}$$

where a_u, $\sigma_u > 0$ are positive constants and θ_u is a non–negative constant.

Assumption 3.2.3
The dynamics of the short rate spread (the short rate spread is supposed to be the defaultable short rate minus the non-defaultable short rate) is given by the following stochastic differential equation:

$$ds(t) = [b_s u(t) - a_s s(t)]\,dt + \sigma_s \sqrt{s(t)}dW_s(t), \ 0 \le t \le T^*, \tag{3.3}$$

where a_s, $b_s, \sigma_s > 0$ are positive constants.

Additionally, we assume that

$$\begin{aligned} Cov(dW_r(t), dW_s(t)) &= Cov(dW_r(t), dW_u(t)) \\ &= Cov(dW_s(t), dW_u(t)) = 0. \end{aligned}$$

Note, that although we assume uncorrelated standard Brownian motions W_r, W_s, and W_u, the short rate spread $s(t)$ and the uncertainty index $u(t)$ are correlated through the stochastic differential equation for the short rate spread.

First we show that the definition of r, s, and u, makes sense from the mathematical point of view. Afterwards we give some economical motivation and interpretation.

Lemma 3.2.1.
Let r_t, u_t, and s_t be stochastic processes defined by equations (3.1), (3.2), and (3.3), respectively. Assume that $\theta_r(t)$ is bounded[24] *on $[0, T^*]$, i.e. $\theta_r(t) \le \theta_r \forall$ $t \in [0, T^*]$. In addition, let*

[24] The assumption that $\theta_r(t)$ is bounded on $[0, T^*]$ is not too restrictive. As we show later, we infer $\theta_r(t)$ from market data by applying methods that ensure that $\theta_r(t)$ is a continuous function on $[0, T^*]$. Hence, in all our cases $\theta_r(t)$ is bounded on $[0, T^*]$.

$$dX_t = b(X_t)\,dt + \sigma(X_t)\,dW_t,\ 0 \le t \le T^*, \tag{3.4}$$

define a three-dimensional stochastic differential equation[25]*, where*

$$\begin{aligned} b(X_t) &= b(r_t, u_t, s_t) \\ &= (b_i(r_t, u_t, s_t))_{1\le i\le 3} = \begin{pmatrix} \theta_r(t) - a_r r_t \\ \theta_u - a_u u_t \\ b_s u_t - a_s s_t \end{pmatrix}, \end{aligned}$$

$$\begin{aligned} \sigma(X_t) &= \sigma(r_t, u_t, s_t) \\ &= (\sigma_{ij}(r_t, u_t, s_t))_{1\le i,j\le 3} = \begin{pmatrix} \sigma_r r_t^\beta & 0 & 0 \\ 0 & \sigma_u\sqrt{u_t} & 0 \\ 0 & 0 & \sigma_s\sqrt{s_t} \end{pmatrix}, \end{aligned}$$

and

$$W_t = (W_r(t), W_u(t), W_s(t))'.$$

Then, given the $\mathcal{F}_0-$measurable random variable $(r_0, u_0, s_0)'$, equation (3.4) has a unique weak solution[26] $X = (X_t)_{0\le t\le T^*} = (r_t, u_t, s_t)_{0\le t\le T^*}$.

[25] Let

- $W = (W_1, ..., W_p)$ an $\mathbf{R}^p-$ valued $\mathcal{F}_t-$Brownian motion.
- $b : \mathbf{R}^+ \times \mathbf{R}^n \to \mathbf{R}^n$, $b(s,x) = (b_1(s,x), ..., b_n(s,x))$.
- $\sigma : \mathbf{R}^+ \times \mathbf{R}^n \to \mathbf{R}^{n\times p}$, $\sigma(s,x) = (\sigma_{i,j}(s,x))_{1\le i\le n, 1\le j\le p}$.
- $Z = (Z_1, ..., Z_n)$ an $\mathcal{F}_0-$measurable random variable in $\mathbf{R}^n$.

Then

$$X_t = Z + \int_0^t b(s, X_s)\,ds + \int_0^t \sigma(s, X_s)\,dW_s$$

is called a multi-dimensional stochastic differential equation. In other words, a multi-dimensional stochastic process is a process $(X_t)_{0\le t\le T^*}$ with values in $\mathbf{R}^n$, adapted to the filtration $(\mathcal{F}_t)_{t\ge 0}$ and such that $\mathbf{P}$ a.s., for any t and for any $i \le n$

$$X_i(t) = Z_i + \int_0^t b_i(s, X_s)\,ds + \sum_{j=1}^p \int_0^t \sigma_{i,j}(s, X_s)\,dW_j(s).$$

[26] A weak solution of the stochastic differential equation (3.4) is a triple (X, W), $(\Omega, \mathcal{F}, \mathbf{P})$, $\mathbf{F} = (\mathcal{F}_t)$, where

1. $(\Omega, \mathcal{F}, \mathbf{P})$ is a probability space, and $\mathbf{F} = (\mathcal{F}_t)$ is a filtration of sub-σ-fields of $\mathcal{F}$ satisfying the usual conditions,
2. X is a continuous, $\mathcal{F}_t-$adapted $\mathbf{R}^3$-valued process, W is a three-dimensional Brownian motion,
3. $\mathbf{P}\left[\int_0^t \{|b_i(X_s)| + \sigma_{ij}^2(X_s)\}\,ds < \infty\right] = 1$ holds for every $1 \le i,j \le 3$ and $0 \le t \le T^*$,
4. the integral version of (3.4) $X_t = X_0 + \int_0^t b(X_s)\,ds + \int_0^t \sigma(X_s)\,dW_s$, $0 \le t \le T^*$, holds almost surely.

Proof.
See appendix B.

Lemma 3.2.2.
r, s and u are $\mathcal{F}_t$–progressively measurable processes on $[0, T^*]$.

Proof.
All three processes are continuous and as such progressively measurable[27] on $[0, T^*]$.

The assumption of the dynamics of the non-defaultable short rate can be replaced by any other short rate specification without major changes. To determine the parameters of the non-defaultable short rate one can use either the swap curve or the Treasury curve. But for the pricing of credit derivatives, the market uses as its base non-defaultable curve the LIBOR-based swap curve rather than the Treasury curve. The uncertainty index can be interpreted as a measure for the quality of the obligor: the larger the value of the uncertainty index the worse the quality. In case of corporates one could use data from rating agencies or firm values to fit the uncertainty index and estimate the parameters. In case of sovereigns one could use data from rating agencies or some kind of macroeconomic data. The model admits various interpretations and is very flexible to capture the characteristics of many different types of obligors. The assumption of mean reversion of the uncertainty index is motivated by several empirical observations. For example, Elsas, Ewert, Krahnen, Rudolph & Weber (1999) mention that a downgrading usually makes the management of a firm start taking actions to improve the firm's quality to reach the previous level again. In addition, the assumption of mean reversion of the short rate spread agrees with the prior beliefs of many academics and practitioners. For example, Taurén (1999) points out, that his empirical studies support the opinion that models which do not have mean reversion should be strongly rejected. Our model generalizes previous models in that the mean reversion level is time-dependent and may depend on the uncertainty index. Thus, we take into consideration that the rating has a great impact on credit spreads. There are some credit spread issues which shouldn't be ignored: Often, the yield spread between defaultable and non-defaultable assets is not a pure credit spread. Loans and bonds can contain explicit or implicit options. In that case, the observed spread must be adjusted for the value of these options. In addition, the observed spread can reflect liquidity or other forms of risk as well. Ideally, these risk components should be taken out of observed credit spreads.

As usual our first task is to find a convenient characterization of the no-arbitrage assumption. Absence of arbitrage is guaranteed by the existence of

[27] Korn & Korn (1999), p.36: If all paths of a stochastic process are right continuous the process is progressively measurable.

an equivalent martingale measure $\mathbf{Q}$. By definition, an equivalent martingale measure has to satisfy $\mathbf{Q} \sim \mathbf{P}$[28] and the discounted security price processes have to be local $\mathbf{Q}$–martingales with respect to a suitable numéraire[29].

Definition 3.2.1.
The non-defaultable money market account is defined by

$$B(t) = e^{\int_0^t r(l)dl}.$$

Taking the non-defaultable money market account as numéraire we have:

Definition 3.2.2.
There are no locally bounded arbitrage opportunities if and only if there is a probability measure $\mathbf{Q}$ defined on $(\Omega, \mathcal{F}, \mathbf{P})$ equivalent to $\mathbf{P}$ under which the discounted security price processes become local $\mathbf{Q}$–martingales. This measure $\mathbf{Q}$ is called an equivalent martingale measure, and for any security price process $X(t)$ the discounted price process is defined as $\frac{X(t)}{B(t)}$.

In our Brownian setting (basically $\mathcal{F}_t = \sigma(W(\tau), 0 \leq \tau \leq t)$ slightly enlarged to satisfy the usual conditions) we know that each equivalent martingale measure $\mathbf{Q}$ is given in terms of a Radon-Nikodym-Derivative[30]

$$\frac{d\mathbf{Q}}{d\mathbf{P}} \text{ and } \frac{d\mathbf{Q}_t}{d\mathbf{P}_t}$$

where $\mathbf{Q}_t = \mathbf{Q}|\mathcal{F}_t$ and $\mathbf{P}_t = \mathbf{P}|\mathcal{F}_t$ are the restrictions of $\mathbf{Q}$ and $\mathbf{P}$ on $\mathcal{F}_t$, with

$$\frac{d\mathbf{Q}_t}{d\mathbf{P}_t} = \exp\left(-\int_0^t \gamma(\tau)' \, dW(\tau) - \frac{1}{2}\int_0^t \|\gamma(\tau)\|^2 \, d\tau\right),$$

where $\|\cdot\|$ denotes the Euclidean norm and

$$\left\{\gamma(t)' = (\gamma_r(t), \gamma_s(t), \gamma_u(t)) : 0 \leq t \leq T^*\right\}$$

is an adapted measurable three-dimensional process satisfying

$$\int_0^{T^*} \gamma_i^2(t) \, dt < \infty \text{ for } i = r, s, u \quad \mathbf{P} - a.s.$$

[28] A probability measure $\mathbf{Q}$ on $(\Omega, \mathcal{F})$ is absolutely continuous relative to $\mathbf{P}$ if

$$\forall\, A \in \mathcal{F} \quad \mathbf{P}(A) = 0 \Rightarrow \mathbf{Q}(A) = 0.$$

The probabilities $\mathbf{P}$ and $\mathbf{Q}$ are equivalent $(\mathbf{P} \sim \mathbf{Q})$ if each one is absolutely continuous relative to the other.

[29] A numéraire is a price process $X(t)$ almost surely strictly positive foreach $t \in [0, T]$.

[30] For details see, e.g., Bingham & Kiesel (1998), §5.8.

More precisely, we assume (e.g., compare to Chen (1996), p.5)

$$\gamma_r(t) = \lambda_r \sigma_r r(t)^{1-\beta},$$
$$\gamma_s(t) = \lambda_s \sigma_s \sqrt{s(t)}, \text{ and}$$
$$\gamma_u(t) = \lambda_u \sigma_u \sqrt{u(t)}, \ 0 \le t \le T^*,$$

where λ_r, λ_s and λ_u are real constants and assume that Novikov's condition

$$E\left(\exp\left(\frac{1}{2}\int_0^{T^*} \|\gamma(\tau)\|^2 d\tau\right)\right) < \infty$$

is satisfied. Then by application of Girsanov's theorem[31] the process

$$\left\{\hat{W}(t)' = \left(\hat{W}_r(t), \hat{W}_s(t), \hat{W}_u(t)\right) : 0 \le t \le T^*\right\}$$

defined by

$$\hat{W}_i(t) = W_i(t) + \int_0^t \gamma_i(\tau)\, d\tau, \ i = r, s, u, \ 0 \le t \le T^*,$$

is a three-dimensional standardized Brownian Motion for the filtered probability space $(\Omega, \mathcal{F}, \mathbf{F}, \mathbf{Q})$ restricted to the time interval $[0, T^*]$. Under the measure $\mathbf{Q}$ the dynamics of $r(t)$, $s(t)$ and $u(t)$ are given by

$$dr(t) = [\theta_r(t) - \hat{a}_r r(t)]\, dt + \sigma_r r(t)^\beta \ d\hat{W}_r(t), \tag{3.5}$$
$$ds(t) = [b_s u(t) - \hat{a}_s s(t)]\, dt + \sigma_s \sqrt{s(t)} d\hat{W}_s(t), \tag{3.6}$$
$$du(t) = [\theta_u - \hat{a}_u u(t)]\, dt + \sigma_u \sqrt{u(t)} d\hat{W}_u(t), \ 0 \le t \le T^*, \tag{3.7}$$

where $\hat{a}_i = a_i + \lambda_i \sigma_i^2$.

Remark 3.2.1.
Obviously, existence and uniqueness of a solution of equations (3.5), (3.6), and (3.7) in the sense of lemma 3.2.1 is satisfied for the following reasons:

- $Cov\left(d\hat{W}_r(t), d\hat{W}_s(t)\right) = Cov\left(d\hat{W}_r(t), d\hat{W}_u(t)\right)$
  $= Cov\left(d\hat{W}_s(t), d\hat{W}_u(t)\right) = 0.$
- $\theta_r(t)$ doesn't change under the measure transformation.
- The basic structures of $b(r_t, u_t, s_t)$ and $\sigma(r_t, u_t, s_t)$ doesn't change under the measure transformation. We only have to replace the constants a_i, $i = r, s, u$, by the constants $\hat{a}_i$, $i = r, s, u$.

[31] See, e.g., Karatzas & Shreve (1988), pp. 190-201.

3.2.2 Valuation Formulas For Contingent Claims

In general, a contingent claim (or just a claim) or derivative asset is a financial instrument whose payoffs are exactly determined by the payoffs on one or more underlying assets (for a more detailed definition see, e.g., Ingersoll (1987), pages 50-51). Technically speaking, a simple (European) non-defaultable contingent $T-$claim is a pair (Y,T) consisting of a non-negative $\mathcal{F}_T-$measurable random variable Y and the time $T \leq T^*$, at which Y is paid. This concept can be generalized to defaultable claims:

Definition 3.2.3.
A simple (European) defaultable claim is a triple $\left[(Y,T), Z, T^d\right]$ consisting of

- *a simple (European) non-defaultable contingent claim (Y,T) yielding a payoff Y at time T, provided there has been no default, i.e. (Y,T) is describing the obligation of the issuer, and satisfying $E^{\mathbf{Q}}\left[|Y|^q\right] < \infty$ for some $q > 1$;*
- *a $\mathcal{F}_t-$predictable process Z describing the payoff upon default, and satisfying $E^{\mathbf{Q}}\left[\sup_t |Z_t|^q\right] < \infty$;*
- *a $\mathbf{F}-$stopping time T^d valued in $[0,\infty)$, describing the stochastic structure of the default time.*

The default time may be a surprise, i.e. totally inaccessible. With positive probability it can't be foreseen immediately before it occurs. As in section 2.3.4 the default indicator function $H(t) = H_t$ is defined by

$$H_t = 1_{\{T^d \leq t\}},\ t \geq 0.$$

In addition, we define

$$L_t = 1 - H_t,\ t \geq 0, \tag{3.8}$$

and let $\tau = \min\left(T, T^d\right)$. In terms of the default indicator function, the cumulative dividend process of the defaultable security is given by

$$\int_0^{t\wedge T} Z_u dH_u + Y 1_{\{T^d > T, t \geq T\}},\ t \geq 0.$$

The arbitrage free price at time t, $F(t)$, of the simple defaultable contingent claim $\left[(Y,T), Z, T^d\right]$ can be obtained as the discounted expected value of the future cash flows[32]. This expectation has to be taken with respect to $\mathbf{Q}$, that is

$$F(t) = E^{\mathbf{Q}}\left[\int_t^T e^{-\int_t^u r(l)dl} Z_u dH_u + e^{-\int_t^T r(l)dl}\, Y L_T \middle| \mathcal{F}_t\right],\ 0 \leq t < \tau, \tag{3.9}$$

and $F(t) = 0$ for $t \geq \tau$ since there are no dividends after time τ.

[32] See, e.g., Duffie, Schroder & Skiadas (1996).

In the following we derive a representation for F which doesn't explicitly involve the stopping time T^d. Therefore we have to state some assumptions, definitions and lemmas first:

Assumption 3.2.4
We assume that the payoff of the claim upon default is given by

$$Z_t(\omega) = Z(\omega, t, F) = w(\omega, t) F(\omega, t-), \; 0 \leq w(\omega, t) \leq 1,$$

where $w(t)$ is a $\mathcal{F}_t$–predictable process (such that $E^{\mathbf{Q}}[\sup_t |Z_t|^q] < \infty$) describing the recovery rate process, i.e. we assume partial recovery of market value[33].

Now we can define a defaultable money market account to be the value of 1 invested at $t = 0$ in a defaultable zero coupon bond of very short maturity, and if there is no default up to t rolled over until that time. Hence, the defaultable money market account can be compared to the non-defaultable money market account $B(t)$ in non-defaultable interest rate modelling.

Definition 3.2.4.
The defaultable money market account B^d is defined as

$$B^d(t) = \left(1 + \int_0^t (w_l - 1)\, dH_l\right) e^{\int_0^t (r(l)+s(l))dl}.$$

Lemma 3.2.3.
$M^d(t) = \int_0^t s(l)\, dl + \int_0^t (w_l - 1)\, dH_l$ *is a $\mathcal{F}_t$–(local) martingale.*

Proof.
According to definition 3.2.2 and our no-arbitrage assumption, under the measure $\mathbf{Q}$, the discounted process

$$\frac{B^d(t)}{B(t)} = \left(1 + \int_0^t (w_l - 1)\, dH_l\right) e^{\int_0^t s(l)dl}$$

must be a (local) martingale. But this is the Doléans Dade exponential[34] of

[33] See section 2.4.

[34] See Musiela & Rutkowski (1997), p.245: Let U be a real-valued semimartingale, right continuous with existing left limmits (RCLL, sometimes also called càdlàg), defined on $(\Omega, \mathcal{F}, \mathbf{Q})$ with $U_0 = U_{0-} = 0$. We write $\mathcal{E}(U)$ to denote the Doléans Dade exponential of U; that is, the unique solution of the stochastic differential equation

$$d\mathcal{E}_t(U) = \mathcal{E}_{t-}(U)\, dU_t, \tag{3.10}$$

with $\mathcal{E}_0(U) = 1$.The solution to equation (3.10) is explicitely known, namely

$$\mathcal{E}_t(U) = e^{U_t - \frac{1}{2}[U]_t^c} \prod_{u \leq t} (1 + \Delta_u U)\, e^{-\Delta_u U},$$

where $\Delta_u U = U_u - U_{u-}$, and $[U]^c$ is the path-by-path continuous part of $[U]$.

$$M^d(t) = \int_0^t s(l)\,dl + \int_0^t (w_l - 1)\,dH_l,$$

which in turn must also be a (local) martingale[35]: Observe that $M^d(t)$ is of finite variation[36]. Hence, the Doléans Dade exponential of $M^d(t)$ is given by

$$\begin{aligned}
\mathcal{E}_t\left(M^d\right) &= e^{M_t^d} \prod_{u \le t} \left(1 + \Delta_u M^d\right) e^{-\Delta_u M^d} \\
&= e^{\int_0^t s(l)dl + \int_0^t (w_l - 1)dH_l} \prod_{u \le t} \left(1 + \int_{u-}^{u} (w_l - 1)\,dH_l\right) e^{-\int_{u-}^{u}(w_l - 1)dH_l} \\
&= e^{\int_0^t s(l)dl} \prod_{u \le t} \left(1 + \int_{u-}^{u} (w_l - 1)\,dH_l\right) \\
&= \left(1 + \int_0^t (w_l - 1)\,dH_l\right) e^{\int_0^t s(l)dl}.
\end{aligned}$$

Lemma 3.2.4.
For a given continuous function $f : \mathbb{R} \times \Omega \times [0, \infty) \to \mathbb{R}$, an $\mathcal{F}_T$-measurable random variable Y, and a process of finite variation $\{D_t : 0 \le t \le T\}$, suppose there is some $q \in [1, \infty)$ such that $E^{\mathbf{Q}}\left[\left(\int_0^T |f(0, \omega, t)|\,dt\right)^q\right] < \infty$, $E^{\mathbf{Q}}\left[|Y|^q\right] < \infty$, and suppose there is some constant $K > 0$ such that

$$|f(x, \omega, t) - f(y, \omega, t)| \le K\,|x - y|$$

for all (ω, t) and all $x, y \in \mathbb{R}$. Then there exists a unique solution V to the recursive stochastic integral equation

$$V_t = E^{\mathbf{Q}}\left[\int_t^T f(V_l, \omega, l)\,dl + \int_t^T dD_l + Y \,\middle|\, \mathcal{F}_t\right],\ t \le T,$$

in the space of all RCLL adapted processes that satisfy $E^{\mathbf{Q}}\left[\left(\int_0^T |V_t|\,dt\right)^q\right] < \infty$.

Proof.
See Duffie & Huang (1996), page 941.

Lemma 3.2.5.
Let M be a $\mathbf{Q}$–martingale. If Y is predictable and $E^{\mathbf{Q}}\left[\sup_t |Y_t|^q\right] < \infty$ for some $q > 1$, then $\int Y dM$ is a $\mathbf{Q}$–martingale.

[35] See Lando (1995), p.4: Given a semimartingale U with $U_0 = U_{0-} = 0$. U is a local martingale iff $\mathcal{E}(U)$ is a local martingale.

[36] Jacod & Shiryaev (1987), page 59: If U is of finite variation,

$$\mathcal{E}_t(U) = e^{U_t} \prod_{u \le t} (1 + \Delta_u U)\, e^{-\Delta_u U}.$$

Proof.
See Duffie et al. (1996), page 1086.

Lemma 3.2.6.
Let Y be a semimartingale (see definition 2.2.1) satisfying $E^{\mathbf{Q}}\left[\int_0^T |Y_t|\,dt\right] < \infty$, let D be a semimartingale satisfying $E^{\mathbf{Q}}\left[\int_0^T |dD_t|\right] < \infty$, where by definition $\int_0^T |dD_t| = \int_0^T d\,|D|_t$ and $|D|_t = VAR_t(D)$ is the variation process of D (see footnote 7), and let G be a progressively measurable process such that $E^{\mathbf{Q}}\left[\int_0^T |G_t|\,dt\right] < \infty$. There exists a martingale m such that

$$dY_t = -G_t dt - dD_t + dm_t, \; t \leq T,$$

if and only if

$$Y_t = E^{\mathbf{Q}}\left[\int_t^T G_u du + \int_t^T dD_u + Y_T \middle| \mathcal{F}_t\right], \; t \leq T.$$

Proof.
See Duffie et al. (1996), page 1086, and Duffie & Huang (1996), page 942.

Corollary 3.2.1.
Let Y be a semimartingale satisfying $E^{\mathbf{Q}}\left[\int_0^T |Y_t|\,dt\right] < \infty$. Suppose that D is an adapted RCLL process of integrable variation[37], and ξ is a progressively measurable process. In addition, assume that the properties of ξ guarantee that all processes are well defined[38]. Then

$$dY_t = -dD_t - Y_t \xi_t dt + dm_t, \; t \leq T,$$

for some martingale m, if and only if

$$Y_t = E^{\mathbf{Q}}\left[\int_t^T e^{\int_t^u \xi_v dv} dD_u + e^{\int_t^T \xi_v dv} Y_T \middle| \mathcal{F}_t\right].$$

Proof. See Duffie et al. (1996), page 1086.

Remark 3.2.2.

1. If D is an adapted *RCLL* process of integrable variation it is a semimartingale satisfying $E^{\mathbf{Q}}\left[\int_0^T |dD_t|\right] < \infty$ (see, e.g., Protter (1992), page 47).

[37] The stochastic process D is of integrable variation if

$$E^{\mathbf{Q}}\left[VAR(D)_\infty\right] < \infty,$$

where $VAR(D)_\infty = \lim_{t\to\infty} VAR(D)_t$. $VAR(D)_t$ is defined in footnote 7.

[38] See lemma 3.2.6.

2. If D is of integrable variation or if D satisfies $E^{\mathbf{Q}}\left[\int_0^T |dD_t|\right] < \infty$ it is of finite variation (see, e.g., Jacod & Shiryaev (1987), page 29).

Using lemma 3.2.3 and corollary 3.2.1 we can prove the following important proposition:

Proposition 3.2.1.
Let $E^{\mathbf{Q}}\left[|Y|^q\right] < \infty$ for some $q > 1$. Under assumption 3.2.4 and the dynamics specified by equations (3.5), (3.6) and (3.7) the price process, $F(t)$, given by equation (3.9), satisfies

$$F(t) = V(t)\, 1_{\{t<\tau\}}, \tag{3.11}$$

where the adapted continuous process V is given by

$$V(t) = E^{\mathbf{Q}}\left[e^{-\int_t^T (r(l)+s(l))dl} Y \mid \mathcal{F}_t\right], \; 0 \leq t < T, \tag{3.12}$$

and $V(t) = 0$ for $t \geq T$, i.e. if there has been no default until time t, $F(t)$ must equal the expected value of riskless cash flows discounted at risky discount rates. Equation (3.12) has a unique solution in the space consisting of every semimartingale, J, such that $E^{\mathbf{Q}}\left[\sup_t |J_t|^q\right] < \infty$ for some $q > 1$.

Proof.
Existence and uniqueness of equation (3.12) follow immediately from lemma 3.2.4. It remains to show that equation (3.11) is valid.

- Because V satisfies the integral equation (3.12) only on $[0, T)$, we define a modified process $\widehat{V}$ by

$$\widehat{V}(t) = V_t 1_{\{t<T\}} + Y 1_{\{t \geq T\}},$$

  to extend the definition on the compact interval $[0, T]$.
- Apply corollary 3.2.1 to $\widehat{V}$ with $\xi = -(r+s)$ and $dX_t = 0$ (by lemma 3.2.2 ξ is progressively measurable):

$$\begin{aligned} d\widehat{V}(t) &= \widehat{V}_t (r_t + s_t)\, dt + dm_t \\ &= \widehat{V}_t r_t dt + \widehat{V}_t (1 - w_t)\, dH_t + \widehat{V}_t dM_t^d + dm_t \end{aligned}$$

  for some martingale m and M_t^d as defined in lemma 3.2.3.
- Define $U(t) = \widehat{V}_t L_t$ with $L_t = L(t)$ as defined by equation (3.8). Using integration by parts[39],

[39] See, e.g., Protter (1992), p. 60: Let X, Y be two semimartingales. Then XY is a semimartingale and

$$XY = \int X_- dY + \int Y_- dX + [X, Y].$$

$$\begin{aligned}dU(t) &= \widehat{V}_{t-}dL_t + L_{t-}d\widehat{V}_t + d\left[L,\widehat{V}\right]_t\\ &= \widehat{V}_t dL_t + L_{t-}d\widehat{V}_t\\ &= \widehat{V}_t dL_t + U_t r_t dt + \widehat{V}_t L_{t-}(1-w_t)\,dH_t + \widehat{V}_t L_{t-}dM_t^d + L_{t-}dm_t\\ &= \widehat{V}_t dL_t + U_t r_t dt + \widehat{V}_t L_{t-}(1-w_t)\,dH_t + d\widetilde{m}_t.\end{aligned}$$

as $\widehat{V}$ is continuous and L is a quadratic pure jump semimartingale[40]. Note, that $\widetilde{m}_t$ with $d\widetilde{m}_t = \widehat{V}_t L_{t-}dM_t^d + L_{t-}dm_t$ is a martingale[41].

- Apply corollary 3.2.1 with $\xi = -r$ and $dX_t = -\widehat{V}_t L_{t-}(1-w_t)\,dH_t - \widehat{V}_t dL_t$, i.e.

$$dX_t = \begin{cases} 0 & ,\ \text{if } t \neq T^d, \\ \widehat{V}_{T^d} w_{T^d} & ,\ \text{if } t = T^d, \end{cases}$$

(by lemma 3.2.2 ξ is progressively measurable; by the definition of H and L, X is an adapted $RCLL$ process; it is of integrable variation as it is adapted $RCLL$, increasing and $E\left(VAR(X)_\infty\right) \leq \widehat{V}_{T^d} < \infty$):

$$\begin{aligned}&U(t)\\ &= E^{\mathbf{Q}}\left[-\int_t^T e^{-\int_t^u r(l)dl}\widehat{V}_u\left(L_{u-}(1-w_u)-1\right)dH_u + e^{-\int_t^T r(l)dl}Y L_T \middle| \mathcal{F}_t\right]\\ &= E^{\mathbf{Q}}\left[-\int_t^T e^{-\int_t^u r(l)dl}\widehat{V}_{u-}\left(L_{u-}(1-w_u)-1\right)dH_u\right.\\ &\quad \left. + e^{-\int_t^T r(l)dl}Y L_T \middle| \mathcal{F}_t\right]\\ &= E^{\mathbf{Q}}\left[\int_t^T e^{-\int_t^u r(l)dl}\widehat{V}_{u-}w_u dH_u + e^{-\int_t^T r(l)dl}Y L_T \middle| \mathcal{F}_t\right].\end{aligned}$$

The formula follows trivially from the definition of the quadratic covariation $[X,Y]$ of two semimartingales X and Y:

$$[X,Y] = XY - \int X_{\_}dY - \int Y_{\_}dX.$$

[40] See, e.g., Protter (1992), p.68: Let L be a quadratic pure jump semimartingale. Then for any semimartingale $\widehat{V}$ we have

$$\left[L,\widehat{V}\right]_t = L_0\widehat{V}_0 + \sum_{0<s\leq t}\Delta L_s \Delta\widehat{V}_s.$$

A semimartingale L will be called quadratic pure jump if $[L,L]^c = 0$.

[41] $\int L_{t-}dm_t$ is a martingale since L is bounded and m is a martingale (see, e.g., Jacod & Shiryaev (1987), p. 47, 4.34 (b)). $\int \widehat{V}_t L_{t-}dM_t^d$ is a martingale by lemma 3.2.5: because V is continuous on $(0,T)$ it must be predictable. In addition, V is in the space of semimartingales, Y, such that $E^{\mathbf{Q}}\left[\sup_t |Y_t|^q\right] < \infty$. By proposition 2.6 in Jacod & Shiryaev (1987), p.17, L_{t-} is predictable.

- Because $U(t) = V(t)$ for $t < \tau$,

$$F(t) = V(t)\,1_{\{t<\tau\}}.$$

We calculate equation (3.12) by relating $V(t)$ to the solution of a partial differential equation. Under mild regularity conditions (see, e.g., Duffie (1992)) and by using the Feynman-Kac (see, e.g., Duffie (1992)) formula, we get the following lemma:

Lemma 3.2.7.
Assuming the dynamics specified by equations (3.5), (3.6), and (3.7), the pre-default value at time t, $V(r,s,u,t)$, of a defaultable claim $\left[(Y,T), Z, T^d\right]$ with Z like in assumption 3.2.4, is the solution to the partial differential equation (PDE)[42]

$$\begin{aligned} 0 = &\frac{1}{2}\left[\sigma_r^2 r^{2\beta} V_{rr} + \sigma_s^2 s V_{ss} + \sigma_u^2 \,\mathrm{V}_{uu}\right] \\ &+ \left[\theta_r(t) - \hat{a}_r r\right] V_r + \left[b_s u - \hat{a}_s s\right] V_s \\ &+ \left[\theta_u - \hat{a}_u u\right] V_u + V_t - (r+s) V, \quad (r,s,u,t) \in \mathbb{R}^3 \times [0,\mathrm{T}), \end{aligned} \tag{3.13}$$

with boundary condition

$$V(r,s,u,T) = Y(r,s,u), \quad (r,s,u) \in \mathbb{R}^3. \tag{3.14}$$

Similarly, assuming the dynamics specified by equation (3.5) the time t value, $F(r,t)$, of a non-defaultable claim (Y,T) is the solution to the PDE

$$0 = \frac{1}{2}\sigma_r^2 r^{2\beta} F_{rr} + \left[\theta_r(t) - \hat{a}_r r\right] F_r + F_t - rF, \quad (r,t) \in \mathbb{R} \times [0,\mathrm{T}),$$

with boundary condition

[42] If we assumed

$$\begin{aligned} Cov\left(dW_r(t), dW_s(t)\right) &= \rho_{rs} dt, \\ Cov\left(dW_r(t), dW_u(t)\right) &= \rho_{ru} dt, \\ Cov\left(dW_s(t), dW_u(t)\right) &= \rho_{su} dt, \end{aligned}$$

for some constants $\rho_{rs}, \rho_{ru}, \rho_{su}$, instead of PDE (3.13) we would have to consider the following PDE (see section 3.5.3):

$$\begin{aligned} 0 = &\frac{1}{2}\left[\sigma_r^2 r^{2\beta} V_{rr} + \sigma_s^2 s V_{ss} + \sigma_u^2 \,\mathrm{V}_{uu}\right] \\ &+ \rho_{rs}\sigma_r\sigma_s r^\beta \sqrt{s} V_{rs} + \rho_{ru}\sigma_r\sigma_u r^\beta \sqrt{u} V_{ru} + \rho_{us}\sigma_u\sigma_s\sqrt{su} V_{us} \\ &+ \left[\theta_r(t) - \hat{a}_r r\right] V_r + \left[b_s u - \hat{a}_s s\right] V_s \\ &+ \left[\theta_u - \hat{a}_u u\right] V_u + V_t - (r+s) V, \quad (r,s,u,t) \in \mathbb{R}^3 \times [0,\mathrm{T}). \end{aligned}$$

$$F(r,T) = Y(r), \; r \in \mathbb{R}.$$

Hence, the time t value of a non-defaultable discount bond with maturity T, $P(t,T) = P(r,t,T)$, is given by (compare to Vasicek (1977), Hull & White (1990), and Hull (1997))

$$P(r,t,T) = A(t,T)\, e^{-B(t,T)r}, \tag{3.15}$$

where $A(t,T)$ and $B(t,T)$ are defined by

$$B(t,T) = \begin{cases} \frac{1}{\hat{a}_r}\left[1 - e^{-\hat{a}_r(T-t)}\right], & \text{if } \beta = 0, \\ \frac{1-e^{-\delta_r(T-t)}}{\kappa_1^{(r)} - \kappa_2^{(r)} e^{-\delta_r(T-t)}}, & \text{if } \beta = \frac{1}{2}, \end{cases} \text{ and,} \tag{3.16}$$

$$\ln A(t,T) = \begin{cases} \int_t^T \left(\frac{1}{2}\sigma_r^2 B(\tau,T)^2 - \theta_r(\tau) B(\tau,T)\right) d\tau \\ = \ln \frac{P(0,T)}{P(0,t)} - B(t,T) \frac{\partial \ln P(0,t)}{\partial t} & \text{if } \beta = 0, \\ -\frac{\sigma_r^2}{4\hat{a}_r^3}\left(e^{-\hat{a}_r T} - e^{-\hat{a}_r t}\right)^2 \left(e^{2\hat{a}_r t} - 1\right), \\ -\int_t^T \theta_r(\tau) B(\tau,T)\, d\tau, & \text{if } \beta = \frac{1}{2}, \end{cases} \tag{3.17}$$

with

$$\delta_x = \sqrt{\hat{a}_x^2 + 2\sigma_x^2} \text{ and } \kappa_{1/2}^{(x)} = \frac{\hat{a}_x}{2} \pm \frac{1}{2}\delta_x. \tag{3.18}$$

Equations (3.15), (3.16) and (3.17) define the price of a discount bond at a future time t in terms of the short rate at time t and the prices of non-defaultable discount bond prices today. The latter can be calculated from today's term structure. The partial derivative $\frac{\partial \ln P(0,t)}{\partial t}$ in equation (3.17) can be approximated by $\frac{\ln P(0,t+\varepsilon) - \ln P(0,t-\varepsilon)}{2\varepsilon}$ where ε is a small length of time. In addition, if $\beta = 0$, the deterministic function $\theta_r(t)$ is given by

$$\theta_r(t) = f_t(0,t) + \hat{a}_r f(0,t) + \frac{\sigma_r^2}{2\hat{a}_r}\left(1 - e^{-2\hat{a}_r t}\right),$$

where $f(0,t)$ denotes the instantaneous forward rate as seen at time 0 for a contract maturing at time t. If $\beta = \frac{1}{2}$, $\theta_r(t)$ can be obtained iteratively from

$$-\int_0^t \theta_r(\tau) B(\tau,t)\, d\tau = \ln A(0,t)$$

by time discretization.

3.3 The Pricing of Defaultable Fixed and Floating Rate Debt

3.3.1 Introduction

In the following we determine pricing formulas for defaultable zero coupon bonds, coupon bonds, floating rate notes, and interest rate swaps. If not otherwise stated we always assume face values of 1.

3.3.2 Defaultable Discount Bonds

A defaultable discount bond is a financial instrument promising to pay 1 at some pre-defined maturity date T. Trivially, such a financial instrument satisfies definition 3.2.3 of a simple defaultable claim. So we can use the results of the previous section to determine the time t ($t < T$) price of the claim. Applying lemma 3.2.7 to a defaultable discount bond yields the following theorem:

Theorem 3.3.1.
Assuming the dynamics specified by equations (3.5), (3.6) and (3.7), the value at time $t < \tau$, $P^d(t,T) = P^d(r,s,u,t,T)$ of a defaultable discount bond is given by

$$P^d(t,T) = A^d(t,T)\, e^{-B(t,T)r(t)-C^d(t,T)s(t)-D^d(t,T)u(t)} \tag{3.19}$$

where

$$\begin{aligned} C^d(t,T) &= \frac{1-e^{-\delta_s(T-t)}}{\kappa_1^{(s)} - \kappa_2^{(s)} e^{-\delta_s(T-t)}}, \\ D^d(t,T) &= \frac{-2v'(t,T)}{\sigma_u^2 v(t,T)}, \\ \ln A^d(t,T) &= \ln A(t,T) + \frac{2\theta_u}{\sigma_u^2} \ln \left| \frac{v(T,T)}{v(t,T)} \right|, \end{aligned}$$

where $v(t,T)$ is defined as in equations (3.31) and (3.33) below.

Proof.
According to lemma 3.2.7, the value at time t, $P^d(r,s,u,t,T)$, of a defaultable discount bond is the solution to the PDE

$$\begin{aligned} 0 &= \frac{1}{2}\sigma_r^2 r^{2\beta} P_{rr}^d + \frac{1}{2}\sigma_s^2 s P_{ss}^d + \frac{1}{2}\sigma_u^2 u P_{uu}^d \\ &\quad + [\theta_r - \hat{a}_r r] P_r^d + [b_s u - \hat{a}_s s] P_s^d \\ &\quad + [\theta_u - \hat{a}_u u] P_u^d + P_t^d - (r+s) P^d, \end{aligned}$$

with boundary condition $P^d(r,s,u,T,T) = 1$.

If $\beta = 0$, plugging in the partial derivatives of P^d yields the following system of ODEs

$$\hat{a}_r B^d - B_t^d - 1 = 0 \tag{3.20}$$

$$\frac{1}{2}\sigma_s^2 \left(C^d\right)^2 + \hat{a}_s C^d - C_t^d - 1 = 0 \tag{3.21}$$

$$\frac{1}{2}\sigma_u^2 \left(D^d\right)^2 + \hat{a}_u D^d - D_t^d - b_s C^d = 0 \tag{3.22}$$

$$A^d \left(\theta_r B^d + \theta_u D^d - \frac{1}{2}\sigma_r^2 \left(B^d\right)^2\right) - A_t^d = 0. \tag{3.23}$$

Equation (3.21) has Ricatti form $C_t^d = \frac{1}{2}\sigma_s^2 \left(C^d\right)^2 + \hat{a}_s C^d - 1$. The solution is

$$C^d(t,T) = \frac{-2w'(t,T)}{\sigma_s^2 w(t,T)}$$

where $w(t,T)$ satisfies

$$w'' - \hat{a}_s w' - \frac{1}{2}\sigma_s^2 w = 0. \tag{3.24}$$

From $\hat{a}_s^2 + 2\sigma_s^2 > 0$ it follows that all solutions of the ODE (3.24) are given by $w = \alpha_1 e^{\kappa_1^{(s)} t} + \alpha_2 e^{\kappa_2^{(s)} t}$, where α_1 and α_2 are some constants and $\kappa_1^{(s)}$ and $\kappa_2^{(s)}$ are given by

$$\kappa_{1/2}^{(x)} = \frac{\hat{a}_x}{2} \pm \frac{1}{2}\sqrt{\hat{a}_x^2 + 2\sigma_x^2}. \tag{3.25}$$

Then all solutions to equation (3.21) are given by

$$C^d(t,T) = -\frac{2}{\sigma_s^2}\frac{\alpha_1 \kappa_1^{(s)} e^{\kappa_1^{(s)} t} + \alpha_2 \kappa_2^{(s)} e^{\kappa_2^{(s)} t}}{\alpha_1 e^{\kappa_1^{(s)} t} + \alpha_2 e^{\kappa_2^{(s)} t}}. \tag{3.26}$$

In order to satisfy the boundary condition

$$C^d(T,T) = 0,$$

the constant α_1 equals

$$\alpha_1 = -\alpha_2 \frac{\kappa_2^{(s)}}{\kappa_1^{(s)}} e^{-\delta_s T},$$

and therefore

$$C^d(t,T) = \frac{1 - e^{-\delta_s (T-t)}}{\kappa_1^{(s)} - \kappa_2^{(s)} e^{-\delta_s (T-t)}}, \tag{3.27}$$

where

$$\delta_x = \sqrt{\hat{a}_x^2 + 2\sigma_x^2}. \tag{3.28}$$

Equation (3.22) has Ricatti form $D_t^d = \frac{1}{2}\sigma_u^2 \left(D^d\right)^2 + \hat{a}_u D^d - b_s C^d$. The solution is

$$D^d(t,T) = \frac{-2v'(t,T)}{\sigma_u^2 v(t,T)}, \tag{3.29}$$

where $v(t,T)$ satisfies

$$v'' - \hat{a}_u v' - \frac{1}{2} b_s \sigma_u^2 C^d v = 0. \tag{3.30}$$

The solutions to equation (3.30) are given by

$$\begin{aligned} v(t,T) = {} & \vartheta_1 \left(\sigma_u^2 e^{-\delta_s (T-t)}\right)^{\frac{\hat{a}_u}{2\delta_s} - \phi\left(\kappa_1^{(s)}\right)} F_1(t,T) \\ & + \vartheta_2 \left(\sigma_u^2 e^{-\delta_s (T-t)}\right)^{\frac{\hat{a}_u}{2\delta_s} + \phi\left(\kappa_1^{(s)}\right)} F_3(t,T), \end{aligned} \tag{3.31}$$

where ϑ_1 and ϑ_2 are some constants and

$$\begin{aligned} F_1(t,T) = F \Big(& -\phi\left(\kappa_1^{(s)}\right) - \phi\left(\kappa_2^{(s)}\right), -\phi\left(\kappa_1^{(s)}\right) + \phi\left(\kappa_2^{(s)}\right), \\ & 1 - 2\phi\left(\kappa_1^{(s)}\right), \kappa_2^{(s)}/\kappa_1^{(s)} e^{-\delta_s (T-t)} \Big), \\ F_3(t,T) = F \Big(& \phi\left(\kappa_1^{(s)}\right) - \phi\left(\kappa_2^{(s)}\right), \phi\left(\kappa_1^{(s)}\right) + \phi\left(\kappa_2^{(s)}\right), \\ & 1 + 2\phi\left(\kappa_1^{(s)}\right), \kappa_2^{(s)}/\kappa_1^{(s)} e^{-\delta_s (T-t)} \Big), \end{aligned}$$

with

$$\phi(g) = \sqrt{\frac{\hat{a}_u^2 g + 2 b_s \sigma_u^2}{4\delta_s^2 g}}$$

and $F(a,b,c,z)$ is the hypergeometric function[43].
Differentiation of $v(t,T)$ yields

$$v'(t,T) = y_1(t,T) + y_2(t,T), \tag{3.32}$$

[43] The hypergeometric function, usually denoted by F, has series expansion

$$F(a,b,c,z) = \sum_{k=0}^{\infty} \frac{(a)_k (b)_k}{(c)_k} \frac{z^k}{k!},$$

where$(a)_0 = 1$, $(a)_n = a(a+1)(a+2)\dots(a+n-1)$, $n \in \mathbf{N}$, and is the solution of the hypergeometric differential equation

$$z(1-z)y'' + [c - (a+b+1)z]y' - aby = 0.$$

The hypergeometric function can be written as an integral

$$F(a,b,c,z) = \frac{\Gamma(c)}{\Gamma(b)\Gamma(c-b)} \int_0^1 t^{b-1} (1-t)^{c-b-1} (1-tz)^{-a} dt, \quad (c > b > 0),$$

and is also known as the Gauss series or the Kummer series.

where

$$y_1(t,T) = \vartheta_1 \left(\sigma_u^2 e^{-\delta_s(T-t)}\right)^{\frac{\hat{a}_u}{2\delta_s} - \phi\left(\kappa_1^{(s)}\right)} \varphi_2(t,T),$$
$$y_2(t,T) = -\vartheta_2 \left(\sigma_u^2 e^{-\delta_s(T-t)}\right)^{\frac{\hat{a}_u}{2\delta_s} + \phi\left(\kappa_1^{(s)}\right)} \varphi_1(t,T),$$

with

$$\varphi_1(t,T) = \zeta_2 e^{-\delta_s(T-t)} F_4(t,T) - \xi_1 F_3(t,T),$$
$$\varphi_2(t,T) = \xi_2 F_1(t,T) - \zeta_1 e^{-\delta_s(T-t)} F_2(t,T),$$

where

$$F_2(t,T) = F\left(1 - \phi\left(\kappa_1^{(s)}\right) - \phi\left(\kappa_2^{(s)}\right), 1 - \phi\left(\kappa_1^{(s)}\right) + \phi\left(\kappa_2^{(s)}\right), 2 - 2\phi\left(\kappa_1^{(s)}\right), \kappa_2^{(s)}/\kappa_1^{(s)} e^{-\delta_s(T-t)}\right),$$
$$F_4(t,T) = F\left(1 + \phi\left(\kappa_1^{(s)}\right) - \phi\left(\kappa_2^{(s)}\right), 1 + \phi\left(\kappa_1^{(s)}\right) + \phi\left(\kappa_2^{(s)}\right), 2 + 2\phi\left(\kappa_1^{(s)}\right), \kappa_2^{(s)}/\kappa_1^{(s)} e^{-\delta_s(T-t)}\right),$$

and

$$\xi_{1/2} = \left(\frac{\hat{a}_u}{2} \pm \delta_s \phi\left(\kappa_1^{(s)}\right)\right), \quad \zeta_{1/2} = \delta_s \frac{\kappa_2^{(s)}}{\kappa_1^{(s)}} \frac{\phi^2\left(\kappa_2^{(s)}\right) - \phi^2\left(\kappa_1^{(s)}\right)}{1 \mp 2\phi\left(\kappa_1^{(s)}\right)}.$$

In order to satisfy the boundary condition

$$D^d(T,T) = 0,$$

ϑ_1 equals

$$\vartheta_1 = \vartheta_2 \left(\sigma_u^2\right)^{2\phi(\kappa_1(s))} \frac{\varphi_1}{\varphi_2}, \tag{3.33}$$

where $\varphi_1 = \varphi_1(T,T)$ and $\varphi_2 = \varphi_2(T,T)$. From equations (3.29), (3.31), (3.32) and (3.33), $D^d(t,T)$ can be determined as

$$D^d(t,T) = \frac{2}{\sigma_u^2} \cdot \frac{\varphi_2 e^{-2\delta_s \phi\left(\kappa_1^{(s)}\right)(T-t)} \varphi_1(t,T) - \varphi_1 \varphi_2(t,T)}{\varphi_1 F_1(t,T) + \varphi_2 e^{-2\delta_s \phi\left(\kappa_1^{(s)}\right)(T-t)} F_3(t,T)}.$$

Consider the case $\beta = 0$:
The solution of equation (3.20) that satisfies the boundary condition

$$B^d(T,T) = 0$$

is

$$B^d(t,T) = \frac{1}{\hat{a}_r}\left[1 - e^{-\hat{a}_r(T-t)}\right].$$

By direct substitution, the solution of equation (3.23) for A^d that satisfies the boundary condition

$$A^d(T,T) = 1$$

is

$$A^d(t,T)$$
$$= \exp\left[-\int_t^T \left(\theta_r(\tau) B^d(\tau,T) + \theta_u D^d(\tau,T) - \frac{1}{2}\sigma_r^2 \left(B^d(\tau,T)\right)^2\right) d\tau\right].$$

According to equation (3.17),

$$-\int_t^T \left(\theta_r(\tau) B^d(\tau,T) - \frac{1}{2}\sigma_r^2 \left(B^d(\tau,T)\right)^2\right) d\tau = \ln A(t,T),$$

and in addition, according to equation (3.29),

$$\theta_u \int_t^T D^d(\tau,T)\, d\tau = \frac{-2\theta_u}{\sigma_u^2}\left[\ln\left|\frac{v(T,T)}{v(t,T)}\right|\right],$$

where $\vartheta_1 = \vartheta_2 \left(\sigma_u^2\right)^{2\phi(\kappa_1(s))} \frac{\varphi_1}{\varphi_2}$.

The case $\beta = \frac{1}{2}$ is considered in appendix B.2.

Remark 3.3.1.
If we extend the definition of the uncertainty index from a constant parameter θ_u to a time-dependent parameter $\theta_u(t)$, the values of $\theta_u(t)$ can be determined iteratively from

$$\ln\frac{A^d(0,t)}{A(0,t)} = \int_0^t \theta_u(\tau) D^d(\tau,t)\, d\tau.$$

Although the bond pricing and credit spread formulas are rather complex and there are many parameters involved it is easy to prove that they show realistic features: $\lim_{T\to\infty} P^d(r,s,u,t,T) = 0$; for $T > t$: $lim_{r\to\infty} P^d(r,s,u,t,T) = \lim_{s\to\infty} P^d(r,s,u,t,T) = 0$, since $B(t,T) > 0$ and $C^d(t,T) > 0$; the price of a defaultable bond is a decreasing function of r and a decreasing function of s; further more, it is a convex function of r and a convex function of s.

Factor Loadings. The yield to maturity of a defaultable discount bond is given by

$$R^d(r,s,u,t,T)$$
$$= -\frac{1}{T-t}\left[\ln A^d(t,T) - B(t,T)\,r - C^d(t,T)\,s - D^d(t,T)\,u\right].$$

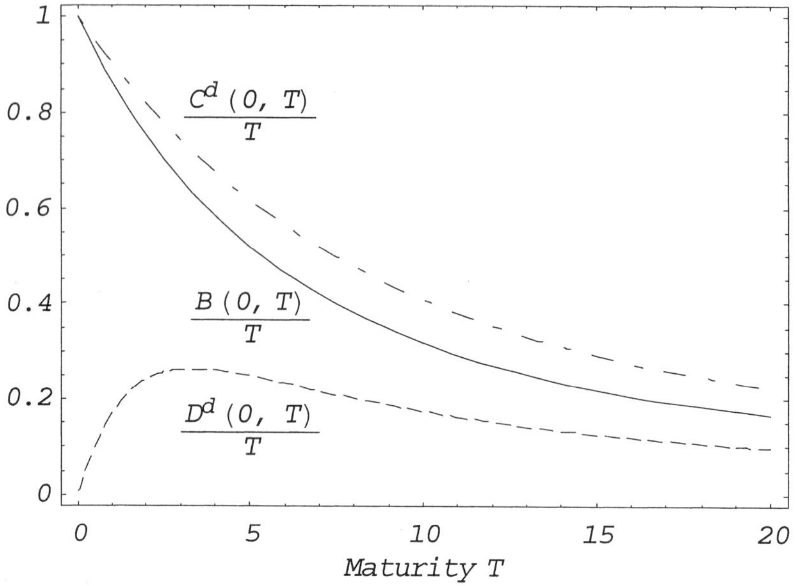

Fig. 3.14. Term structure of $\frac{B(0,T)}{T}$, $\frac{C^d(0,T)}{T}$, and $\frac{D^d(0,T)}{T}$. The values of the parameters are $\hat{a}_r = 0.3$, $\hat{a}_s = 0.2$, $\sigma_s = 0.1$, $b_s = 0.5$, $\hat{a}_u = 1$, $\sigma_u = 0.4$, $\theta_u = 1.5$.

The functions B, C^d and D^d determine the sensitivity of a defaultable zero coupon bond's yield to the factors r, s, and u. We call them factor loadings for r, s, and u, respectively.

Figure 3.14 shows that the sensitivity of a bond's yield to the factors r and s is greater for short and intermediate maturities. The sensitivity to u is greatest for intermediate maturities. All sensitivities die out as maturities approach infinity. This is consistent with the well-known effect of flattening yield curves for long maturities.

The Term Structure of Credit Spreads. The credit spread is defined as the difference between the yields of a defaultable and its corresponding non-defaultable bond. Since $A^d(t,T) = A(t,T)\, e^{\int_t^T \theta_u D^d(\tau,T)d\tau}$, the defaultable bond pricing formula can be written as

$$P^d(r,s,u,t,T) = P(r,t,T)\, e^{\int_t^T \theta_u D^d(\tau,T)d\tau - C^d(t,T)s - D^d(t,T)u}. \tag{3.34}$$

Hence, the default premium of the defaultable bond is given by

$$P(r,t,T)\left(1 - e^{\int_t^T \theta_u D^d(\tau,T)d\tau - C^d(t,T)s - D^d(t,T)u}\right).$$

If we denote the time t yield to maturity of a non-defaultable discount bond with maturity T by $R(r,t,T)$ and the time t yield to maturity of a defaultable discount bond with maturity T by $R^d(r,s,u,t,T)$, the credit spread, $S(r,s,u,t,T)$, is given by

$$
\begin{aligned}
& S(r,s,u,t,T) \\
&= R^d(r,s,u,t,T) - R(r,t,T) \\
&= \frac{1}{T-t}\left[-\int_t^T \theta_u D^d(\tau,T)\,d\tau + C^d(t,T)\,s + D^d(t,T)\,u\right]. \qquad (3.35)
\end{aligned}
$$

It is obvious from equation (3.35) that the credit spreads implied by our model are independent of the level of the non-defaultable short rate, although the influence of the non-defaultable short rate to the prices of defaultable and non-defaultable bonds is crucial. In addition, the credit spread tends to $\frac{-\int_t^T \theta_u D^d(\tau,T)d\tau}{T-t}$ as s and u tend to 0. $\frac{-\int_t^T \theta_u D^d(\tau,T)d\tau}{T-t}$ can be either positive or negative depending on the values of the parameters. It reflects the fact that there is a certain probability that the quality of the firm under consideration will decrease (i.e. the uncertainty index will increase) between time t and maturity although its current quality is excellent and therefore the current short rate spread is 0. There will always remain a certain amount of default risk and the buyer of the defaultable bond should get a compensation for it. Nevertheless, if $\theta_u \equiv 0$, zero becomes an absorbing state for u. Then, if s tends to 0 the yield spread will also tend to 0. Finally, the model is consistent in that the short rate spread implied by the credit spreads equals[44]

$$
\lim_{T\to t}\left[S(r,s,u,t,T)\right] = s(t). \qquad (3.36)
$$

Two immediate implications can be drawn from the wider set of parameters influencing the term structure of credit spreads compared to previous models. First, we can expect larger spreads which are closer to those observed in practice. Second, our model captures more complex properties of credit spreads. In order to better understand these properties we consider the following specific parameter values and study the effects of varying them: $s(0) = 0.0008$, $u(0) = 3$, $\theta_u = 1$, $\hat{a}_u = 1$, $\sigma_u^2 = 0.16$, $b_s = 0.0001$, $\hat{a}_s = 0.1$, $\sigma_s^2 = 0.01$. In the following we will refer to these parameters as the base case parameters.

The Effect of the Mean Reversion Parameter θ_u. Figure 3.15 shows that the parameter θ_u and therefore the mean-reversion level of the uncertainty index behave as expected: an increase in θ_u widens the credit spread. The parameter represents the long term expectation of the quality of the firm. The lower this expectation is the smaller the spreads are. As the actual quality of the firm ($u(0) = 3$) is much worse than the long-run levels of the uncertainty index: $\frac{\theta_u}{\hat{a}_u} = 1.5,\ 1.0,\ 0.5,\ 0.1$, the credit spreads narrow for long maturities. For

[44] $\lim_{T\to t} \frac{-\int_t^T \theta_u D^d(\tau,T)d\tau}{T-t} = -\theta_u D^d(T,T) = 0$,
$\lim_{T\to t} \frac{C^d(t,T)}{T-t} = \lim_{T\to t} \frac{\left(1-e^{-\delta_s(T-t)}\right)s(t)}{\left(\kappa_1^{(s)}-\kappa_2^{(s)}e^{-\delta_s(T-t)}\right)(T-t)} \overset{L'Hospital}{=} s(t)$,
$\lim_{T\to t} \frac{D^d(t,T)u(t)}{T-t} = \lim_{T\to t} \frac{-2v'(t,T)u(t)}{\sigma_u^2 v(t,T)(T-t)} \overset{L'Hospital}{=} 0$, as
$v''(t,t) = -\frac{1}{2}\sigma_u^2\left(\hat{a}_u D^d(t,t) - b_s C^d(t,t)\right)v(t,t) = 0$ and $v(t,t) \neq 0$.

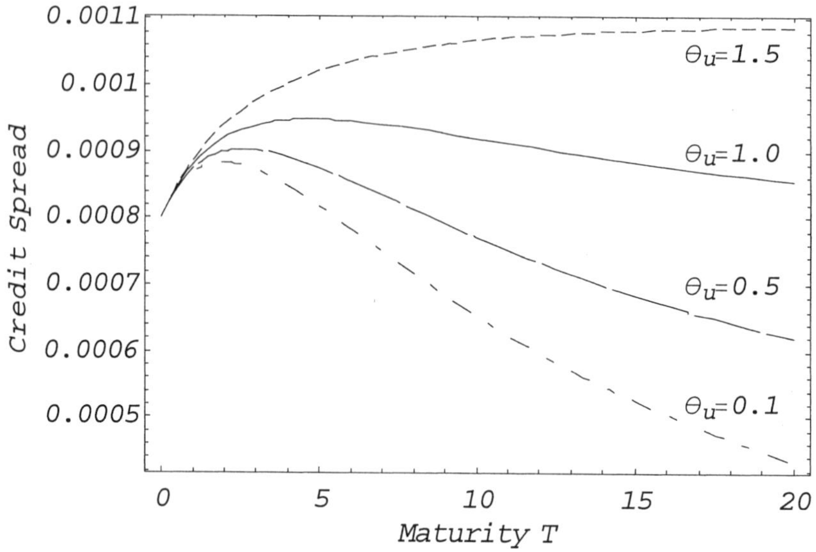

Fig. 3.15. Credit spread term structure vs. θ_u.

small values of θ_u the credit spread term structures are humped shaped. For larger values of θ_u, i.e. for values of θ_u such that $\frac{\theta_u}{\hat{a}_u}$ is closer to $u(0)$, the term structure changes to an upward-sloping shape.

The Effect of the Speed of Mean Reversion Parameter $\hat{a}_u$. Figure 3.16 shows that an increase of the mean reversion speed parameter $\hat{a}_u$ narrows the credit spreads. In the cases $\hat{a}_u = 1.5$, 1.0, and 0.5, the actual quality of the firm ($u(0) = 3$) is much worse than the long-run levels of the uncertainty index: $\frac{\theta_u}{\hat{a}_u} = \frac{2}{3}$, 1, and 2. For $\hat{a}_u = 1.5$ and 1.0 the credit spreads widen for short maturities and narrow for long maturities. The credit spread term structure is humped shaped. In case of $\hat{a}_u = 0.1$, the long-run level of the uncertainty index is worse than the actual quality of the firm. Hence, the long-run expectation on the quality of the firm is to deteriorate further. We get an upward-sloping credit spread term structure. The larger $\hat{a}_u$ the faster is the returning to the mean reversion level. In the case of $\hat{a}_u = 0.1$, this increases the credit spread widening effect even more. For $\hat{a}_u = 1.5$, 1.0, and 0.5, the acceleration effect increases the credit spread narrowing.

The Effect of the Uncertainty Index $u(0)$. Figure 3.17 shows that credit spreads of short term debt are sensitive to the current quality of the firm. For long term debt the long-run level of the quality of the firm is more important than its current quality. The bigger the actual uncertainty index values the bigger the credit spreads. The maximal credit spread is observed for a defaultable bond with a maturity of approximately four years.

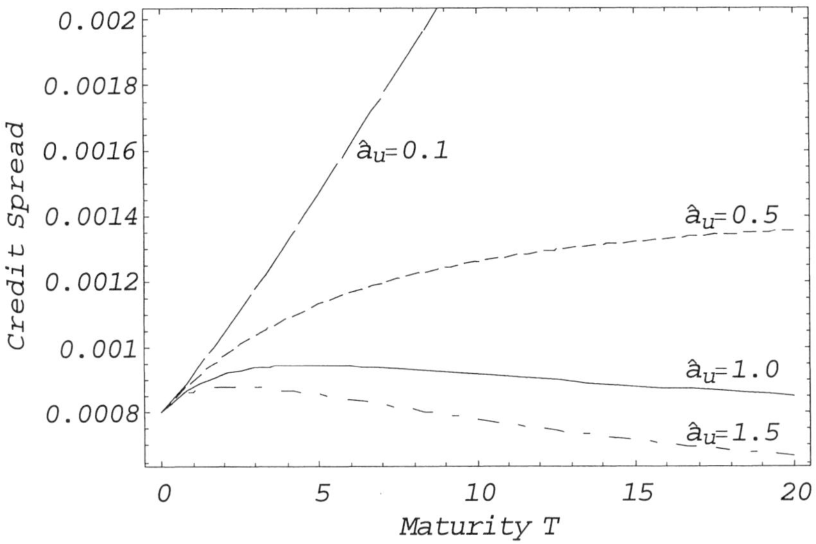

Fig. 3.16. Credit spread term structure vs. $\hat{a}_u$.

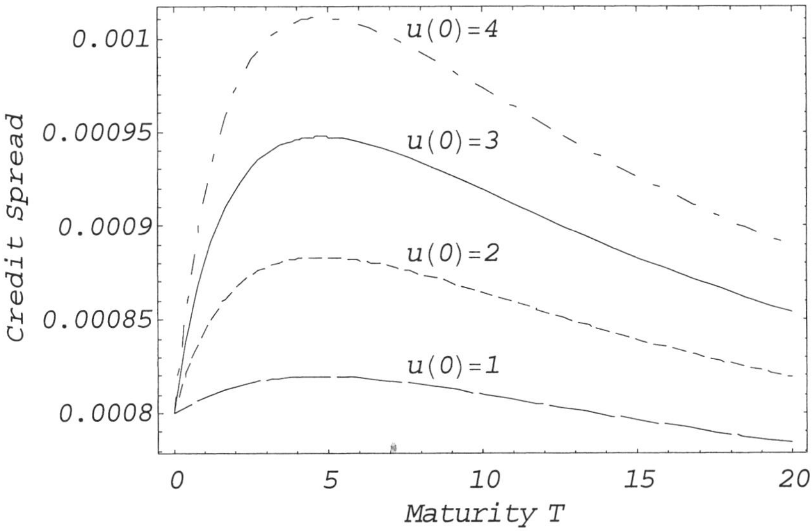

Fig. 3.17. Credit spread term structure vs. $u(0)$.

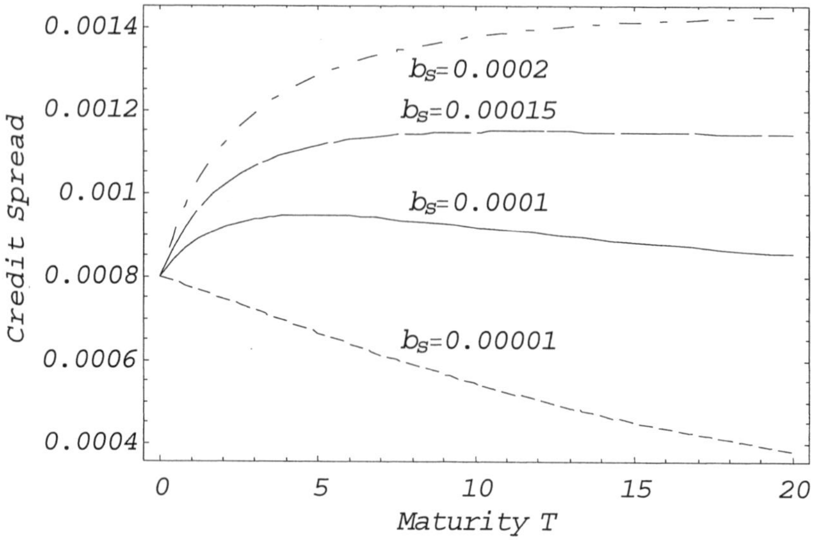

Fig. 3.18. Credit spread term structure vs. b_s.

The Effect of the Parameter b_s. Figure 3.18 shows that an increase in b_s has a great impact on the term structure of credit spreads. In general, the larger b_s the greater the influence of the uncertainty index on the term structure of the short rate spread and the credit spread. For $b_s = 0.0001$ and $b_s = 0.00015$ the curves of figure 3.18 are humped-shaped: for $b_s = 0.00001$ the curve is downward-sloping, for $b_s = 0.0002$ upward-sloping.

The Effect of the Parameter $\hat{a}_s$. The larger $\hat{a}_s$ the narrower the credit spreads. In the cases $\hat{a}_s = 0.2$ and 0.5, the actual short rate credit spread $s(0) = 0.0008$ is wider than the long-run levels of $\frac{b_s}{\hat{a}_s}\frac{\theta_u}{\hat{a}_u} = 0.0005$ and 0.0002. Hence, the credit spreads widen for short maturities and narrow for long maturities. The credit spread term structure is humped shaped. In the cases of $\hat{a}_s = 0.1$, and 0.01, the actual short rate credit spread is narrower than the long-run levels of the long-run level of $\frac{b_s}{\hat{a}_s}\frac{\theta_u}{\hat{a}_u} = 0.001$ and 0.01. Hence, the long-run expectation on the credit spreads is not to narrow much or even to widen further.

The Effect of the Volatility Parameter σ_s *of the Short Rate Spread.* For our set of base case parameters an increase of σ_s narrows the credit spreads. This can mainly be explained by the fact that the actual short rate credit spread and firm quality are worse than the long-run levels. A larger volatility parameter increases the probability of a fast return to this level.

The Effect of the Short Rate Spread $s(0)$. Figure 3.21 shows that credit spreads are an increasing function in s. This fits to the fact that the price of a

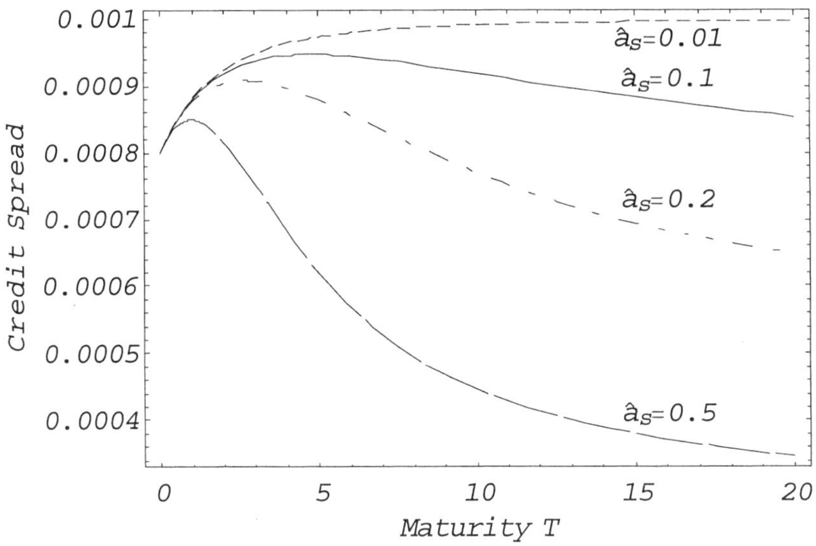

Fig. 3.19. Credit spread term structure vs. $\hat{a}_s$.

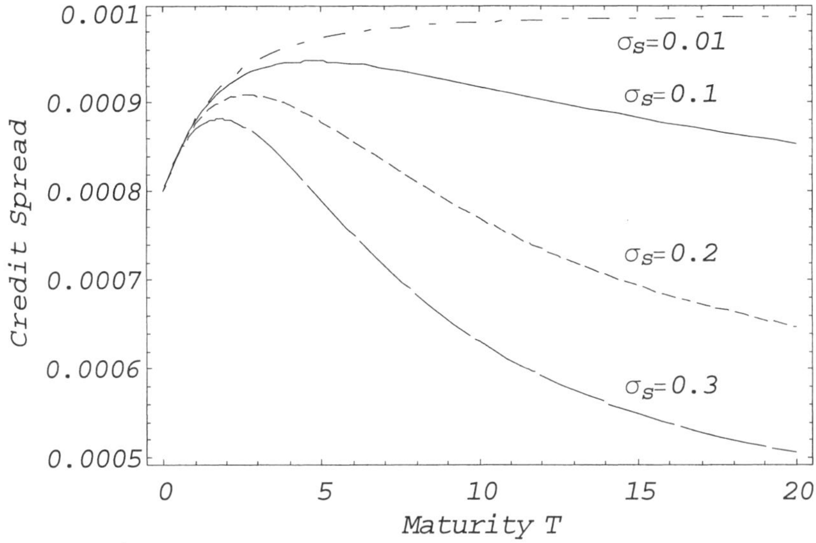

Fig. 3.20. Credit spread term structure vs. σ_s.

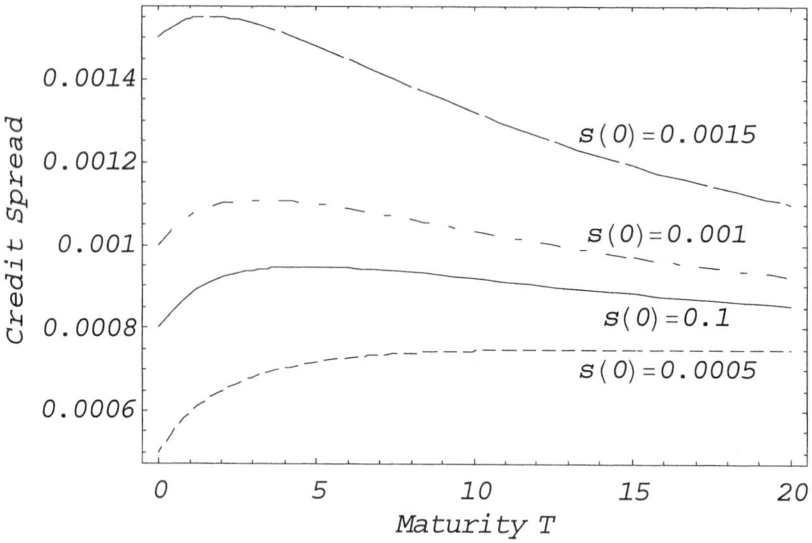

Fig. 3.21. Credit spread term structure vs. $s(0)$.

defaultable bond is a decreasing function in s. In contrast with Merton's and many other models we get positive credit spreads even for very short maturities. Thus, our model takes into consideration that instantaneous default is possible. In addition, expected as well as unexpected defaults are captured by the methodology.

Our model is capable of producing upward-sloping, downward-sloping and humped term structures of credit spreads meeting the properties suggested by the empirical results of Sarig & Warga (1989). We are able to produce a wide range of levels of credit spreads and are not faced with the problem of the traditional Merton model which can't reproduce the entire range of spreads observed in the market.

Implied Recovery Rates. One of the key components of the default process is the recovery by bond holders in the event of default. According to assumption 3.2.4 we assume fractional recovery of market value. In addition, for simplicity we assume that the stochastic recovery rate w and the default process are independent and that the recovery rate is paid at maturity (if there is a default prior to maturity). Then we can easily determine an implicit expected recovery rate. These assumptions are not too restrictive as most models assume constant recovery rates. By our assumptions, the price of a risky bond is given by

$$P^d(t,T) = P(t,T)\,E^{\mathbf{Q}}\left[w1_{\{\tau\leq T\}} + 1_{\{\tau>T\}}|\mathcal{F}_t\right] \tag{3.37}$$
$$= P(t,T)\left[E^{\mathbf{Q}}\left[w|\mathcal{F}_t\right](1-\mathbf{Q}(\tau>T|\mathcal{F}_t)) + \mathbf{Q}(\tau>T|\mathcal{F}_t)\right],$$

where $P(t,T)$ denotes the value at time t of a non-defaultable discount bond assuming the dynamics of the riskless short rate specified by equation (3.1). Using equations (3.34) and (3.37), we get

$$E^{\mathbf{Q}}\left[w(t)|\mathcal{F}_t\right] = \frac{e^{\int_t^T \theta_u D^d(\tau,T)d\tau - C^d(t,T)s - D^d(t,T)u} - \mathbf{Q}(\tau>T|\mathcal{F}_t)}{1-\mathbf{Q}(\tau>T|\mathcal{F}_t)}. \tag{3.38}$$

If we assumed a constant recovery rate (as we do, e.g., in section 3.4), the right hand side of equation 3.38 is exactly the recovery rate. Thus, our model yields an alternative way for finding recovery rates if there is only scarce empirical data available (in chapter 3.6 we show how the risk-neutral survival probabilities can be calculated).

3.3.3 Defaultable (Non-Callable) Fixed Rate Debt

The theory for the pricing of simple (European) defaultable contingent claims can't be used to price defaultable fixed rate bonds. Therefore, we extend our theory to the pricing of general (European) defaultable contingent claims. A general (European) non-defaultable contingent claim is a triple (Y,D,T) consisting of a cumulative dividend process D (any $\mathcal{F}_t$−adapted process of integrable variation), the $\mathcal{F}_T$−measurable random variable Y and the time $T \leq T^*$, at which Y is paid. This concept can be generalized to defaultable claims:

Definition 3.3.1.
A general (European) defaultable claim is a triple $\left[(Y,D,T), Z, T^d\right]$ consisting of

- *a general (European) non-defaultable contingent claim (Y,D,T) yielding payoffs $\int_t^{T\wedge T^d} dD_u$ over the time interval $\left[t, T\wedge T^d\right]$, and a final payoff Y at time T, provided there has been no default until time T, i.e. (Y,D,T) is describing the obligation of the issuer, and satisfying*

$$E^{\mathbf{Q}}\left[\int_0^T |dD_t|^q\right] < \infty \text{ as well as } E^{\mathbf{Q}}\left[|Y|^q\right] < \infty \text{ for some } q>1;$$

- *a $\mathcal{F}_t$−predictable process Z describing the payoff upon default, and satisfying $E^{\mathbf{Q}}\left[\sup_t |Z_t|^q\right] < \infty$;*
- *a $\mathbf{F}$−stopping time T^d valued in $[0,\infty)$, describing the stochastic structure of the default time.*

Hence, a simple (European) defaultable contingent claim $\left[(Y,T), Z, T^d\right]$ equals a general (European) defaultable contingent claim $\left[(Y,D,T), Z, T^d\right]$, where $dD_t = 0$, $0 \leq t \leq T$. For simplicity, we will refer to a general defaultable contingent claim as a defaultable contingent claim. In terms of the default indicator function, the cumulative dividend process of the defaultable security is given by

$$\int_0^{t\wedge T} Z_u dH_u + \int_0^{t\wedge T} L_u dD_u + Y 1_{\{T^d > T, t \geq T\}}, \; t \geq 0.$$

The arbitrage free price at time t, $F(t)$, of the defaultable contingent claim $\left[(Y,D,T), Z, T^d\right]$ can be obtained as the discounted expected value of the future cash flows. This expectation has to be taken with respect to $\mathbf{Q}$, that is for $0 \leq t < \tau$,

$$\begin{aligned} &F(t) \\ &= E^{\mathbf{Q}}\left[\int_t^T e^{-\int_t^u r(l)dl} Z_u dH_u + \int_t^T e^{-\int_t^u r(l)dl} L_u dD_u \right. \qquad (3.39) \\ &\left. + e^{-\int_t^T r(l)dl}\, Y L_T \right| \mathcal{F}_t \Bigg], \end{aligned}$$

and $F(t) = 0$ for $t \geq \tau$ since there are no dividends after time τ.

Proposition 3.3.1.
Under assumption 3.2.4 and the dynamics specified by equations (3.5), (3.6) and (3.7) the price process, $F(t)$, given by equation (3.39), satisfies

$$F(t) = V(t)\, 1_{\{t<\tau\}}, \tag{3.40}$$

if V is predictable or if $\Delta V_{T^d} = 0$ a.s., and where the adapted process V is given by

$$V(t) = E^{\mathbf{Q}}\left[\int_t^T e^{-\int_t^u (r(l)+s(l))dl} dD_u + e^{-\int_t^T (r(l)+s(l))dl} Y \right| \mathcal{F}_t \Bigg], \; 0 \leq t < T, \tag{3.41}$$

and $V(t) = 0$ for $t \geq T$, i.e. if there has been no default until time t, $F(t)$ must equal the expected value of riskless cash flows discounted at risky discount rates. Equation (3.41) has a unique solution in the space consisting of every semimartingale, J, such that $E^{\mathbf{Q}}\left[\sup_t |J_t|^q\right]$ for some $q > 1$.

Proof.
All prerequisites of lemma 3.2.4 are satisfied by the definition of a defaultable claim and the characteristics of r and s. Hence, existence and uniqueness of equation (3.41) follows immediately from lemma 3.2.4. It remains to show that equation (3.40) is valid.

- Because V satisfies the integral equation (3.12) only on $[0,T)$, we define a modified process $\widehat{V}$ by

$$\widehat{V}(t) = V_t 1_{\{t<T\}} + 1_{\{t\geq T\}} dD_T + Y 1_{\{t\geq T\}},$$

to extend the definition on the compact interval $[0,T]$.
- Apply corollary 3.2.1 to $\widehat{V}$ with $\xi = -(r+s)$ and $dX_t = dD_t$ (by lemma 3.2.2 ξ is progressively measurable):

$$\begin{aligned} d\widehat{V}(t) &= -dD_t + \widehat{V}_t (r_t + s_t) dt + dm_t \\ &= -dD_t + \widehat{V}_t r_t dt + \widehat{V}_t (1 - w_t) dH_t + \widehat{V}_t dM_t^d + dm_t \end{aligned}$$

for some martingale m and M_t^d as defined in lemma 3.2.3.
- Define $U(t) = \widehat{V}_t L_t$ with $L_t = L(t)$ as defined above. Using integration by parts,

$$\begin{aligned} dU(t) &= \widehat{V}_{t-} dL_t + L_{t-} d\widehat{V}_t + d\left[L, \widehat{V}\right]_t \\ &= \widehat{V}_t dL_t + L_{t-} d\widehat{V}_t \\ &= \widehat{V}_t dL_t - L_{t-} dD_t + U_t r_t dt + \\ &\quad \widehat{V}_t L_{t-} (1 - w_t) dH_t + \widehat{V}_t L_{t-} dM_t^d + L_{t-} dm_t \\ &= \widehat{V}_t dL_t - L_{t-} dD_t + U_t r_t dt + \\ &\quad \widehat{V}_t L_{t-} (1 - w_t) dH_t + d\widetilde{m}_t. \end{aligned}$$

As in the proof of proposition 3.2.1 $\widetilde{m}_t$ with $d\widetilde{m}_t = \widehat{V}_t L_{t-} dM_t^d + L_{t-} dm_t$ is a martingale.
- Apply corollary 3.2.1 with $\xi = -r$ and

$$dX_t = L_{t-} dD_t - \widehat{V}_t L_{t-} (1 - w_t) dH_t - \widehat{V}_t dL_t,$$

(by lemma 3.2.2 ξ is progressively measurable; by the definition of H and L, X is an adapted $RCLL$ process; it is of integrable variation as it is adapted $RCLL$, increasing and $E(Var(X)_\infty) \leq \widehat{V}_{T^d} < \infty$):

$$\begin{aligned} &U(t) \\ &= E^{\mathbf{Q}} \left[-\int_t^T e^{-\int_t^u r(l)dl} \widehat{V}_u (L_{u-}(1 - w_u) - 1) dH_u \right. \\ &\quad \left. + \int_t^T e^{-\int_t^u r(l)dl} L_{u-} dD_u + e^{-\int_t^T r(l)dl} Y L_T \right| \mathcal{F}_t \Bigg] \\ &= E^{\mathbf{Q}} \left[\int_t^T e^{-\int_t^u r(l)dl} \widehat{V}_{u-} w_u dH_u \right. \\ &\quad \left. + \int_t^T e^{-\int_t^u r(l)dl} L_{u-} dD_u + e^{-\int_t^T r(l)dl} Y L_T \right| \mathcal{F}_t \Bigg], \end{aligned}$$

- Because $U(t) = V(t)$ for $t < \tau$,

$$F(t) = V(t) 1_{\{t<\tau\}}.$$

Remark 3.3.2.
The assumption $\Delta V_{T^d} = 0$ *a.s.* is not very restrictive. E.g., in case of defaultable coupon bonds default is usually not announced exactly at a coupon payment date but some time earlier.

Suppose we want to price a defaultable coupon bond promising to make discrete coupon payments c_i occurring at dates $t < t_i \leq T$, $i = 1, ..., n$, and a final payment of 1 at maturity T. Trivially, a defaultable coupon bond satisfies the characteristics of a defaultable claim. Hence, by using proposition 3.3.1 we find easily that the time t price of a coupon bond that hasn't defaulted yet, $P_c^d(t,T) = P_c^d(r,s,u,t,T)$, is given by

$$P_c^d(t,T) = \sum_{i=1}^{n} c_i P^d(t,t_i) + P^d(t,T). \tag{3.42}$$

3.3.4 Defaultable Callable Fixed Rate Debt

Many corporate bonds are callable. Thus, it is important to extend our pricing theory to capture fixed rate bonds with embedded call options. We assume that it is optimal for the bond issuer to call the bond when its market value is minimal. If we denote the feasible call policies in the time interval $[t,T]$ by $\mathcal{CP}(t,T)$ and assume that the bond hasn't been called and hasn't defaulted until time t, the time t price of a defaultable callable fixed rate bond with discrete coupon payments c_i occurring at dates $t < t_i \leq T$, $i = 1, ..., n$, and maturity T, $P_{cc}^d(t,T) = P_{cc}^d(r,s,u,t,T)$, is given by

$$\begin{aligned} &P_{cc}^d(t,T) \\ &= \min_{T^c \in \mathcal{CP}(t,T)} E^{\mathbf{Q}} \left(\sum_{t<t_i\leq T^c} c_i e^{-\int_t^{t_i}(r(l)+s(l))dl} + e^{-\int_t^{T^c}(r(l)+s(l))dl} \middle| \mathcal{F}_t \right), \end{aligned} \tag{3.43}$$

assuming that the minimum in the equation above is attained by some stopping time. Technical regularity conditions are given in Karatzas (1988). This stopping time approach to callable bond pricing in a quite different context was first proposed by Merton (1974). Equation (3.43) can be solved, e.g., by using discretization techniques (see, e.g., Duffie & Singleton (1997)).

3.3.5 Building a Theoretical Framework for Pricing One-Party Defaultable Interest Rate Derivatives

We consider a simple (European) defaultable claim $[(Y,T), Z, T^d]$ as stated in definition 3.2.3 and assume recovery of market value (see assumption 3.2.4).

As usual we denote the price of the defaultable claim at time t by $F(t)$, where $F(t)$ is given in proposition 3.2.1. $V(t)$ is the solution of equation

$$0 = \frac{1}{2}\left[\sigma_r^2 r^{2\beta} V_{rr} + \sigma_s^2 s V_{ss} + \sigma_u^2 \mathrm{V}_{uu}\right] + \left[\theta_r(t) - \hat{a}_r r\right] V_r + \left[b_s u - \hat{a}_s s\right] V_s + \left[\theta_u - \hat{a}_u u\right] V_u + V_t - (r+s) V, \quad (r,s,u,t) \in \mathbb{R}^3 \times [0, \mathrm{T}), \tag{3.44}$$

with boundary condition

$$V(r,s,u,T) = Y(r,s,u), \quad (r,s,u) \in \mathbb{R}^3. \tag{3.45}$$

Now assume that $G\left(y, \check{t}, z, t\right)$ is the solution to the problem

$$0 = \frac{1}{2}\sigma_r^2 r^{2\beta} G_{rr} + \frac{1}{2}\sigma_s^2 s G_{ss} + \frac{1}{2}\sigma_u^2 u G_{uu} + \left[\theta_r(t) - \hat{a}_r r\right] G_r + \left[b_s u - \hat{a}_s s\right] G_s + \left[\theta_u - \hat{a}_u u\right] G_u + G_t - (r+s) G, \tag{3.46}$$

with boundary condition

$$G\left(y, \check{t}, z, \check{t}\right) = \delta(r - y_r)\,\delta(s - y_s)\,\delta(u - y_u), \tag{3.47}$$

where $\delta(.)$ is the Dirac function[45], and $x = (x_1, x_2, x_3)$, $y = (y_r, y_s, y_u)$ and $z = (r,s,u)$. Then it is straightforward to show[46] that the solution to the PDE (3.44) with boundary condition (3.45) can be written as

[45] We use the definition of the Dirac function given in Wilmott, Dewynne & Howison (1993), pp.94 ff.: The Dirac function δ is not in fact a function, but is rather a generalized function. It is the limit as $\varepsilon \to 0$ of any one-parameter family of functions $\delta_\epsilon(t)$ with the following properties:

- for each ϵ, $\delta_\epsilon(t)$ is piecewise smooth;
- $\int_{-\infty}^{\infty} \delta_\epsilon(t)\,dt = 1$;
- for each $t \neq 0$, $\lim_{\epsilon \to 0} \delta_\epsilon(t) = 0$.

Such a sequence of functions is called a delta-sequence. For any smooth function $f(x)$,

$$\int_{-\infty}^{\infty} \delta(x - x_0) f(x)\,dx = f(x_0),$$

so multiplying by $\delta(x - x_0)$ and integrating picks out the value of f at x_0. Furthermore, if $\mathcal{H}(x)$ is the unit step function,

$$\mathcal{H}(x) = \begin{cases} 0 \text{ for } x < 0, \\ 1 \text{ for } x \geq 0, \end{cases}$$

then $\int_{-\infty}^{x} \delta(\xi)\,d\xi = \mathcal{H}(x)$, and conversely, $\mathcal{H}'(x) = \delta(x)$. Sometimes $\mathcal{H}(x)$ is called Heaviside function.

[46] Compare, e.g., to Chen (1996) or Cathcart & El-Jahel (1998). Chen (1996) uses a similar approach for the pricing of non-defaultable bonds.

$$V(z,t) = \iiint\limits_{\mathbf{R}^3} G(y,T,z,t)\, Y(y)\, dy. \tag{3.48}$$

As a first step we show that V - as defined in equation (3.48) - satisfies the PDE (3.44):

$$\begin{aligned}
&\frac{1}{2}\left[\sigma_r^2 r^{2\beta} V_{rr} + \sigma_s^2 s V_{ss} + \sigma_u^2 V_{uu}\right] + \left[\theta_r(t) - \hat{a}_r r\right] V_r + \left[b_s u - \hat{a}_s s\right] V_s \\
&+ \left[\theta_u - \hat{a}_u u\right] V_u + V_t - (r+s) V \\
= &\iiint\limits_{\mathbf{R}^3} \Big\{ \frac{1}{2}\left[\sigma_r^2 r^{2\beta} G_{rr}(y,T,z,t) + \sigma_s^2 s G_{ss}(y,T,z,t) + \sigma_u^2 u G_{uu}(y,T,z,t)\right] \\
&+ \left[\theta_r(t) - \hat{a}_r r\right] G_r(y,T,z,t) + \left[b_s u - \hat{a}_s s\right] G_s(y,T,z,t) \\
&+ \left[\theta_u - \hat{a}_u u\right] G_u(y,T,z,t) + G_t(y,T,z,t) - (r+s) G(y,T,z,t) \Big\} Y(y)\, dy \\
= &\iiint\limits_{\mathbf{R}^3} 0 \cdot Y(y)\, dy = 0.
\end{aligned}$$

The first equality follows by interchanging the order of integration and differentiation. Therefore G must satisfy some appropriate smoothness conditions. The second equality follows directly from equation (3.46).
As a second step we check that the boundary condition (3.45) is satisfied:

$$\begin{aligned}
V(z,T) &= \iiint\limits_{\mathbf{R}^3} G(y,T,z,T)\, Y(y)\, dy \\
&= \iiint\limits_{\mathbf{R}^3} \delta(r - y_r)\, \delta(s - y_s)\, \delta(u - y_u)\, Y(y)\, dy \qquad (3.49) \\
&= Y(z)\,. \qquad (3.50)
\end{aligned}$$

Equation (3.49) uses equation (3.47), and equation (3.50) follows immediately from the properties of the Dirac function.

Corollary 3.3.1.

$$F(z,t) = 1_{\{t<\tau\}} \iiint\limits_{\mathbf{R}^3} G(y,T,z,t)\, Y(y)\, dy.$$

Especially, if $t < \tau$,

$$P^d(z,t,T) = \iiint\limits_{\mathbf{R}^3} G(y,T,z,t)\, dy.$$

Hence, if $t < \tau$,

$$\iiint\limits_{\mathbf{R}^3} G(y,T,z,t)\, dy = A^d(t,T)\, e^{-B(t,T)r(t) - C^d(t,T)s(t) - D^d(t,T)u(t)}.$$

If we define

$$L(y,T,z,t) = \frac{G(y,T,z,t)}{P^d(z,t,T)},$$

we get

$$F(z,t) = 1_{\{t<\tau\}} P^d(z,t,T) \iiint_{\mathbf{R}^3} L(y,T,z,t)\, Y(y)\, dy.$$

By construction $L(y,T,z,t)$ is positive and integrates to 1 with respect to y. Therefore we can think of L as of a probability density, the joint density of $r(T)$, $s(T)$ and $u(T)$ under some measure $\mathbf{Q}^L$. Hence,

$$F(z,t) = 1_{\{t<\tau\}} P^d(z,t,T)\, E^{\mathbf{Q}^L}\left[Y(y)\,|\mathcal{F}_t\right].$$

Corollary 3.3.2.
The arbitrage free price at time t, $F(t)$, of the simple defaultable contingent claim $\left[(Y,T),Z,T^d\right]$ is given by

$$\begin{aligned}
F(t) &= E^{\mathbf{Q}}\left[\int_t^T e^{-\int_t^u r(l)dl} Z_u dH_u + e^{-\int_t^T r(l)dl}\, Y L_T \,\middle|\, \mathcal{F}_t\right] \\
&= 1_{\{t<\tau\}} E^{\mathbf{Q}}\left[e^{-\int_t^T (r(l)+s(l))dl}\, Y \,\middle|\, \mathcal{F}_t\right] \\
&= 1_{\{t<\tau\}} \iiint_{\mathbf{R}^3} G(y,T,z,t)\, Y(y)\, dy \\
&= 1_{\{t<\tau\}} P^d(z,t,T)\, E^{\mathbf{Q}^L}\left[Y(y)\,|\mathcal{F}_t\right].
\end{aligned}$$

So we can conclude that if we know the function G we can determine the price of the derivative easily.

Lemma 3.3.1.
$G\left(y,\check{t},z,t\right)$, is given by

$$G\left(y,\check{t},z,t\right) = \frac{1}{(2\pi)^{3/2}} \iiint_{\mathbf{R}^3} e^{-ixy'}\, \tilde{G}\left(x,\check{t},z,t\right) dx \tag{3.51}$$

where

$$\tilde{G}\left(x,\check{t},z,t\right) = A^{\tilde{G}}\left(x,t,\check{t}\right) e^{-B^{\tilde{G}}\left(x,t,\check{t}\right)r - C^{\tilde{G}}\left(x,t,\check{t}\right)s - D^{\tilde{G}}\left(x,t,\check{t}\right)u}$$

with $z=(r,s,u)$, $x=(x_1,x_2,x_3)$, $y=(y_r,y_s,y_u)$, and

$$B^{\tilde{G}}\left(x,t,\check{t}\right)=\begin{cases}-ix_1e^{-\hat{a}_r\left(\check{t}-t\right)}+\frac{1}{\hat{a}_r}\left(1-e^{-\hat{a}_r\left(\check{t}-t\right)}\right), & if\ \beta=0,\\ -\frac{2}{\sigma_r^2}\frac{\varpi(x_1)\kappa_1^{(r)}e^{-\kappa_1^{(r)}\left(\check{t}-t\right)}+\kappa_2^{(r)}e^{-\kappa_2^{(r)}\left(\check{t}-t\right)}}{\varpi(x_1)e^{-\kappa_1^{(r)}\left(\check{t}-t\right)}+e^{-\kappa_2^{(r)}\left(\check{t}-t\right)}}, & if\ \beta=\frac{1}{2},\end{cases} \tag{3.52}$$

$$C^{\tilde{G}}\left(x,t,\check{t}\right)=\frac{\kappa_3^{(s)}\left(x\right)-e^{-\delta_s\left(\check{t}-t\right)}}{\kappa_4^{(s)}\left(x\right)-\kappa_5^{(s)}\left(x\right)e^{-\delta_s\left(\check{t}-t\right)}},$$

$$D^{\tilde{G}}\left(x,t,\check{t}\right)=\frac{-2}{\sigma_u^2}\left(\pi_1\left(x\right)\varphi_2\left(x,t,\check{t}\right)\right.$$
$$\left.-e^{-2\delta_s\phi\left(\kappa_4^{(s)}(x),\kappa_3^{(s)}(x)\right)\left(\check{t}-t\right)}\pi_2\left(x\right)\varphi_1\left(x,t,\check{t}\right)\right)/$$
$$\left(\pi_1\left(x\right)F_1^{\tilde{G}}\left(x,t,\check{t}\right)\right.$$
$$\left.+e^{-2\delta_s\phi\left(\kappa_4^{(s)}(x),\kappa_3^{(s)}(x)\right)\left(\check{t}-t\right)}\pi_2\left(x\right)F_3^{\tilde{G}}\left(x,t,\check{t}\right)\right),$$

if $\beta=\frac{1}{2}$:

$$A^{\tilde{G}}\left(x,t,\check{t}\right)=\tilde{A}\left(x,t,\check{t}\right),$$

with

$$\ln\tilde{A}\left(x,t,\check{t}\right)=\int_{\check{t}}^{t}\left(\theta_r\left(\tau\right)B^{\tilde{G}}\left(x,\tau,\check{t}\right)+\theta_uD^{\tilde{G}}\left(x,\tau,\check{t}\right)\right)d\tau,$$

if $\beta=0$:

$$A^{\tilde{G}}\left(x,t,\check{t}\right)=\tilde{A}\left(x,t,\check{t}\right)e^{-\int_{\check{t}}^{t}\frac{1}{2}\sigma_r^2\left(B^{\tilde{G}}\left(x,\tau,\check{t}\right)\right)^2d\tau},$$

and $F\left(a,b,c,z\right)$ *is the hypergeometric function.* ϖ, $\kappa_3^{(s)}$, $\kappa_4^{(s)}$, $\kappa_5^{(s)}$, π_1, π_2, φ_1, *and* φ_2 *are defined in the proof below.* δ_s, $\kappa_1^{(r)}$, *and* $\kappa_2^{(r)}$ *are given by equation (3.18).*

Proof.
We apply the proof of appendix B.3 with $\alpha=1$. Then

$$\begin{array}{ll}G\left(y,\check{t},z,t\right)=G^{(1)}\left(y,\check{t},z,t\right), & \tilde{G}\left(x,\check{t},z,t\right)=\widetilde{G}^{(1)}\left(x,\check{t},z,t\right),\\ A^{\tilde{G}}\left(x,t,\check{t}\right)=A^{\widetilde{G}^{(1)}}\left(x,t,\check{t}\right), & B^{\tilde{G}}\left(x,t,\check{t}\right)=B^{\widetilde{G}^{(1)}}\left(x,t,\check{t}\right),\\ C^{\tilde{G}}\left(x,t,\check{t}\right)=C^{\widetilde{G}^{(1)}}\left(x,t,\check{t}\right), & D^{\tilde{G}}\left(x,t,\check{t}\right)=D^{\widetilde{G}^{(1)}}\left(x,t,\check{t}\right),\\ \pi_1\left(x\right)=\pi_1^{(1)}\left(x\right), & \pi_2\left(x\right)=\pi_2^{(1)}\left(x\right),\\ \varphi_1\left(x,t,\check{t}\right)=\varphi_1^{(1)}\left(x,t,\check{t}\right), & \varphi_2\left(x,t,\check{t}\right)=\varphi_2^{(1)}\left(x,t,\check{t}\right),\\ \kappa_3^{(s)}\left(x\right)=\kappa_3^{(s,1)}\left(x\right), & \kappa_4^{(s)}\left(x\right)=\kappa_4^{(s,1)}\left(x\right),\\ \kappa_5^{(s)}\left(x\right)=\kappa_5^{(s,1)}\left(x\right), & \end{array}$$

and ϖ is given by equation (B.21).

In the following we summarize the steps necessary to calculate prices of defaultable interest rate derivatives under the assumption that the prices for defaultable bonds are given[47]:

1. Determine the Fourier transform[48] $\tilde{G}$ of G by using lemma 3.3.1.
2. Determine the probability density function L in the following way:
   a) Calculate the Fourier transform $\widetilde{L}$ of L by using $\tilde{G}$:

$$\widetilde{L}\left(x,\check{t},z,t\right)=\frac{1}{\left(2\pi\right)^{3/2}}\frac{\tilde{G}\left(x,\check{t},z,t\right)}{\tilde{G}\left(0,\check{t},z,t\right)},$$

where 0 denotes the three-dimensional zero vector.

Proof.

$$\begin{aligned}\tilde{G}\left(x,\check{t},z,t\right)&=\frac{1}{\left(2\pi\right)^{3/2}}\iiint\limits_{\mathbf{R}^3}e^{ixy'}G\left(y,\check{t},z,t\right)dy\\&=\frac{1}{\left(2\pi\right)^{3/2}}\iiint\limits_{\mathbf{R}^3}e^{ixy'}L\left(y,\check{t},z,t\right)P^d\left(z,t,\check{t}\right)dy\\&=\frac{1}{\left(2\pi\right)^{3/2}}P^d\left(z,t,\check{t}\right)\iiint\limits_{\mathbf{R}^3}e^{ixy'}L\left(y,\check{t},z,t\right)dy\\&=P^d\left(z,t,\check{t}\right)\widetilde{L}\left(x,\check{t},z,t\right).\end{aligned}$$

Hence,

$$\widetilde{L}\left(x,\check{t},z,t\right)=\frac{\tilde{G}\left(x,\check{t},z,t\right)}{P^d\left(z,t,\check{t}\right)}.$$

Finally,

$$\begin{aligned}P^d\left(z,t,\check{t}\right)&=\iiint\limits_{\mathbf{R}^3}G\left(y,\check{t},z,t\right)dy\\&=\left(2\pi\right)^{3/2}\tilde{G}\left(0,\check{t},z,t\right).\end{aligned}$$

---

[47] If defaultable bond prices are not available we can use theorem 3.3.1 to determine them. Therefore the three factor defaultable term structure model must be calibrated first.

[48] The Fourier transform of a function $f:\mathbf{R}\rightarrow\mathbf{R}$, which satisfies Dirichlet's conditions (see, e.g., Bronstein & Semendjajew (1991), page 608) in each finite subinterval of $\mathbf{R}$ and $\int_{-\infty}^{\infty}|f(x)|<\infty$, is defined by

$$\frac{1}{\sqrt{2\pi}}\int_{-\infty}^{\infty}f(x)\,e^{iyx}\,dx.$$

b) Evaluate the Fourier inverse L of $\widetilde{L}$:

$$L\left(y, \check{t}, z, t\right) = \frac{1}{(2\pi)^{3/2}} \iiint\limits_{\mathbf{R}^3} e^{-ixy'} \widetilde{L}\left(x, \check{t}, z, t\right) dx.$$

If an analytical result can't be determined we can use numerical techniques such as the evaluation of L by numerical inversion of the characteristic function.

3. Use defaultable bond prices and L to get prices of defaultable interest rate derivatives:

$$F\left(z, t\right) = 1_{\{t<\tau\}} P^d\left(z, t, T\right) \iiint\limits_{\mathbf{R}^3} L\left(y, T, z, t\right) Y\left(y\right) dy.$$

3.3.6 Defaultable Floating Rate Debt

In the following we consider a defaultable floating rate note with a given sequence of reset dates $t_1 \leq t < t_i \leq T$, $i = 2, ..., n$, and a promised sequence of payment dates $t < t_p\left(t_i\right) \leq T$, $i = 1, ..., n$, such that $t_i \leq t_p\left(t_i\right)$ for all i. Let $\tau_p^1 = t_p\left(t_1\right) - t$ and $\tau_p^i = t_p\left(t_i\right) - t_p\left(t_{i-1}\right)$, $i = 2, ..., n$. In practice, floating rate debt spreads are usually relative to some agreed-upon floating index such as the three-month LIBOR, that need not be purely default-free. There is no problem in the further analysis if the pure default-free floating rate and the reference differ by a constant. We assume that the periodic floating payments float with LIBOR plus a constant spread S. The index yield fixed at time t_i and the time to maturity of the index are denoted by $I\left(t_i\right)$ and τ^I, respectively. For the annualized LIBOR, we have

$$I\left(t_i\right) = \frac{1}{\tau^I}\left(\frac{1}{P\left(t_i, t_i + \tau^I\right)} - 1\right),$$

where the non-defaultable bond price $P\left(t_i, t_i + \tau^I\right)$ is given by equation (3.15). At time $t_p\left(t_i\right)$ there is a floating rate payment of $\tau_p^i I\left(t_i\right) + S$. Without any loss of generality we assume the standard market practice of $\tau_p^i = \tau^I$ for all $i = 1, ..., n$. Trivially, defaultable floating rate notes qualify as defaultable claims. Hence, we can apply the framework of section 3.3.5 to the pricing of this financial instrument. Let us first consider a special case where the reset dates equal the payment dates:

Special case: There are only payments $t_p\left(t_i\right) = t_i$ for $i = 2, ..., n$:. Applying proposition 3.3.1, the time t price of $\tau^I I\left(t_i\right)$ (denoted by $f_i\left(t\right)$) is given by

$$\begin{aligned} f_i\left(t\right) &= E^{\mathbf{Q}}\left[\left. e^{-\int_t^{t_i}(r(l)+s(l))dl} \tau^I I\left(t_i\right) \right| \mathcal{F}_t\right] \\ &= E^{\mathbf{Q}}\left[\left. e^{-\int_t^{t_i}(r(l)+s(l))dl} \left(\frac{1}{P\left(t_i, t_i + \tau^I\right)} - 1\right) \right| \mathcal{F}_t\right]. \end{aligned}$$

We determine the expectation by using the PDE techniques described in section 3.3.5. By the Feynman-Kac Formula, f_i satisfies the PDE

$$\begin{aligned}0 &= \frac{1}{2}\sigma_r^2 r^{2\beta}(f_i)_{rr} + \frac{1}{2}\sigma_s^2 s(f_i)_{ss} + \frac{1}{2}\sigma_u^2 u(f_i)_{uu} \\ &+ [\theta_r(t) - \hat{a}_r r](f_i)_r + [b_s u - \hat{a}_s s](f_i)_s \\ &+ [\theta_u - \hat{a}_u u](f_i)_u + (f_i)_t - (r+s) f_i, \quad (r,s,u,t) \in \mathbb{R}^3 \times [0,\mathrm{T})\end{aligned} \tag{3.53}$$

with boundary condition

$$f_i(z, t_i) = \frac{1}{P(z, t_i, t_i + \tau^I)} - 1. \tag{3.54}$$

The solution of equations (3.53) and (3.54) is given by

$$f_i(t) = f_i(z,t) = \iiint_{\mathbf{R}^3} G(y, t_i, z, t)\left(\frac{1}{P(y, t_i, t_i + \tau^I)} - 1\right) dy. \tag{3.55}$$

With

$$L(y, t_i, z, t) = \frac{G(y, t_i, z, t)}{P^d(t, t_i)}, \tag{3.56}$$

$$f_i(t) = f_i(z,t) = P^d(t, t_i) \iiint_{\mathbf{R}^3} L(y, t_i, z, t)\left(\frac{1}{P(y, t_i, t_i + \tau^I)} - 1\right) dy.$$

Finally, the time t price of the floating rate note is given by

$$P_f^d(t,T) = 1_{\{t<\tau\}} \sum_{i=2}^{n} \left(f_i(t) + S \cdot P^d(t, t_i)\right) + 1_{\{t<\tau\}} P^d(t,T). \tag{3.57}$$

General case:. For $i = 1$ the payment of $\tau^I I(t_1)$ is already known at time t and the pricing problem reduces to the pricing of a fixed rate coupon. Hence, the time t price of $\tau^I I(t_1)$ (denoted by $f_1(t)$) is given by

$$f_1(t) = P^d(t, t_p(t_1))\left(\frac{1}{P(t_1, t_1 + \tau^I)} - 1\right).$$

For $i \geq 2$, the situation is more complicated. The time t price of $\tau^I I(t_i)$ (denoted by $f_i(t)$) is given by

$$\begin{aligned}f_i(t) &= E^{\mathbf{Q}}\left[e^{-\int_t^{t_p(t_i)}(r(l)+s(l))dl} \tau^I I(t_i) \middle| \mathcal{F}_t \right] \\ &= E^{\mathbf{Q}}\left[e^{-\int_t^{t_i}(r(l)+s(l))dl} \left(\frac{P^d(t_i, t_p(t_i))}{P(t_i, t_i + \tau^I)} - P^d(t_i, t_p(t_i))\right) \middle| \mathcal{F}_t \right].\end{aligned}$$

Proof.

$$E^{\mathbf{Q}}\left[e^{-\int_t^{t_p(t_i)}(r(l)+s(l))dl}\tau^I I(t_i)\middle|\mathcal{F}_{t_i}\right]$$
$$=E^{\mathbf{Q}}\left[e^{-\int_t^{t_i}(r(l)+s(l))dl}e^{-\int_{t_i}^{t_p(t_i)}(r(l)+s(l))dl}\tau^I I(t_i)\middle|\mathcal{F}_{t_i}\right]$$
$$=e^{-\int_t^{t_i}(r(l)+s(l))dl}\tau^I I(t_i)P^d(t_i,t_p(t_i)).$$

By using the tower law we get

$$E^{\mathbf{Q}}\left[e^{-\int_t^{t_p(t_i)}(r(l)+s(l))dl}\tau^I I(t_i)\middle|\mathcal{F}_t\right]$$
$$=E^{\mathbf{Q}}\left[e^{-\int_t^{t_i}(r(l)+s(l))dl}\tau^I I(t_i)P^d(t_i,t_p(t_i))\middle|\mathcal{F}_t\right].$$

Solving PDE (3.53) with boundary condition

$$f_i(z,t_i)=\frac{P^d(z,t_i,t_p(t_i))}{P(z,t_i,t_i+\tau^I)}-P^d(z,t_i,t_p(t_i))$$

by applying the results of section 3.3.5 yields

$$f_i(t)=f_i(z,t)$$
$$=P^d(t,t_i)\iiint_{\mathbf{R}^3}L(y,t_i,z,t)\left(\frac{P^d(z,t_i,t_p(t_i))}{P(z,t_i,t_i+\tau^I)}-P^d(z,t_i,t_p(t_i))\right)dy.$$

Finally, the time t price of the floating rate note is given by

$$P_f^d(t,T)=1_{\{t<\tau\}}\sum_{i=1}^{n}\left(f_i(t)+S\cdot P^d(t,t_i)\right)+1_{\{t<\tau\}}P^d(t,T). \tag{3.58}$$

3.3.7 Defaultable Interest Rate Swaps

An interest rate swap is an agreement between two counterparties in which each of them promises to make fixed or floating periodic payments to the other in the same currency. Each series of floating payments is based on a specific interest rate (index). In a typical swap contract, a fixed rate payer makes fixed payments every year, whereas a floating rate payer makes several payments a year. The payments due on any date are usually netted against each other before payment is made. The generic interest rate swap refers to a floating to fixed swap in which the payment of one counterparty is based on a floating interest rate index and the payment of the other is based on a predetermined fixed interest rate. If there is no default risk, a generic swap can be characterized as an exchange of two riskless bonds. According to Bicksler

& Chen (1986), the swap transaction is identical to an agreement where the counterparty promising to make fixed payments exchanges a fixed coupon default-free bond with coupon-dates and maturity equal to that of the swap for a default-free floating rate note with index, payment dates and maturity equal to that of the swap with the counterparty promising to make floating payments. In practice, the counterparties to swaps are usually not default riskless. But there is only coupon default risk. Netting usually reduces the credit risk even further. There is no exposure to the loss of principal, because the exchange of principals on the two sides of the swaps is avoided by the terms of the swap contract. The price of the default risk in swaps is highly dependent on the default triggering events and the settlement in bankruptcy. Conditions under which swap agreements are terminated are set out in the International Swap Dealers Association (ISDA) Master Agreement. In a swap settled under the "fault" rule, the bankruptcy rules are such that if default occurs, all future payments are null and void. Especially, the non-defaulting counterparty is not obligated to compensate the defaulting counterparty if the remaining market value of the swap contract is positive for the defaulting counterparty. In a swap settled under the "no fault" rule, the counterparty with negative remaining market value is obligated to compensate the other counterparty based on the remaining market value of the swap independent of the fact of the identity of the defaulting counterparty.

Sundaresan (1991) was the first one to consider the pricing of defaultable interest rate swaps. He models both, the non-defaultable short rate and a default premium, as Cox-Ingersoll-Ross processes (see, e.g., Cox et al. (1985)). Cooper & Mello (1991) calculate defaultable swap prices for structural models but only allow for one sided default risk. They don't allow for netting and only consider the "no fault" rule. Sorensen & Bollier (1994) analyze two sided default risk, but not within an advanced credit risk model. Duffie & Huang (1996) are the first to model two sided credit risk for an advanced credit risk model, especially for intensity based models. They apply basic concepts developed by Rendleman (1992). We analyze two sided default risk in interest rate swaps for our hybrid model.

In the following, we model two counterparties A and B, A making fixed payments and B making floating payments. Given is a sequence of reset dates t_i, $i = 1, ..., n$, and a sequence of payment dates $t_p(t_i)$, $i = 1, ..., n$, such that $t_1 \leq t \leq t_p(t_1) \leq t_2 \leq t_p(t_2) \leq ... \leq t_n \leq t_p(t_n) = T$. The periodic floating payments float with an agreed-upon floating index such as the three-month LIBOR. The index yield fixed at time t_i and the time to maturity of the index are denoted by $I(t_i)$ and τ^I, respectively. For the annualized LIBOR, we have

$$I(t_i) = \frac{1}{\tau^I}\left(\frac{1}{P(t_i, t_i + \tau^I)} - 1\right),$$

where the non-defaultable bond price $P\left(t_i, t_i + \tau^I\right)$ is given by equation (3.15). The periodic finite fixed payments are denoted by c. A generic interest rate swap is then an exchange of a sequence of fixed payments $\{c\}$ with a sequence of floating payments $\left\{\tau^I I\left(t_i\right)\right\}$ at times $\left\{t_p\left(t_i\right)\right\}$. Note that the floating payment $\tau^I I\left(t_i\right)$ at time $t_p\left(t_i\right)$ depends on the non-defaultable short rate $r\left(t_i\right)$ at time t_i and not on the defaultable short rate $r\left(t_p\left(t_i\right)\right)$ at time $t_p\left(t_i\right)$. As in the case of floating rate notes we could also consider floating payments that float with $\tau^I I\left(t_i\right)$ plus a constant spread S. Because we take into account possible asynchronous swap payments, at time $t_p\left(t_i\right)$, there are three payment procedures possible:

- counterparty A receives a floating rate payment of $\tau^I I\left(t_i\right)$, i.e. the counterparty A netted payment is given by $C^A_{t_p(t_i)} = \tau^I I\left(t_i\right)$.
- counterparty A makes a fixed rate payment of c, i.e. the counterparty A netted payment is given by $C^A_{t_p(t_i)} = -c$.
- there is a floating rate payment of $\tau^I I\left(t_i\right)$ and a fixed rate payment of c, i.e. the counterparty A netted payment is given by $C^A_{t_p(t_i)} = \tau^I I\left(t_i\right) - c$. If $c - \tau^I I\left(t_i\right) > 0$, counterparty B is the receiver of the cash flow, otherwise counterparty A.

We denote the value of the swap contract to counterparty i, $i \in \{A, B\}$, at time t by $F^i\left(t\right)$. Obviously, $F^A\left(t\right) = -F^B\left(t\right)$. Because the standard market practice is the "no fault" rule, we concentrate on that case.

One Sided Default Risk.

Assumption 3.3.1 *There is only default risk associated with one of the counterparties, say counterparty i, where $i \in \{A, B\}$.*

For counterparty i we assume the dynamics specified by equations (3.5), (3.6) and (3.7). Because there is no default risk associated with the other counterparty, its interest rate dynamics are fully described by equation (3.5). Using the notations of definition 3.3.1, to counterparty A the swap contract is a triple $\left[\left(Y^A, D^A, T\right), Z^A, T^d_A\right]$ with $Y^A = 0$, pre-default payments of

$$dD^A_t = \begin{cases} C^A_{t_p(t_j)}, & t = t_p\left(t_j\right),\ j = 1, ..., n \\ 0, & \text{in all other cases} \end{cases}, \tag{3.59}$$

and predictable settlement payoffs of

$$Z^A_t = \begin{cases} w^A\left(t\right) F^A\left(t-\right), & F^A\left(t-\right) < 0,\ A \text{ defaults}, \\ F^A\left(t-\right), & F^A\left(t-\right) \geq 0,\ A \text{ defaults}, \\ w^B\left(t\right) F^A\left(t-\right), & F^A\left(t-\right) \geq 0,\ B \text{ defaults}, \\ F^A\left(t-\right), & F^A\left(t-\right) < 0,\ B \text{ defaults}, \end{cases} \tag{3.60}$$

$w^i\left(t\right)$ is the recovery rate process of counterparty i as defined in assumption 3.2.4. Note, that all characteristics of a defaultable claim are satisfied by our specification of Y^A, D^A, and T_A^d. Hence, we can apply our general theory. For $t < \tau$ the price of the defaultable interest rate swap, $F^A(t)$, is given by

$$F^A(t) = E^{\mathbf{Q}}\left[\int_t^T e^{-\int_t^u r(l)dl} Z_u^A dH_u^i + \int_t^T e^{-\int_t^u r(l)dl} L_u^i dD_u^A \,\middle|\, \mathcal{F}_t\right] \quad (3.61)$$

where H_t^i is the default indicator function of counterparty i and $L_t^i = 1 - H_t^i$. Because a swap contract is not a one-party claim we can't use proposition 3.3.1 and the framework developed in section 3.3.5 to value the contract. We have to consider the default characteristics of both counterparties. But we can extend proposition 3.3.1 to this more general setting:

Proposition 3.3.2.
If we assume

- *the pre-default payments of equation (3.59) and the settlement payoffs of equation (3.60)*
- *the dynamics specified by equations (3.5), (3.6) and (3.7) for the defaultable counterparty i*
- *the dynamics specified by equation (3.5) for the non-defaultable counterparty*

then the price process, $F^A(t)$, given by equation (3.61), satisfies

$$F^A(t) = V(t)\, 1_{\{t<\tau\}},$$

where for $0 \leq t < T$ the adapted continuous process V is given by

$$V(t) = \begin{cases} E^{\mathbf{Q}}\left[\int_t^T e^{-\int_t^u \left(r(l)+s(l)\cdot 1_{\{F_{l-}^A<0\}}\right)dl} dD_u^A \,\middle|\, \mathcal{F}_t\right], & A \text{ defaults} \\ E^{\mathbf{Q}}\left[\int_t^T e^{-\int_t^u \left(r(l)+s(l)\cdot 1_{\{F_{l-}^A\geq 0\}}\right)dl} dD_u^A \,\middle|\, \mathcal{F}_t\right], & B \text{ defaults} \end{cases} \quad (3.62)$$

and $V(t) = 0$ for $t \geq T$. Equation (3.62) has a unique solution in the space consisting of every semimartingale, J, such that $E^{\mathbf{Q}}\left[\sup_t |J_t|^q\right] < \infty$ for some $q > 1$.

Proof.
See proof of proposition 3.3.4.

Remark 3.3.3.
Further pricing techniques are described in section 3.3.7.

Two Sided Symmetric Default Risk.

Assumption 3.3.2
Before default the two counterparties always have the same default risk, but there is no simultaneous default possible.

Let us extend our definition of default from section 3.2.2 to the case of two counterparties A and B. We model the stochastic default times as $\mathbf{F}-$stopping times T_i^d, $i \in \{A, B\}$, valued in $[0, \infty)$. The default time T^d of the swap contract is defined as $T^d = \min\{T_A^d, T_B^d\}$. If T is the maturity of the swap, we set $\tau = \min(T, T^d)$. The event $\{T^d > \tau\}$ is the event of no default. We assume that the interest rate dynamics of both counterparties are driven by identical processes specified by equations (3.5), (3.6) and (3.7). For $t < \tau$ the price of the defaultable swap can be calculated by

$$F^A(t) = E^{\mathbf{Q}}\left[\int_t^T e^{-\int_t^u r(l)dl} 1_{\{u \le T^d\}} Z_u^A \left(dH_u^A + dH_u^B\right) \right.$$
$$\left. + \int_t^T e^{-\int_t^u r(l)dl} L_u^A L_u^B dD_u^A \right| \mathcal{F}_t \Bigg],$$

where D^A and Z^A are given by equations (3.59) and (3.60), respectively, and H_t^i, $i \in \{A, B\}$, are the default indicator functions of counterparties A and B. In addition, $L_t^i = 1 - H_t^i$. Given all these assumptions the following proposition holds:

Proposition 3.3.3.
For $0 \le t < T$,

$$F^A(t) = V(t) 1_{\{t<\tau\}},$$

with

$$V(t) = E^{\mathbf{Q}}\left[\int_t^T e^{-\int_t^u (r(l)+s(l))dl} dD_u^A \right| \mathcal{F}_t \Bigg], \tag{3.63}$$

and $V(t) = 0$ *for* $t \ge T$. *Equation (3.63) has a unique solution in the space consisting of every semimartingale,* J, *such that* $E^{\mathbf{Q}}[\sup_t |J_t|^q] < \infty$ *for some* $q > 1$.

Proof.
See proof of proposition 3.3.4.

Remark 3.3.4.
In the case of two sided symmetric default risk, $F^A(t)$ can be calculated with the same techniques as in the pricing of defaultable fixed rate bonds and defaultable floating rate notes.

Two Sided Asymmetric Default Risk. Finally, we generalize the pricing of defaultable swap contracts to the case of two counterparties A and B with individual default risks. Again, we assume that there is no simultaneous default possible[49].

Assumption 3.3.3
Under the measure $\mathbf{Q}$, the dynamics of the non-defaultable short rate are given by equation (3.5).

Assumption 3.3.4
Under the measure $\mathbf{Q}$, the developments of the uncertainty indices of counterparties $i = A$ and B are given by the following stochastic differential equations:

$$du_t^i = \left[\theta_u^i - \hat{a}_u^i u_t^i\right] dt + \sigma_u^i \sqrt{u_t^i} d\hat{W}_u^i(t), \quad 0 \le t \le T^*, \ i = A, \ B,$$

where $\hat{a}_u^i$, $\sigma_u^i > 0$, $i = A$, B, are positive constants and θ_u^i, $i = A$, B, are non–negative constants.

Assumption 3.3.5
Under the measure $\mathbf{Q}$, the dynamics of the short rate spreads of counterparties $i = A$ and B are given by the following stochastic differential equations:

$$ds_t^i = \left[b_s^i u_t^i - \hat{a}_s^i s_t^i\right] dt + \sigma_s^i \sqrt{s_t^i} d\hat{W}_s^i(t), \quad 0 \le t \le T^*, \ i = A, \ B,$$

where $\hat{a}_s^i$, $b_s^i, \sigma_s^i > 0$ are positive constants.

Additionally, we assume that the Brownian Motions $\hat{W}_r, \hat{W}_s^A, \hat{W}_s^B, \hat{W}_u^A$ and $\hat{W}_u^B$ are uncorrelated in pairs.
As in the case of symmetric default risk, $F^A(t)$ is given by

$$F^A(t) = E^{\mathbf{Q}}\left[\int_t^T e^{-\int_t^u r(l)dl} 1_{\{u \le \tau\}} Z_u^A \left(dH_u^A + dH_u^B\right) + \int_t^T e^{-\int_t^u r(l)dl} L_u^A L_u^B dD_u^A \,\middle|\, \mathcal{F}_t\right],$$

where D^A and Z^A are given by equations (3.59) and (3.60), respectively. Under these circumstances the following proposition holds:

Proposition 3.3.4.
For $0 \le t < T$,

$$F^A(t) = V(t)\, 1_{\{t < \tau\}},$$

with

[49] In practice a simultaneous default of two swap contract counterparties with positive probability is very unlikely.

$$V(t) = E^{\mathbf{Q}}\left[\left.\int_t^T e^{-\int_t^u\left(r_l+s_l^A\cdot 1_{\{F_{l-}^A<0\}}+s_l^B\cdot 1_{\{F_{l-}^A\geq 0\}}\right)dl} dD_u^A\right| \mathcal{F}_t\right], \quad (3.64)$$

and $V(t) = 0$ *for* $t \geq T$.

Proof.
Existence and uniqueness of equation (3.64) follow immediately from lemma 3.2.4. Because $e^{-\int_t^T r_u du} F_T^A = 0$, for $t < \tau$:

$$\begin{aligned}
F_t^A &= E^{\mathbf{Q}}\left[\left.\int_t^T e^{-\int_t^l r_u du}\left(L_l^A L_l^B dD_l^A + 1_{\{l\leq\tau\}} Z_l^A\left(dH_l^A + dH_l^B\right)\right)\right| \mathcal{F}_t\right] \\
&= E^{\mathbf{Q}}\left[\int_t^T e^{-\int_t^l r_u du}\left(L_l^A L_l^B dD_l^A + 1_{\{l\leq\tau\}} Z_l^A\left(dH_l^A + dH_l^B\right)\right)\right. \\
&\quad \left.\left. + e^{-\int_t^T r_u du} F_T^A \right| \mathcal{F}_t\right].
\end{aligned}$$

Applying corollary 3.2.1 to F^A, using equation (3.60), lemma 3.2.3 with $M_t^{d,A}$ and $M_t^{d,B}$, and $F_t^A = F_t^A \cdot 1_{\{t\leq\tau\}}$ yields

$$\begin{aligned}
dF_t^A &= r_t F_t^A dt - L_t^A L_t^B dD_t^A - 1_{\{t\leq\tau\}} Z_t^A\left(dH_t^A + dH_t^B\right) + dm_t \\
&= r_t F_t^A dt - L_t^A L_t^B dD_t^A - 1_{\{t\leq\tau\}} F_{t-}^A\left(1_{\{F_{t-}^A<0\}}\left(w_t^A - 1\right) + 1\right) dH_t^A \\
&\quad - 1_{\{t\leq\tau\}} F_{t-}^A\left(1_{\{F_{t-}^A\geq 0\}}\left(w_t^B - 1\right) + 1\right) dH_t^B + dm_t \\
&= r_t F_t^A dt - L_t^A L_t^B dD_t^A - 1_{\{t\leq\tau\}} 1_{\{F_{t-}^A<0\}} F_{t-}^A\left(w_t^A - 1\right) dH_t^A \\
&\quad - 1_{\{t\leq\tau\}} F_{t-}^A dH_t^A - 1_{\{t\leq\tau\}} 1_{\{F_{t-}^A\geq 0\}} F_{t-}^A\left(w_t^B - 1\right) dH_t^B \\
&\quad - 1_{\{t\leq\tau\}} F_{t-}^A dH_t^B + dm_t \\
&= r_t F_t^A dt - L_t^A L_t^B dD_t^A - 1_{\{t\leq\tau\}} 1_{\{F_{t-}^A<0\}} F_{t-}^A\left(dM_t^{d,A} - s_t^A dt\right) \\
&\quad - 1_{\{t\leq\tau\}} F_{t-}^A dH_t^A - 1_{\{t\leq\tau\}} 1_{\{F_{t-}^A\geq 0\}} F_{t-}^A\left(dM_t^{d,B} - s_t^B dt\right) \\
&\quad - 1_{\{t\leq\tau\}} F_{t-}^A dH_t^B + dm_t \\
&= 1_{\{t\leq\tau\}} r_t F_t^A dt - L_t^A L_t^B dD_t^A \\
&\quad + 1_{\{t\leq\tau\}} F_{t-}^A\left(s_t^A 1_{\{F_{t-}^A<0\}} + s_t^B 1_{\{F_{t-}^A\geq 0\}}\right) dt \\
&\quad - 1_{\{t\leq\tau\}} F_{t-}^A\left(dH_t^A + dH_t^B\right) + d\widetilde{m}_t \\
&= 1_{\{t\leq\tau\}} F_t^A\left(r_t + s_t^A 1_{\{F_{t-}^A<0\}} + s_t^B 1_{\{F_{t-}^A\geq 0\}}\right) dt - L_t^A L_t^B dD_t^A \\
&\quad - 1_{\{t\leq\tau\}} F_{t-}^A\left(dH_t^A + dH_t^B\right) + d\widetilde{m}_t.
\end{aligned}$$

for some (local) $\mathbf{Q}$−martingales m and $\widetilde{m}$, where

$$d\widetilde{m}_t = -L_{t-}^A L_{t-}^B F_{t-}^A 1_{\{F_{t-}^A<0\}} \left(dM_t^{d,A} - dM_t^{d,B}\right)$$
$$-L_{t-}^A L_{t-}^B F_{t-}^A dM_t^{d,B} + dm_t.$$

Applying lemma 3.2.6 to F^A yields (the prerequisites of the lemma are satisfied by similar arguments as in the proof of propositions 3.2.1 and 3.3.1)

$$\begin{aligned}F_t^A \cdot 1_{\{t<\tau\}} &= F_t^A \\ &= E^{\mathbf{Q}}\left[\int_t^T -\left(r_l + s_l^A 1_{\{F_{l-}^A<0\}} + s_l^B 1_{\{F_{l-}^A\geq 0\}}\right) 1_{\{l\leq\tau\}} F_l^A dl\right. \\ &\qquad \left. + L_l^A L_l^B dD_l^A + 1_{\{l\leq\tau\}} F_{l-}^A \left(dH_l^A + dH_l^B\right) \mid \mathcal{F}_t\right].\end{aligned}$$

On the other hand, applying corollary 3.2.1 to $V(t)$ yields

$$dV_t = \left(r_t + s_t^A \cdot 1_{\{F_{t-}^A<0\}} + s_t^B \cdot 1_{\{F_{t-}^A\geq 0\}}\right) V_t dt - dD_t^A + d\widehat{m}_t,$$

for some $\mathbf{Q}$–martingale $\widehat{m}$. Using integration by parts,

$$\begin{aligned}&d\left(V_t 1_{\{t<\tau\}}\right) \\ &= d\left(V_t L_t^A L_t^B\right) \\ &= L_{t-}^A L_{t-}^B dV_t - V_{t-}\left(L_{t-}^B dH_t^A + L_{t-}^A dH_t^B\right) \\ &= L_{t-}^A L_{t-}^B \left(\left(r_t + s_t^A \cdot 1_{\{F_{t-}^A<0\}} + s_t^B \cdot 1_{\{F_{t-}^A\geq 0\}}\right) V_t dt - dD_t^A + d\widehat{m}_t\right) \\ &\quad - V_{t-}\left(L_{t-}^B dH_t^A + L_{t-}^A dH_t^B\right) \\ &= -L_{t-}^A L_{t-}^B dD_t^A + L_{t-}^A L_{t-}^B \left(r_t + s_t^A \cdot 1_{\{F_{t-}^A<0\}} + s_t^B \cdot 1_{\{F_{t-}^A\geq 0\}}\right) V_t dt \\ &\quad - 1_{\{t\leq\tau\}} V_{t-}\left(dH_t^A + dH_t^B\right) + L_{t-}^A L_{t-}^B d\widehat{m}_t.\end{aligned}$$

Applying lemma 3.2.6 to $V_t 1_{\{t<\tau\}}$ yields (the prerequisites of the lemma are satisfied by similar arguments as in the proof of propositions 3.2.1 and 3.3.1)

$$\begin{aligned}V_t 1_{\{t<\tau\}} &= E^{\mathbf{Q}}\left[\int_t^T -\left(r_l + s_l^A 1_{\{F_{t-}^A<0\}} + s_l^B 1_{\{F_{l-}^A\geq 0\}}\right) 1_{\{l\leq\tau\}} V_l dl\right. \\ &\qquad \left. + L_l^A L_l^B dD_l^A + 1_{\{l\leq\tau\}} V_{l-}\left(dH_l^A + dH_l^B\right) \middle| \mathcal{F}_t\right].\end{aligned}$$

Because of the uniqueness of a solution we can conclude for $t < \tau$,

$$F^A(t) = V(t) 1_{\{t<\tau\}}.$$

A solution for equation (3.64) can be determined, e.g., by choosing its Feynman-Kac representation and solving the appropriate PDE, e.g., by applying a finite-difference algorithm such as the Crank-Nicholson method[50]. Alternatively Monte-Carlo simulations can be used.

[50] See, e.g., Lamberton & Lapeyre (1996).

3.4 The Pricing of Credit Derivatives

3.4.1 Introduction

Credit derivatives will lead to a revolution in banking. One is definitely true: the volume of the credit derivatives market has increased enormously (see, e.g., table 3.1) since credit derivatives have been first publicly introduced in 1992, at the International Swaps and Derivatives Association annual meeting in Paris, and the end of this tendency is not about to come. Credit derivatives are one of the most important types of new financial products introduced during the last decade. Meanwhile, there is a great variety of products: The most important ones are credit options (section 3.4.3), credit spread products (section 3.4.4), default swaps/options (section 3.4.5), total rate of return swaps (section 3.4.8), and credit-linked notes (section 3.4.9). Credit derivatives can be based on a broad set of credit sensitive underlyings:

- Derivatives based on sovereign bonds: E.g., Brady bond derivatives allow investors to take a view on the narrowing of sovereign credit spreads.
- Derivatives based on corporate bonds: E.g., derivatives based on a single company's bond are often used for liability management.
- Derivatives based on bank loans: E.g., derivatives based on loans are used by banks to diversify or neutralize concentrations of issuer specific risk and offer investors favorable risk-return profiles.

Traditionally, exposure to credit risk was managed by trading in the underlying asset itself. Or even worse: when a loan was made in the past, the credit risk remained on the lender's balance sheet till the obligation matured, was paid or charged off. Like other derivatives, credit derivatives facilitate the separate trading of individual attributes of an underlying asset in isolation from the asset itself. They have been developed for transferring, replicating and hedging credit risk. They can change the credit risk profile of an underlying asset by isolating specific aspects of credit risk without selling the asset itself. This is even possible for highly illiquid instruments which couldn't have been traded regularly otherwise. Hence, they allow credit risk to be disaggregated and traded. Their payoff usually depends on the credit risk of a particular counterparty or a group of counterparties, or is based on the credit performance of some credit-sensitive instrument. Credit performance is measured by yield spreads relative to benchmarks (e.g., basis points over Treasuries or LIBOR), credit ratings or default status. And as Masters (1998), global head of credit derivatives marketing at J. P. Morgan, points out:

> "In bypassing barriers between different classes, maturities, rating categories, debt seniority levels and so on, credit derivatives are creating enormous opportunities to exploit and profit from associated discontinuities in the pricing of credit risk."

In addition, credit derivatives

- have a market-wide impact. They
  - have encouraged more participants in many markets such as high-yield debt, bank loans and credit enhancement products
  - have helped to make pure credit risk markets more liquid and well-developed
  - have enabled more efficient pricing across several market sectors
  - have led to a reduction in credit spreads
  - have improved institutional portfolio diversification
- allow banks maintaining banking relationships and diversification at the same time
- create new arbitrage opportunities
- allow investments based on credit views
- can be used for
  - risk protection, exchange of one set of risks for another, and speculation
  - offsetting over-the-counter counterparty exposure
  - loan portfolio hedging
  - extending lines of business
  - changing the maturity or currency of credit risks
  - getting access to classes of assets in which an institution may otherwise find it difficult to invest and trade

Example 3.4.1.
During Asia's debt crisis at the end of the 1990's many banks were offering short-term protection (by pitching short-term credit default swaps) on some Asian corporate bonds to entice buyers back into Asia's fixed-income markets. There was the view that if a corporate could survive the upcoming year, it would most probably survive in the long term. Short-term default swaps shortened the yield curve out to a year, while leaving the underlying corporate bond unhedged for later credit events. To get default protection investors paid a high premium for the first year of exposure to the Asian corporate bond, but in return they could lock in enormously high yields (up to 1200 basis points over US$ LIBOR) for the rest of the life of the bond.

Not very surprisingly, the volumes traded in the global credit derivatives market have enormously risen during the last years. Based on an Canadian Imperial Bank of Commerce (CIBC) estimate[51], the credit derivatives market volume was about US$ 5 billion and US$ 40 billion in 1994 and 1995, respectively. According to a J.P. Morgan estimate[52] the outstanding volume doubled in 1996 again. A March 1998 RISK magazine's survey (Green, Locke & Paul-Choudhury 1998) estimates the global volumes ranging from US$ 140 billion to US$ 325 billion in 1997. The March 1999 RISK magazine's survey (Baldwin 1999) gives an average figure of all outstanding credit derivatives of US$ 477 billion, and in the RISK survey published in March 2000

[51] See, e.g., Wilson (1998), page 225, exhibit 5.
[52] See, e.g., Wilson (1998), page 225, exhibit 5.

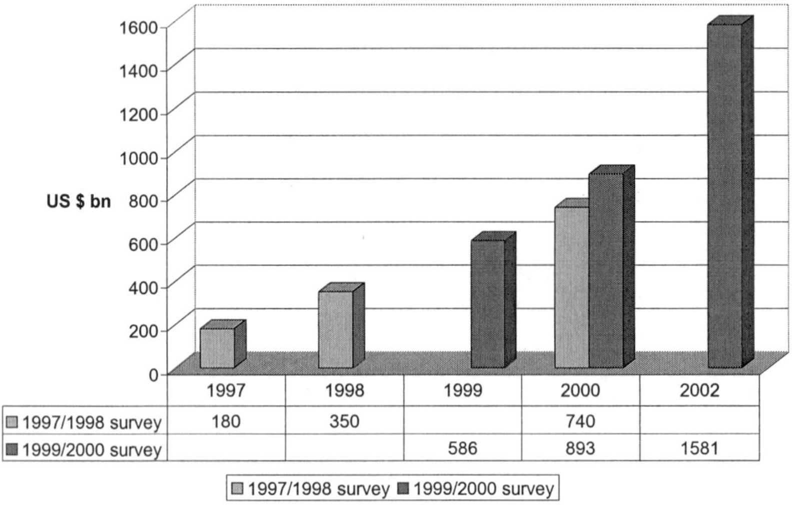

Fig. 3.22. Global credit derivatives market size. Source: (*BBA Credit Derivatives Report 1999/2000* 2000).

(Hargreaves 2000) this figure has increased by 39% to US$ 661 billion. For the year 2000 RISK (Patel 2001) reports a total notional amount of outstanding contracts around US$ 810 billion. The British Bankers' Association's credit derivatives surveys[53] of the years 1997/1998 and 1999/2000 show even higher numbers which are summarized in figure 3.22.

Not only the market size is increasing but also the range of products used. Although standard credit default products still account for the largest market share by far, more and more hybrid products are being developed. Figure 3.23 shows the proportions of the global derivative market which is accounted for by the specific products.

[53] According to *BBA Credit Derivatives Report 1999/2000* (2000) over 30 institutions from Australia, Canada, France, Germany, Italy, Japan, Netherlands, Switzerland, United Kingdom and United States submitted detailed questionnaires to the British Bankers' Association. 85% of them considered themselves as Intermediary/market makers. The survey used the following definiton of credit derivatives:

> "Any instrument that enables the trading/management of credit risk in isolation from the other types of risk associated with an underlying asset. These instruments may include: credit default products, credit spread products, total return products, basket products, credit linked notes and asset swaps." (*BBA Credit Derivatives Report 1999/2000* (2000), page 6)

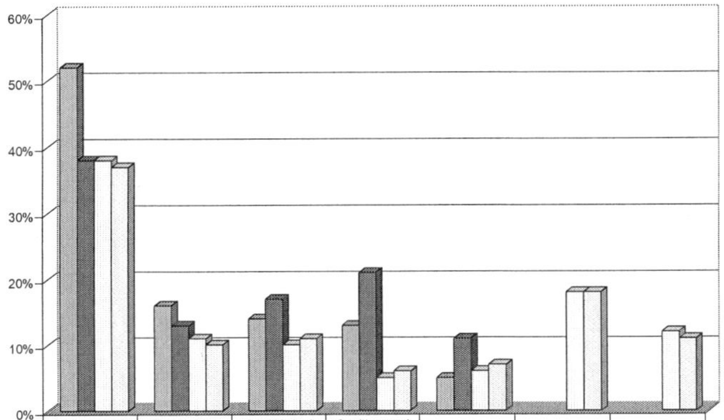

	Credit default products	Total return swaps	Credit linked notes	Credit spread products	Baskets	Portfolio/ CLOs	Asset Swaps
End 1997 actual	52%	16%	14%	13%	5%		
End 2000 estimated	38%	13%	17%	21%	11%		
End 1999 actual	38%	11%	10%	5%	6%	18%	12%
End 2002 estimated	37%	10%	11%	6%	7%	18%	11%

End 1997 actual ■ End 2000 estimated □ End 1999 actual □ End 2002 estimated

Fig. 3.23. Credit derivatives products market share. Source: (*BBA Credit Derivatives Report 1999/2000* 2000), page 13.

According to figure 3.24, currently the biggest credit derivatives market is Europe, as the euro has helped to develop European debt markets. In less developed derivatives markets, due to the Asian and Russian crises, the use of credit derivatives has fallen from 34% in 1998 to 5% in 1999, but has recovered again to 18% in 2000. In emerging markets the fastest growing geographical sector is central and eastern Europe. The region accounts for 11% of the global market in 2000. Hungary, for example, is the region's most active market for credit derivatives and also has the greatest number of liquid bonds.
Besides such estimates, there are only a few official credit derivatives volumes figures reported yet. The US Office of the Comptroller of the Currency began publishing US commercial banks' credit derivatives volumes in 1997. Table 3.1 shows the absolute outstanding notional amounts in billion US$ and the number of US banks that had outstanding credit derivatives positions. The notional amounts have grown from less than US$ 20 billion in the first quarter of 1997 to about US$ 426 billion in the fourth quarter of 2000. The main reasons for the enormous credit derivatives' growth are a much greater awareness of these products, the better understanding and wider usage of risk management techniques and an increasing market liquidity. End-users of credit derivatives[54] are banks (in 2000: 64%), reinsurance companies (11%),

[54] See, e.g., Patel (2001).

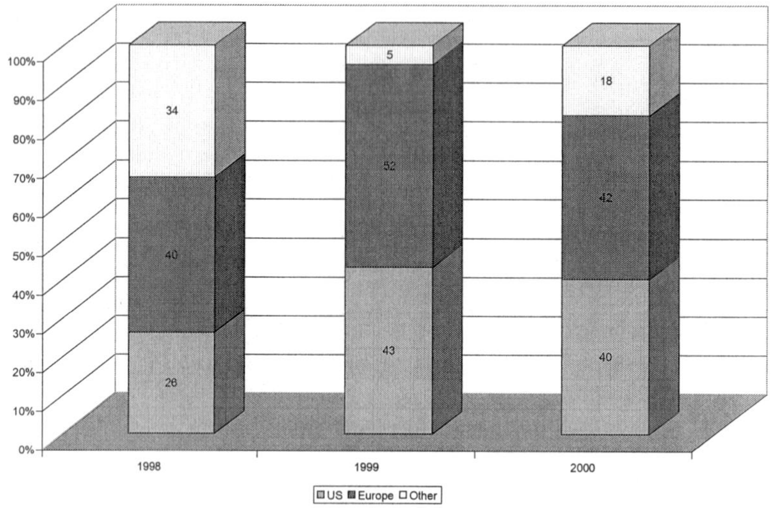

Fig. 3.24. Estimated geographical distribution of credit derivatives market 1998-2000. Source: (Hargreaves 2000).

corporates (8%), asset managers (7%), hedge funds (5%), insurance companies (3%), and special purpose vehicles (2%).

The main problem of credit derivatives is that they still suffer from price-discovery problems. James (1999), vice president and head of research, strategic risk management advisory, at First National Bank of Chicago in London, explains:

> "Perhaps the closest analogy with the credit derivatives market today is the options market some 25 years ago, shortly before the Black-Scholes pricing model was developed. The credit derivatives market seems to be waiting for a similar revolution. There is a feeling that just around the corner lies some "Black-Scholes model for credit derivatives" and, after it is found, pricing will become simple."

There are basically three approaches used by market participants to price credit derivatives today:

- Pricing based on guarantee product markets:
  The amount by which a guarantor should be compensated is determined by looking to other forms of credit enhancement as a reference. For example, if counterparty A is willing to pay counterparty B 100 basis points annually to guarantee the debt of counterparty C, a credit default swap should be

Table 3.1. US credit derivatives market (notional amounts in US$ billions).

	Notional Amounts	*Number of Banks*
1st Qtr 97	19.139	504
2nd Qtr 97	25.649	463
3rd Qtr 97	38.880	475
4th Qtr 97	54.729	459
1st Qtr 98	91.419	451
2nd Qtr 98	129.202	461
3rd Qtr 98	161.678	464
4th Qtr 98	144.006	447
1st Qtr 99	190.990	439
2nd Qtr 99	210.351	435
3rd Qtr 99	234.131	426
4th Qtr 99	286.584	416
1st Qtr 00	301.913	389
2nd Qtr 00	361.685	416
3rd Qtr 00	378.585	421
4th Qtr 00	425.848	400
1st Qtr 01	352.405	395
2nd Qtr 01	351.235	367

Source: Office of the Comptroller of the Currency bank call reports. Credit derivatives data were being reported in the call reports in 1997 for the first time. Statistics include all US commercial banks holding derivatives. Call reports do not differentiate credit derivatives by contract type.

priced similarly as it provides more or less the same form of protection. The insurance community, e.g., offers a variety of traditional insurance or guarantee products priced by using historical default tables. Of course, this approach can't be used for all types of credit derivatives, and doesn't take into account whatever specific market information about default may exist.

- Pricing based on replication and funding costs:
  This approach prices credit derivatives based on the price of the positions necessary to hedge the derivative contract and how much it costs to enter in these positions. The net hedging cost plus reserves and the dealer's profit and loss is the price of the credit derivative. The strength of this approach is that it is easy to use and very intuitive. If a hedge can be constructed, the result is most useful for a dealer, but for many structures, a complete hedge is not available, or would be too costly.
- Pricing based on stochastic models such as structural, intensity based or hybrid models:
  Although the structural models have intuitive appeal, they are not widely used in trading rooms. Intensity based models are quite common in dealing rooms now. In the following we will apply our three-factor term structure model to the pricing of credit derivatives.

Most of the papers in the field of credit/default risk pricing are concerned with the pricing of defaultable bonds. There still have been only a few works especially on the pricing of credit derivatives. Das (1995) basically shows that in an asset based framework credit options are the expected forward values of put options on defaultable bonds with a credit level adjusted exercise price. Longstaff & Schwartz (1995a) develop a pricing formula for credit spread options in a setting where the logarithm of the credit spread and the non defaultable short rate follow Vasicek processes. Das & Tufano (1996) apply their model, which is an extension to stochastic recovery rates of the model of Jarrow et al. (1997), to the pricing of credit-sensitive notes. Das (1997) summarizes the pricing of credit derivatives in various credit risk models (e.g., the models of Jarrow et al. (1997), and Das & Tufano (1996)). All models are presented in a simplified discrete fashion. Duffie (1998a) uses simple no arbitrage arguments to determine approximate prices for default swaps. Hull & White (2000) provide a methodology for valuing credit default swaps when the payoff is contingent on default by a single reference entity and there is no counterparty default risk. Schönbucher (2000) develops various pricing formulas for credit derivatives in the intensity based framework.

In the following we develop pricing formulas for credit options, spread options, and default options/swaps based on our three-factor defaultable term structure model. Our work is different from all other results in that we apply our new three-factor model and PDE methods similar to those introduced in section 3.3.5 to the pricing of credit derivatives. Throughout this section we assume that $\beta = \frac{1}{2}$ to make sure that the non-defaultable short rate r always stays positive. We discuss the case $\beta = 0$ in appendix C.

3.4.2 Technical Definitions and Pricing Issues

Definition 3.4.1.

- *A credit derivative is a derivative security that has at least one payoff that is conditioned on the occurrence of a credit event (default payment). The credit event is defined with respect to a reference credit or a basket of reference credits and the reference credit assets issued by the reference credit. The maturity date of a credit derivative is deemed to be which ever is earlier - the originally agreed maturity date or the credit event related payment date. In some cases there is a pre-agreed time interval between the credit event and the payout calculation. Credit derivatives can be either quoted in terms of an up-front fee, that is payable at the beginning of the contract, or as a fee, that has to be paid in regular intervals until default or maturity.*
- *A credit event is a precisely defined default event, determined by negotiation between the parties at the outset of a credit derivative. Market standards typically specify the existence of publicly available information confirming*

the occurrence, with respect to the reference credit, of bankruptcy, insolvency, repudiation, restructuring, moratorium, failure-to-pay, cross-default or cross-acceleration. There is some risk of disagreement over whether the credit event has in fact occurred. For pricing issues we will ignore this enforceability risk.

- *A reference credit is an issuer whose default triggers the credit event.*
- *The reference credit assets are a set of assets issued by the reference credit.*
- *Default payments are the payments which must be made in the case of a credit event.*

The key issues related to credit derivatives transactions are the exact definitions of the credit event and the credit event payout or settlement mechanism. Usually the payout mechanism is based on the market bid price of the reference credit asset at the declaration of the credit event, or it is a binary payout (i.e. there is a pre-determined amount of cash payout), or there is a physical sale or delivery of the defaulted reference credit asset at a pre-arranged price. If the reference credit asset is a loan, it is usually very difficult to obtain a market price, and binary payments are more common. In most cases these payouts are based on pre-agreed assessments of the potential changes in price of the reference loans. Naturally, this may expose the credit protection buyer to basis risk between the payout and the actual change in price until and including the credit event. In addition, binary payouts may expose the counterparties to additional tax payments. Although physical settlement mechanisms may overcome some of the problems of the other two forms of payout mechanisms, there may be other risks like settlement risk (the credit protection seller may not be long the reference credit asset at the time of the credit event) or there may be a ban on the delivery of the reference credit asset after the credit event. This may, e.g., happen if there is a court-imposed freeze on the reference credit assets of the defaulted reference credit. In the case of loans it may take a long time to transfer these, due to their administrative complexity, which often includes a requirement that the lender secures the consent of the borrower to reassign its loan. If a settlement period is not exactly specified, the protection seller may not know when it will receive the asset and therefore will be unable to estimate and hedge its risk. In addition, many credit derivatives bear credit risk by themselves. In the following we assume that we can neglect this risk. For the pricing of credit derivatives at time t we apply our three-factor defaultable term structure model. But we have to make some extensions first. Suppose we want to price an option on a defaultable zero-coupon bond (a so called credit option). If the option is knocked out at default of the zero-coupon bond, the buyer of the option receives nothing. Hence, we can interpret the option as a defaultable investment with zero recovery. We show that we can determine the price of the option as the expected value of the promised cash flow at maturity of the option discounted at risky discount rates. But which risky discount rates do we have to use ? As the recovery rate of the option is different from the recovery rate of the reference defaultable zero-coupon bond the risky discount rates are not the same as in the case of the pricing of defaultable zero-coupon bonds. Hence, we have to find a short rate credit spread s^{zero} describing the credit spread process of an obligor which is equivalent to the issuer of the zero-coupon bond (especially of the same quality) but with zero recovery rate. Therefore, for pricing credit derivatives such as credit options we need the following data for all maturities $T > 0$:

- the default-free term structure of bond prices $P(t,T)$,
- the defaultable term structure of bond prices $P^d(t,T)$,
- the defaultable term structure of bond prices under zero recovery $P^{d,zero}(t,T)$.

The first piece of information, the default-free term structure, is easily obtained. Possible choices are government curves or swap curves in developed economies. The second piece is the defaultable term structure of the reference credit. Ideally it is obtained directly from the prices of the reference credit's bonds. Finally, the third piece of input data are the defaultable bond prices under zero recovery. These prices are usually unobservable. But we can derive the zero recovery term structure of bond prices from the default-free and defaultable term structures of bond prices. Therefore we use our three-factor defaultable term structure model. Obviously, the uncertainty index u and the non defaultable short rate r do not depend on the recovery rate, but the recovery rate should implicitly change the short rate spread. Hence, we have to introduce an additional stochastic process to our model, describing the zero recovery short rate spread. We do this consistently to our definition of a defaultable money market account (see definition 3.2.4).

Assumption 3.4.1
The zero recovery short rate spread s^{zero} is given by:

$$s^{zero}(t) = \frac{s(t)}{1-w(t)}, \quad 0 \leq t \leq T^*, \tag{3.65}$$

where $s(t)$ is the short rate spread process defined in equation (3.3) and $0 \leq w(t) < 1$ is the recovery rate process of the reference credit asset introduced in assumption 3.2.4.

Definition 3.4.2 (corresponds to definition 3.2.4).
The zero recovery defaultable money market account $B^{d,zero}$ is defined as

$$B^{d,zero}(t) = \left(1 - \int_0^t dH_l\right) e^{\int_0^t (r(l)+s^{zero}(l))dl},$$

where H_t is the default indicator function of the reference credit asset.

Lemma 3.4.1 (corresponds to lemma 3.2.3).
$M^{d,zero}(t) = \int_0^t s^{zero}(l)\,dl - \int_0^t dH_l$ is a $\mathcal{F}_t-$(local) martingale. H_t is the default indicator function of the reference credit asset.

Proof.
See proof of lemma 3.2.3.

Using lemma 3.2.4, lemma 3.2.5, lemma 3.2.6, lemma 3.4.1, and corollary 3.2.1, it can be shown that the following proposition is valid:

Proposition 3.4.1 (corresponds to proposition 3.2.1).
Let $E^{\mathbf{Q}}\left[|Y|^q\right] < \infty$ for some $q > 1$. Under the zero recovery assumption (i.e. under the assumption that the contingent claim is knocked out at default of the reference credit asset) and the stochastic processes specified by equations (3.5), (3.6), (3.7), and (3.65), the price process, $F(t)$:

$$F(t) = E^{\mathbf{Q}}\left[e^{-\int_t^T r(l)dl}\, Y L_T \middle|\, \mathcal{F}_t\right],\ 0 \le t < \tau,$$

where $L_T = 1 - H_T$, is given by

$$F(t) = V(t)\, 1_{\{t<\tau\}}, \tag{3.66}$$

where the adapted continuous process V is defined by

$$V(t) = E^{\mathbf{Q}}\left[e^{-\int_t^T (r(l)+s^{zero}(l))dl}\, Y \mid \mathcal{F}_t\right],\ 0 \le t < T, \tag{3.67}$$

and $V(t) = 0$ for $t \ge T$, i.e. if there has been no default until time t, $F(t)$ must equal the expected value of riskless cash flows discounted at zero recovery risky discount rates. Equation (3.67) has a unique solution in the space consisting of every semimartingale, J, such that $E^{\mathbf{Q}}\left[\sup_t |J_t|^q\right] < \infty$ for some $q > 1$.

Proof.
See proof of proposition 3.2.1.

Remark 3.4.1.

1. Suppose we want to price a contingent claim that promises to pay off Y at maturity time T of the contingent claim, if the reference credit asset hasn't defaulted until then and zero in case of a default. Then the time t price of the reference credit asset, given there has been no default so far, depends on the stochastic processes r, s, and u. But in addition, the price of the contingent claim depends on s^{zero}, because discounting is done with $e^{-\int_t^T (r(l)+s^{zero}(l))dl}$.
2. Similarly to proposition 3.4.1 a proposition corresponding to proposition 3.3.1 can be formulated.

For all the pricing formulas developed in the previous sections we haven't used recovery rates explicitly. Especially, we haven't made any specific assumptions on the dynamics of $w(t)$. In the following we assume that $w(t)$ is a known constant, i.e. $w(t) = w$ for all $0 \leq t \leq T^*$. Then the dynamics of the zero recovery short rate spread are given by

$$\begin{aligned} ds^{zero}(t) &= \frac{1}{1-w} ds(t) \\ &= \left[\frac{b_s}{1-w} u(t) - \frac{a_s}{1-w} s(t)\right] dt + \frac{\sigma_s}{1-w}\sqrt{s(t)}dW_s(t) \\ &= \left[\frac{b_s}{1-w} u(t) - a_s s^{zero}(t)\right] dt + \frac{\sigma_s}{\sqrt{1-w}}\sqrt{s^{zero}(t)}dW_s(t) \\ &= \left[b_s^{zero} u(t) - a_s s^{zero}(t)\right] dt + \sigma_s^{zero}\sqrt{s^{zero}(t)}dW_s(t), \ 0 \leq t \leq T^*, \end{aligned}$$

where $b_s^{zero} = \frac{b_s}{1-w}$ and $\sigma_s^{zero} = \frac{\sigma_s}{\sqrt{1-w}}$. Under the measure $\mathbf{Q}$, the dynamics of s^{zero} are given by

$$ds^{zero}(t) = \left[b_s^{zero} u(t) - \widehat{a}_s s^{zero}(t)\right] dt + \sigma_s^{zero}\sqrt{s^{zero}(t)}d\hat{W}_s(t), \ 0 \leq t \leq T^*.$$

To summarize, the following steps are necessary to determine the defaultable term structure of bond prices under zero recovery at time t:

1. Determination of the time t default-free and defaultable term structures of bond prices from observable market data.
2. Determination of $r(t)$, $s(t)$, and $u(t)$.
3. Estimation of the parameters of the processes r, s and u (for details see section 3.6).
4. Calculation of the parameters b_s^{zero} and σ_s^{zero}.
5. Calculation of the zero recovery zero-coupon bond prices

$$\begin{aligned} &P^{d,zero}(t,T) \qquad (3.68) \\ &= A^{d,zero}(t,T)\, e^{-B(t,T)r(t)-C^{d,zero}(t,T)s^{zero}(t)-D^{d,zero}(t,T)u(t)}, \end{aligned}$$

where $A^{d,zero}(t,T)$, $C^{d,zero}(t,T)$, and $D^{d,zero}(t,T)$ are given by the corresponding formulas for $A^d(t,T)$, $C^d(t,T)$, and $D^d(t,T)$ with b_s and σ_s substituted by b_s^{zero} and σ_s^{zero}, respectively.

So far nothing has been said about the credit quality of the protection seller. The price of a credit derivative should be lower for lower quality protection sellers. The higher the default correlation between the reference credit and the protection seller the less the default swap should be worth. If not otherwise stated, we assume that the protection seller is default-free.

3.4.3 Credit Options

Definition 3.4.3.
A credit option is a put or call option on the price of either

1. *a floating rate note, fixed rate bond, or loan,*

2. *an asset swap package, consisting of a credit-risky instrument with any payment characteristics and a corresponding derivative contract that exchanges the cash flows of that instrument for a floating rate cash flow stream, typically three or six month LIBOR plus a spread.*

Settlement may be on a cash or physical basis.

Credit options offer protection against changing default free interest rates and changing credit spreads. Hence, they allow hedging of mark-to-market exposure to fluctuations in spreads: hedging long positions with puts, and short positions with calls. For investors they are a good source of yield enhancement. Borrowers can lock in future borrowing costs without inflating their balance sheet by entering into credit options on their own name. They can buy the right to put their own paper to a dealer at a pre-agreed spread.

Let us now price a European call and put option with maturity $T_O \leq T$ and exercise price K, on a defaultable zero-coupon bond with maturity T, and denote their values by $F^{cc}(z,t,T;T_O,K)$ and $F^{cp}(z,t,T;T_O,K)$, respectively, where $z = (r,s,u)$. As with other options, the credit option premium is highly sensitive to the volatility of the market price of the underlying, and the extent to which the spread between strike and bond price is in or out of the money relative to the applicable current forward yield curve. Depending on the specification, the option can either survive a default or be knocked out by it. In the first case it doesn't suffice to consider P^d alone but we must consider the post-default bond price behavior as well. Basically there are two possibilities: either the obligor survives the default, e.g., some kind of restructuring takes place, and the bonds are still traded with a market value dropped to the recovery rate times the pre-default market value of the debt, or the proceeds from default recovery are reinvested at the default-free short rate and rolled over until expiration. If credit options survive a credit event, default risk and spread risk are transferred between the counterparties. Otherwise only spread risk is transferred. In the following we will assume throughout that options are knocked out at default of the underlying.

Definition 3.4.4.

1. *A European call option with maturity $T_O \leq T$ and exercise price K on a defaultable zero-coupon bond $P^d(t,T)$ pays off*

$$1_{\{T_O<T^d\}}\left(P^d(T_O,T)-K\right)_+,$$

if the call is knocked out at default.

2. *A European put option with maturity $T_O \leq T$ and exercise price K on a defaultable zero-coupon bond $P^d(t,T)$ pays off*

$$1_{\{T_O<T^d\}}\left(K-P^d(T_O,T)\right)_+,$$

if the put is knocked out at default.

If we assume that there is no default risk with the issuer of the option and the call is knocked out at default, by proposition 3.4.1 the call price at time $t \leq T_O$ is given by

$$\begin{aligned} & F^{cc}(z,t,T;T_O,K) \\ &= E^{\mathbf{Q}}\left[e^{-\int_t^{T_O} r(l)dl} 1_{\{T_O<T^d\}}\left(P^d(T_O,T)-K\right)_+ \Big| \mathcal{F}_t\right] \\ &= E^{\mathbf{Q}}\left[e^{-\int_t^{T_O}(r(l)+s^{zero}(l))dl}\left(P^d(T_O,T)-K\right)\cdot 1_{\{\mathcal{B}_1\}}\Big| \mathcal{F}_t\right], \end{aligned}$$

where $\mathcal{B}_1$ is the range of values[55] of r, s and u over which the option is in the money at the expiration date T_O, that is,

$$\begin{aligned} \mathcal{B}_1 &= \left\{z \in \mathbb{R}_+^3 | P^d(z,T_O,T) - K \geq 0\right\} \\ &= \left\{z \in \mathbb{R}_+^3 | B(T_O,T)r + C^d(T_O,T)s + D^d(T_O,T)u \leq K^*\right\}. \end{aligned}$$

$K^* = \ln \frac{A^d(T_O,T)}{K}$ and $P^d(T_O,T)$ is the bond price given by equation (3.19). Similarly, by proposition 3.4.1 the put price is given by

$$\begin{aligned} & F^{cp}(z,t,T;T_O,K) \\ &= E^{\mathbf{Q}}\left[e^{-\int_t^{T_O}(r(l)+s^{zero}(l))dl}\left(K-P^d(T_O,T)\right)\cdot 1_{\{\mathcal{B}_2\}}\Big| \mathcal{F}_t\right], \end{aligned}$$

where $\mathcal{B}_2$ is the range of values of r, s and u over which the option is in the money at the expiration date T_O, that is,

$$\mathcal{B}_2 = \left\{z \in \mathbb{R}_+^3 | K^* \leq B(T_O,T)r + C^d(T_O,T)s + D^d(T_O,T)u\right\}.$$

We determine $F^{cc}(z,t,T;T_O,K)$ by using PDE techniques. Under mild regularity conditions and by the Feynman-Kac Formula, $F^{cc}(z,t,T;T_O,K)$ satisfies the PDE

$$\begin{aligned} 0 &= \frac{1}{2}\sigma_r^2 r^{2\beta} F_{rr}^{cc} + \frac{1}{2}\sigma_s^2 s F_{ss}^{cc} + \frac{1}{2}\sigma_u^2 u F_{uu}^{cc} \\ &+ \left[\theta_r(t) - \hat{a}_r r\right] F_r^{cc} + \left[b_s u - \hat{a}_s s\right] F_s^{cc} \\ &+ \left[\theta_u - \hat{a}_u u\right] F_u^{cc} + F_t^{cc} - \left(r + \frac{s}{1-w}\right) F^{cc}, \end{aligned} \tag{3.69}$$

with boundary condition

$$F^{cc}(z,T_O,T;T_O,K) = \left(P^d(z,T_O,T) - K\right)_+. \tag{3.70}$$

If $\overrightarrow{G}(y,\check{t},z,t)$ is the solution of the problem

[55] Since we have set β to $\frac{1}{2}$ we can make sure that r always stays positive. In addition, the definitions of s and u guarantee that s and u are positive processes. Hence, throughout section 3.4 $(r,s,u) \in \mathbb{R}_+^3$. In appendix C we discuss the case that $\beta = 0$. This implies that r may become negative.

$$\begin{aligned} 0 &= \frac{1}{2}\sigma_r^2 r^{2\beta}\overrightarrow{G}_{rr} + \frac{1}{2}\sigma_s^2 s\overrightarrow{G}_{ss} + \frac{1}{2}\sigma_u^2 u\overrightarrow{G}_{uu} \\ &\quad + \left[\theta_r(t) - \hat{a}_r r\right]\overrightarrow{G}_r + \left[b_s u - \hat{a}_s s\right]\overrightarrow{G}_s \\ &\quad + \left[\theta_u - \hat{a}_u u\right]\overrightarrow{G}_u + \overrightarrow{G}_t - \left(r + \frac{s}{1-w}\right)\overrightarrow{G}, \end{aligned}$$

with boundary condition

$$\overrightarrow{G}\left(y, \check{t}, z, \check{t}\right) = \delta\left(r - y_r\right)\delta\left(s - y_s\right)\delta\left(u - y_u\right),$$

where $\delta(.)$ is the Dirac function, the solution of the PDE (3.69) with boundary condition (3.70) can be written as

$$\begin{aligned} &F^{cc}\left(z, t, T; T_O, K\right) \\ &= \iiint\limits_{\mathbf{R}^3} \overrightarrow{G}\left(y, T_O, z, t\right)\left(P^d\left(y, T_O, T\right) - K\right)_+ dy. \end{aligned} \tag{3.71}$$

If we know $\overrightarrow{G}$ we can determine $F^{cc}\left(z, t, T; T_O, K\right)$ easily.

Lemma 3.4.2.
$\overrightarrow{G}\left(y, \check{t}, z, t\right)$, is given by

$$\overrightarrow{G}\left(y, \check{t}, z, t\right) = \frac{1}{(2\pi)^{3/2}} \iiint\limits_{\mathbf{R}^3} e^{-ixy'}\overleftarrow{G}\left(x, \check{t}, z, t\right)dx, \tag{3.72}$$

where

$$\overleftarrow{G}\left(x, \check{t}, z, t\right) = A^{\overleftarrow{G}}\left(x, t, \check{t}\right)e^{-B^{\tilde{G}}\left(x,t,\check{t}\right)r - C^{\overleftarrow{G}}\left(x,t,\check{t}\right)s - D^{\overleftarrow{G}}\left(x,t,\check{t}\right)u},$$

with

$$C^{\overleftarrow{G}}\left(x, t, \check{t}\right) = \frac{\kappa_3^{\left(s,\frac{1}{1-w}\right)}(x) - e^{-\delta_s^{\left(\frac{1}{1-w}\right)}\left(\check{t}-t\right)}}{\kappa_4^{\left(s,\frac{1}{1-w}\right)}(x) - \kappa_5^{\left(s,\frac{1}{1-w}\right)}(x)\,e^{-\delta_s^{\left(\frac{1}{1-w}\right)}\left(\check{t}-t\right)}},$$

$$D^{\overleftarrow{G}}\left(x, t, \check{t}\right) = \frac{-2\left(v^{\overleftarrow{G}}\right)'\left(x, t, \check{t}\right)}{\sigma_u^2 v^{\overleftarrow{G}}\left(x, t, \check{t}\right)}.$$

If $\beta = 0$:

$$\begin{aligned} &A^{\overleftarrow{G}}\left(x, t, \check{t}\right) \\ &= e^{-\int_t^{\check{t}}\left(-\frac{1}{2}\sigma_r^2\left(B^{\tilde{G}}\right)^2\left(x,\tau,\check{t}\right) + \theta_r(\tau)B^{\tilde{G}}\left(x,\tau,\check{t}\right) + \theta_u D^{\overleftarrow{G}}\left(x,\tau,\check{t}\right)\right)d\tau}. \end{aligned}$$

If $\beta = \frac{1}{2}$:

$$A^{\overleftarrow{G}}\left(x,t,\check{t}\right) = e^{-\int_t^{\check{t}}\left(\theta_r(\tau)B^{\tilde{G}}\left(x,\tau,\check{t}\right)+\theta_u D^{\overleftarrow{G}}\left(x,\tau,\check{t}\right)\right)d\tau}.$$

$v^{\overleftarrow{G}}\left(x,\check{t},t\right)$ *and* $\left(v^{\overleftarrow{G}}\right)'\left(x,\check{t},t\right)$ *are complicated functions defined in the proof below.* $\kappa_3^{\left(s,\frac{1}{1-w}\right)}(x)$, $\kappa_4^{\left(s,\frac{1}{1-w}\right)}(x)$, $\kappa_5^{\left(s,\frac{1}{1-w}\right)}(x)$, *and* $\delta_s^{\left(\frac{1}{1-w}\right)}(t)$ *are defined by equations (B.23), (B.24), (B.25), and (B.22), respectively.* $B^{\tilde{G}}\left(x,t,\check{t}\right)$ *is given by equation (3.52).*

Proof.
We apply the proof of appendix B.3 with $\alpha = \frac{1}{1-w}$. Then

$$\overrightarrow{G}\left(y,\check{t},z,t\right) = G^{\left(\frac{1}{1-w}\right)}\left(y,\check{t},z,t\right), \quad \overleftarrow{G}\left(x,\check{t},z,t\right) = \tilde{G}^{\left(\frac{1}{1-w}\right)}\left(x,\check{t},z,t\right),$$
$$A^{\overleftarrow{G}}\left(x,t,\check{t}\right) = A^{\tilde{G}^{\left(\frac{1}{1-w}\right)}}\left(x,t,\check{t}\right), \quad C^{\overleftarrow{G}}\left(x,t,\check{t}\right) = C^{\tilde{G}^{\left(\frac{1}{1-w}\right)}}\left(x,t,\check{t}\right),$$
$$D^{\tilde{G}}\left(x,t,\check{t}\right) = D^{\tilde{G}^{\left(\frac{1}{1-w}\right)}}\left(x,t,\check{t}\right).$$

$v^{\overleftarrow{G}}\left(x,\check{t},t\right) = v^{\tilde{G}^{\left(\frac{1}{1-w}\right)}}\left(x,\check{t},t\right)$ and $\left(v^{\overleftarrow{G}}\right)'\left(x,\check{t},t\right)$ are defined as in equations (B.26), (B.27), and (B.28) of appendix B.3.

Equation (3.71) together with lemma (3.4.2) yields the following closed-form solution for $F^{cc}\left(z,t,T_B;T_O,K\right)$:

Theorem 3.4.1.

1. *The price of a European call option (knocked out at default of the underlying) with maturity* $T_O \leq T$ *and exercise price* K *on a defaultable zero-coupon bond* $P^d(t,T)$ *is given by*

$$\begin{aligned}&F^{cc}\left(z,t,T;T_O,K\right)\\&= P^d\left(z,t,T\right)\cdot\\&\quad \Phi^C\left(\phi_1,\phi_2,\phi_3,\psi_0,\psi_1,\psi_2,\psi_3,\varphi_0,\varphi_1,\varphi_2,\varphi_3,z\right)\\&\quad -KP^d\left(z,t,T_O\right)\cdot\\&\quad \Phi^C\left(\phi_4,\phi_5,\phi_6,\psi_4,\psi_5,\psi_6,\psi_7,\varphi_0,\varphi_1,\varphi_2,\varphi_3,z\right),\end{aligned}$$

where

$$\begin{aligned}&\Phi^C\left(a_1,a_2,a_3,b_0,b_1,b_2,b_3,c_0,c_1,c_2,c_3,z\right)\\&= \frac{1}{(2\pi)^{3/2}}\iiint_{\mathbf{R}^3} \Lambda^C\left(a_1,a_2,a_3,c_0,c_1,c_2,c_3\right)\cdot\\&\quad b_0\left(x\right)\cdot e^{-b_1(x)r-b_2(x)s-b_3(x)u}dx\end{aligned} \tag{3.73}$$

with

$$\Lambda^C(a_1,a_2,a_3,c_0,c_1,c_2,c_3) \tag{3.74}$$
$$= \iiint_{\mathbf{R}^3_+} e^{-ia_1(x)y_r-ia_2(x)y_s-ia_3(x)y_u}\cdot$$
$$1_{\{c_1y_r+c_2y_s+c_3y_u\le c_0\}}dy.$$

$$\begin{aligned}
&\phi_1 = x_1 - iB(T_O,T), && \phi_2 = x_2 - iC^d(T_O,T),\\
&\phi_3 = x_3 - iD^d(T_O,T), && \phi_4 = x_1,\\
&\phi_5 = x_2, && \phi_6 = x_3,\\
&\psi_0 = A^d(T_O,T)\tfrac{A^{\overleftarrow{G}}(x,t,T_O)}{A^d(t,T)}, && \psi_1 = B^{\widetilde{G}}(x,t,T_O) - B(t,T),\\
&\psi_2 = C^{\overleftarrow{G}}(x,t,T_O) - C^d(t,T), && \psi_3 = D^{\overleftarrow{G}}(x,t,T_O) - D^d(t,T),\\
&\psi_4 = \tfrac{A^{\overleftarrow{G}}(x,t,T_O)}{A^d(t,T_O)}, && \psi_5 = B^{\widetilde{G}}(x,t,T_O) - B(t,T_O),\\
&\psi_6 = C^{\overleftarrow{G}}(x,t,T_O) - C^d(t,T_O), && \psi_7 = D^{\overleftarrow{G}}(x,t,T_O) - D^d(t,T_O),\\
&\varphi_0 = \ln\tfrac{A^d(T_O,T)}{K}, && \varphi_1 = B(T_O,T),\\
&\varphi_2 = C^d(T_O,T), && \varphi_3 = D^d(T_O,T).
\end{aligned}$$

$B^{\widetilde{G}}$ is given by equation (3.52), $A^{\overleftarrow{G}}$, $C^{\overleftarrow{G}}$, and $D^{\overleftarrow{G}}$ are defined like in lemma 3.4.2, and A^d, B, C^d, and D^d are defined in theorem 3.3.1. $\Lambda^C(a_1,a_2,a_3,c_0,c_1,c_2,c_3)$ can be computed analytically (lemma 3.4.3).

2. *The price of a European put option (knocked out at default of the underlying) with maturity $T_O \le T$ and exercise price K on a defaultable zero-coupon bond $P^d(t,T)$ is given by*

$$F^{cp}(z,t,T;T_O,K)$$
$$= KP^d(z,t,T_O)\cdot$$
$$\Phi^P(\phi_4,\phi_5,\phi_6,\psi_4,\psi_5,\psi_6,\psi_7,\varphi_0,\varphi_1,\varphi_2,\varphi_3,z)$$
$$-P^d(z,t,T)\cdot$$
$$\Phi^P(\phi_1,\phi_2,\phi_3,\psi_0,\psi_1,\psi_2,\psi_3,\varphi_0,\varphi_1,\varphi_2,\varphi_3,z),$$

where

$$\Phi^P(a_1,a_2,a_3,b_0,b_1,b_2,b_3,c_0,c_1,c_2,c_3,z)$$
$$= \frac{1}{(2\pi)^{3/2}}\iiint_{\mathbf{R}^3} \Lambda^P(a_1,a_2,a_3,c_0,c_1,c_2,c_3)\cdot$$
$$b_0(x)\cdot e^{-b_1(x)r-b_2(x)s-b_3(x)u}dx$$

with

$$\Lambda^{P}\left(a_1,a_2,a_3,c_0,c_1,c_2,c_3\right) = \iiint\limits_{\mathbf{R}_+^3} e^{-ia_1y_r-ia_2y_s-ia_3y_u} \cdot 1_{\{c_1y_r+c_2y_s+c_3y_u\geq c_0\}}dy.$$

Proof.
The value $F^{cc}\left(z,t,T;T_O,K\right)$ can be written as

$$\begin{aligned}
&F^{cc}\left(z,t,T;T_O,K\right)\\
&=\iiint\limits_{\mathbf{R}^3}\left(P^d\left(y,T_O,T\right)-K\right)\overrightarrow{G}\left(y,T_O,z,t\right)1_{\{y\in\mathcal{B}_1\}}dy\\
&=\iiint\limits_{\mathbf{R}^3}P^d\left(y,T_O,T\right)\overrightarrow{G}\left(y,T_O,z,t\right)1_{\{y\in\mathcal{B}_1\}}dy\\
&\quad -K\iiint\limits_{\mathbf{R}^3}\overrightarrow{G}\left(y,T_O,z,t\right)1_{\{y\in\mathcal{B}_1\}}dy\\
&=I_1-I_2
\end{aligned}$$

where $\mathcal{B}_1$ is defined as above and $\overrightarrow{G}\left(y,T_O,z,t\right)$ is given in lemma 3.4.2.
Determination of I_1 :

$$\begin{aligned}
I_1&=\iiint\limits_{\mathbf{R}^3}P^d\left(y,T_O,T\right)\overrightarrow{G}\left(y,T_O,z,t\right)1_{\{y\in\mathcal{B}_1\}}dy\\
&=\frac{1}{(2\pi)^{3/2}}\iiint\limits_{\mathbf{R}^3}\iiint\limits_{\mathbf{R}^3}P^d\left(y,T_O,T\right)e^{-iyx'}1_{\{y\in\mathcal{B}_1\}}dy\cdot\overleftarrow{G}\left(x,T_O,z,t\right)dx\\
&=\frac{P^d\left(z,t,T\right)}{(2\pi)^{3/2}}\iiint\limits_{\mathbf{R}^3}\iiint\limits_{\mathbf{R}^3}A^d\left(T_O,T\right)\cdot\\
&\quad e^{-iy_r(x_1-iB(T_O,T))-iy_s\left(x_2-iC^d(T_O,T)\right)-iy_u\left(x_3-iD^d(T_O,T)\right)}\cdot 1_{\{y\in\mathcal{B}_1\}}dy\cdot\\
&\quad \frac{A^{\overleftarrow{G}}\left(x,t,T_O\right)}{A^d\left(t,T\right)}e^{-\left(B^{\overleftarrow{G}}(x,t,T_O)-B(t,T)\right)r}\cdot\\
&\quad e^{-\left(C^{\overleftarrow{G}}(x,t,T_O)-C^d(t,T)\right)s-\left(D^{\overleftarrow{G}}(x,t,T_O)-D^d(t,T)\right)u}dx.
\end{aligned}$$

Determination of I_2 :
Similarly the second integral can be written as

$$
\begin{aligned}
I_2 &= \iiint\limits_{\mathbf{R}^3} K\overrightarrow{G}(y, T_O, z, t)\, 1_{\{y\in\mathcal{B}_1\}} dy \\
&= \frac{K}{(2\pi)^{3/2}} \iiint\limits_{\mathbf{R}^3} \iiint\limits_{\mathbf{R}^3} e^{-iyx'} 1_{\{y\in\mathcal{B}_1\}} dy \\
&\quad e^{-B^{\overleftarrow{G}}(x,t,T_O)r} A^{\overleftarrow{G}}(x,t,T_O)\, e^{-C^{\overleftarrow{G}}(x,t,T_O)s - D^{\overleftarrow{G}}(x,t,T_O)u} dx \\
&= \frac{KP^d(r,s,u,t,T_O)}{(2\pi)^{3/2}} \iiint\limits_{\mathbf{R}^3} \iiint\limits_{\mathbf{R}^3} e^{-iyx'} 1_{\{y\in\mathcal{B}_1\}} dy \cdot \\
&\quad \frac{A^{\overleftarrow{G}}(x,t,T_O)}{A^d(t,T_O)} e^{-\left(B^{\overleftarrow{G}}(x,t,T_O) - B(t,T_O)\right)r} \cdot \\
&\quad e^{-\left(C^{\overleftarrow{G}}(x,t,T_O) - C^d(t,T_O)\right)s - \left(D^{\overleftarrow{G}}(x,t,T_O) - D^d(t,T_O)\right)u} dx.
\end{aligned}
$$

The proof for the put works identically.

Lemma 3.4.3.

$$
\begin{aligned}
&\Lambda^C(a_1, a_2, a_3, c_0, c_1, c_2, c_3) \\
&= -\frac{ic_0^3}{c_1 c_2 c_3 \widetilde{a}_1} \cdot \\
&\left(\frac{e^{-i\widetilde{a}_3} - e^{-i\widetilde{a}_2}}{(\widetilde{a}_3 - \widetilde{a}_2)(\widetilde{a}_2 - \widetilde{a}_1)} - \frac{e^{-i\widetilde{a}_3} - e^{-i\widetilde{a}_1}}{(\widetilde{a}_3 - \widetilde{a}_1)(\widetilde{a}_2 - \widetilde{a}_1)} + \frac{e^{-i\widetilde{a}_3} - 1}{\widetilde{a}_2 \widetilde{a}_3} - \frac{e^{-i\widetilde{a}_3} - e^{-i\widetilde{a}_2}}{\widetilde{a}_2(\widetilde{a}_3 - \widetilde{a}_2)} \right),
\end{aligned}
$$

where

$$
\widetilde{a}_i = \frac{c_0 a_i}{c_i} \text{ for } i = 1, 2, 3.
$$

A similar result can be obtained for Λ^P.

Proof.
See appendix B.

Remark 3.4.2.

1. If we assumed that the call option survived a default, and after some restructuring the bonds were still traded with a market value dropped to the bond recovery rate times the pre-default market value of the debt, the price would be given by

$$
\begin{aligned}
&F^{cc}(z, t, T; T_O, K) \\
&= E^{\mathbf{Q}}\left[e^{-\int_t^{T_O} r(l)dl} 1_{\{T_O < T^d\}} \left(P^d(T_O, T) - K\right)_+ \middle| \mathcal{F}_t \right] \\
&\quad + E^{\mathbf{Q}}\left[e^{-\int_t^{T_O} r(l)dl} 1_{\{T_O \geq T^d\}} \left(\widetilde{P}^d(T_O, T) - K\right)_+ \middle| \mathcal{F}_t \right],
\end{aligned}
$$

where $\widetilde{P}^d(t,T)$ is the defaultable zero-coupon bond price adjusted for a possible default before t, i.e. it is the price of a zero-coupon bond which hasn't defaulted yet but is equivalent to the defaulted bond with the face value reduced to the bond recovery rate (which we assumed to be constant) times the pre-default market value of the debt.

$$E^{\mathbf{Q}}\left[e^{-\int_t^{T_O} r(l)dl}1_{\{T_O \geq T^d\}}\left(\widetilde{P}^d(T_O,T)-K\right)_+\middle|\mathcal{F}_t\right]$$

$$= E^{\mathbf{Q}}\left[e^{-\int_t^{T_O} r(l)dl}\left(\widetilde{P}^d(T_O,T)-K\right)_+\middle|\mathcal{F}_t\right] \quad (3.75)$$

$$-E^{\mathbf{Q}}\left[e^{-\int_t^{T_O} r(l)dl}1_{\{T_O < T^d\}}\left(\widetilde{P}^d(T_O,T)-K\right)_+\middle|\mathcal{F}_t\right] \quad (3.76)$$

Because (3.76) can be calculated similarly to

$$E^{\mathbf{Q}}\left[e^{-\int_t^{T_O} r(l)dl}1_{\{T_O < T^d\}}\left(P^d(T_O,T)-K\right)_+\middle|\mathcal{F}_t\right],$$

we leave the calculations to the interested reader. For the determination of the value of (3.75) one can use PDE techniques similar to those described above. The necessary mathematical tools are given in lemma B.5.1.

2. Corresponding formulas are valid for put options.
3. The structure of the pricing formulas in the defaultable case is the same as the structure of the bond option pricing formulas in the classical term structure models.

3.4.4 Credit Spread Options

Definition 3.4.5.

1. *A credit spread call option on a defaultable bond $P^d(t,T)$ with maturity $T_O < T$ and strike spread K gives the holder the right to buy the defaultable bond at time T_O at a price that corresponds to a yield spread of K above the yield of an otherwise identical non defaultable bond $P(t,T)$.*
2. *A credit spread put option on a defaultable bond $P^d(t,T)$ with maturity $T_O < T$ and strike spread K gives the holder the right to sell the defaultable bond at time T_O at a price that corresponds to a yield spread of K above the yield of an otherwise identical non defaultable bond $P(t,T)$.*

Credit spread options offer investors whose portfolio values are highly sensitive to shifts in the spread between defaultable and non-defaultable yields an important tool for managing and hedging their exposure to this type of risk. Credit spread puts enable investors who are not allowed to invest in assets of too low quality to switch out of a defaultable bond investment as soon as the credit quality of the reference credit asset falls below some boundary. They can be viewed as an exchange option that give one counterparty the right to exchange one defaultable bond for a certain number of non defaultable bonds. Again, depending on the specification, the option can either survive a default or be knocked out by it. We use the same pricing methodology as in the previous section.

Definition 3.4.6.

1. *A European credit spread call option with maturity $T_O \leq T$ and strike spread K on a defaultable zero-coupon bond $P^d(t,T)$ pays off*

$$1_{\{T_O<T_B^d\}}\left(P^d(T_O,T)-e^{-(T-T_O)K}P(T_O,T)\right)_+,$$

if the call is knocked out at default.

2. *A European credit spread put option with maturity $T_O \leq T$ and exercise price K on a defaultable zero-coupon bond $P^d(t,T)$ pays off*

$$1_{\{T_O<T_B^d\}}\left(e^{-(T-T_O)K}P(T_O,T)-P^d(T_O,T)\right)_+,$$

if the put is knocked out at default.

If we assume that there is no default risk with the issuer of the option and the call is knocked out at default, the call price at time $t \leq T_O$ is given by

$$\begin{aligned}
&F^{csc}(z,t,T;T_O,K)\\
&=E^{\mathbf{Q}}\left[e^{-\int_t^{T_O}r(l)dl}1_{\{T_O<T^d\}}\left(P^d(T_O,T)-e^{-(T-T_O)K}P(T_O,T)\right)_+\middle|\mathcal{F}_t\right]\\
&=E^{\mathbf{Q}}\left[e^{-\int_t^{T_O}(r(l)+s^{zero}(l))dl}1_{\{\mathcal{B}_3\}}\left(P^d(T_O,T)-e^{-(T-T_O)K}P(T_O,T)\right)\middle|\mathcal{F}_t\right],
\end{aligned}$$

where $\mathcal{B}_3$ is the range of values of r, s, and u over which the option is in the money at the expiration date T_O, that is,

$$\begin{aligned}
\mathcal{B}_3&=\left\{z\in\mathbb{R}_+^3\,\middle|\,P^d(T_O,T)-e^{-(T-T_O)K}P(T_O,T)\geq 0\right\}\\
&=\left\{z\in\mathbb{R}_+^3\,\middle|\,C^d(T_O,T)s+D^d(T_O,T)u\leq(T-T_O)K+\ln\frac{A^d(T_O,T)}{A(T_O,T)}\right\}.
\end{aligned}$$

Similarly, the put price is given by

$$\begin{aligned}
&F^{csp}(z,t,T;T_O,K)\\
&=E^{\mathbf{Q}}\left[e^{-\int_t^{T_O}(r(l)+s^{zero}(l))dl}1_{\{\mathcal{B}_4\}}\left(e^{-(T-T_O)K}P(T_O,T)-P^d(T_O,T)\right)\middle|\mathcal{F}_t\right],
\end{aligned}$$

where $\mathcal{B}_4$ is the range of values of r, s, and u over which the option is in the money at the expiration date T_O, that is,

$$\mathcal{B}_4 = \left\{ z \in \mathbb{R}_+^3 \,\middle|\, (T - T_O)\, K + \ln \frac{A^d (T_O, T)}{A (T_O, T)} \le C^d (T_O, T)\, s + D^d (T_O, T)\, u \right\}.$$

Then the time t value of the call option is

$$\begin{aligned} &F^{\mathrm{csc}} (z, t, T_O, K) \\ &= \int_{\mathcal{B}_3} \left(P^d (y, T_O, T) - e^{-(T-T_O)K} P (y_r, T_O, T) \right) \overrightarrow{G} (y, T_O, z, t)\, dy \\ &= I_3 - I_4, \end{aligned}$$

where $\overrightarrow{G} (y, T_O, z, t)$ is given by equation (3.72), $\mathcal{B}_3$ is the range of values over which the credit spread option is in the money at the expiration date T. I_3 and I_4 can be calculated by similar methods as I_1 and I_2:

$$\begin{aligned} I_3 = &\frac{P^d (z, t, T)}{(2\pi)^{3/2}} \iiint\limits_{\mathbf{R}^3} \iiint\limits_{\mathbf{R}^3} \\ &e^{-iy_r(x_1 - iB(T_O,T)) - iy_s\left(x_2 - iC^d(T_O,T)\right) - iy_u\left(x_3 - iD^d(T_O,T)\right)} \cdot 1_{\{y \in \mathcal{B}_3\}} dy \cdot \\ &A^d (T_O, T) \frac{A^{\overleftarrow{G}} (x, t, T_O)}{A^d (t, T)} e^{-\left(B^{\overleftarrow{G}}(x,t,T_O) - B(t,T)\right) r} \cdot \\ &e^{-\left(C^{\overleftarrow{G}}(x,t,T_O) - C^d(t,T)\right) s - \left(D^{\overleftarrow{G}}(x,t,T_O) - D^d(t,T)\right) u} dx, \end{aligned}$$

and

$$\begin{aligned} I_4 = &\frac{e^{-(T-T_O)K} P^d (z, t, T_O)}{(2\pi)^{3/2}} \iiint_{\mathbf{R}^3} \\ &\iiint_{\mathbf{R}^3} e^{-iy_r(x_1 - iB(T_O,T)) - iy_s x_2 - iy_u x_3} 1_{\{y \in \mathcal{B}_3\}} dy \cdot \\ &A (T_O, T) \frac{A^{\overleftarrow{G}} (x, t, T_O)}{A^d (t, T_O)} e^{-\left(B^{\overleftarrow{G}}(x,t,T_O) - B(t,T_O)\right) r} \cdot \\ &e^{-\left(C^{\overleftarrow{G}}(x,t,T_O) - C^d(t,T_O)\right) s - \left(D^{\overleftarrow{G}}(x,t,T_O) - D^d(t,T_O)\right) u} dx. \end{aligned}$$

Therefore the following theorem is obtained.

Theorem 3.4.2.

1. *The price of a European call option (knocked out at default of the underlying) with maturity $T_O \le T$ and exercise price K on a defaultable zero-coupon bond $P^d (t, T)$ is given by*

$$
\begin{aligned}
&F^{csc}(z,t,T;T_O,K)\\
&= P^d(z,t,T)\cdot\\
&\quad \Phi^C(\phi_1,\phi_2,\phi_3,\psi_0,\psi_1,\psi_2,\psi_3,\varphi_4,\varphi_5,\varphi_2,\varphi_3,z)\\
&\quad -\overline{K}P^d(z,t,T_O)\cdot\\
&\quad \Phi^C(\phi_1,\phi_5,\phi_6,\psi_8,\psi_5,\psi_6,\psi_7,\varphi_4,\varphi_5,\varphi_2,\varphi_3,z),
\end{aligned}
$$

where $\overline{K} = e^{-(T-T_O)K}$, Φ^C is given in theorem 3.4.1, and

$$
\begin{aligned}
\psi_8 &= A(T_O,T)\,\frac{A^{\overleftarrow{G}}(x,t,T_O)}{A^d(t,T_O)},\\
\varphi_4 &= (T-T_O)\,K + \ln\frac{A^d(T_O,T)}{A(T_O,T)},\ \varphi_5 = 0.
\end{aligned}
$$

$A^{\overleftarrow{G}}$, A^d, and A are defined in lemma 3.4.2, theorem 3.3.1, and by equation (3.17), respectively. All other parameters are defined in theorem 3.4.1.

2. *The price of a European put option (knocked out at default of the underlying) with maturity $T_O \le T$ and exercise price K on a defaultable zero-coupon bond $P^d(t,T)$ is given by*

$$
\begin{aligned}
&F^{csp}(z,t,T;T_O,K)\\
&= \overline{K}P^d(z,t,T_O)\cdot\\
&\quad \Phi^P(\phi_1,\phi_5,\phi_6,\psi_8,\psi_5,\psi_6,\psi_7,\varphi_4,\varphi_5,\varphi_2,\varphi_3,z)\\
&\quad -P^d(z,t,T)\cdot\\
&\quad \Phi^P(\phi_1,\phi_2,\phi_3,\psi_0,\psi_1,\psi_2,\psi_3,\varphi_4,\varphi_5,\varphi_2,\varphi_3,z).
\end{aligned}
$$

Remark 3.4.3.

1. Credit spreads are usually very volatile. That is why issuers of credit spread put options often include an additional feature. If the market spread $S(t,T)$ is greater than or equal to some pre-agreed spread $K^* > K$ at any time t before maturity of the option, then the put option immediately pays

$$
e^{-(T-t)K}P(t,T) - e^{-(T-t)K^*}P(t,T).
$$

2. If we allow the option to survive a default, we must model the post-default bond behavior as well. Similar techniques as for credit options can be applied.

3.4.5 Default Swaps and Default Options

Figure 3.25 shows the general structure of a default swap and option.
The following definition gives an overview of the most important default swap and default option structures:

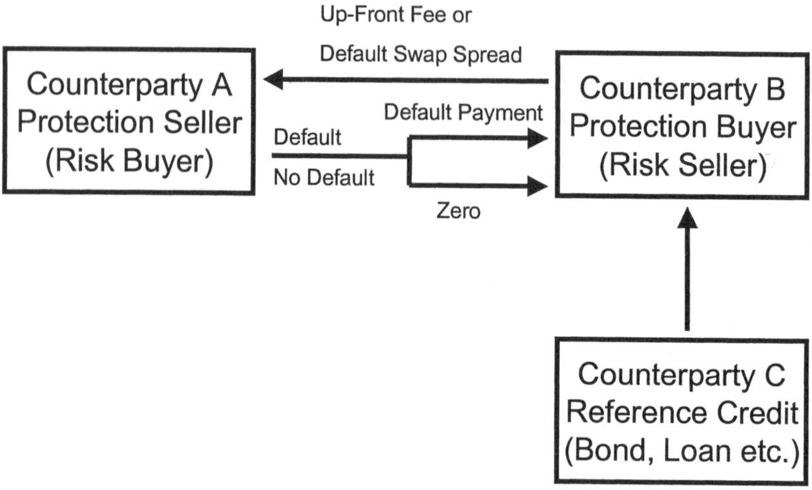

Fig. 3.25. Basic structure of a credit default swap and option.

Definition 3.4.7.

1. *A default digital (put) option has a pre-agreed payoff at the time of default, e.g., expressed as a fixed percentage of the notional amount or as absolute value. The beneficiary pays the guarantor a lump-sum fee up-front.*
2. *A default digital swap has a pre-agreed payoff at the time of default, e.g., expressed as a fixed percentage of the notional amount or as absolute value. The beneficiary pays the guarantor regular fees instead of a single up-front payment.*
3. *A default option (put) is a credit derivative under which one party (the beneficiary) pays the other party (the guarantor) a fixed amount (lump-sum fee up-front). This is in exchange for the guarantor's promise to make a fixed or variable payment in the event of default in one or more reference assets to cover the full loss in default.*
4. *A default swap is a swap under which one party (the beneficiary) pays the other party (the guarantor) regular fees, amounts that are based on a generic interest rate, called the default swap spread or the default swap premium. This is in exchange for the guarantor's promise to make a fixed or variable payment in the event of default in one or more reference assets to cover the full loss in default.*
5. *A default swap with a dynamic notional is a default swap which for a fixed fee provides the protection buyer with a contingent payment that matches the mark-to-market value on any given day of a specified derivative.*
6. *A first-loss default swap is a default swap whereby the protection seller commits to indemnify the protection buyer for a predefined amount of*

losses incurred following one or more credit events in a specified reference portfolio.

7. *A first-to-default swap or basket swap is a default swap where the protection seller takes on exposure to the first entity suffering a credit event within a basket. The credit position in each name in the basket is typically equal to the notional of the first-to-default default swap. Losses are capped at the notional amount and the protection seller does not have exposure to subsequent credit events.*

Default Digital Swaps and Default Digital Put Options. We consider a default digital put option that pays off 1 in case of a credit event. First we assume that the payoff takes place at maturity of the contract. If there has been no default until time t, the time t price of the contract is given by

$$\begin{aligned} F^{ddp}(t) &= E^{\mathbf{Q}}\left[e^{-\int_t^T r(l)dl} 1_{\{T^d \leq T\}} \middle| \mathcal{F}_t \right] \\ &= E^{\mathbf{Q}}\left[e^{-\int_t^T r(l)dl} \left(1 - 1_{\{T^d > T\}}\right) \middle| \mathcal{F}_t \right] \\ &= P(t,T) - E^{\mathbf{Q}}\left[e^{-\int_t^T r(l)dl} 1_{\{T^d > T\}} \middle| \mathcal{F}_t \right] \\ &= P(t,T) - P^{d,zero}(t,T). \end{aligned}$$

If the payoff takes place at default of the reference credit asset and there has been no default until time t, the time t price of the contract is given by

$$F^{ddp}(t) = E^{\mathbf{Q}}\left[\int_t^T e^{-\int_t^{\tilde{t}} r(l)dl} dH_{\tilde{t}} \middle| \mathcal{F}_t \right].$$

Hence, since $L_T F_T^{ddp} = 0$,

$$L_t F_t^{ddp} = E^{\mathbf{Q}}\left[\int_t^T e^{-\int_t^{\tilde{t}} r(l)dl} dH_{\tilde{t}} + e^{-\int_t^T r(l)dl} L_T F_T^{ddp} \middle| \mathcal{F}_t \right]. \tag{3.77}$$

Applying corollary 3.2.1 to equation (3.77) yields

$$d\left(L_t F_t^{ddp}\right) = -dH_t + r_t L_t F_t^{ddp} dt + dm_t \tag{3.78}$$

for some martingale m. Together with lemma 3.4.1 equation (3.78) becomes

$$d\left(L_t F_t^{ddp}\right) = -s_t^{zero} d_t + r_t L_t F_t^{ddp} dt + d\widetilde{m}_t$$

for some martingale $\widetilde{m}$ with $d\widetilde{m}_t = dm_t + dM_t^{d,zero}$. Finally, as

$$\int L_t F_t^{ddp} dM_t^{d,zero} = \int L_t F_t^{ddp} s_t^{zero} dt - \int L_t F_t^{ddp} dH_t$$

is a martingale by the arguments we have used before,

$$
\begin{aligned}
d\left(L_t F_t^{ddp}\right) &= -L_t F_t^{ddp} dH_t - s_t^{zero} dt + \left(r_t + s_t^{zero}\right) L_t F_t^{ddp} dt + d\widehat{m}_t \\
&= -s_t^{zero} dt + \left(r_t + s_t^{zero}\right) L_t F_t^{ddp} dt + d\widehat{m}_t \qquad (3.79)
\end{aligned}
$$

for some martingale $\widehat{m}$ with $d\widehat{m} = d\widehat{m}_t - L_t F_t^{ddp} dM_t^{d,zero}$. Equation (3.79) holds because $L_t F_t^{ddp} dH_t = 0$. By applying corollary 3.2.1 again, we get

$$
\begin{aligned}
&L_t F_t^{ddp} \\
&= E^{\mathbf{Q}}\left[\int_t^T e^{-\int_t^{\widetilde{t}}(r(l)+s^{zero}(l))dl} s_{\widetilde{t}}^{zero} d\widetilde{t} + e^{-\int_t^T (r(l)+s^{zero}(l))dl} L_T F_T^{ddp} \middle| \mathcal{F}_t\right].
\end{aligned}
$$

Thus,

$$
\begin{aligned}
L_t F_t^{ddp} &= E^{\mathbf{Q}}\left[\int_t^T e^{-\int_t^{\widetilde{t}}(r(l)+s^{zero}(l))dl} s_{\widetilde{t}}^{zero} d\widetilde{t} \middle| \mathcal{F}_t\right] \qquad (3.80) \\
&= \int_t^T E^{\mathbf{Q}}\left[e^{-\int_t^{\widetilde{t}}(r(l)+s^{zero}(l))dl} s_{\widetilde{t}}^{zero} \middle| \mathcal{F}_t\right] d\widetilde{t},
\end{aligned}
$$

as there is sufficient regularity to allow the interchange of expectation and integration[56]. Using the independence of r and s^{zero}, we finally get

$$
\begin{aligned}
L_t F_t^{ddp} &= \int_t^T P\left(t,\widetilde{t}\right) E^{\mathbf{Q}}\left[e^{-\int_t^{\widetilde{t}} s^{zero}(l)dl} s_{\widetilde{t}}^{zero} \middle| \mathcal{F}_t\right] d\widetilde{t} \\
&= \int_t^T P^{d,zero}\left(t,\widetilde{t}\right) f^{d,zero}\left(t,\widetilde{t}\right) d\widetilde{t}, \qquad (3.81)
\end{aligned}
$$

which follows immediately from a well-known result (see, e.g., Sandmann & Sondermann (1997)) in non-defaultable interest rate theory, saying basically

$$
E^{\mathbf{Q}}\left[e^{-\int_t^{\widetilde{t}} r(l)dl} r\left(\widetilde{t}\right) \middle| \mathcal{F}_t\right] = -E^{\mathbf{Q}}\left[e^{-\int_t^{\widetilde{t}} r(l)dl} \middle| \mathcal{F}_t\right] \cdot \frac{\partial}{\partial T} \ln P(t,T)\bigg|_{T=\widetilde{t}},
$$

and $f^{d,zero}\left(t,\widetilde{t}\right)$ is the zero recovery spread forward rate, i.e.

$$
f^{d,zero}\left(t,\widetilde{t}\right) = -\frac{\partial}{\partial \widetilde{t}} \ln \frac{P^{d,zero}\left(t,\widetilde{t}\right)}{P\left(t,\widetilde{t}\right)}. \qquad (3.82)
$$

Hence, plugging in equation (3.82) into equation (3.81) yields

---

56 $E^{\mathbf{Q}}\left[\int_t^T \left|e^{-\int_t^{\widetilde{t}}(r(l)+s^{zero}(l))dl} s_{\widetilde{t}}^{zero}\right| d\widetilde{t}\right] \leq E^{\mathbf{Q}}\left[\int_t^T \left|s_{\widetilde{t}}^{zero}\right| d\widetilde{t}\right] < \infty$ and $e^{-\int_t^{\widetilde{t}}(r(l)+s^{zero}(l))dl} s_{\widetilde{t}}^{zero}$ is product measurable on $\Omega \times [t,T]$ (see, e.g., Duffie (1992), p. 234).

$$
\begin{aligned}
L_t F_t^{ddp} &= -\int_t^T P^{d,zero}\left(t,\tilde{t}\right)\frac{\partial}{\partial\tilde{t}}\left(\ln\frac{P^{d,zero}\left(t,\tilde{t}\right)}{P\left(t,\tilde{t}\right)}\right)d\tilde{t} \\
&= \int_t^T \frac{P^{d,zero}\left(t,\tilde{t}\right)\frac{\partial}{\partial\tilde{t}}\left(P\left(t,\tilde{t}\right)\right)}{P\left(t,\tilde{t}\right)} - \frac{\partial}{\partial\tilde{t}}\left(P^{d,zero}\left(t,\tilde{t}\right)\right)d\tilde{t} \\
&= L_t - \int_t^T \frac{P^{d,zero}\left(t,\tilde{t}\right)}{P\left(t,\tilde{t}\right)}\frac{\partial}{\partial\tilde{t}}\left(P\left(t,\tilde{t}\right)\right)d\tilde{t} - P^{d,zero}\left(t,T\right) \\
&= L_t - P^{d,zero}\left(t,T\right) \\
&\quad + \int_t^T P^{d,zero}\left(t,\tilde{t}\right)\left(\frac{A_{\tilde{t}}\left(t,\tilde{t}\right)}{A\left(t,\tilde{t}\right)} - B_{\tilde{t}}\left(t,\tilde{t}\right)r_t\right)d\tilde{t},
\end{aligned}
\tag{3.83}
$$

We can conclude:

Theorem 3.4.3. *If there has been no default until time t, the price of a default digital put option paying off* 1 *in case of a credit event, is given by*

$$
\begin{aligned}
F_t^{ddp} &= 1 - P^{d,zero}\left(t,T\right) \\
&\quad + \int_t^T P^{d,zero}\left(t,\tilde{t}\right)\left(\frac{A_{\tilde{t}}\left(t,\tilde{t}\right)}{A\left(t,\tilde{t}\right)} - B_{\tilde{t}}\left(t,\tilde{t}\right)r_t\right)d\tilde{t}.
\end{aligned}
$$

Remark 3.4.4.

1. Equation (3.83) is a closed form solution for the price of a default digital put:
   a) $P^{d,zero}\left(t,\tilde{t}\right)$ is given by equation (3.68) for all $t \leq \tilde{t} \leq T$.
   b) $A_{\tilde{t}}\left(t,\tilde{t}\right) = \frac{\partial}{\partial\tilde{t}}A\left(t,\tilde{t}\right)$ can be easily calculated from $A\left(t,\tilde{t}\right)$ which is given by equation (3.17).
   c) $B_{\tilde{t}}\left(t,\tilde{t}\right) = \frac{\partial}{\partial\tilde{t}}B\left(t,\tilde{t}\right)$ can be easily calculated from $B\left(t,\tilde{t}\right)$ which is given by equation (3.16).
   d) L_t and r_t are known at time t.
2. Alternatively, without demanding any regularity conditions for the interchange of expectation and integration, we can solve equation (3.80) by applying PDE techniques.

Default Swaps and Default Puts. In practice, default swap and default put contracts differ in their specific default payments:

- Replacement of the difference to an equivalent default-free bond. That is, the payoff at the default time T^d is

$$
\begin{aligned}
&P\left(T^d,T\right) - P^d\left(T^d,T\right) \\
&= P\left(T^d,T\right) - w\left(T^d\right)P^d\left(T^d-,T\right).
\end{aligned}
$$

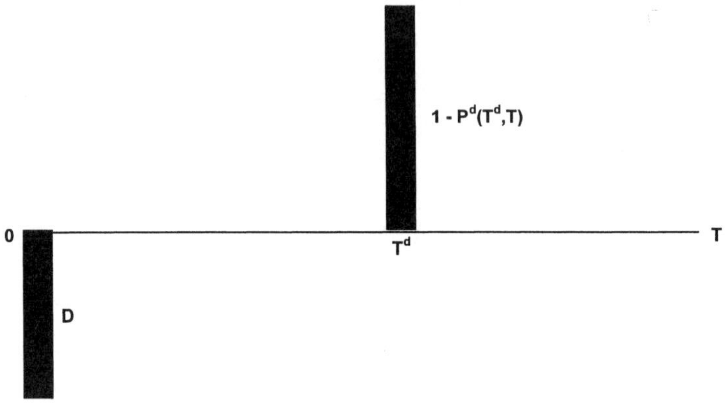

Fig. 3.26. Cash flows of a default put with a default event at time T^d. The default put up-front fee is denoted by D. Replacement of the difference to par: $1 - P^d\left(T^d, T\right)$. The reference credit asset is a defaultable zero coupon bond.

- Replacement of the difference to par: if termination is triggered, there is a payoff that is the difference between the face value and the market value (at default) of a reference credit asset (cash settlement). That is, the payoff at the time T^d of default is

$$\begin{aligned} & 1 - P^d\left(T^d, T\right) \\ & = 1 - w\left(T^d\right) P^d\left(T^d -, T\right). \end{aligned}$$

  A default swap on a defaultable coupon bond only pays off the difference between the post-default coupon bond price and par. There is only principal but not coupon protection. For the case that a default happens, figures 3.26 and 3.27 show the cash flows of a default put and default swap, respectively.

The pricing of a default swap consists of two problems. At origination there is no exchange of cash flows, and we have to determine the default swap spread S that makes the market value of the default swap zero. After origination, the market value of the default swap will change due to changes in the underlying variables. So given the default swap spread S, we have to determine the current market value of the default swap. We assume throughout that the credit swap counterparties (beneficiary and guarantor) are default-free, and

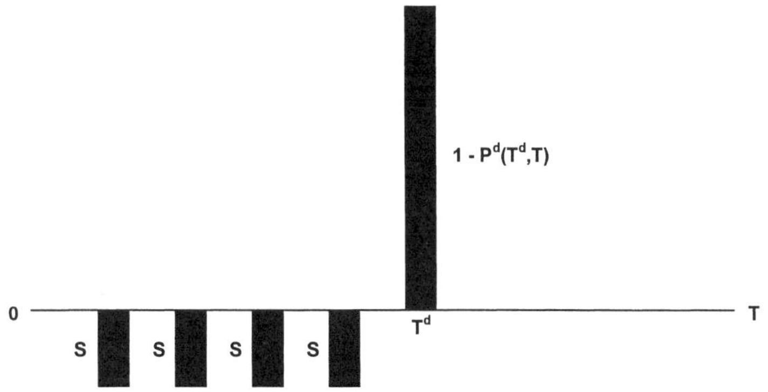

Fig. 3.27. Cash flows of a default swap with a default event at time T^d. The default swap spread is denoted by S. Replacement of the difference to par: $1 - P^d\left(T^d, T\right)$. The underlying reference credit asset is a defaultable zero coupon bond.

that there is a replacement to the difference of par (which is currently market standard).

The underlying reference credit asset is a defaultable zero-coupon bond. We assume that there has been no credit event until time t.

1. Default put options and replacement of the difference to par:
   The time t price is given by

$$\begin{aligned}
F^{dp}(t) &= E^{\mathbf{Q}}\left[\int_t^T e^{-\int_t^u r(l)dl}\left(1 - Z(u)\right) dH_u \middle| \mathcal{F}_t\right] \\
&= F^{ddp}(t) - E^{\mathbf{Q}}\left[\int_t^T e^{-\int_t^u r(l)dl} Z(u)\, dH_u \middle| \mathcal{F}_t\right] \\
&= F^{ddp}(t) - E^{\mathbf{Q}}\left[\int_t^T e^{-\int_t^u r(l)dl} Z(u)\, dH_u + e^{-\int_t^T r(l)dl} L_T \middle| \mathcal{F}_t\right] \\
&\quad + E^{\mathbf{Q}}\left[e^{-\int_t^T r(l)dl} L_T \middle| \mathcal{F}_t\right] \\
&= F^{ddp}(t) - P^d(t,T) + P^{d,zero}(t,T).
\end{aligned}$$

2. Default put options and replacement of the difference to an equivalent default-free bond:

There is a simple no-arbitrage argument that can be used to determine the value of a credit default option on a defaultable zero-coupon bond that - in case of a credit event - replaces the difference to an equivalent default-free bond . Assume that an investor forms a portfolio consisting of a defaultable zero-coupon bond with maturity T and a credit default option that pays the difference to a default-free zero-coupon bond with maturity T in case of a default. This construction eliminates the entire default risk from the defaultable zero-coupon bond. Hence, the value of the portfolio must always be equal to the value of a non defaultable zero-coupon bond with maturity T, i.e.

$$F^{dp}(t) = P(t,T) - P^{d}(t,T).$$

This equation is valid in the most general assumptions on the processes r, s, and u.

3. Default swaps:
In case of a credit default swap there are regular payments S (the credit swap spread) instead of an up-front fee F_0^{dp}. The value of paying F_0^{dp} at the origination of the credit default put option must be the same as paying S at some predefined times t_i, $i = 1, ..., m$, until a default happens. Note, that t_i, $i = 1, ..., m$, are all possible payment dates. Hence, by using remark 3.4.1 (2.),

$$F^{dp}(0) = S \sum_{i=1}^{m} P^{d,zero}(0,t_i).$$

This is equivalent to a credit swap spread of

$$S = \frac{F^{dp}(0)}{\sum_{i=1}^{m} P^{d,zero}(0,t_i)}.$$

The underlying reference credit asset is a defaultable fixed rate bond. In the following we want to ignore any accrued premiums that may be outstanding at the time of default. In addition, we assume that there has been no credit event until time t.

1. Default put options and replacement to the difference to par:
The reference credit asset is a coupon bond with discrete coupon payments c_i occurring at dates $t < t_i \leq T$, $i = 1, ..., n$, and maturity T. Then the pricing argument for the default put is exactly the same as in the case of the zero-coupon bond, and we get

$$F_c^{dp}(t) = F^{ddp}(t) - P_c^{d}(t,T) + P_c^{d,zero}(t,T),$$

where

$$P_c^{d,zero}(t,T) = \sum_{i=1}^{n} c_i P^{d,zero}(t,t_i) + P^{d,zero}(t,T).$$

2. Default put options and replacement of the difference to an equivalent default-free bond:
   We can use the same no-arbitrage argument as in the case of zero-coupon bonds, and get
   $$F_c^{dp}(t) = P_c(t,T) - P_c^d(t,T).$$
3. Default swaps:
   The credit swap spread can be calculated by the same argument as in the case of zero-coupon bonds. Hence, if there are regular payments S at some predefined times t_i, $i = 1, ..., m$, until a default happens, S is given by
   $$S = \frac{F_c^{dp}(0)}{\sum_{i=1}^{m} P_0^d(0,t_i)}.$$

The underlying note is a defaultable par floating rate note with the maturity of the default swap. We assume that default is only possible at coupon dates or at maturity and that there exists a default-free floating rate note with floating rate C_t at date t. The coupon payments of the underlying defaultable floating rate note are $C_t + \overline{S}$ at date t, where $\overline{S}$ is a fixed spread. Both floating rate notes have a final payoff of 1 (if there is no credit event). If both floaters trade at par at $t = 0$, we can use an arbitrage argument to price the default swap. We short the par issued defaultable floating rate note and invest the money in a par issued default-free floating rate note and hold this portfolio either until to maturity or a credit event occurs, receiving the coupons on the default-free floating rate note and paying the coupons on the defaultable floating rate note. If there is no credit event before maturity, both floating rate notes mature at par. So there is no net cash flow at maturity. If there is default before maturity, we liquidate the portfolio immediately receiving 1 from the default-free floating rate note, which is par on a coupon date, and paying the remaining market value $P_f^d(T^d,T)$ of the defaulted floating rate note. Hence, the net cash flow equals $1 - P_f^d(T^d,T)$, which is exactly the same as that specified in a default swap contract. The absence of arbitrage implies that the unique arbitrage free default swap spread S is given by $S = \overline{S}$. Table 3.2 compares the cash flows of the default swap to the cash flows of the portfolio at any time until default or maturity.

If we allow for default not only at coupon times we liquidate the portfolio at the coupon date immediately after default. Then the relationship

$$Default\ Swap = Default\text{-}Free\ FRN \ - \ Defaultable\ FRN$$

is only approximately valid.

Conclusion 3.4.1

Because the market value of a default swap on a defaultable floating rate note at origination equals zero, the arbitrage free default swap spread S equals the coupon spread of the reference defaultable floating rate note spread $\overline{S}$ over

Table 3.2. Payoffs of a default swap with a defaultable floating rate note as a reference asset and payoffs of a portfolio consisting of a default free floating rate note (long) and a defaultable floating rate note (short).

	Default Swap	*Default Free FRN - Defaultable FRN*
t=0	0	$1-1=0$
Coupon dates before default including maturity	$-S$	$C_t - (C_t + \overline{S}) = -\overline{S}$
$t = T^d$ *(without coupons)*	$1 - P_f^d(T^d, T)$	$1 - P_f^d(T^d, T)$
$t = T$ *(without coupons)*	0	$1-1=0$

an equivalent default-free floating rate note. The price of the default swap after origination equals the market value of the default-free floating rate note minus the market value of the defaultable floating rate note.

Remark 3.4.5.

1. We can relax the assumption that the underlying floating rate note has the same maturity as the default swap. The relevant par spread $\overline{S}$ for fixing the default swap spread is that of a different floating rate note issued by counterparty C which is of the same maturity as the default swap, and of the same priority as the underlying floating rate note. If there is no available par floating rate note of the same credit quality and seniority with the same maturity as the default swap, often the default swap spread S can be deduced from other spreads.
2. One of the important elements of the arbitrage argument is to short the par issued counterparty C defaultable floating rate note freely. Shorting a floating rate note can be done, e.g., via a reverse repo combined with a cash sale. Through the reverse repo one can receive the floating rate note as a collateral on a loan. Instead of holding the collateral one can sell the note immediately. But there may be some possible additional problems:
   - Transaction costs;
   - Big bid-ask spreads for the counterparty C floating rate note;
   - One may be forced in a special repo, i.e. one may be forced to offer a repo rate that is substantially below the general collateral rate (GCR). Then the default swap spread should be increased by the difference between the GCR and the special repo rate;
   - In practice, for illiquid instruments, the default swap spread can vary from the reference credit counterparty C floating rate note;
3. Sometimes the default swap contract is specified such that the protection buyer must pay the default swap premium that has accrued since the last coupon date.

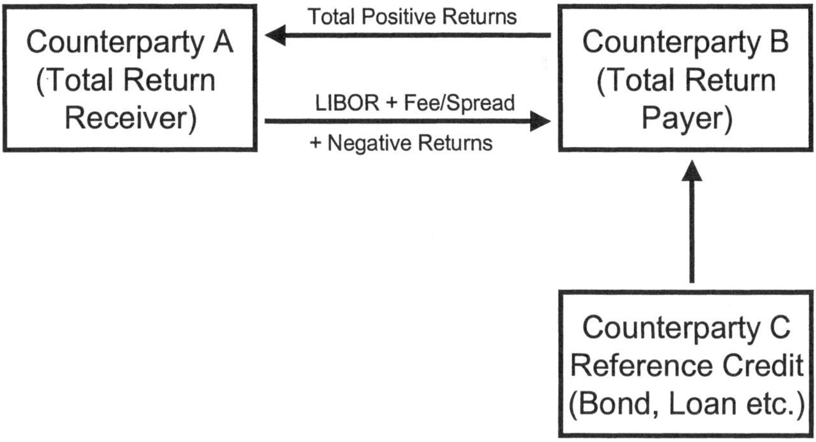

Fig. 3.28. Basic structure of a total return swap.

4. The typical default swap specifies payment at default of the difference between face value without accrued interest and market value of the underlying floating rate note. The arbitrage portfolio described above is worth face value plus accrued interest on the non defaultable floating rate note, less recovery on the underlying defaultable floating rate note.

3.4.6 Other Credit Derivatives

Total Rate of Return Swaps (Total Return Swaps)

Definition 3.4.8.
A total rate of return swap is a swap under which two parties periodically pay each other the total return on one or two reference assets or baskets of assets which they do not necessarily hold. When at least one of the reference assets is a credit-sensitive instrument, the swap is a credit derivative. The payments of the two parties are netted.

A total return swap is a means of duplicating cash flows of either selling or buying an asset, without ever necessarily possessing the asset itself. It is distinct from the default swap in that it exchanges either the total economic performance of a specified asset for another cash flow or the total economic performances of two specified assets. Hence, payments between the counterparties to a total rate of return swap are based upon changes in the market

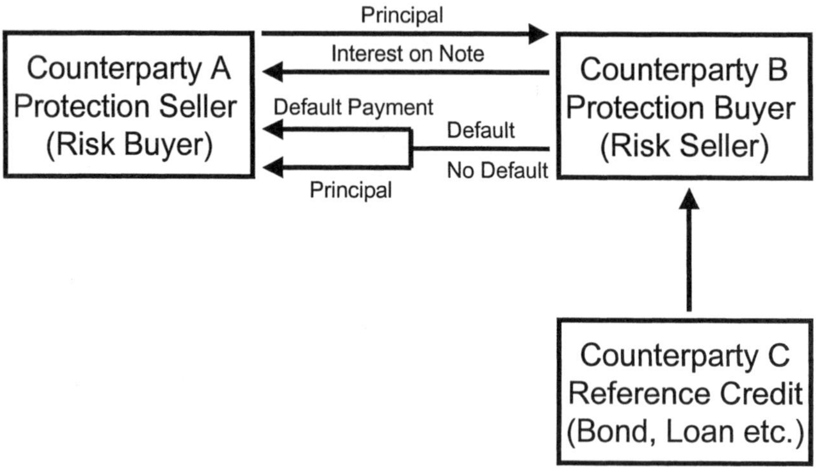

Fig. 3.29. Basic structure of a credit-linked note.

valuation of one or more specific credit instruments, irrespective of whether a credit event has occurred. In contrast to the default swap, the total return swap doesn't only transfer credit risk but also market risk of the reference credit asset. Figure 3.28 shows the structure of a typical total return swap. Counterparty A pays counterparty B at regular intervals (usually weekly, monthly, or quarterly) a regular rate of LIBOR plus a fee, a possible price depreciation of the counterparty C bond since the last payment date, and in case of a default of the counterparty C bond the par value of the bond. Counterparty B pays counterparty A at the same regular intervals all coupon payments of the counterparty C bond, a possible price appreciation of the counterparty C bond since the last payment, the principal repayment of the counterparty C bond (in case of no default) and the recovery value of the bond (in case of a default). To determine the cash flows, the total rate of return swap has to be marked to market at the regular payment dates. As an alternative to cash settlement total rate of return swaps allow for physical delivery of the reference credit asset at maturity. Maturity of the total return swap is not required to match that of the reference credit asset, and, in practice, rarely does.

Credit-Linked Notes

Definition 3.4.9.
A credit-linked note is a security that is typically issued from a collateralized special purpose vehicle, which may be a company or business trust, with re-

demption and/or coupon payments linked to the occurrence of a credit event. Credit-linked notes may also be issued on an unsecured basis directly by a corporation or financial institution. A capital-protected credit-linked note is a credit-linked note where the principal is partly or fully guaranteed to be repaid at maturity. In a 100% principal-guaranteed credit-linked note, only the coupons paid under the note bear credit risk.

The pricing of total return swaps and credit-linked notes as well as other credit derivatives can be done by applying similar methods as those described in sections 3.4.3, 3.4.4, and 3.4.5. For a survey of additional credit derivative products see, e.g., Schmid (1998b). Because some of the closed form solutions developed in this section are very complicated one should decide from case to case if it is better to apply these closed form solutions or to use numerical methods which we show in section 3.5

3.5 A Discrete-Time Version of the Three-Factor Model

3.5.1 Introduction

This section presents a discrete-time version of the model presented in section 3.2. It is a discrete time approximation of the continuous-time model, which enables us to determine prices for default related instruments that don't have any closed form solutions, e.g., caused by callability features or because they are American. In addition, it is a computational tool for extensive numerical investigations of our model. As the defaultable term structure model consists of three stochastic processes, the lattice we have to build involves four dimensions. One dimension in time and the other three in the state space. We assume that the process of the non defaultable short rate is independent of the other two processes. The uncertainty index process affects the process of the short rate credit spread process. So the construction of the four dimensional lattice basically consists of two parts: building the tree for the non defaultable short rate and building the combined tree for the short rate credit spread and the uncertainty index. First, the lattice for the uncertainty index is expanded one step further, than this value is used as an input to extend the lattice for the short rate credit spread.

3.5.2 Constructing the Lattice

In this subsection, we show how credit derivatives can be priced using a four dimensional lattice based on our three-factor model. The building method is a modification of the two-stage procedure proposed by Hull & White (1994) for representing a wide range of one-factor interest rate models. Especially, their procedure is applied for building an interest rate tree corresponding to the non-defaultable short rate model defined by equation (3.5) for $\beta = 0$.

All processes are assumed to be considered under the equivalent martingale measure $\mathbf{Q}$. As a first step, let us suppose we had to build up a trinomial tree for the one dimensional stochastic process $X(t)$ defined by

$$dX(t) = (\mu(X,t) - a \cdot X(t))\,dt + \sigma dW_*(t), \tag{3.84}$$

where $W_*(t)$ denotes a one-dimensional Brownian motion, $a > 0$ and $\sigma > 0$ are constants and $\mu(X,t)$ is a progressively measurable stochastic process which may depend on $X(t)$. Note that $W_*(t)$ may be any of the Brownian motions we consider in our three factor model. Hence, we consider $\mathcal{F}_t$ as defined in the previous sections. Working with time steps of size Δt we know that

$$\Delta X(t) = X(t+\Delta t) - X(t) = (\mu(X,t) - a \cdot X(t)) \cdot \Delta t + \sigma \cdot \Delta W_*(t),$$

which is normally distributed conditional on $\mathcal{F}_t$, with an expected value of

$$E^{\mathbf{Q}}[\Delta X(t)\,|\mathcal{F}_t] = (\mu(X,t) - a \cdot X(t)) \cdot \Delta t, \tag{3.85}$$

and a conditional variance of

$$Var^{\mathbf{Q}}[\Delta X(t)\,|\mathcal{F}_t] = \sigma^2 \cdot \Delta t. \tag{3.86}$$

There are two main conditions for a sequence of discrete-time processes to converge in distribution to the corresponding continuous-time diffusion process (see, e.g., Amin (1995)):

a) The (conditional) mean, variance and covariance terms per time unit Δt of the discrete sequence of processes must converge to that of the continuous-time diffusion process.
b) The limiting process must have continuous sample paths, i.e., as $\Delta t \to 0$, the maximum of the absolute increment to the process (jump size) at any date must converge to zero.

Since we are dealing with the assumption of uncorrelated Brownian motions, i.e. $\rho_{rs} = \rho_{ru} = \rho_{su} = 0$, these conditions are satisfied for our three factor model if we ensure the mean and variance conditions for each single one factor model. The basic building block to do this is to consider the flat stochastic process $X^*(t)$ defined by equation (3.84) with $\mu \equiv 0$. With respect to error minimization (see, e.g., Hull & White (1994)) we choose a constant step size of $\Delta x^* = \sigma \cdot \sqrt{3 \cdot \Delta t}$ for the distance between the nodes of $X^*(t)$ at each time step. If we define (i,j) as the tree node with $t = i \cdot \Delta t$ and $X^*(t) = X^*(i \cdot \Delta t) = j \cdot \Delta x^*$, $j_{\max}$ to be the smallest integer greater than $\frac{0.184}{a \cdot \Delta t}$, and $j_{\min} = -j_{\max}$, we can ensure that, for the flat tree, the mean and variance condition holds, and all probabilities are positive if we apply the following branching methods: standard branching for $j_{\min} \leq j \leq j_{\max}$ from node (i,j) to nodes $u = (i+1, j+1)$, $m = (i+1, j)$ and $d = (i+1, j-1)$ with probabilities

$$p_u = \frac{1}{6} + \frac{a^2 j^2 \Delta t^2 - aj\Delta t}{2}, \; p_m = \frac{2}{3} - a^2 j^2 \Delta t^2, \; p_d = \frac{1}{6} + \frac{a^2 j^2 \Delta t^2 + aj\Delta t}{2},$$

upward branching[57] for $j < j_{\min}$ and downward branching[58] for $j > j_{\max}$. Note that the probabilities at each node only depend on j, a and Δt which makes the procedure very robust with respect to the sensitivity analysis of changing yield or spread curves.

In the second building block we shift each node in the flat tree to ensure that conditions *a)* and *b)* from above hold in the resulting tree. Let us therefore define the shift size $\alpha(t)$ at each node by $\alpha(t) = X(t) - X^*(t)$, $t \in [0, T^*]$, which can be described by the differential equation

$$d\alpha(t) = (\mu(X,t) - a \cdot \alpha(t))\, dt \text{ with } \alpha(0) = X(0).$$

The corresponding discrete time version is given by

$$\begin{aligned} \Delta\alpha(t) &= \alpha(t + \Delta t) - \alpha(t) = [\mu(X,t) - a \cdot \alpha(t)] \cdot \Delta t \\ &= [\mu(X^* + \alpha, t) - a \cdot \alpha(t)] \cdot \Delta t. \end{aligned} \tag{3.87}$$

Hence,

$$\alpha(t + \Delta t) = \mu(X^* + \alpha, t) \cdot \Delta t + (1 - a \cdot \Delta t) \cdot \alpha(t).$$

Note, that $\alpha(t + \Delta t)$ via $\mu(X,t)$ depends on the predecessor node of the specific node in the tree that has to be shifted. Using equations (3.85) with $\mu \equiv 0$ and (3.87), we get

$$\begin{aligned} E^{\mathbf{Q}}[\Delta X(t) | \mathcal{F}_t] &= E^{\mathbf{Q}}[X^*(t + \Delta t) + \alpha(t + \Delta t) - (X^*(t) + \alpha(t)) | \mathcal{F}_t] \\ &= [\mu(X,t) - a \cdot X(t)] \cdot \Delta t. \end{aligned}$$

Similarly, we get

$$Var^{\mathbf{Q}}[\Delta X(t) | \mathcal{F}_t] = Var^{\mathbf{Q}}[\Delta X^*(t) | \mathcal{F}_t] = \sigma^2 \cdot \Delta t,$$

---

[57] Upward branching for $j < j_{\min}$ from node (i,j) to nodes $d = (i+1, j)$, $m = (i+1, j+1)$ and $u = (i+1, j+2)$ with probabilities

$$p_u = \frac{1}{6} + \frac{a^2 j^2 \Delta t^2 + aj\Delta t}{2}, \; p_m = -\frac{1}{3} - a^2 j^2 \Delta t^2 - 2aj\Delta t,$$
$$p_d = \frac{7}{6} + \frac{a^2 j^2 \Delta t^2 + 3aj\Delta t}{2}.$$

[58] Downward branching for $j > j_{\max}$ from node (i,j) to nodes $d = (i+1, j-2)$, $m = (i+1, j-1)$ and $u = (i+1, j)$ with probabilities

$$p_u = \frac{7}{6} + \frac{a^2 j^2 \Delta t^2 - 3aj\Delta t}{2}, \; p_m = -\frac{1}{3} - a^2 j^2 \Delta t^2 + 2aj\Delta t,$$
$$p_d = \frac{1}{6} + \frac{a^2 j^2 \Delta t^2 - aj\Delta t}{2}.$$

which ensures that our sequence of discrete-time processes converges in distribution to the corresponding continuous-time diffusion process. For the practical application we start at time $t = 0$ and shift the node $(0,0)$ by $\alpha(0) = X(0)$. Suppose we shifted the flat tree up to time $t = i \cdot \Delta t$ getting the node values $x_{i,j}$ from $x^*_{i,j}$. Then, the value $x^*_{i+1,j+k}$, $k = -1, 0, 1$, of each node $(i+1, j+k)$, which is reached by node (i,j), is shifted by

$$\alpha_{i+1,j+k} = \mu(x_{i,j}, t) \cdot \Delta t + (1 - a \cdot \Delta t) \cdot \alpha_{i,j}$$

to the value $x_{i+1,j+k}$. Note that the dependence of $\alpha_{i+1,j+k}$ on $x_{i,j}$ can destroy the recombining property of the flat tree.
The third building block is only necessary for Cox-Ingersoll-Ross processes defined by

$$dY(t) = (\theta(Y,t) - \hat{a} \cdot Y(t))\,dt + \sigma \cdot \sqrt{Y(t)}dW(t).$$

Setting $X(t) = G(y,t)$ and using the transformation

$$G(y,t) = 2 \cdot \sqrt{y(t)},$$

with Itô´s lemma, we get

$$dX(t) = \left[\frac{1}{\sqrt{Y(t)}} \cdot (\theta(Y,t) - \hat{a} \cdot Y(t)) - \frac{1}{4} \cdot \frac{1}{\sqrt{Y(t)}} \cdot \sigma^2\right] dt + \sigma dW(t).$$

Now, since $Y(t) = \frac{1}{4} \cdot X^2(t)$,

$$\begin{aligned} dX(t) &= \left[\frac{2 \cdot \theta\left(\frac{1}{4} \cdot X^2, t\right) - \frac{1}{2} \cdot \sigma^2}{X(t)} - \frac{\hat{a}}{2} \cdot X(t)\right] dt + \sigma dW(t) \\ &= [\mu(X,t) - a \cdot X(t)]\,dt + \sigma dW(t), \end{aligned}$$

with

$$\mu(X,t) = \frac{2 \cdot \theta\left(\frac{1}{4} \cdot X^2, t\right) - \frac{1}{2} \cdot \sigma^2}{X(t)} \quad \text{and} \quad a = \frac{\hat{a}}{2}.$$

Therefore, we can apply the previous building blocks to build up a representing trinomial tree for the stochastic process $X(t)$. We get the corresponding tree for $Y(t)$ by setting $Y(t) = \frac{1}{4} \cdot X^2(t)$ in each node of the tree for $X(t)$.
Let us now apply the proposed method for our three factor model. We start with the uncertainty process

$$du(t) = [\theta_u - \hat{a}_u \cdot u(t)]\,dt + \sigma_u \cdot \sqrt{u(t)}d\hat{W}_u(t).$$

It can be transformed to the process

$$dX_u(t) = \left[\frac{2 \cdot \theta_u - \frac{1}{2} \cdot \sigma^2}{X_u(t)} - \frac{\hat{a}_u}{2} \cdot X_u(t)\right] dt + \sigma_u d\hat{W}_u(t)$$

and

$$\alpha_u (t + \Delta t) = \alpha_u (t) + \left[\frac{2 \cdot \theta_u - \frac{1}{2} \cdot \sigma^2}{X_u (t)} - \frac{\hat{a}_u}{2} \cdot \alpha_u (t) \right] \cdot \Delta t$$
$$= \frac{2 \cdot \theta_u - \frac{1}{2} \cdot \sigma^2}{X_u^* (t) + \alpha_u (t)} \cdot \Delta t + \left(1 - \frac{\hat{a}_u}{2} \cdot \Delta t \right) \cdot \alpha_u (t)$$

with $\alpha_u (0) = X_u (0) = 2 \cdot \sqrt{u (0)}$.
Similarly, given $u (t)$ at time t, for the spread process

$$ds (t) = [b_s \cdot u (t) - \hat{a}_s \cdot s (t)] \, dt + \sigma_s \cdot \sqrt{s (t)} d\hat{W}_s (t)$$

we get the transformations

$$dX_s (t) = \left[\frac{2 \cdot b_s \cdot u (t) - \frac{1}{2} \cdot \sigma_s^2}{X_s (t)} - \frac{\hat{a}_s}{2} \cdot X_s (t) \right] dt + \sigma_s d\hat{W}_s (t)$$

and

$$\alpha_s (t + \Delta t) = \frac{2 \cdot b_s \cdot u (t) - \frac{1}{2} \cdot \sigma_s^2}{X_s^* (t) + \alpha_s (t)} \cdot \Delta t + \left(1 - \frac{\hat{a}_s}{2} \cdot \Delta t \right) \cdot \alpha_s (t)$$

with $\alpha (0) = X_s (0) = 2 \cdot \sqrt{s (0)}$.
The short rate process is given by

$$dr (t) = [\theta_r (t) - \hat{a}_r \cdot r (t)] \, dt + \sigma_s \cdot r^{\beta} (t) \, d\hat{W}_r (t)$$

with $\beta \in \left\{ 0, \frac{1}{2} \right\}$. For $\beta = \frac{1}{2}$ we have to transform the short rate process to

$$dX_r (t) = \left[\frac{2 \cdot \theta (t) - \frac{1}{2} \cdot \sigma_r^2}{X_r (t)} - \frac{\hat{a}_r}{2} \cdot X_r (t) \right] dt + \sigma_r d\hat{W}_r (t) ,$$

for $\beta = 0$ the transformation is not necessary and we may consider

$$dX_r (t) = [\theta (t) - \hat{a}_r \cdot X_r (t)] \, dt + \sigma_r d\hat{W}_r (t) ,$$

i.e., $X (t) = r (t)$. The corresponding α's are given by

$$\alpha_r (t + \Delta t) = \frac{2 \cdot \theta (t) - \frac{1}{2} \cdot \sigma_r^2}{X_r^* (t) + \alpha_r (t)} \cdot \Delta t + \left(1 - \frac{\hat{a}_r}{2} \cdot \Delta t \right) \cdot \alpha_r (t)$$

with $\alpha_r (0) = X_r (0) = 2 \cdot \sqrt{r (0)}$ for $\beta = \frac{1}{2}$ and

$$\alpha_r (t + \Delta t) = \theta (t) \cdot \Delta t + (1 - \hat{a}_r \cdot \Delta t) \cdot \alpha_r (t)$$

with $\alpha_r (0) = X_r (0) = r (0)$ for $\beta = 0$.
Note that the short rate model can be fitted to the yield curve as $\theta (t)$ is time-dependent. Also note that for the Hull-White model ($\beta = 0$) the shift

size $\alpha_r(t)$ is the same for all nodes (i,j) at time $t = i \cdot \Delta t$. To build up an interest rate tree for this case, Hull & White (1994) propose a slightly different method than that just described which they claim to be numerically more efficient.

We are now able to build up a three dimensional trinomial tree for the process $(r(t), s(t), u(t))$. In contrast to the trinomial trees proposed by Chen (1996), Amin (1995), or Boyle (1988) the branching as well as the probabilities don´t change with a changing drift, which makes the tree more efficient, especially under risk management purposes. The probabilities for each node in the three dimensional tree are simply given by the product of the one dimensional processes. Note that despite the fact that we have to consider all possible combinations (r_{ij}, s_{ij}, u_{ij}) at time $t = i \cdot \Delta t$ and nodes $j_r \cdot \Delta r$, $j_s \cdot \Delta s$ and $j_u \cdot \Delta u$ the total number is limited by the branching method.

3.5.3 General Interest Rate Dynamics

If we want to allow for correlated Brownian motion, i.e.

$$\begin{aligned} Cov\left(dW_r(t), dW_s(t)\right) &= \rho_{rs} dt, \\ Cov\left(dW_r(t), dW_u(t)\right) &= \rho_{ru} dt, \\ Cov\left(dW_s(t), dW_u(t)\right) &= \rho_{su} dt, \end{aligned}$$

the fundamental PDE can be written as

$$\begin{aligned} &-\left(\rho_{rs}\sigma_r\sigma_s r^{\beta}\sqrt{s}F_{rs} + \rho_{ru}\sigma_r\sigma_u r^{\beta}\sqrt{u}F_{ru} + \rho_{us}\sigma_u\sigma_s\sqrt{su}F_{us}\right) \\ &= \frac{1}{2}\sigma_r^2 r^{2\beta} F_{rr} + \frac{1}{2}\sigma_s^2 s F_{ss} + \frac{1}{2}\sigma_u^2 u F_{uu} \\ &+ \left[\theta_r(t) - \hat{a}_r r\right] F_r + \left[b_s u - \hat{a}_s s\right] F_s \\ &+ \left[\theta_u - \hat{a}_u u\right] F_u + F_t - (r+s) F, \quad (r,s,u,t) \in \mathbb{R}^3 \times [0, \mathrm{T}), \end{aligned} \tag{3.88}$$

with a boundary condition

$$F(r,s,u,T) = h(r,s,u). \tag{3.89}$$

It is possible to show that a solution for PDE (3.88) with boundary condition (3.89) can be found by applying a recursive algorithm involving the function G defined in lemma 3.3.1. But as this method is very inconvenient for several reasons[59], we suggest to use tree based methods for the correlated case. Therefore, the procedure proposed in section 3.5.2 should be slightly modified. The extension of tree based methods from the case where the Brownian motions are uncorrelated to the case where they are correlated have been already discussed in depth in the literature. Hence, we omit this discussion here and refer, e.g., to Hull & White (1994).

[59] E.g., the algorithm involves the calculation of a large number of integrals all dealing with the complicated function G. In addition, the speed of convergence is not a priori known.

3.6 Fitting the Model to Market Data

3.6.1 Introduction

Whether we have closed-form solutions for pricing default related instruments or we use numerical methods, in both cases we need estimates of the parameters of the underlying stochastic processes that determine the interest rate dynamics. The ultimate success or failure in implementing pricing formulas is directly related to the ability to collect the necessary information for determining good model parameter values. In the following we suggest two different ways how meaningful values for the parameters of the three processes r, s, and u can be found. The first one is the method of least squared minimization. Basically, we compare market prices and theoretical prices at one specific point in time and calculate the implied parameters by minimization of the sum of the squared deviations of the market from the theoretical prices. The second one is the Kalman filter method.

3.6.2 Method of Least Squared Minimization

The uncertainty index. Many practitioners use ratings of rating agencies as a proxy for the quality of a firm: Usually the better the rating the smaller the probability of default. We assume that there are 6 rating classes which we denote by $1, 2, ..., 6$. Rating class 6 corresponds to default, rating class 1 consists of the instruments with the highest quality (i.e. the lowest uncertainty) of defaultable bonds. Each firm (or more specific each debt instrument) belongs to exactly one rating class depending on its quality or its "uncertainty" given by the uncertainty index of the firm. There is a one-to-one mapping from the value of the uncertainty index onto the set of rating classes, i.e. there are thresholds ξ_j $, j = 1, ..., 5$, such that a firm is in default if $u > \xi_5$, has rating j if $\xi_{j-1} < u \leq \xi_j$, $j = 2, ..., 5$, or has rating 1 if $u \leq \xi_1$. We call ξ_5 the default boundary and denote it sometimes by ξ^d. Using the non-central χ^2-distribution property of $u(t)$ (for details see, e.g., Lamberton & Lapeyre (1996), pages 129 ff.) the unknown parameters of the process u and the unknown thresholds can be expressed by the transition probabilities of the firm. If we suppose that the transition probabilities are given for the time interval $[0, t]$, the following equations hold:

$$\mathbf{P}\left(u(t) \leq \xi_1 | u(0)\right) = \mathbf{F}_{\frac{4\theta_u}{\sigma_u^2}, \varsigma}\left(\frac{\xi_1}{L}\right) \quad (3.90)$$

$$\mathbf{P}\left(u(t) \leq \xi_1 | u(0)\right) + \sum_{k=2}^{j} \mathbf{P}\left(\xi_{k-1} < u(t) \leq \xi_k | u(0)\right) = \mathbf{F}_{\frac{4\theta_u}{\sigma_u^2}, \varsigma}\left(\frac{\xi_j}{L}\right) \quad (3.91)$$

$$\mathbf{P}\left(u(t) > \xi_5 | u(0)\right) = 1 - \mathbf{F}_{\frac{4\theta_u}{\sigma_u^2}, \varsigma}\left(\frac{\xi_5}{L}\right)$$

where $L = \frac{\sigma_u^2}{4a_u}\left(1 - e^{-a_u t}\right)$, $\varsigma = \frac{4u(0)a_u}{\sigma_u^2\left(e^{a_u t}-1\right)}$ and $\mathbf{F}_{\frac{4\theta_u}{\sigma_u^2},\varsigma}$ denotes the distribution function of the non-central chi-squared law with $\frac{4\theta_u}{\sigma_u^2}$ degrees of freedom and parameter ς. The transition probabilities are the same within each rating class. To embed this discrete setting in our continuous framework we assume that for each possible initial rating the rating agencies' probabilities correspond to a certain initial value of the uncertainty process within the range of admissible values, i.e., rating 1 corresponds to some uncertainty process value $u_1(0) = \alpha_1 \xi_1$ for some $0 \le \alpha_1 \le 1$ and rating k, $2 \le k \le 5$, corresponds to some uncertainty process value $u_k(0) = (1 - \alpha_k)\,\xi_{k-1} + \alpha_k \xi_k$ for some $0 \le \alpha_k \le 1$. If we set up equations (3.90) and (3.91) for each rating class (besides rating class 6) we get a system of 25 equations with 25 unknown variables which we must solve under the constraints $\xi_1 < \xi_2 < \xi_3 < \xi_4 < \xi_5$ and $0 \le \alpha_k \le 1$, $1 \le k \le 5$. One possibility to solve this system of equations is by applying the multidimensional Downhill Simplex method which was introduced by Nelder & Mead (1965). Because we use real world transition probabilities we can only estimate a_u but not $\hat{a}_u$. But for pricing purposes we are rather interested in $\hat{a}_u$ than in a_u. Therefore, we estimate λ_u together with the parameters for the short rate spread from market prices of observed credit spreads.

The non-defaultable short rate. The most intuitive procedure to fit the non-defaultable short rate to market prices (e.g., broker quotes) is to choose the values for $\hat{a}_r$ and σ_r that best fit a series of non-defaultable interest rate options such as caps. The parameter σ_r determines the overall volatility of the non-defaultable short rate. The parameter $\hat{a}_r$ determines the relative volatilities of long and short rates. The procedure is to choose the values of $\hat{a}_r$ and σ_r that minimize

$$\sum_i \left(P_i^*\left(\hat{a}_r, \sigma_r\right) - V_i\right)^2,$$

where P_i^* is the price given by the model for the i-th interest rate option and V_i is the market price of the i-th interest rate option. The procedure is quite easy for the Hull/White model, where cap prices can be calculated analytically. Again, the problem can be solved by applying the multidimensional Downhill Simplex method.

The short rate credit spread. The remaining parameters to be estimated are b_s, $\hat{a}_s$, σ_s and λ_u. We choose the values for these parameters that best fit a series of observed credit spreads. Like with the estimation for the parameters of the non-defaultable short rate the procedure is to choose the values of b_s, $\hat{a}_s$, σ_s and λ_u that minimize

$$\sum_i \left(S_i\left(b_s, \hat{a}_s, \sigma_s, \lambda_u\right) - Y_i\right)^2,$$

Table 3.3. Average one-year transition rates (%) by S&P (July 1998).

	AAA	*AA*	*A*	*BBB*	*BB*	*B*	*CCC*	*D*
AAA	90.82	8.26	0.74	0.06	0.11	0.00	0.00	0.00
AA	0.65	90.88	7.69	0.58	0.05	0.13	0.02	0.00
A	0.08	2.42	91.30	5.23	0.68	0.23	0.01	0.05
BBB	0.03	0.31	5.87	87.45	4.96	1.08	0.12	0.18
BB	0.02	0.12	0.64	7.70	81.08	8.39	0.98	1.08
B	0.00	0.10	0.24	0.44	6.81	82.90	3.90	5.60
CCC	0.20	0.00	0.40	1.19	2.56	11.24	61.97	22.50

Table 3.4. Modified transition matrix.

	1	*2*	*3*	*4*	*5*
1	95.31	4.22	0.40	0.07	0.00
2	2.50	91.30	5.91	0.24	0.05
3	0.24	3.26	90.59	5.28	0.63
4	0.15	0.30	5.50	80.00	14.05

where S_i is the model value of the i-th credit spread and Y_i is its observed market value. Again, for the optimization procedure we can use a multidimensional Downhill Simplex method.

Example. We want to apply our theoretical framework and our calibration methods to set up a firm specific model for General Motors. Therefore we use data from Reuters, Bloomberg and S&P to estimate the model parameters.

1. The non-defaultable short rate:
   Using the US Cap-Volas (May 4th, 1999) from Reuters
   $$1 \text{ year } 11.25\ \%,\ 2 \text{ years } 15.25\ \%,$$
   we get the estimations $\hat{a}_r = 1.05 \cdot 10^{-8}$ and $\sigma_r = 1.01949464\ \%$.
2. The uncertainty index:
   We assume that $\alpha_k = \frac{1}{2}\ \forall k$ (i.e. ratings correspond to the average quality within a rating class) and that there are 5 rating classes.
   The average one-year transition rates (%) by S&P (July 1998) are given by the transition matrix in table 3.3. We modify the matrix by aggregating the rating classes AAA and AA to rating class 1, A to rating class 2, BBB and BB to rating class 3, B and CCC to rating class 4. D corresponds to rating class 5. Hence, the modified transition matrix[60] is given by table 3.4.

[60] We assume that the number of obligors in each rating class is the same.

In S&P's notation General Motors' rating is A which corresponds to our rating class 2. Using the Downhill Simplex algorithm we get the following parameter estimates for this rating class:

$$\theta_u = 0.0653562131910263,$$
$$\sigma_u = 0.09999999994330677,$$
$$a_u = 0.13499953576965013,$$

and the threshold values

$$\xi_1 = 0.0436501349994976,$$
$$\xi_2 = 0.2540403487950756,$$
$$\xi_3 = 0.6491354397214147,$$
$$\xi_4 = 1.1806484698650033.$$

3. The short rate spread:
   For estimating the remaining parameters we use the following US$ - fixed rate bond data (semiannual coupons, S&P rating class A of General Motors which corresponds to our rating class 2) from Bloomberg (May 4th, 1999):
   a) 9 1/8, 07/18/00, Clean Price: 104.15, Yield: 5.497,
   b) 9.02, 06/07/01, Clean Price: 106.32, Yield: 5.758,
   c) 8 7/8, 06/11/01, Clean Price: 106.07, Yield: 5.760,
   d) 9.2, 07/02/01, Clean Price: 106.86, Yield: 5.769.
   Using $s(0) = 80$ basis points the Downhill Simplex algorithm yields the estimates $b_s = 0.0000997$, $\hat{a}_s = 0.328893$, $\sigma_s = 0.2$ and $\lambda_u = 0.19$.

3.6.3 The Kalman Filtering Methodology

Whereas in the previous section we determined the parameter values for the three-factor defaultable term structure model from market data at one specific day, this section is devoted to estimating parameter values by looking at time series of market values of bonds. Therefore we apply the Kalman filtering technique (see, e.g., Oksendal (1998), pages 79-106, and Harvey (1989)). As the number of parameters in our model is quite big, the idea is to apply the method twice. First, we estimate the parameters $\hat{a}_r$ and σ_r by applying the Kalman filter technique to the non-defaultable bond data corresponding to the non-defaultable short-rate model (see equations (3.1) and (3.5)). As a second step, using the obtained estimators for the non-defaultable model to apply the Kalman filter to different time series of defaultable bonds to get the estimators for the remaining parameters. We apply this method to zero coupon bond data of German and Italian Government bonds and coupon bond data of Greek Government bonds between January 1, 1999 and October 23, 2000. For that time frame the exchange rates between the German and Italian currencies have already been fixed due to the membership of the two countries to the European Monetary Union. The German, Italian, and Greek coupon bonds in our sample are all denominated in Euro. So we don't have to consider any exchange rate risk in our study. We assume that there is no default risk with the German bonds, and assume the Italian and Greek bonds to be risky. We analyze the development of the credit spreads between German and Italian and German and Greek bonds through time, and examine for the ability of our three-factor defaultable term structure model to describe these dynamics realistically. Especially Germany and Italy are appropriate for our analysis because they are one of the most liquid markets for Government bonds within the European Monetary Union. The daily coupon bond prices (from January $1st$, 1999 until October $23rd$, 2000,) are provided by Reuters Information Services.

The application of Kalman filtering methods in the estimation of term structure models using time-series data has been analyzed (among others) by Chen & Scott (1995), Geyer & Pichler (1996) and Babbs & Nowman (1999). Up to our knowledge we are the first ones to apply this method to defaultable term structure models, especially to our model. The great advantage of the application of the Kalman filter to (defaultable) term structure models is that it allows the underlying state variables (in our case the default free short rate, the short rate credit spread and the uncertainty index) to be completely unobservable. Other approaches usually need to work with proxies for the short rates which induces noise in the parameter estimation process. Which proxy one could use for the values of the uncertainty index would be a serious problem.

All yields in our analysis are adjusted to the continuously compounded yields to maturity assuming 365 days a year. Credit spreads are then calculated as the differences between Italian and German and Greek and German zero coupon bond yields. We analyze the development of these credit spreads through time and analyze the performance of our model to explain these dynamics. Empirical investigation of credit spreads - mostly for corporates - has been done by, e.g., Longstaff & Schwartz (1995a), Duffee (1996b), Wei & Guo (1997), and Düllmann & Windfuhr (2000). Our analysis offers some advantages:

- We use daily data for credit spreads.
- (To our knowledge) we are the first ones to apply Kalman filtering techniques to credit spread investigation.
- We don't use proxies for the unobservable state variables but filter their values from observable data.
- We apply many different in - sample and, most important, out - of - sample tests.

Table 3.5. Summary statistics for the sample of German, Italian and Greek sovereign bonds.

	Germany	*Italy*	*Greece*
Number of bonds	33	36	38
Minimal maturity	0.5 years	0.36 years	2.4 years
Maximal maturity	11.5 years	12.2 years	20.8 years
Average maturity	4.9 years	3.5 years	7.46 years

The Data. In the following analysis we use observed data of credit spreads between German and Italian zero coupon Government bonds and German and Greek coupon Government bonds. The S&P ratings of the German, Italian and Greek bonds are AAA, AA, and $A-$, respectively. Hence, all of the bonds are investment grade, and we can assume that the German bonds are default risk free whereas the Italian and Greek bonds are defaultable. The credit spreads are calculated as the differences of the zero rates of the appropriate bonds. We consider a 22 months time series of daily bond prices from January 1*st*, 1999, until October 23*rd*, 2000, provided by Reuters Information Services[61]. All prices are denominated in Euro. As Germany and Italy are both members of the European Monetary Union, we don't have to take care of possible currency risks involved in these credit spreads. Note further, that our sample for Germany and Italy only consists of pure zero coupon bonds without any special embedded options such as callability features. The Greek bonds are all pure fixed rate bonds paying annual coupons between 3% p.a. and 9.7% p.a. From table 3.5 it can be seen that we use a universe of 33 German, 36 Italian, and 38 Greek bonds. The ranges of maturities of the bonds span from 0.5 years to 11.5 years, from 0.36 years to 12.2 years, and from 2.4 years to 20.8 years for Germany, Italy, and Greece, respectively.

To determine the parameter values of the three-factor model we need the complete German, Italian and Greek zero curves at each time step (i.e. at each observation day), at least up to some maximal time of maturity. But unfortunately only a finite number of points on these zero curves is observable. To infer the entire German, Italian, and Greek zero curves from the daily prices of the 33 German, 36 Italian, and 38 Greek bonds on a daily basis, we apply the method of Nelson & Siegel (1987). The parsimonious model of Nelson and Siegel is widely used and suggested:

- Litterman & Scheinkman (1991) examine Treasury bonds and find that level, slope, and curvature explain most of the returns on the examined Treasury bonds.

[61] Most of the previous empirical studies use weekly or monthly data. Besides Düllmann & Windfuhr (2000) we are the only ones to use daily data - at least up to our knowledge.

- Jones (1991) shows that the yield curve can be mainly explained by shifts (parallel changes) and twists (changes in the slope).
- Barrett, Gosnell & Heuson (1995) apply it to daily Treasury note and bond data. From the investigation of shifts in the yield curve they draw conclusions for the selection of immunization strategies.
- Willner (1996) uses Nelson and Siegel's approach to extend traditional duration measurement methods to level, slope, and curvature durations.
- The Bundesbank has moved away from its in-house model to the Nelson and Siegel method for estimating the par yield curve (see, e.g., *Estimating the Term Structure of Interest Rates* (1997)).
- Brooks & Yan (1999) show that the Nelson-Siegel functional form can be used to fit the forward curve and the spot curve as well.
- Jordan & Mansi (2000) show that the Nelson and Siegel functional form performs better than other yield-smoothing methods.
- Mansi (2000) compares the use of constant-maturity Treasuries as an alternative to on-the-run yields obtained from the Treasury market. He finds that a continuous bootstrapping methodology with the Nelson and Siegel functional form as the interpolation method can reduce pricing errors dramatically.

Nelson and Siegel fit the yield curve using an exponential decay specification and reduce the problem to a four-parameter model: level, slope, curvature, and a time constant. Besides the construction of the zero curves we expect from the Nelson and Siegel methodology a smoothing effect of our data, especially for the Greek data which we expect to include more noise than the German and Italian data. Such an interest rate smoothing model avoids the problem inherent in spline-based models of choosing the optimal knot point specification. Nelson and Siegel take the following four parameter approximation model to determine zero curves from bond prices:

$$R(t,T) = \beta_0(t) + (\beta_1(t) + \beta_2(t)) \frac{1 - e^{-\frac{(T-t)}{\beta_3}}}{\frac{(T-t)}{\beta_3}} - \beta_2(t)\, e^{-\frac{(T-t)}{\beta_3}}, \qquad (3.92)$$

where

$$P(t,T) = 100e^{-R(t,T)(T-t)}, \; 0 \le t \le T.$$

The components in equation (3.92) determine the appropriate choices of weights that can be used to generate zero curves of a variety of shapes. $\beta_0(t)$ stands for the level or long term factor. $-\beta_1(t)$ stands for the slope or the short term factor. $\beta_2(t)$ stands for the curvature or the medium term component. β_3 is the time constant associated with curve hump positioning. It determines the rate of decay towards the long term rate. We estimate the parameters $\beta_i(t)$, $i = 0, 1, 2$, for each day t based on the non-defaultable German zero coupon bond data from a non-linear regression and based on β_3. We choose the specific β_3 value that yields the best results. As table 3.5

shows, the German bonds cover a range of maturities from half a year up to 11.5 years with an average maturity of 4.9 years.

Afterwards we apply the same methodology to the defaultable Italian zero coupon bond data and the defaultable Greece coupon bond data. The Italian bonds cover maturities from three months up to 12.2 years with an average of 3.5 years, the Greece bonds from 2.4 years up to 20.8 years with an average of 7.46 years. For each t we fit the parameters $\beta_i^{d,j}(t)$, $i = 0, 1, 2$, $j \in \{I = Italy,\ G = Greece\}$, and $\beta_3^{d,j}$ of the Nelson and Siegel model

$$R^{d,j}(t,T) = \beta_0^{d,j}(t) + (\beta_1^{d,j}(t) + \beta_2^{d,j}(t)) \frac{1 - e^{-\frac{(T-t)}{\beta_3^{d,j}}}}{\frac{(T-t)}{\beta_3^{d,j}}} - \beta_2^{d,j}(t)\, e^{-\frac{(T-t)}{\beta_3^{d,j}}}, \quad (3.93)$$

where

$$P^{d,I}(t,T) = 100 e^{-R^{d,I}(t,T)(T-t)}, \quad 0 \le t \le T,$$

and

$$P_c^{d,G}(t,T) = \sum_{k=1}^{n} c_k e^{-R^{d,G}(t,t_k)(t_k - t)} + 100 e^{-R^{d,G}(t,T)(T-t)},$$

to the available Italian and Greece defaultable bond data. The Greek coupon bonds pay discrete coupons c_i at dates $t < t_k \le T$, $k = 1, ..., n$. To make the three models better comparable we assume that $\beta_3 = \beta_3^{d,j}$ for $j \in \{I,\ G\}$. Finally, based on the estimated parameter values $\beta_i(t)$ and $\beta_i^{d,j}(t)$, $i = 0, 1, 2$, $j \in \{I,\ G\}$, for each t and β_3, we can calculate the estimated zero rates for non-defaultable German and defaultable Italian and Greek Government bonds for each maturity $T \ge t$. It turns out that the best results can be achieved by setting the constant parameter β_3 equal to 3. After having estimated the zero curves we apply a robust outlier test removing all the curves which couldn't be fitted well enough by the Nelson and Siegel methodology[62]. Table 3.6 presents the quality statistics of our zero curve estimations for Germany and Italy, i.e. we summarize the analysis of the deviations of the observed German and Italian bond data from the estimated term structures of interest rates. The mean average absolute errors[63] are 18.8 basis points

[62] Let SSR_t be the sum of the squared deviations of the observed zero rates from the zero rates estimated with the Nelson-Siegel methodology at time t divided by the number of observations. We assume that the curve at time t^* is an outlier if the deviation of SSR_{t^*} from the mean of all SSR_t is more than three times the standard deviation of the values SSR_t, $\forall t$.

[63] By average absolute error of the Nelson-Siegel estimated curve at time t we mean

$$\sqrt{\frac{SSR_t}{\text{Number of bonds used for estimating time } t \text{ curve}}},$$

where SSR_t is the sum of squared deviations of the observed zero rates from the Nelson-Siegel estimated yields at time t.

Table 3.6. Summary statistics for the deviations of the estimated zero rates (continuous compounding) from the observed German and Italian zero rates. The deviation results are in basis points.

	Germany	*Italy*
Average number of bonds per estimated curve	23.8	15.4
Mean of average absolute deviation	18.8	9.0
Standard deviation of average absolute deviation	11.0	10.3
Maximum of average absolute deviation	49.8	39.2

for Germany and 9.0 basis points for Italy, with standard deviations of 11.0 basis points and 10.3 basis points, correspondingly. Hence, all the curves fit the data fairly well.

Tables 3.7, 3.8, and 3.9 show the parameter summary results of the curve fittings for Germany, Italy, and Greece, respectively. The results show that the German long term spot rate is, on average, 5.532%, and the spot curve is, on average, upward-sloping, since the mean of the slope is 2.245%. In addition, on average, the German spot curve shows a curvature of 0.102%. The Italian long term spot rate is, on average, 6.048%, and the spot curve is, on average, upward-sloping, since the mean of the slope is 2.795%. In addition, on average, the Italian spot curve shows a curvature of 0.385%. Hence, on average, the level of the Italian zero rates is higher than the level of the German zero rates. Some of the German and Italian spot curves are downward-sloping, most of them are upward-sloping. The Italian curves tend to be steeper. The Greek long term spot rate is, on average, 7.046%, and the spot curve is, on average, downward-sloping, since the mean of the slope is −1.435%. In addition, on average, the Greek spot curve shows a curvature of −5.684%. On average, the level of the Greece yields is higher than the level of the German and Italian yields. That's exactly what the ratings of the three countries would suggest. In addition, the lower the rating the higher the standard deviation of level, slope and curvature. Most of the Greece curves are downward-sloping and concave. Figures 3.30 and 3.31 show graphically the results of the German and Italian spot curve fittings on October 3*rd*, 1999, and August 24*th*, 2000. On October 3*rd*, 1999, both curves are humped, deeply upward-sloping, convex, and fit the data very well: the level, slope, and curvature parameters of the German and Italian spot curves are 5.345%, 2.989%, and 2.942%, and 6.220%, 3.686%, and 1.532%, respectively. Hence, level and slope parameters of the Italian spot curve are higher than the corresponding quantities of the German spot curve. Obviously, that can be explained by the lower rating of the Italian bonds. On August 24*th*, 2000, the situation is quite different. Although the German curve is upward-sloping for short maturities and downward-sloping for long maturities, over all it is very flat. The Italian curve is steeply upward-sloping for short maturities, humped,

Table 3.7. Summary statistics for the Nelson-Siegel parameters, results of fitting the German spot curve. All numbers are given in percent.

	Mean	*Standard Deviation*	*Maximum*	*Minimum*
Level β_0	5.532	0.257	6.414	4.042
Slope -β_1	2.245	0.994	3.788	−0.556
Curvature β_2	0.102	1.682	4.343	−3.492

Table 3.8. Summary statistics for the Nelson-Siegel parameters, results of fitting the Italian spot curve. All numbers are given in percent

	Mean	*Standard Deviation*	*Maximum*	*Minimum*
Level β_0^d	6.048	0.435	9.967	4.305
Slope -β_1^d	2.795	0.965	7.478	−0.239
Curvature β_2^d	0.385	2.041	8.391	−4.759

Table 3.9. Summary statistics for the Nelson-Siegel parameters, results of fitting the Greek spot curve. All numbers are given in percent.

	Mean	*Standard Deviation*	*Maximum*	*Minimum*
Level β_0	7.046	0.501	8.400	5.620
Slope -β_1	−1.435	1.777	2.350	−5.977
Curvature β_2	−5.684	3.533	3.352	−18.905

and downward-sloping for long maturities. For maturities less than a year, the estimated Italian curve lies below the estimated German curve although all observed Italian zero rates are higher than the appropriate German zero rates. Nevertheless, both curves fit the data fairly well. The level, slope, and curvature parameters of the German and Italian spot curves are 5.055%, 0.120%, and 0.602%, and 6.088%, 3.548%, and 2.247%, respectively.

To study the relationship between the German and Italian, and the German and Greek zero curves, we calculate the correlation matrices of the three-, six-, and nine-year German and Italian, and German and Greek zero rates first. The results in table 3.10 show that all German and Italian rates are highly correlated. The correlation of the zero rates of different countries but with the same maturity is almost always higher than the correlation between curves of the same country with different maturities. Overall, we can say, the greater the difference between the maturities the less the correlation of the appropriate curves. For Germany and Greece the situation is quite different.

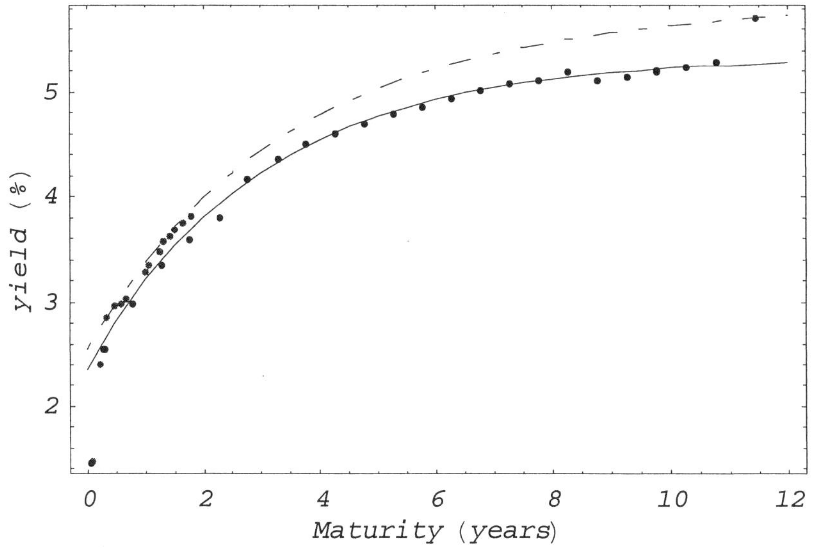

Fig. 3.30. Nelson-Siegel spot curve fitting on October, 3rd, 1999. The line and the dashed line refer to the fitted spot rates of Germany and Italy, respectively. The dots refer to the estimated zero rates of Germany and Italy.

The Greek three year rates show a negative correlation with all German rates and very low correlations with the other Greek rates. There is a high correlation between the six year and nine year Greek rates, and medium correlations of these rates with all German rates. Figures 3.32 for Germany and Italy and 3.33 for Germany and Greece show the co-movements of the rates across time. According to the high correlations between Germany and Italy, the curves mainly differ in their absolute level whereas the shapes are more or less all the same. The longer the maturity of the German and Italian rates the higher the level of the corresponding curves. While the German and Italian rates are mainly increasing over the observation period, the Greek rates are mainly decreasing. The level of all Greek curves is higher than the level of the German and Italian curves. The levels of the Greek curves which correspond to longer maturity rates is lower than the levels of curves which correspond to shorter maturity rates. The German, Italian and Greek rates are converging. The reason for this convergence lies in the announcement that Greece will become a member of the EMU. Because Germany and Italy have belonged to the EMU from the very beginning their rates have already converged prior to the observation period.

To further understand the structural differences between the German, Italian and Greek spot curves we investigate the spreads between them. The

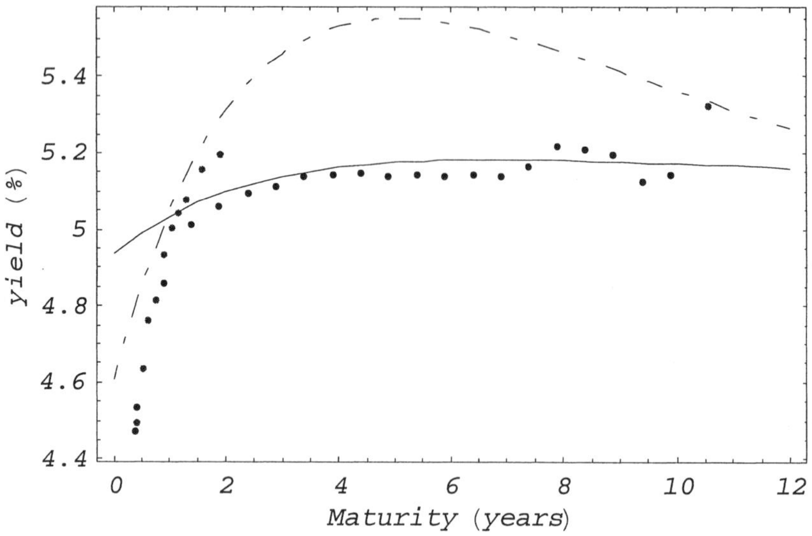

Fig. 3.31. Nelson-Siegel spot curve fitting on August 24th, 2000. The line and the dashed line refer to the fitted spot rates of Germany and Italy, respectively. The dots refer to the estimated zero rates of Germany and Italy.

Table 3.10. Correlation matrix of 3Y, 6Y, 9Y German and 3Y, 6Y, 9Y Italian zero rates.

	3Y Ger	*6Y Ger*	*9Y Ger*	*3Y Italy*	*6Y Italy*	*9Y Italy*
3Y Ger	1.000					
6Y Ger	0.967	1.000				
9Y Ger	0.924	0.990	1.000			
3Y Italy	0.996	0.956	0.911	1.000		
6Y Italy	0.976	0.991	0.973	0.976	1.000	
9Y Italy	0.949	0.990	0.978	0.944	0.992	1.000

estimated spread processes for various maturities, calculated as differences between Italian and German yield processes, are presented in figures 3.34, 3.35, and 3.36. The spreads between the Greek and German bonds are shown in figures 3.37, 3.38, and 3.39. The spreads are very volatile for all maturities and all countries. The Greek spreads have fallen from levels as high as 400 basis points to levels below 100 basis points. Because Germany and Italy are one of the most liquid Government bond markets in Europe we can assume that these spreads are real credit spreads and that liquidity risk can be neglected.

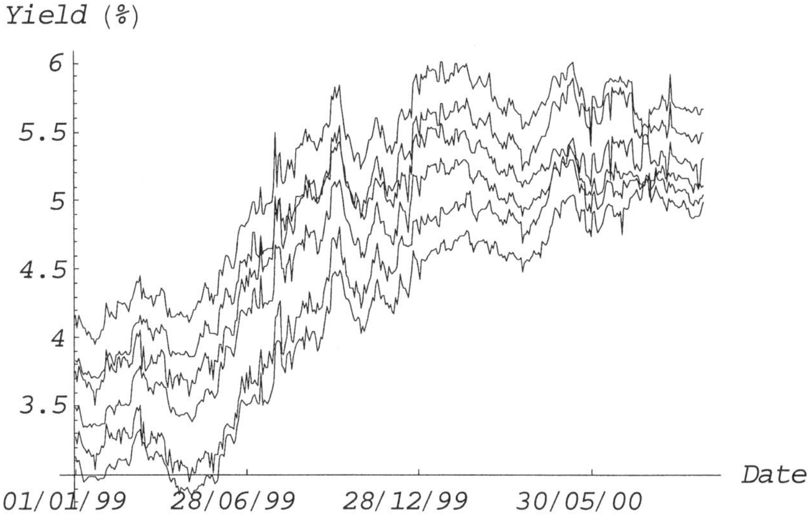

Fig. 3.32. From below: 3Y German, 3Y Italian, 6Y German, 6Y Italian, 9Y German, 9Y Italian zero rates.

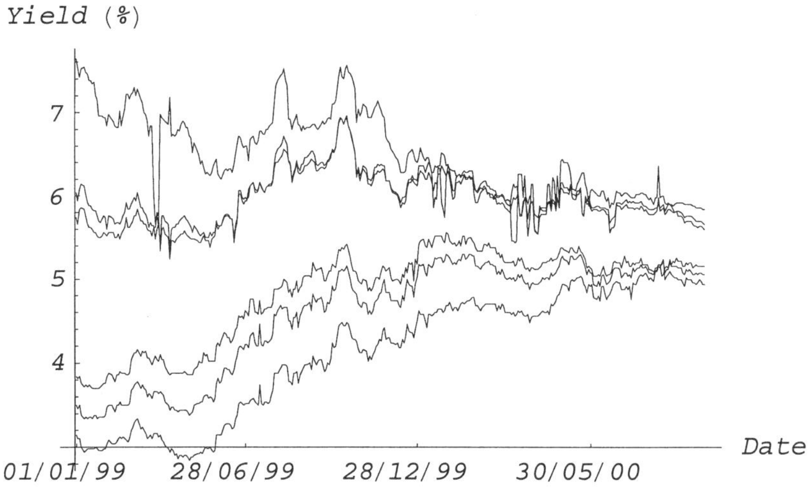

Fig. 3.33. From below: 3Y German, 6Y German, 9Y German, 9Y Greek, 6Y Greek, 3Y Greek zero rates.

Table 3.11. Correlation matrix of 3Y, 6Y, 9Y German and 3Y, 6Y, 9Y Greece zero rates.

	3Y Ger	*6Y Ger*	*9Y Ger*	*3Y Greece*	*6Y Greece*	*9Y Greece*
3Y Ger	1.000					
6Y Ger	0.967	1.000				
9Y Ger	0.924	0.990	1.000			
3Y Greece	−0.486	−0.441	−0.424	1.000		
6Y Greece	0.482	0.574	0.601	0.391	1.000	
9Y Greece	0.649	0.746	0.778	0.118	0.951	1.000

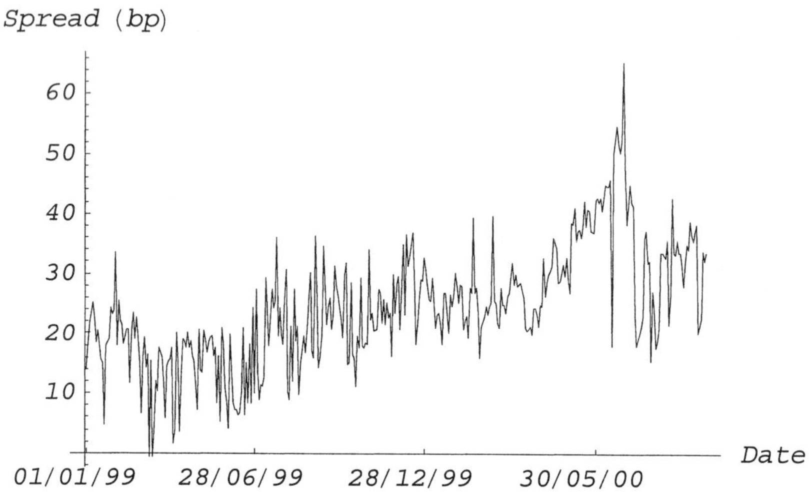

Fig. 3.34. Estimated credit spreads between Italian and German Government zero coupon bonds with maturity of 3 years. Time period: from January 1*st*, 1999, until October 23*rd*, 2000.

In the following we partition the credit spread by using the Nelson-Siegel formulas (3.92) and (3.93). First, we observe that we can rewrite equation (3.92) as:

$$R(t,T) = \beta_0(t) + \beta_1(t)\frac{\beta_3}{(T-t)}\left(1 - e^{-\frac{(T-t)}{\beta_3}}\right)$$
$$+\beta_2(t)\frac{\beta_3}{(T-t)}\left(1 - e^{-\frac{(T-t)}{\beta_3}}\left(\frac{(T-t)}{\beta_3}+1\right)\right).$$

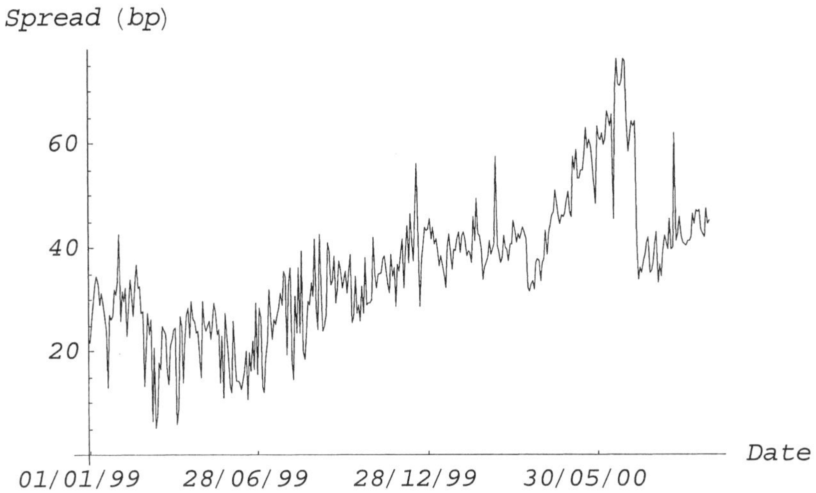

Fig. 3.35. Estimated credit spreads between Italian and German Government zero coupon bonds with maturity of 6 years. Time period: from January $1st$, 1999, until October $23rd$, 2000.

We can obtain corresponding formulas for $R^{d,j}(t,T)$, $j \in \{I, G\}$. Then the credit spread $S^j(t,T) = R^{d,j}(t,T) - R(t,T)$ can be partitioned into three parts:

$$S^j(t,T) = \left(\beta_0^{d,j}(t) - \beta_0(t)\right) + \left(\beta_1^{d,j}(t) - \beta_1(t)\right) \frac{\beta_3}{(T-t)} \left(1 - e^{-\frac{(T-t)}{\beta_3}}\right) + \left(\beta_2^{d,j}(t) - \beta_2(t)\right) \frac{\beta_3}{(T-t)} \left(1 - e^{-\frac{(T-t)}{\beta_3}} \left(\frac{(T-t)}{\beta_3} + 1\right)\right) \quad (3.94)$$

The first term on the right-hand side of equation (3.94) is the level component, the second term is the slope component and the third term is the curvature component for the credit spread at time t with maturity T. In our sample set, $\left(\beta_0^{d,j}(t) - \beta_0(t)\right) > 0$ for all t. In case of Italy, the mean level component contributes to most of the mean credit spread. The mean slope component offsets the mean level component. The mean credit spread increases with maturity. The mean curvature component plays a less important role. In case of Greece, the mean level and the mean slope components contribute to most of the mean credit spread. The mean curvature component offsets the mean level component. The credit spreads coincide almost with the slope component.

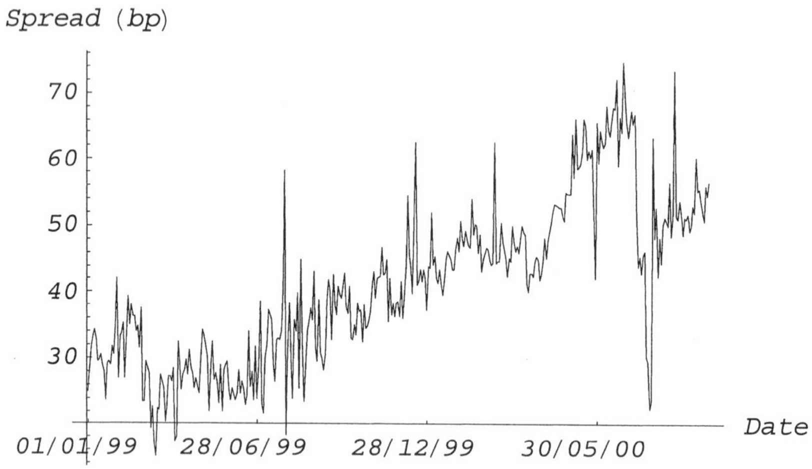

Fig. 3.36. Estimated credit spreads between Italian and German Government zero coupon bonds with maturity of 9 years. Time period: from January 1*st*, 1999, until October 23*rd*, 2000.

All together we get Italian and Greek credit spread curves for 370 days between January 1*st*, 1999 and October 23*rd*, 2000. Figure 3.42 shows the plot of the Italian curves: over the observed time period, we get a range of different shapes: monotonic, humped and S shaped. Figure 3.43 shows the tightening of the Greek spreads over time.

Table 3.12 shows the summary statistics for the credit spreads between the German and Italian zero coupon bonds for different maturities. Again, the statistics are based on 370 observation days. The range of expected spreads between the two markets spans from 24 to 41 basis points depending on the time to maturity. Spreads are usually higher for longer maturities. The standard deviation of the credit spreads is more or less the same for all maturities (around 12 basis points). The skewness parameters[64] are all positive

[64] See, e.g., Larsen & Marx (2001), p. 233: Let X be a random variable with mean μ and variance σ^2. The skewness of a probability density function (pdf) can be measured in terms of its third moment about the mean. If a pdf is symmetric, $E\left[(X-\mu)^3\right]$ will obviously be 0; for pdf's not symmetric $E\left[(X-\mu)^3\right]$ will not be zero. In practice, the symmetry (or lack of symmetry) of a pdf is often measured by the coefficient of skewness, γ_1, where

$$\gamma_1 = \frac{E\left[(X-\mu)^3\right]}{\sigma^3}.$$

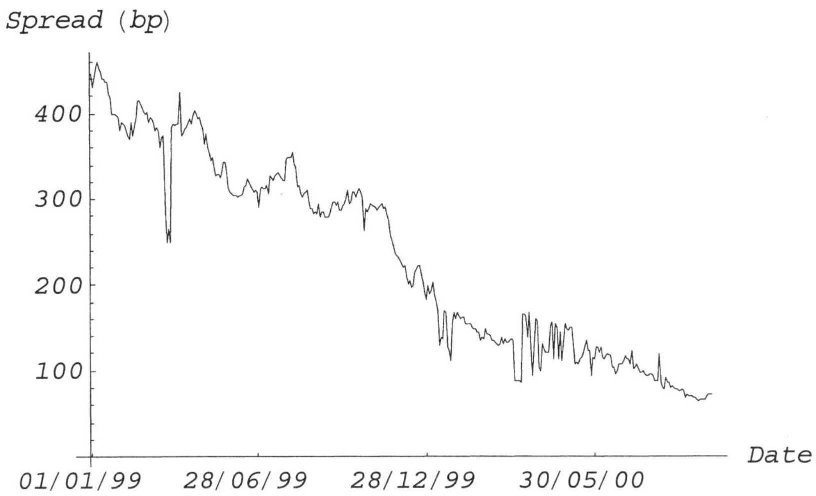

Fig. 3.37. Estimated credit spreads between Greek and German Government zero coupon bonds with maturity of 3 years. Time period: from January 1*st*, 1999, until October 23*rd*, 2000.

and suggest that the credit spreads are more likely to be above the mean. The excess kurtosis[65] parameters suggest that the probability density functions are platykurtic for all maturities. For short term debt (maturities of 1 and 2 years) we find very high standard deviations of the spreads. That's why we exclude these maturities from the further analysis. For Greece we have summarized the credit spread statistics in table 3.13. The range of expected spreads between Greece and Germany spans from 113 to 232 basis points and is much higher than the Italian spread range. In opposite to the Ital-

A variable with a negative skew is more likely to be far below the mean than it is to be far above the mean.

[65] See, e.g., Larsen & Marx (2001), p. 233: Let X be a random variable with mean μ and variance σ^2. The excess kurtosis of a probability density function (pdf) can be measured in terms of its fourth moment about the mean. The coefficient of kurtosis, γ_2, is defined by

$$\gamma_2 = \frac{E\left[(X-\mu)^4\right]}{\sigma^4} - 3.$$

A pdf whose excess kurtosis is positive has more mass in the tails than a Gaussian pdf with the same variance. Hence, γ_2, is a useful measure of peakedness: relatively "flat" pdf's are said to be platykurtic; more peaked pdf's are called leptokurtic.

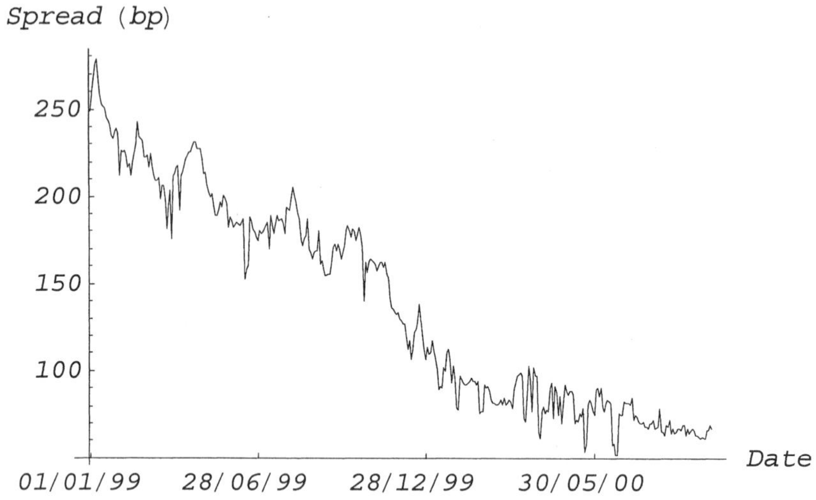

Fig. 3.38. Estimated credit spreads between Greek and German Government zero coupon bonds with maturity of 6 years. Time period: from January 1*st*, 1999, until October 23*rd*, 2000.

ian case the spreads tend to be higher for shorter maturities. The standard deviations of the Greece spreads decrease with the maturity and are much higher than for Italy. The Greece credit spreads are more likely to be above than below the mean, and the probability density functions are leptokurtic for all maturities. One method that has been suggested for testing whether the distribution underlying a sample of n elements is normal, is to refer the statistic

$$L = n\left(\frac{skewness^2}{6} + \frac{excess\ kurtosis^2}{24}\right) \tag{3.95}$$

to the chi-squared distribution with two degrees of freedom[66]. The critical values for 5% and 1% are 5.99 and 9.21, respectively. We carry out the test using our credit spread data for the maturities between 3 and 9 years. According to the Italian values of L given in table 3.12 and the Greece values of L given in table 3.13, we can reject the normality hypothesis for the credit spread samples (for all maturities between 3 and 9 years) on a 1% level. In summary, we find that the distributions of the Italian and Greek spreads are completely different, and that both we cannot accept a normal distribution hypothesis.

[66] See, e.g., Greene (2000), p. 161.

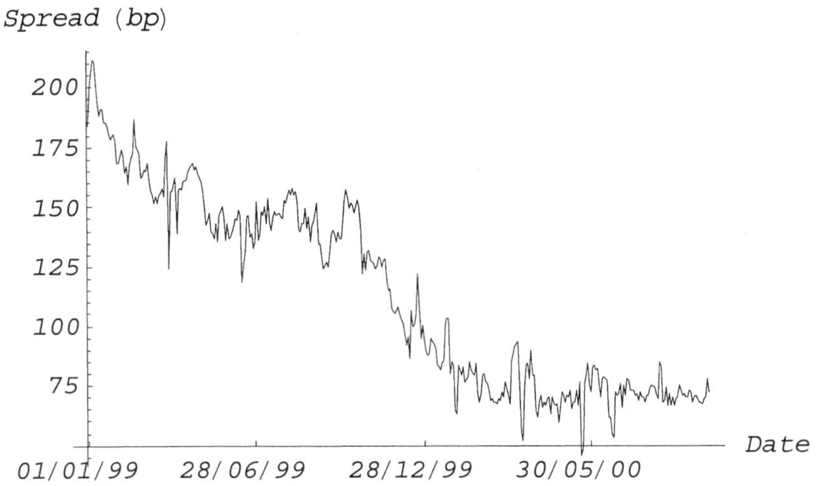

Fig. 3.39. Estimated credit spreads between Greek and German Government zero coupon bonds with maturity of 9 years. Time period: from January 1*st*, 1999, until October 23*rd*, 2000.

Table 3.12. Summary statistics for German - Italian credit spreads for different maturities. Mean, standard deviation and maximum values are given in basis points.

Maturity	*Mean*	*Std. Dev.*	*Maximum*	*Skewness*	*Excess Kurtosis*	*L*
3 years	24.35	10.00	65.33	0.46	0.73	21.02
4 years	29.30	11.97	72.40	0.47	0.89	25.29
5 years	33.05	12.88	75.48	0.47	0.79	22.74
6 years	35.89	13.08	76.24	0.45	0.56	17.33
7 years	38.06	12.91	77.05	0.43	0.23	12.12
8 years	39.75	12.62	76.38	0.40	−0.14	10.01
9 years	41.06	12.39	74.73	0.36	−0.46	11.33

In addition to the analysis of the credit spread levels we investigate the first-differences in the credit spread levels. The results in tables 3.14 and 3.15 suggest that credit spread changes are far away from being normally distributed. As, e.g., Duffie & Pan (1997) and Pedrosa & Roll (1998) point out, this implies troubling implications for risk management. The large values of the excess kurtosis are caused by fat tails in the probability density function. There are much more extreme events than would have been in the case of

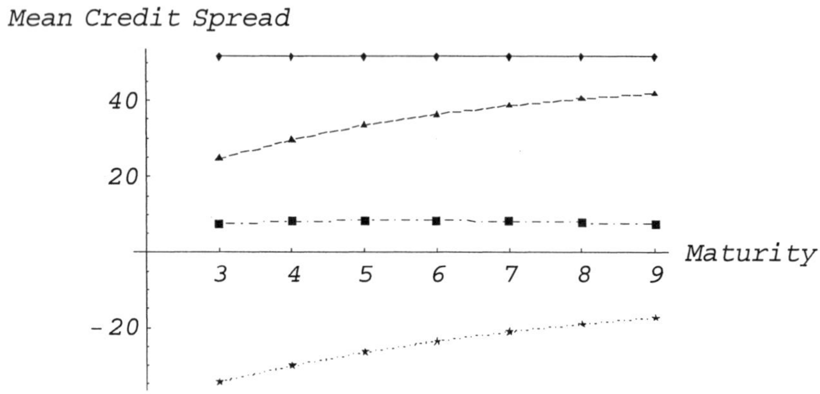

Fig. 3.40. Components of Italian mean credit spreads for different maturities. From below: mean slope component, mean curvature component, mean credit spread, mean level component. Maturity in years, mean credit spreads and credit spread components in basis points.

Table 3.13. Summary statistics for German - Greek credit spreads for different maturities. Mean, standard deviation and maximum values are given in basis points.

Maturity	*Mean*	*Std. Dev.*	*Maximum*	*Skewness*	*Excess Kurtosis*	*L*
3 years	232.16	114.70	460.16	0.15	−1.40	31.28
4 years	188.20	90.12	378.75	0.19	−1.37	31.52
5 years	158.51	72.70	320.30	0.23	−1.36	31.53
6 years	138.80	60.29	278.31	0.26	−1.34	31.43
7 years	126.04	51.40	248.12	0.26	−1.32	31.26
8 years	118.10	45.02	226.41	0.26	−1.32	31.05
9 years	113.46	40.46	211.17	0.24	−1.33	30.92

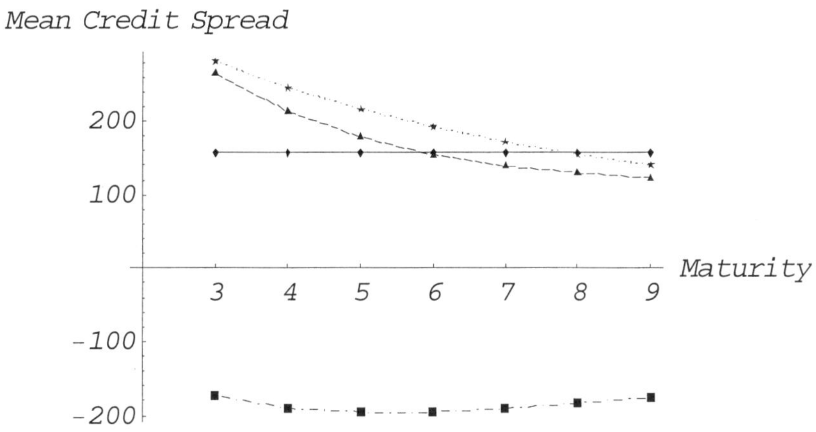

Fig. 3.41. Components of Greek mean credit spreads for different maturities. From below: mean curvature component, mean level component, mean credit spread, mean slope component. Maturity in years, mean credit spreads and credit spread components in basis points.

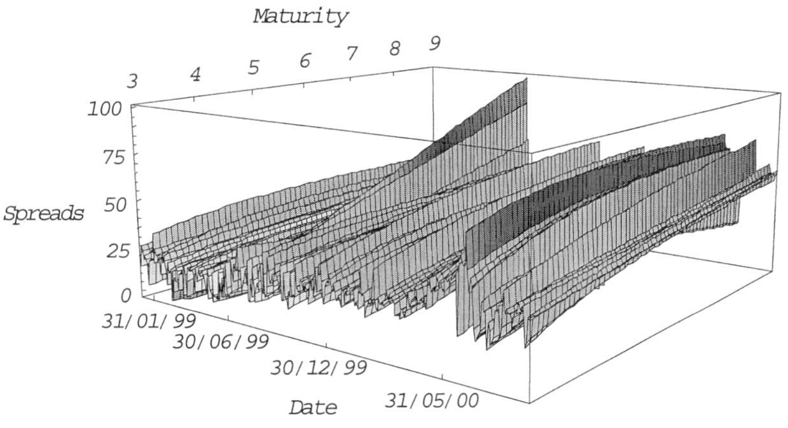

Fig. 3.42. Evolution of Italian credit spread curves. Credit spreads (bps), maturity (years).

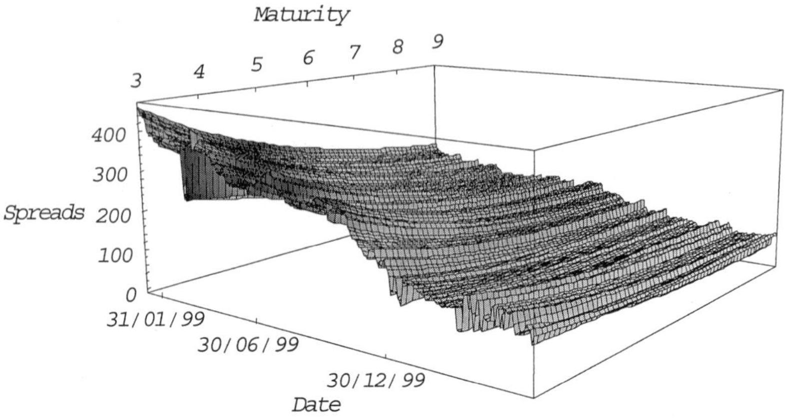

Fig. 3.43. Evolution of Greek credit spread curves. Credit spreads (bps), maturity (years).

Table 3.14. Summary statistics for the credit spread changes between Germany and Italy for different maturities. Mean, standard deviation and maximum are given in basis points.

Maturity	*Skewness*	*Excess Kurtosis*
3 years	−0.60	16.17
4 years	−1.05	23.71
5 years	−0.93	11.14
6 years	−0.54	6.31
7 years	−0.35	4.08
8 years	−0.31	4.17
9 years	−0.26	8.18

a normal distribution. The skewness is negative for all maturities but the 3−year Greece credit spread changes.

A prerequisite for producing reliable statistical results is that the credit spread time series is inter-temporal stationary, i.e. that there is no unit root. We use the augmented Dickey-Fuller regression (Dickey & Fuller 1981) to test for unit roots:

$$\begin{aligned}\Delta S_t^j(\tau) &= S_t^j(\tau) - S_{t-1}^j(\tau)\\ &= a_0^j + \gamma^j S_{t-1}^j(\tau) + a_2^j t + \sum_{i=2}^{p} \beta_i^j \Delta S_{t-i+1}^j(\tau) + \varepsilon_t^j,\ j \in \{I,\ G\}\end{aligned}$$

where $S_t^j(\tau) = S^j(t, t+\tau)$ denotes the time t credit spread between $\tau-$year Italian and German zero coupon government bonds. The drift term parameter a_0^j, the linear time trend parameter a_2^j, γ^j, and β_i^j are parameters which have

Table 3.15. Summary statistics for the credit spread changes between Germany and Greece for different maturities. Mean, standard deviation and maximum are given in basis points.

Maturity	*Skewness*	*Excess Kurtosis*
3 years	0.69	11.74
4 years	−0.05	7.36
5 years	−0.26	6.89
6 years	−0.22	6.95
7 years	−0.21	8.07
8 years	−0.24	9.18
9 years	−0.26	9.21

Table 3.16. Unit root tests for credit spreads between Italian and German zero coupon government bonds.

Maturity	p	γ	*Standard Error*	*Test Statistic*
3 years	5	−0.283617	0.0561638	−5.04982
4 years	5	−0.211004	0.048394	−4.36013
5 years	5	−0.187264	0.0450996	−4.15224
6 years	5	−0.187931	0.0443555	−4.23693
7 years	5	−0.212585	0.0461903	−4.60237
8 years	4	−0.266	0.049571	−5.36603
9 years	4	−0.346507	0.0558706	−6.20196

Table 3.17. Unit root tests for credit spreads between Greece and German zero rates.

Maturity	p	γ	*Standard Error*	*Test Statistic*
3 years	1	−0.46146	0.0479452	−9.62474
4 years	1	−0.483547	0.0479009	−10.0948
5 years	1	−0.49087	0.0480069	−10.225
6 years	1	−0.484757	0.0481268	−10.0725
7 years	1	−0.473419	0.0481574	−9.83066
8 years	1	−0.46307	0.0481434	−9.61856
9 years	1	−0.455755	0.0481921	−9.45706

to be estimated by regression. ε_t^j is the spherical disturbance. We choose p to be the highest significant lag from the autocorrelation function of S^j. The coefficient of interest is γ^j. If $\gamma^j = 0$, the sequence $\left\{S_t^j(\tau)\right\}$ contains a unit root. Tables 3.16 and 3.17 report the Dickey-Fuller t-test results of $H_0 : \gamma^j = 0$ for Italy and Greece, respectively. The critical 95% and 99% values are -3.43 and -3.99, respectively. A smaller t-statistic rejects H_0. Hence, according to tables 3.16 and 3.17 we can reject the existence of unit roots for Italy and Greece for all maturities at the 99% level.

The Kalman Filter Methodology for the Parameter Estimation of the Non-Defaultable Short Rate. The application of Kalman filtering methods to the parameter estimation of term structure models has the great advantage that it allows the underlying state variables to be handled as completely unobservable, whereas other methods often must use some short term rates as proxies, which introduces additional noise. In the following we use the Kalman filtering method to estimate the parameters of the Hull and White term structure model defined in section 3.2 using the German zero coupon bond data described in section 3.6.3. First we derive the state space model formulation[67] of the non-defaultable term structure model defined by equation (3.1) and then present the Kalman filter algorithm. This is used in the calculation of the likelihood function of the observed zero rates and the computation of the unobserved state variables and parameters of the model. Because we use real world zero rate observations for the Kalman filter, we must describe the zero rate dynamics under the "real world" measure $\mathbf{P}$. We follow the assumptions of section 3.2 with the additional assumption that $\beta = 0$, and model the dynamics of $r(t)$ under $\mathbf{P}$ the following way:

$$dr(t) = [\theta_r(t) - a_r r(t)]\, dt + \sigma_r dW_r(t), \quad 0 \le t \le T^*.$$

In addition,

$$a_r = \hat{a}_r - \lambda_r \sigma_r^2, \text{ and } \hat{W}_r(t) = W_r(t) + \int_0^t \gamma_r(l)\, dl,$$

with

$$\gamma_r(t) = \lambda_r \sigma_r r(t),$$

for some constant λ_r. We denote the parameter vector consisting of the unknown non-defaultable short rate process parameters by $\Phi_r = (a_r, \sigma_r, \lambda_r)$. The German zero coupon bond prices follow the non-defaultable Hull-White model (see equations (3.15), (3.16), and (3.17)), and the continuous zero rates of the non-defaultable discount bonds are given by

$$\begin{aligned} R(t,T) &= -\frac{1}{T-t} \ln P(t,T) \\ &= a_1(t,\tau) + b_1(\tau)\, r(t), \end{aligned}$$

where $\tau = T - t$, $a_1(t,\tau) = -\frac{\ln A(t,t+\tau)}{\tau}$, and $b_1(\tau) = \frac{B(t,t+\tau)}{\tau}$. Note, that $B(t,T)$ only depends on the time to maturity τ. We fix N different times to maturity $\tau_1, \ldots, \tau_N$, and denote the vector of the zero rates of the corresponding N different bonds by $RV(t)$:

$$RV(t) = \begin{pmatrix} R(t, t+\tau_1) \\ R(t, t+\tau_2) \\ \vdots \\ R(t, t+\tau_N) \end{pmatrix}.$$

[67] For a general definition of state space models see, e.g., Harvey (1989), chapter 3.

Let

$$A_1(t) = A_1(t, \Phi_r) = \begin{pmatrix} a_1(t,\tau_1) \\ a_1(t,\tau_2) \\ \vdots \\ a_1(t,\tau_N) \end{pmatrix}, \quad B_1 = B_1(\Phi_r) = \begin{pmatrix} b_1(\tau_1) \\ b_1(\tau_2) \\ \vdots \\ b_1(\tau_N) \end{pmatrix}.$$

Then the observable vector $RV(t)$ of zero rates and the unobservable non-defaultable short rates are related through the measurement equation:

$$RV(t) = A_1(t) + B_1 r(t).$$

We consider n time instances $t_1, \ldots, t_n$ on the time interval $(t, T]$ with $t_0 = t$ and $t_n = T$, and denote the time increments by $\Delta t_k = t_k - t_{k-1}$, $k = 1, \ldots, n$. At each time step t_k, $k = 1, \ldots, n$, we observe a vector consisting of N different zero rates (of N different maturities) :

$$RV_k = RV(t_k) = \begin{pmatrix} R(t_k, t_k + \tau_1) \\ R(t_k, t_k + \tau_2) \\ \vdots \\ R(t_k, t_k + \tau_N) \end{pmatrix}.$$

We allow for noise in the sampling process of the data. Hence, we assume that the zero rates are observed with measurement errors ε_k, that are jointly normally distributed with zero mean and $(N \times N)$–dimensional covariance matrix H. We choose the covariance matrix to be diagonal but allow for maturity-specific diagonal elements of H, i.e.

$$H = \begin{pmatrix} h_1^2 & 0 & \cdots & 0 \\ 0 & h_2^2 & \cdots & 0 \\ \vdots & \vdots & \ddots & \vdots \\ 0 & 0 & \cdots & h_N^2 \end{pmatrix}.$$

These diagonal elements h_i, $1 \leq i \leq N$, must be estimated together with Φ_r, and the vector consisting of these diagonal elements is denoted by $\Psi_r = (h_1, ..., h_N)$. Let $r_k = r(t_k)$ and $A_{1,k} = A_1(t_k)$. Then the measurement equation is given by

$$RV_k = A_{1,k} + B_1 r_k + \varepsilon_k, \ \varepsilon_k \sim N(0, H). \tag{3.96}$$

Applying Itó's formula to $v(t) = e^{a_r t} r(t)$ yields:

$$dv(t) = e^{a_r t}\theta_r(t)dt + \sigma_r e^{a_r t} dW_r(t).$$

The solution of this SDE is given by

$$v(t) = v(0) + \int_0^t e^{a_r x}\theta_r(x)dx + \sigma_r \int_0^t e^{a_r x} dW_r(x).$$

Hence, $r(t)$ is given by

$$r(t) = r(0)e^{-a_r t} + \int_0^t e^{a_r(x-t)}\theta_r(x)dx + \sigma_r \int_0^t e^{a_r(x-t)} dW_r(x),$$

which can also be written as

$$\begin{aligned} r(t) &= r(s)e^{-a_r(t-s)} + \int_s^t e^{a_r(x-t)}\theta_r(x)dx + \sigma_r \int_s^t e^{a_r(x-t)} dW_r(x) \\ &= r(s)e^{-a_r(t-s)} + \int_0^{t-s} e^{a_r(x-(t-s))}\theta_r(x+s)dx \\ &\quad +\sigma_r \int_0^{t-s} e^{a_r(x-(t-s))} dW_r(x). \end{aligned}$$

Thus, with respect to the time increments,

$$\begin{aligned} r_{k+1} &= r_k e^{-a_r \Delta t_{k+1}} + \int_0^{\Delta t_{k+1}} e^{-a_r(\Delta t_{k+1}-x)}\theta_r(x+t_k)dx \\ &\quad +\sigma_r \int_0^{\Delta t_{k+1}} e^{-a_r(\Delta t_{k+1}-x)} dW_r(x), \end{aligned}$$

which can be approximated by

$$\begin{aligned} r_{k+1} &= r_k e^{-a_r \Delta t_{k+1}} + \int_0^{\Delta t_{k+1}} e^{-a_r(\Delta t_{k+1}-x)}\theta_r(t_k)dx \\ &\quad +\sigma_r \int_0^{\Delta t_{k+1}} e^{-a_r(\Delta t_{k+1}-x)} dW_r(x). \end{aligned}$$

Let $\widetilde{r}_{k|k-1}$ and $\widetilde{r}_k$denote the optimal estimators[68] of the unknown short rate r_k based upon the observations up to time t_{k-1} and t_k, i.e. given $RV_1, ..., RV_{k-1}$, and $RV_1, ..., RV_k$, respectively. Then,

$$\begin{aligned} \widetilde{r}_{k+1|k} &= E_k[r_{k+1}] \\ &= \widetilde{r}_k e^{-a_r \Delta t_{k+1}} + \int_0^{\Delta t_{k+1}} e^{-a_r(\Delta t_{k+1}-x)}\theta_r(t_k)dx, \end{aligned} \tag{3.97}$$

where $E_k[\cdot]$ denotes the expected value operator conditional on all information up to time t_k, i.e. given the observations $RV_1, ..., RV_k$. The mean squared error between the optimal estimator $\widetilde{r}_{k|k-1}$ and the observation r_{k+1}, conditioned on all observations up to time t_k, and denoted by $Var_{k+1|k}$, is given by[69]

[68] By optimal estimators we mean optimal in the mean squared error sense.

[69] Note, that r_k and the time increments of the standard Brownian motion W are independent for $t \geq t_k$.

$$
\begin{aligned}
&Var_{k+1|k} \\
&= E_k \left[r_{k+1} - \widetilde{r}_{k+1|k} \right]^2 \\
&= E_k \left[r_k e^{-a_r \Delta t_{k+1}} + \sigma_r \int_0^{\Delta t_{k+1}} e^{-a_r(\Delta t_{k+1}-x)} dW_r(x) - \widetilde{r}_k e^{-a_r \Delta t_{k+1}} \right]^2 \\
&= e^{-2a_r \Delta t_{k+1}} E_k \left[r_k - \widetilde{r}_k \right]^2 + \sigma_r^2 \int_0^{\Delta t_{k+1}} e^{-2a_r x} dx.
\end{aligned}
$$

If we denote $E_k \left[r_k - \widetilde{r}_k \right]^2$ by Var_k, then

$$
Var_{k+1|k} = e^{-2a_r \Delta t_{k+1}} Var_k + \sigma_r^2 \int_0^{\Delta t_{k+1}} e^{-2a_r x} dx. \tag{3.98}
$$

Now we can rewrite the measurement equation (3.96) as

$$
RV_{k+1} = A_{1,k+1} + B_1 \left(r_{k+1} - \widetilde{r}_{k+1|k} \right) + B_1 \widetilde{r}_{k+1|k} + \varepsilon_{k+1}.
$$

Then,

$$
\widetilde{RV}_{k+1|k} = A_{1,k+1} + B_1 \widetilde{r}_{k+1|k}.
$$

Let

$$
\upsilon_{k+1} = RV_{k+1} - \widetilde{RV}_{k+1|k} = RV_{k+1} - A_{1,k+1} - B_1 \widetilde{r}_{k+1|k}, \tag{3.99}
$$

and consider the vector $\begin{pmatrix} r_{k+1} \\ RV_{k+1} \end{pmatrix}$, which is normally distributed conditional on $RV_1, \ldots, RV_k$. The conditional mean is given by

$$
E_k \begin{bmatrix} r_{k+1} \\ RV_{k+1} \end{bmatrix} = \begin{pmatrix} \widetilde{r}_{k+1|k} \\ \widetilde{Y}_{k+1|k} \end{pmatrix},
$$

and the conditional covariance matrix by

$$
\begin{aligned}
&Cov_k \begin{bmatrix} r_{k+1} \\ RV_{k+1} \end{bmatrix} \\
&= \begin{pmatrix} Var_{k+1|k} & Cov_k(r_{k+1}, A_{1,k+1} + B_1 r_{k+1}) \\ Cov_k(A_{1,k+1} + B_1 r_{k+1}, r_{k+1}) & Cov_k(RV_{k+1}, RV_{k+1}) \end{pmatrix} \\
&= \begin{pmatrix} Var_{k+1|k} & Var_{k+1|k} B_1' \\ B_1 Var_{k+1|k} & F_{k+1} \end{pmatrix},
\end{aligned}
$$

where

$$
\begin{aligned}
&F_{k+1} \\
&= E_k \left(\upsilon_{k+1} \upsilon_{k+1}' \right) \qquad (3.100) \\
&= E_k \left[\left(B_1 \left(r_{k+1} - \widetilde{r}_{k+1|k} \right) + \varepsilon_{k+1} \right) \left(B_1 \left(r_{k+1} - \widetilde{r}_{k+1|k} \right) + \varepsilon_{k+1} \right)' \right] \\
&= B_1 Var_{k+1|k} B_1' + H.
\end{aligned}
$$

If we apply results from Harvey (1989), chapter 3, we get the updating equations

$$\widetilde{r}_{k+1} = \widetilde{r}_{k+1|k} + K_{k+1} v_{k+1}, \tag{3.101}$$

and

$$Var_{k+1} = Var_{k+1|k} - K_{k+1} B_1 Var_{k+1|k}, \tag{3.102}$$

where

$$K_{k+1} = Var_{k+1|k} B_1^T F_{k+1}^{-1} \tag{3.103}$$

is the Kalman gain vector. Equations (3.97) and (3.98) are prediction equations for r_{k+1} and Var_{k+1}. When the new observation Y_{k+1} becomes available we can obtain more precise estimators using the updating equations (3.101) and (3.102). The Kalman filter determined by the equations (3.96)-(3.103) enables us to evaluate the likelihood function L for the set of parameters Φ_r and Ψ_r :

$$\begin{aligned} L(\Phi_r, \Psi_r | Y_1, \ldots, Y_n) &= \prod_{k=1}^{n} f_{Y_k | Y_1, \ldots, Y_{k-1}} \\ &= \prod_{k=1}^{n} \frac{1}{\left(\sqrt{2\pi}\right)^N} \frac{1}{\sqrt{\det F_k}} \\ &\quad \cdot \exp\left\{ -\frac{1}{2} \left(Y_k - \widetilde{Y}_{k|k-1} \right)' F_k^{-1} \left(Y_k - \widetilde{Y}_{k|k-1} \right) \right\}, \end{aligned}$$

where $f_{Y_k | Y_1, \ldots, Y_{k-1}}$ is the probability density function of Y_k given the observations $Y_1, ..., Y_{k-1}$. Thus, apart from a constant, the log-likelihood function is given by

$$\ln L(\Phi_r, \Psi_r | Y_1, \ldots, Y_n) = -\frac{1}{2} \sum_{k=1}^{n} \ln(\det F_k) - \frac{1}{2} \sum_{k=1}^{n} v_k' F_k^{-1} v_k. \tag{3.104}$$

Parameter Estimation Results for $r(t)$. For the parameter estimation of the non-defaultable short rate model we use two time series of different length:

1. Estimation 1: Seven samples of data, each of length 150, i.e. in the Kalman filter algorithm we set $N = 7$ and $n = 150$. We use a time series with daily German zero rate data from September $30th$, 1999, until May $30th$, 2000, excluding several days for which there is no bond data available, the Nelson-Siegel estimates of the credit spreads appear to be negative or the bond data is identified as an outlier. We consider the times to maturity $\tau_i = i + 2$, $i = 1, ..., 7$ (expressed in years). Thus, the input data consists of 150 observed vectors of zero rates

$$RV_k = \begin{pmatrix} R(t_k, t_k + \tau_1) \\ R(t_k, t_k + \tau_2) \\ \vdots \\ R(t_k, t_k + \tau_7) \end{pmatrix}, \quad 1 \leq k \leq 150.$$

Table 3.18. Kalman filter German maximum likelihood parameter estimates. Estimation 1: Sample period: 150 days from September 30th, 1999, until May 30th, 2000. Estimation 2: Sample period: 300 days from January 1st, 1999, until May 30th, 2000.

Parameter	h_1	h_2	h_3	h_4	h_5	h_6	h_7
Estim. 1	0.00227	0.00119	0.00059	0.00025	0	0.00023	0.00046
Estim. 2	0.00246	0.00139	0.00073	0.00031	0	0.00027	0.00053

Table 3.19. Kalman filter maximum likelihood parameter estimates of the non-defaultable short rate. Estimation 1: Sample period: 150 days from September 30th, 1999, until May 30th, 2000. Estimation 2: Sample period: 300 days from January 1st, 1999, until May 30th, 2000.

Parameter	*Estimation 1*	*Estimation 2*
a_r	0.04481038	0.03398197
σ_r	0.00997727	0.01030943
λ_r	−3.6167735	−2.9502785
Log-Likelihood	7280.2	14219.4

2. Estimation 2: The same time series as in the previous numbered list item but with daily data of German zero rates from January 1, 1999, until May 30, 2000, i.e. with $N = 7$ and $n = 300$.

After initialization we perform the 150 (300) Kalman filter iterations to calculate the log-likelihood function (3.104). Finally, we maximize this function with respect to the two parameter vectors $\Phi_r = (a_r, \sigma_r, \lambda_r)$ and $\Psi_r = (h_1, ..., h_7)$. Therefore, we apply the multi-dimensional downhill simplex method of Nelder & Mead (1965). Tables 3.18 and 3.19 summarize the parameter estimates. The average mean reversion levels of the non-defaultable short rate process implied by our parameter estimates for the first and second estimation equal 4.46% and 4.41%, respectively, which nicely fit to figures 3.44 and 3.45, respectively.

Testing the Assumptions on the Residuals. For the Kalman filter algorithm it is essential that we assume that the standardized residuals (the so called innovations) $\frac{v_k}{\sqrt{F_k}}$ are i.i.d. random variables. To verify this assumption we

1. apply a robust test for normal distribution;
2. calculate the Box-Ljung-statistic (Q-statistic) to test for serial correlation;
3. calculate the H-statistic to test for homoscedasticity;

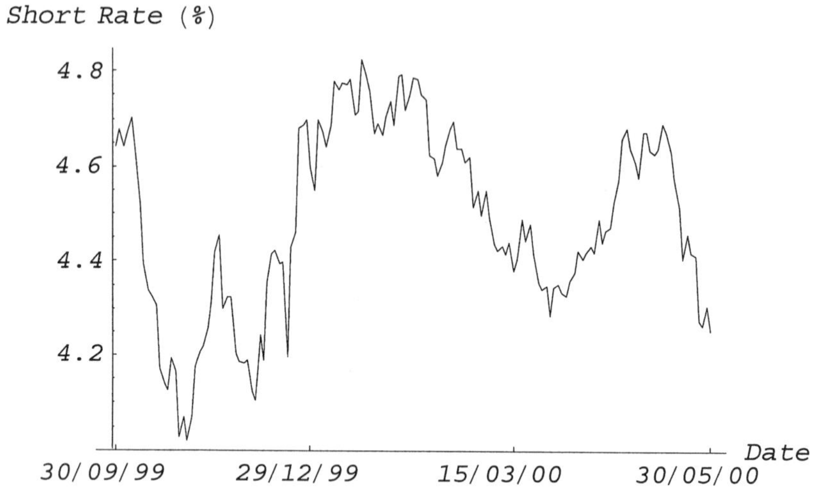

Fig. 3.44. Kalman filtered German short rate process. Time period: 150 days from September 30*th*, 1999, until May 30*th*, 2000.

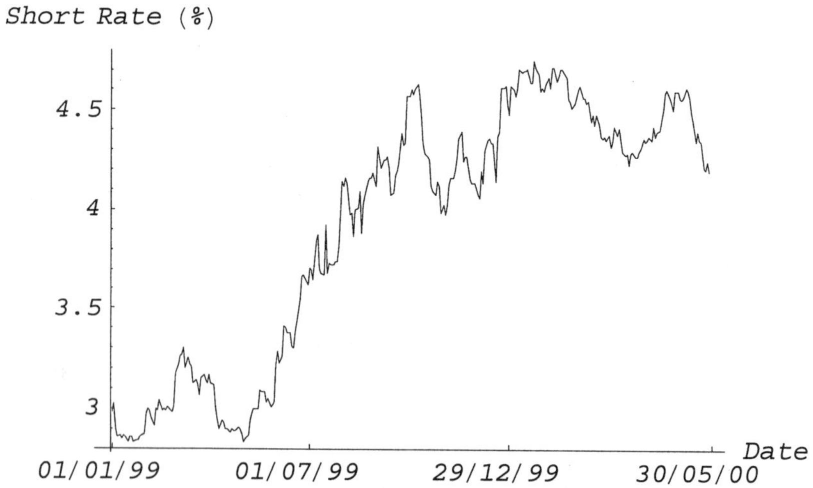

Fig. 3.45. Kalman filtered German short rate process. Time period: 300 days from January 1*st*, 1999, until May 30*th*, 2000.

Table 3.20. Results of the test for normal distribution of the German standardized Kalman filter residuals. Sample period 1: 150 days from September 30th, 1999, until May 30th, 2000. Sample Period 2: 300 days from January 1st, 1999, until May 30th, 2000.

Maturity	*L (Estimation 1)*	*L (Estimation 2)*
3 years	9.53294	7.51221
4 years	7.90222	11.198
5 years	5.20366	9.8423
6 years	1.78387	4.41243
7 years	2.43089	26.1632
8 years	5.0033	10.3134
9 years	4.16506	8.5817

We refer to the statistic (3.95) to test the sample of standardized innovations for normal distribution. The critical values for significance levels of 5% and 1% are 5.99 and 9.21, respectively.

- Estimation 1: According to table 3.20, we reject the normal distribution hypothesis on a 1%-significance level only for the maturity of 3 years. In case of a maturity of 4 years we reject the normal distribution hypothesis on the 5%-significance level. In all other cases we don't reject the hypothesis on 1% and 5% significance levels.
- Estimation 2: For the maturities of 4, 5, 7, and 8 years we reject the normal distribution hypothesis on the 1%−significance level. On the 5%−significance level we have to reject the maturity of 3 years as well.

To test the hypothesis that there is no serial correlation of the standardized residuals (i.e. we consider the standardized residual sample autocorrelations), we apply the Box-Ljung test (see, e.g., Harvey (1989), page 259) on 1% and 5%- significance levels to different maturities. Under the null hypothesis that there is no serial correlation of the standardized Kalman filter residuals, the Box-Ljung Q−statistic has a χ^2−distribution (asymptotically) with

$$\sqrt{n} - number\ of\ estimated\ parameters$$

degrees of freedom, i.e. 2 and 7 for estimations 1 and 2, respectively. We reject the null hypothesis on the α−level only if the test statistic is greater than the $(1-\alpha)$%-quantile of the $\chi^2\left(\sqrt{n}-10\right)$ distribution. The critical values are given in table 3.21.

Table 3.22 summarizes the results of the Q−statistics for several maturities.

- Estimation 1: We reject the null hypothesis that there is no serial correlation on a 1%−significance level only for the maturity of 3 years and on a 5%−significance level for the maturities of 3, 4, 5, and 8 years.

Table 3.21. Critical values of the Box-Ljung test with 150 and 300 data points and 10 estimated parameters.

	$\chi^2(2)$	$\chi^2(7)$
95% quantile	5.99	14.07
99% quantile	9.21	18.48

Table 3.22. Box-Ljung tests for German standardized Kalman filter residuals. Sample period 1: 150 days from September 30th, 1999, until May 30th, 2000. Sample Period 2: 300 days from January 1st, 1999, until May 30th, 2000.

Maturity	*Q – statistic (Estimation 1)*	*Q – statistic (Estimation 2)*
3 years	10.13	10.40
4 years	9.20	18.40
5 years	7.57	15.53
6 years	4.93	6.10
7 years	0.40	4.57
8 years	6.09	16.14
9 years	5.85	17.39

- Estimation 2: We don't reject the null hypothesis that there is no serial correlation on a 1%–significance level for all maturities. On a 5%–significance level we reject the null hypothesis for the maturities of 4, 5, 8, and 9 years.

Finally, we apply a test for homoscedasticity described in Harvey (1981), page 157. If there is homoscedasticity then the H-statistic has a F-Ratio distribution with n_1 numerator and n_2 denominator degrees of freedom where $n_1 = n_2$ is the integer that is closest to $\frac{n}{3}$. The critical values are summarized in table 3.23. If the value of the test statistic (H-statistic) is greater than the $\left(1 - \frac{\alpha}{2}\right)$ –quantile of the $F(n_1, n_2)$ –distribution or smaller than the $\frac{\alpha}{2}$–quantile of the $F(n_1, n_2)$ – distribution, than we reject the null hypothesis. If the value of the test statistic is smaller than the $\left(1 - \frac{\alpha}{2}\right)$ –quantile of the $F(n_1, n_2)$ –distribution and greater than the $\frac{\alpha}{2}$–quantile of the $F(n_1, n_2)$ –distribution, than we don't reject the null hypothesis.

- Estimation 1 : $n_1 = n_2 = 50$. According to table 3.24, we don't reject the hypothesis of homoscedasticity on a 5%–level for the maturities of 4, 5, and 7 years. On the 1%–significance level we don't reject the hypothesis for the 3, 4, 5, and 7 year zero rates.
- Estimation 2 : $n_1 = n_2 = 100$. We don't reject the hypothesis of homoscedasticity on a 5%-level for all maturities but 4 and 9 years. But we don't reject homoscedasticity on a 1%–significance level for these maturities as well.

Table 3.23. Critical values of the test for homoscedasticity.

	$F(50,50)$	$F(100,100)$
0.5% *quantile*	0.476938	0.594923
2.5% *quantile*	0.570791	0.674195
97.5% *quantile*	1.75195	1.48325
99.5% *quantile*	2.09671	1.68089

Table 3.24. Tests for homoscedasticity of German standardized Kalman filter residuals. Sample Period 1: 150 days from September 30th, 1999, until May 30th, 2000. Sample period 2: 300 days from January 1st, 1999, until May 30th, 2000.

Maturity	$H-statistic : H(50)$ *(Estimation 1)*	$H-statistic : H(100)$ *(Estimation 2)*
3 years	0.548653	0.730148
4 years	0.743375	0.605777
5 years	1.51961	0.741434
6 years	2.45601	1.24844
7 years	0.600204	1.32904
8 years	3.11734	1.19796
9 years	3.3072	1.6434

Conclusion 3.6.1
Overall, based on the various tests we can conclude that the assumptions on the Kalman filter algorithm are sufficiently satisfied by the German data sets.

Testing the Model Performance of the Non-Defaultable Short Rate Model. In the following we test the non-defaultable short rate model performance by applying a test[70] used, e.g., by Titman & Torous (1989). We test the power of the model to explain the changes of the observed German zero rates. If the results are satisfactory we can conclude that the model can price non-defaultable bonds accurately. Let $\Delta R_k(\tau) = R(t_k, t_k+\tau) - R(t_{k-1}, t_{k-1}+\tau)$, $2 \leq k \leq 150\ (300)$, denote the changes of the observed zero rates with time to maturity τ, and let $\widehat{\Delta R_k}(\tau)$, $2 \leq k \leq 150\ (300)$, denote the changes of the corresponding fitted German zero rates. The test equation is given by the following linear regression:

$$\Delta R_k(\tau) = a + b\widehat{\Delta R_k}(\tau) + \varepsilon_k^*, \text{ where } \varepsilon_k^* \sim N\left(0, h^2\right). \tag{3.105}$$

We apply the test to the maturities $\tau_i = i+2$, $i = 1, ..., 7$ (expressed in years). If $\widehat{\Delta R_k}(\tau)$ is an unbiased estimate for $\Delta R_k(\tau)$, then a and b should

[70] Because the test is well-known and widely used we refer for any details on the test statistics to the article of Titman & Torous (1989). E.g., testing for $a = 0$ uses the standard t–statistics. The p–values are calculated by comparing the obtained statistic to the t–distribution with $n-p$ degrees of freedom, where n is the sample size and p is the number of predictors.

Table 3.25. Test of model explanatory power for Germany: Linear regression results of estimation 1.

Maturity	a	b	$\overline{R}^2$	*p-Value (a=0)*	*p-Value (a=0,b=1)*
3 years	-0.0000130245	0.71069	0.677014	0.599483	0
4 years	$-7.53239 \cdot 10^{-6}$	0.835213	0.777075	0.736346	0.00007395
5 years	$-6.10068 \cdot 10^{-6}$	0.920887	0.872794	0.722183	0.0242764
6 years	$-5.71593 \cdot 10^{-6}$	0.96917	0.960037	0.544857	0.143196
7 years	$-5.55063 \cdot 10^{-6}$	0.991991	0.999794	0.577653	0.142372
8 years	$-5.34673 \cdot 10^{-6}$	0.997844	0.954494	0.591318	0.139627
9 years	$-5.04453 \cdot 10^{-6}$	0.992707	0.828923	0.802432	0.0482509

be close to 0 and 1, respectively. The adjusted $\overline{R}^2$ statistics are an additional measure for the quality of the model. Table 3.25 and 3.26 show the results of the regression for estimation 1 and 2, respectively.

- Estimation 1:
  - The test of the hypothesis that $a = 0$ is not rejected for all maturities on a 5%–significance level.
  - Except for maturities of 3 and 4 years the parameter values for b are close to 1.
  - The test of the joint hypothesis that $a = 0$ and $b = 1$ is not rejected on a 1%–significance level for all maturities but 3 and 4 years. It is not rejected on a 5%– significance level for 6, 7, and 8 years. Hence, the model prices these zero coupon bonds with acceptable accuracy.
  - The adjusted $\overline{R}^2$ values vary between 67.70 % and 99.98 %.
- Estimation 2:
  The results for the longer time horizon of 300 days are not as good as the results for estimation 1.
  - The test of the hypothesis that $a = 0$ is only rejected for a maturity of 3 years on the 1%–significance level, and, in addition, on the 5%–significance level for a maturity of 4 years.
  - Except for maturities of 3 and 4 years the parameter values for b are close to 1.
  - The test of the joint hypothesis that $a = 0$ and $b = 1$ is not rejected on a 1%–significance level for the maturities of 5, 6, and 7 years. It is not rejected on a 5%– significance level for maturities of 6 and 7 years. Hence, we can assume that the model prices zero coupon bonds with maturities of 5 – 7 years with acceptable accuracy.

Table 3.26. Test of model explanatory power for Germany: Linear regression results of estimation 2.

Maturity	a	b	$\overline{R}^2$	*p-Value (a=0)*	*p-Value (a=0,b=1)*
3 years	−0.0000551972	0.724096	0.75725	0.001371	0
4 years	−0.0000286776	0.885319	0.85426	0.049230	0
5 years	−0.0000168865	0.965857	0.91886	0.129549	0.027711
6 years	−0.0000103833	0.993544	0.97415	0.091742	0.168942
7 years	$-6.22198 \cdot 10^{-6}$	0.986557	0.99988	0.734251	0.145742
8 years	$-3.25004 \cdot 10^{-6}$	0.965154	0.96515	0.625646	0.000266
9 years	$-9.52978 \cdot 10^{-6}$	0.914719	0.85560	0.943822	0.000540

Conclusion 3.6.2
Overall, estimation 1 *yields better results than estimation* 2 *does. This is not very surprising, as figure 3.45 shows that there has been a tremendous change in the level of the filtered non-defaultable German short rate between July* 1999 *and September* 1999. *But even for estimation* 1 *the model performs worse for* 3 *year zero rates. Hence, we can conclude that there may be a structural difference between the* 3 *year zero rates and the zero rates for longer maturities.*

Out-of-Sample Testing Based on the German Data. So far we have done some in-sample-testing to examine the performance of the one-factor non-defaultable term structure model. To complete the analysis of the model we add out-of-sample-tests for estimation 1 and estimation 2. We analyze if we can apply the Kalman filter with the parameters in tables 3.18 and 3.19 to the pricing of zero rates later than May 30*th*, 2000. Therefore we consider 70 additional time steps $t_k^* = 1, ..., 70$, for $k = 1, ..., 70$, from May 30*th*, 2000, until October 23*rd*, 2000, and apply the Kalman filter to the observed zero rates for this time frame. Note, that we keep the parameters of tables 3.18 and 3.19 fixed, i.e. we filter the values for $r(t)$ and determine the non-defaultable short rate predictors with given values for the vectors Φ_r and Ψ_r. To test the performance of the out-of-sample model we apply the linear regression (3.105) to the new data. We test the maturities $\tau_i = i + 2$, $i = 1, ..., 7$ (expressed in years). Tables 3.27 and 3.28 show the results of the regression:

- Estimation 1:
  - The test of the hypothesis that $a = 0$ is not rejected for all maturities on a 5%−significance level.
  - The test of the joint hypothesis that $a = 0$ and $b = 1$ is rejected on a 5%−significance level only for the maturity of 8 and 9 years, on a 1%-

Table 3.27. Test of out-of-sample model explanatory power for Germany: Linear regression results for estimation 1.

Maturity	a	b	$\overline{R}^2$	*p-Value* $(a=0)$	*p-Value* $(a=0, b=1)$
3 years	−0.0000550418	0.864412	0.44628	0.301913	0.245901
4 years	−0.0000314571	0.938133	0.53581	0.484341	0.360516
5 years	−0.0000197269	0.970996	0.68472	0.551017	0.221816
6 years	−0.0000126984	0.985759	0.88139	0.471629	0.270834
7 years	$-7.73987 \cdot 10^{-6}$	0.990779	0.99931	0.567842	0.154642
8 years	$-3.82299 \cdot 10^{-6}$	0.990284	0.85459	0.838539	0.039232
9 years	$-5.15315 \cdot 10^{-7}$	0.986782	0.58180	0.989008	0.008135

Table 3.28. Test of out-of-sample model explanatory power for Germany: Linear regression results for estimation 2.

Maturity	a	b	$\overline{R}^2$	*p-Value* $(a=0)$	*p-Value* $(a=0, b=1)$
3 years	−0.0000561881	0.881174	0.44618	0.292339	0.2902
4 years	−0.0000318168	0.952851	0.53589	0.479379	0.311749
5 years	−0.0000196989	0.981572	0.67975	0.551555	0.189156
6 years	−0.0000124838	0.991632	0.88141	0.479081	0.238614
7 years	$-7.43832 \cdot 10^{-6}$	0.991836	0.99937	0.653212	0.183240
8 years	$-3.48693 \cdot 10^{-6}$	0.986573	0.85699	0.852494	0.051134
9 years	$-1.73726 \cdot 10^{-7}$	0.978417	0.58197	0.996293	0.021683

significance level it is rejected only for a maturity of 9 years. Hence, the model prices these zero coupon bonds with acceptable accuracy.

- The adjusted $\overline{R}^2$ values vary between 44.6 % and 99.9 %.

Overall, the test suggests that the out-of-sample behavior of the model is very encouraging.

- Estimation 2:
  - The test of the hypothesis that $a = 0$ is not rejected for all maturities on a 5%–significance level.
  - The test of the joint hypothesis that $a = 0$ and $b = 1$ is rejected on a 5%–significance level only for the maturity of 9 years. It is not rejected on a 1%-significance level for all maturities. Hence, the model prices these zero coupon bonds with acceptable accuracy.
  - The adjusted $\overline{R}^2$ values vary between 44.6 % and 99.9 %.

  Overall, the test suggests that the out-of-sample behavior of the model is very encouraging.

Conclusion 3.6.3
The out-of-sample tests yield good results for both time series. Only for the 9 *year maturity zero rates in estimation* 1, *the* $p-value(a=0,b=1)<0.01$. *All other p-values are much greater than* 0.01. *The out-of-sample results are even better than the in-sample results. Though, we have considered a shorter time horizon than in the in-sample case.*

Spread Parameter Estimation by Using Kalman Filtering. In the following we apply the Kalman filtering method to estimate the parameters of the three-factor defaultable term structure model described in section 3.2 using the German, Italian, and Greece bond data described in section 3.6.3. First we derive the state space model formulation, and then present the Kalman filter algorithm. This is used in the calculation of the likelihood function of the observed credit spreads and the computation of the unobserved state variables and parameters of the model. We have already shown how we can determine the parameters for the non-defaultable one-factor model, i.e. how to find good estimators for the process $r(t)$. So it suffices to show how to determine the remaining parameters of the Italian and Greece short rate credit spread and uncertainty index processes. Because we use real world credit spread observations, we must describe the credit spread dynamics under the "real world" measure $\mathbf{P}$. We follow the assumptions of section 3.6.3 and model the dynamics of $s^j(t)$ and $u^j(t)$, $j\in\{I,G\}$, under the measure $\mathbf{P}$ the following way:

$$
\begin{aligned}
du^j(t) &= \left[\theta_u^j - a_u^j u^j(t)\right]dt + \sigma_u^j\sqrt{u^j(t)}dW_u^j(t),\\
ds^j(t) &= \left[b_s^j u^j(t) - a_s^j s^j(t)\right]dt + \sigma_s^j\sqrt{s^j(t)}dW_s^j(t),
\end{aligned}
$$

where

$$
a_i^j = \hat{a}_i^j - \lambda_i^j\left(\sigma_i^j\right)^2 \text{ and } \hat{W}_i^j(t) = W_i^j(t) + \int_0^t \gamma_i^j(l)\,dl,\ i=s,u,
$$

with

$$
\gamma_s^j(t) = \lambda_s^j\sigma_s^j\sqrt{s^j(t)} \text{ and } \gamma_u^j(t) = \lambda_u^j\sigma_u^j\sqrt{u^j(t)},
$$

for some constants λ_s^j and λ_u^j. Note, that we assume that $dW_s^I(t)$, $dW_s^G(t)$, $dW_u^I(t)$, $dW_u^G(t)$, and $dW_r(t)$ are pairwise uncorrelated. We denote the parameter vectors consisting of the unknown parameters by

$$
\Phi_{s,u}^j = (a_s^j, a_u^j, \sigma_s^j, \sigma_u^j, b_s^j, \theta_u^j, \lambda_s^j, \lambda_u^j), j\in\{I,G\}.
$$

The theoretical formulas for the observed credit spreads $S^j(t,t+\tau)$, $j\in\{I,G\}$, (compare to equation (3.94)) are given as the differences between the defaultable and non-defaultable continuous zero rates. For country $j\in\{I,G\}$ the zero rate of a defaultable bond $P^{d,j}$ at time $t\in[0,T]$ for a maturity time $T\in[t,T^*]$ is given by

$$\begin{aligned}
&R^{d,j}(t,T)\\
&= -\frac{1}{T-t}\ln P^{d,j}(t,T)\\
&= -\frac{\ln A^{d,j}(t,T)}{T-t} + \frac{B(t,T)}{T-t}r(t) + \frac{C^{d,j}(t,T)}{T-t}s^j(t) + \frac{D^{d,j}(t,T)}{T-t}u^j(t)\\
&= -\frac{\ln A(t,T)}{T-t} - \frac{2\theta_u^j}{\left(\sigma_u^j\right)^2(T-t)}\ln\left|\frac{v^j(T,T)}{v^j(t,T)}\right| + \frac{B(t,T)}{T-t}r(t)\\
&\quad+\frac{C^{d,j}(t,T)}{T-t}s^j(t) + \frac{D^{d,j}(t,T)}{T-t}u^j(t).
\end{aligned}$$

Hence,

$$\begin{aligned}
S^j(t,t+\tau) &= R^{d,j}(t,T) - R(t,T)\\
&= a^j(\tau) + c^j(\tau)s^j(t) + d^j(\tau)u^j(t),\ \tau \geq 0,
\end{aligned}$$

with

$$a^j(\tau) = -\frac{2\theta_u^j}{\left(\sigma_u^j\right)^2\tau}\ln\left|\frac{v^j(T,T)}{v^j(\tau)}\right|,\ c^j(\tau) = \frac{C^{d,j}(\tau)}{\tau},\ \text{and}\ d^j(\tau) = \frac{D^{d,j}(\tau)}{\tau},$$

where $v^j(\tau) = v^j(t,t+\tau)$, $C^{d,j}(\tau) = C^{d,j}(t,t+\tau)$, and $D^{d,j}(\tau) = D^{d,j}(t,t+\tau)$. Note that a^j, c^j, and d^j don't explicitly depend on t. Rather they depend on the time to maturity of the defaultable bond. We consider $N-$dimensional vectors of credit spreads with different maturities $\tau_1, ..., \tau_N \geq 0$ at times $t_1 < t_2 < ... < t_n$:

$$SV^j(t_k) = SV_k^j = \begin{pmatrix} S^j(t_k, t_k+\tau_1)\\ S^j(t_k, t_k+\tau_2)\\ \vdots\\ S^j(t_k, t_k+\tau_N)\end{pmatrix},\ 1 \leq k \leq n,\ j \in \{I, G\}.$$

If we denote

$$A^j = A^j(\Phi_{s,u}^j) = \begin{pmatrix} a^j(\tau_1)\\ a^j(\tau_2)\\ \vdots\\ a^j(\tau_N)\end{pmatrix},\ C^j = C^j(\Phi_{s,u}^j) = \begin{pmatrix} c^j(\tau_1) & d^j(\tau_1)\\ c^j(\tau_2) & d^j(\tau_2)\\ \vdots & \vdots\\ c^j(\tau_N) & d^j(\tau_N)\end{pmatrix},$$

and

$$X^j(t) = X^j(t, \Phi_{s,u}^j) = \begin{pmatrix} s^j(t)\\ u^j(t)\end{pmatrix},$$

where $\Phi_{s,u}^j$ is a subset of the parameter set which we want to estimate, we can define the measurement equation as

$$SV^j(t) = A^j + C^j X^j(t), \; t \geq 0.$$

The system of stochastic differential equations (3.2) and (3.3) with $X^j(t) = \left(s^j(t), u^j(t)\right)'$ can be written in matrix form as

$$dX^j(t) = \left[H^j X^j(t) + J^j\right] dt + V^j(X^j(t))dW^j(t), \tag{3.106}$$

where

$$H^j = H^j\left(\Phi^j_{s,u}\right) = \begin{pmatrix} -a^j_s & b^j_s \\ 0 & -a^j_u \end{pmatrix}, \; J^j = J^j\left(\Phi^j_{s,u}\right) = \begin{pmatrix} 0 \\ \theta^j_u \end{pmatrix},$$

$$V^j(X^j(t)) = V^j\left(X^j(t), \Phi^j_{s,u}\right) = \begin{pmatrix} \sigma^j_s\sqrt{s^j(t)} & 0 \\ 0 & \sigma^j_u\sqrt{u^j(t)} \end{pmatrix},$$

and

$$dW^j = \begin{pmatrix} dW^j_s \\ dW^j_u \end{pmatrix}.$$

We allow for noise in the sampling process of the data. Hence, we assume that for $j \in \{I, G\}$ the spreads SV^j_k are observed with measurement errors ε^j_k that are jointly normally distributed with zero mean and $(N \times N)-$dimensional covariance matrix G^j. Theoretically the matrix G^j can take various forms. But to simplify the calculations of the Kalman filter we choose the covariance matrix to be diagonal. Because trading activity and therefore bid-ask spreads usually vary across maturities (see, e.g., Geyer & Pichler (1996)) we allow for maturity-specific diagonal elements of G^j, i.e.

$$G^j = \begin{pmatrix} \left(g^j_1\right)^2 & 0 & \cdots & 0 \\ 0 & \left(g^j_2\right)^2 & \cdots & 0 \\ \vdots & \vdots & \ddots & \vdots \\ 0 & 0 & \cdots & \left(g^j_N\right)^2 \end{pmatrix}.$$

The diagonal elements g^j_i, $1 \leq i \leq N$, must be estimated together with $\Phi^j_{s,u}$, and the vector consisting of these diagonal elements is denoted by

$$\Psi^j_{s,u} = \left(g^j_1, ..., g^j_N\right).$$

Thus, the measurement equation is given by

$$SV^j_k = A^j + C^j X^j_k + \varepsilon^j_k, \tag{3.107}$$

where

$$X^j_k = X^j(t_k) \text{ and } \varepsilon^j_k \sim N\left(0, G^j\right).$$

ε^j_k is assumed to be a sequence of i.i.d. random vectors. Now, let

$$\Delta t_{k+1} = t_{k+1} - t_k, \ k = 1, ..., n-1,$$

and approximate the variance vector $V^j\left(X^j(t), \Phi^j_{s,u}\right)$ over a subinterval $(t_k, t_{k+1}]$ by its value at the beginning of the subinterval, i.e. by $V^j_k = V^j\left(X^j_k, \Phi^j_{s,u}\right)$. Then the transition equation (3.106) can be approximated by

$$dX^j(t) = \left(H^j X^j(t) + J^j\right) dt + V^j_k dW^j(t), \ t \in (t_k, t_{k+1}]. \qquad (3.108)$$

For $t \in (t_k, t_{k+1}]$ we rewrite equation (3.108) as

$$e^{\left(-H^j t\right)} dX^j(t) - e^{\left(-H^j t\right)} H^j X^j(t)\, dt = e^{\left(-H^j t\right)} \left[J^j dt + V^j_k dW^j(t)\right]. \qquad (3.109)$$

By applying the two-dimensional version of the Itô formula[71] to $e^{\left(-H^j t\right)} X^j(t)$, we get

$$d\left(e^{\left(-H^j t\right)} X^j(t)\right) = e^{\left(-H^j t\right)} dX^j(t) - e^{\left(-H^j t\right)} H^j X^j(t)\, dt. \qquad (3.110)$$

Plugging equation (3.110) into equation (3.109) yields

$$\begin{aligned} & e^{\left(-H^j t_k\right)} X^j_k - e^{\left(-H^j t_{k+1}\right)} X^j_{k+1} \\ &= \int_{t_{k+1}}^{t_k} e^{\left(-H^j l\right)} J^j dl + \int_{t_{k+1}}^{t_k} e^{\left(-H^j l\right)} V^j_k dW^j(l), \end{aligned}$$

which is equivalent to

$$X^j_{k+1} = e^{H^j \Delta t_{k+1}} X^j_k - \int_{t_{k+1}}^{t_k} e^{H^j (t_{k+1} - l)} J^j dl - \int_{t_{k+1}}^{t_k} e^{H^j (t_{k+1} - l)} V^j_k dW^j(l).$$

Easy calculations yield our final transition equation

$$X^j_{k+1} = e^{H^j \Delta t_{k+1}} X^j_k + \int_0^{\Delta t_{k+1}} e^{H^j l} J^j dl + \int_0^{\Delta t_{k+1}} e^{H^j (\Delta t_{k+1} - l)} V^j_k dW^j(l). \qquad (3.111)$$

The measurement equation (3.107) and transition equation (3.111) represent the state space formulation of our model. Now let $\widetilde{X}^j_{k+1|k}$ and $\widetilde{X}^j_{k+1}$ denote the optimal estimators[72] of the unknown state vector X^j_{k+1} based on the available information (i.e. the observed credit spreads) up to and including time t_k and t_{k+1}, respectively. The optimal estimators are the conditional means of X^j_{k+1} which are denoted by $E_k\left[X^j_{k+1}\right]$ and $E_{k+1}\left[X^j_{k+1}\right]$, respectively. Let Cov^j_k denote the covariance matrix of the estimation error, then

[71] See, e.g., Oksendal (1998), p. 48.

[72] Here we mean optimal in the mean squared error sense.

$$Cov_k^j = E_k\left[\left(X_k^j - \widetilde{X}_k^j\right)\left(X_k^j - \widetilde{X}_k^j\right)'\right].$$

Then the prediction equations are

$$\widetilde{X}_{k+1|k}^j = e^{H^j \Delta t_{k+1}} \widetilde{X}_k^j + \int_0^{\Delta t_{k+1}} e^{H^j l} J^j \, dl \tag{3.112}$$

and

$$\begin{aligned}
&Cov_{k+1|k}^j \\
&= E_k\left[(X_{k+1}^j - \widetilde{X}_{k+1|k}^j)(X_{k+1}^j - \widetilde{X}_{k+1|k}^j)'\right] \\
&= E_k\left[\left(e^{H^j \Delta t_{k+1}}\left(X_k^j - \widetilde{X}_k^j\right) + \int_0^{\Delta t_{k+1}} e^{H^j(\Delta t_{k+1}-l)} V_k^j \, dW^j(l)\right)\right. \\
&\quad \left.\cdot\left(e^{H^j \Delta t_{k+1}}\left(X_k^j - \widetilde{X}_k^j\right) + \int_0^{\Delta t_{k+1}} e^{H^j(\Delta t_{k+1}-l)} V_k^j \, dW^j(l)\right)'\right] \\
&= e^{H^j \Delta t_{k+1}} \cdot Cov_k^j \cdot e^{(H^j)' \Delta t_{k+1}} + \int_0^{\Delta t_{k+1}} e^{H^j l} \widetilde{V}_k^j \widetilde{V}_k' e^{(H^j)' l} \, dl, \qquad (3.113)
\end{aligned}$$

where

$$\widetilde{V}_k^j = E_k\left[V_k^j\right] = \begin{pmatrix} \sigma_s^j \sqrt{\widetilde{s}_k^j} & 0 \\ 0 & \sigma_u^j \sqrt{\widetilde{u}_k^j} \end{pmatrix}.$$

Note, that X_k^j and the time increments of the standard Brownian motion are independent for $t \geq t_k$. If we rewrite the credit spread vector as

$$SV_{k+1}^j = A^j + C^j\left(X_{k+1}^j - \widetilde{X}_{k+1|k}^j\right) + C^j \widetilde{X}_{k+1|k}^j + \varepsilon_{k+1}^j,$$

then the optimal estimator of the credit spread vector at time t_{k+1}, given all credit spreads up to time t_k, is given by

$$\widetilde{SV}_{k+1|k}^j = E_k\left[SV_{k+1}^j\right] = A^j + C^j \widetilde{X}_{k+1|k}^j.$$

If we denote the prediction error vector of the credit spreads by v_{k+1}^j, then

$$v_{k+1}^j = SV_{k+1}^j - \widetilde{SV}_{k+1|k}^j = SV_{k+1}^j - A^j - C^j \widetilde{X}_{k+1|k}^j. \tag{3.114}$$

Obviously, given $SV_1^j, \ldots, SV_k^j$ the vector $\begin{pmatrix} X_{k+1}^j \\ SV_{k+1}^j \end{pmatrix}$ is conditionally normally distributed with conditional mean

$$E_k\left[\begin{pmatrix} X_{k+1}^j \\ SV_{k+1}^j \end{pmatrix}\right] = \begin{pmatrix} \widetilde{X}_{k+1|k}^j \\ \widetilde{SV}_{k+1|k}^j \end{pmatrix}$$

and conditional covariance matrix

$$
\begin{aligned}
& Cov_k\left[\begin{pmatrix} X^j_{k+1} \\ SV^j_{k+1}\end{pmatrix}, \begin{pmatrix} X^j_{k+1} \\ SV^j_{k+1}\end{pmatrix}\right] \\
&= \begin{pmatrix} Cov^j_{k+1|k} & Cov_k\left[X^j_{k+1}, A^j + C^j X^j_{k+1}\right] \\ Cov_k\left[A^j + C^j X^j_{k+1}, X^j_{k+1}\right] & Cov_k\left[SV^j_{k+1}, SV^j_{k+1}\right] \end{pmatrix} \\
&= \begin{pmatrix} Cov^j_{k+1|k} & Cov^j_{k+1|k}\left(C^j\right)' \\ C^j Cov^j_{k+1|k} & F^j_{k+1} \end{pmatrix},
\end{aligned}
$$

where - according to equation (3.114) -

$$
\begin{aligned}
F^j_{k+1} &= E_k\left[v^j_{k+1}\left(v^j_{k+1}\right)'\right] \\
&= E_k\left[C^j\left(X^j_{k+1} - \widetilde{X}^j_{k+1|k}\right)\left(X^j_{k+1} - \widetilde{X}^j_{k+1|k}\right)'\left(C^j\right)'\right] + G^j \\
&= C^j Cov^j_{k+1|k}\left(C^j\right)' + G^j.
\end{aligned}
$$

If we apply results from Harvey (1989), chapter 3, we get the updating equations

$$\widetilde{X}^j_{k+1} = \widetilde{X}^j_{k+1|k} + K^j_{k+1} v^j_{k+1} \tag{3.115}$$

and

$$Cov^j_{k+1} = Cov^j_{k+1|k} - K^j_{k+1} C^j Cov^j_{k+1|k}, \tag{3.116}$$

with the so called Kalman gain matrix

$$K^j_{k+1} = Cov^j_{k+1|k}\left(C^j\right)'\left(F^j_{k+1}\right)^{-1}. \tag{3.117}$$

In the update step, the additional information given by SV^j_{k+1} is used to get a better estimate of X^j_{k+1}, the so called filtered estimate. Hence, the Kalman filter is capable of estimating the unobservable short rates s^j and u^j from observable credit spreads. In addition, for parameter estimation, one can define the likelihood function L^j, evaluated with the Kalman filter (3.112)-(3.117), by

$$
\begin{aligned}
& L^j\left(\Phi^j_{s,u}, \Psi^j_{s,u} | SV^j_1, \ldots, SV^j_n\right) \\
&= \prod_{k=1}^{n} f^j_{SV^j_k | SV^j_1, \ldots, SV^j_{k-1}}\left(\Phi^j_{s,u}, \Psi^j_{s,u}\right) \\
&= \prod_{k=1}^{n} \frac{1}{\left(\sqrt{2\pi}\right)^N} \frac{1}{\sqrt{\det F^j_k}} \\
& \quad \cdot \exp\left\{-\frac{1}{2}\left(SV^j_k - \widetilde{SV}^j_{k|k-1}\right)'\left(F^j_k\right)^{-1}\left(SV^j_k - \widetilde{SV}^j_{k|k-1}\right)\right\},
\end{aligned}
$$

where $f^j_{SV^j_k|SV^j_1,\ldots,SV^j_{k-1}}\left(\Phi^j_{s,u},\Psi^j_{s,u}\right)$ denotes the conditional probability density function of SV^j_k given all information up to and including t_{k-1}. Up to a constant, the log-likelihood function can be expressed as

$$\ln L^j\left(\Phi^j_{s,u},\Psi^j_{s,u}|SV^j_1,\ldots,SV^j_n\right) \tag{3.118}$$
$$= -\frac{1}{2}\sum_{k=1}^{n}\ln(\det F^j_k) - \frac{1}{2}\sum_{k=1}^{n}\left(\upsilon^j_k\right)'\left(F^j_k\right)^{-1}\upsilon^j_k.$$

The parameter vectors $\Phi^j_{s,u}$ and $\Psi^j_{s,u}$ can be estimated by maximizing the log-likelihood function (3.118) with respect to $\Phi^j_{s,u}$ and $\Psi^j_{s,u}$. It can be shown that such estimation yields consistent[73] and asymptotically efficient[74] estimators.

Parameter Estimation Results for s^j and $u^j, j \in \{\mathbf{I},\mathbf{G}\}$. For the parameter estimation of the two-factor credit spread model, we use seven samples of data, each of length 150 for each country, i.e. in the Kalman filter algorithm we set $N = 7$ and $n = 150$. We don't consider a time series of length 300 as in the case of non-defaultable parameter estimation because the functions involved in the credit spread parameter estimation are far more complex. We use time series with daily data from September $30th$, 1999, until May $30th$, 2000, excluding several days for which there is no bond data available, the Nelson-Siegel estimates of the credit spreads appear to be negative or the bond data is identified as an outlier. We consider the times to maturity $\tau_i = i+2$, $i = 1, ..., 7$ (expressed in years). Thus, for each $j \in \{I, G\}$ the input data consists of 150 observed spread vectors

$$SV^j_k = \begin{pmatrix} S^j(t_k, t_k+\tau_1) \\ S^j(t_k, t_k+\tau_2) \\ \vdots \\ S^j(t_k, t_k+\tau_7) \end{pmatrix}, \quad 1 \le k \le 150.$$

[73] See, e.g. Larsen & Marx (2001), p. 359: An estimator $\widehat{\Phi}_n$ is said to be consistent for Φ if it converges in probability to Φ, i.e. if for all $\varepsilon > 0$,

$$\lim_{n\to\infty}\left(\mathbf{P}\left\|\widehat{\Phi}_n - \Phi\right\| < \varepsilon\right) = 1.$$

[74] See, e.g. Larsen & Marx (2001), p. 351: Let $\widehat{\Phi}$ be a sample estimate of a parameter vector Φ. The estimate is said to be unbiased if $E\left[\widehat{\Phi}\right] = \Phi$. Now suppose that $\widehat{\Phi}$ is an unbiased estimate of Φ. The estimate $\widehat{\Phi}$ is said to be efficient if it is the case that for any other unbiased estimate $\widehat{\Phi}^*$, the following matrix is positive semidefinite:

$$E\left[\left(\widehat{\Phi}^* - \Phi\right)\left(\widehat{\Phi}^* - \Phi\right)'\right] - E\left[\left(\widehat{\Phi} - \Phi\right)\left(\widehat{\Phi} - \Phi\right)'\right].$$

Table 3.29. Kalman filter maximum likelihood parameter estimates for Italy: Part I. Sample period: 150 days from September 30th, 1999, until May 30th, 2000.

Parameter	g_1^I	g_2^I	g_3^I
Estimation	0.000418245	0.000289569	0.000236120
g_4^I	g_5^I	g_6^I	g_7^I
0.000225986	0.000057738	0.000143889	0.000241359

For the iterative calculation of the log-likelihood function (3.118) we have to initialize the Kalman filter first, i.e. we have to guess some good starting values for $\widetilde{X}^j$ and Cov_0^j. Often they are set to their unconditional expectation and unconditional covariance matrix, respectively. In our case - as the state vector consisting of the short rate spread and the uncertainty index is not observable - we use starting values that are implied by the observable data. Solving the following system of two equations

$$S^j(t_0, t_0 + \tau_1) = a^j(\tau_1) + c^j(\tau_1)\widetilde{s}_0^j + d^j(\tau_1)\widetilde{u}_0^j,$$
$$S^j(t_0, t_0 + \tau_2) = a^j(\tau_2) + c^j(\tau_2)\widetilde{s}_0^j + d^j(\tau_2)\widetilde{u}_0^j,$$

yields $\widetilde{X}_0^j = \begin{pmatrix} \widetilde{s}_0^j \\ \widetilde{u}_0^j \end{pmatrix}$. We initialize the matrix Cov_0^j simply by setting it equal to $\begin{pmatrix} \frac{1}{2} & \frac{1}{2} \\ \frac{1}{2} & \frac{1}{2} \end{pmatrix}$. After initialization we perform the 150 Kalman filter iterations to calculate the log-likelihood function (3.118). Finally, we maximize this function with respect to the two parameter vectors $\Phi_{s,u}^j = \left(a_s^j, a_u^j, \sigma_s^j, \sigma_u^j, b_s^j, \theta_u^j, \lambda_s^j, \lambda_u^j\right)$ and $\Psi_{s,u}^j = \left(g_1^j, \ldots, g_7^j\right)$. To find the maximum we apply the multi-dimensional Downhill Simplex method of Nelder & Mead (1965). Tables 3.29 and 3.30 summarize the parameter estimates of our model derived from the observed credit spreads between Germany and Italy. The average mean reversion level of the Italian short rate credit spread and the mean reversion level of the Italian uncertainty index implied by our parameter estimates equal 25 basis points and 0.049%, respectively, which nicely fit to figures 3.46 and 3.47. In case of Greece the average mean reversion level of the Greek short rate credit spread and the mean reversion level of the Greek uncertainty index are given by 164 basis points and 0.65%.

Testing the Assumptions on the Italian and Greek Kalman Filter Residuals. First we test the assumption that the standardized Kalman filter residuals are normally distributed. We apply the test statistic (3.95) to the residuals with the critical values given in table 3.21 (column $\chi^2(2)$) and find:

- For Italy: According to table 3.33 we don't reject the normal distribution hypothesis on the 5%−significance level for maturities of 3, 4, 5, and 6

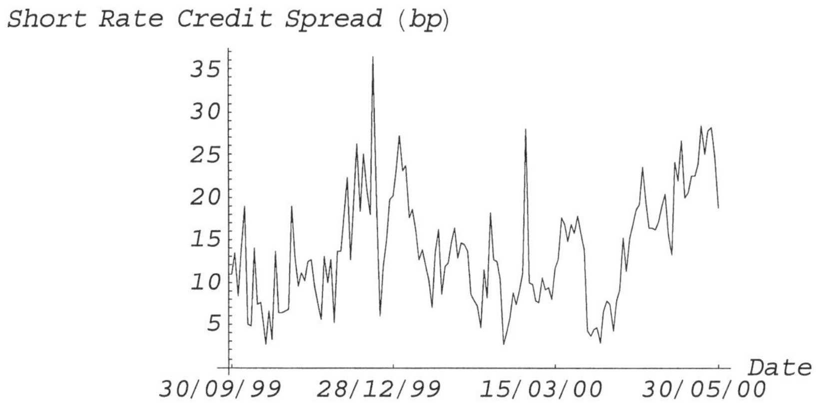

Fig. 3.46. Kalman filtered Italian short rate credit spread process. Time period: 150 days from September 30*th*, 1999, until May 30*th*, 2000.

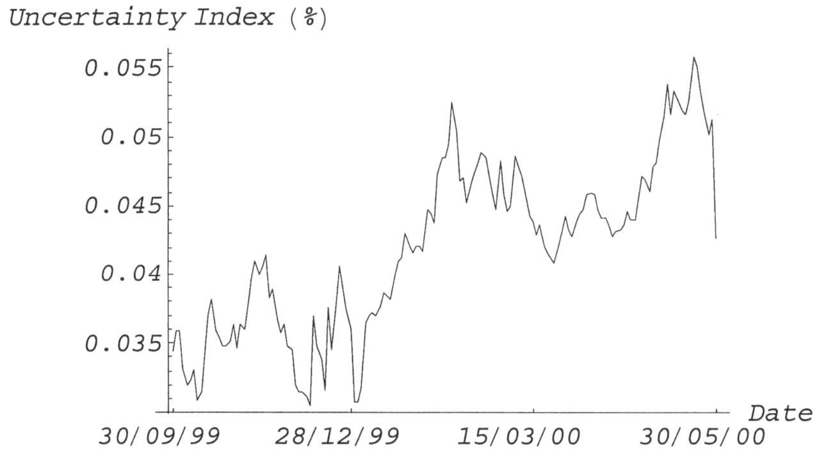

Fig. 3.47. Kalman filtered Italian uncertainty index process. Time period: 150 days from September 30*th*, 1999, until May 30*th*, 2000.

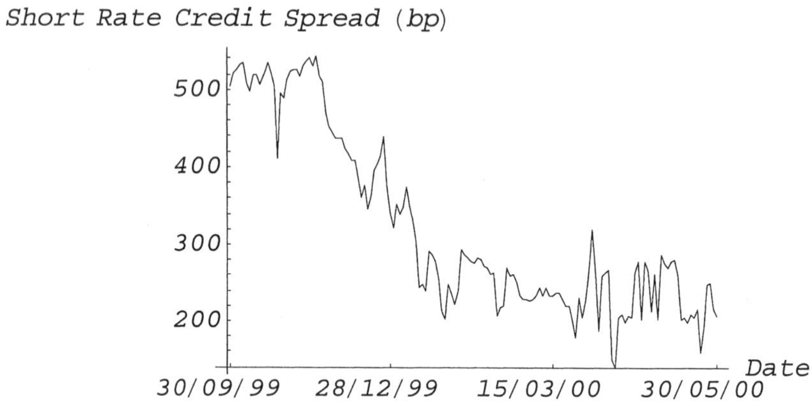

Fig. 3.48. Kalman filtered Greek short rate credit spread process. Time period: 150 days from September 30*th*, 1999, until May 30*th*, 2000.

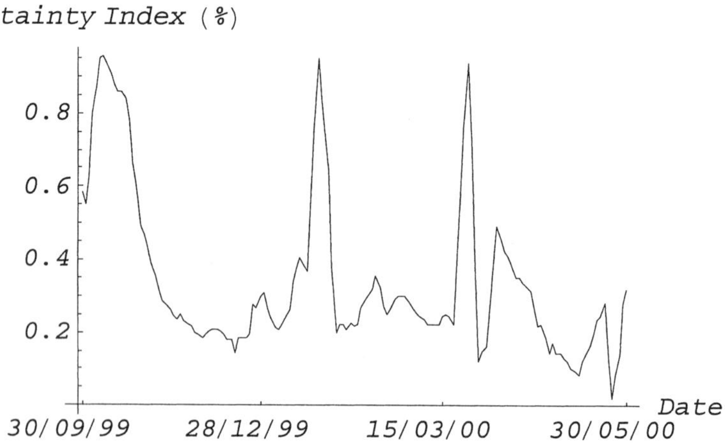

Fig. 3.49. Kalman filtered Greek uncertainty index process. Time period: 150 days from September 30*th*, 1999, until May 30*th*, 2000.

Table 3.30. Kalman filter maximum likelihood parameter estimates for Italy. Part II: Parameters of the short rate credit spread and uncertainty index processes. Sample period: 150 days from September 30th, 1999, until May 30th, 2000.

Parameter	*Estimation*	*Parameter*	*Estimation*
b_s^I	0.273903738	θ_u^I	0.000033835
a_s^I	0.053199919	a_u^I	0.068884441
σ_s^I	0.158772058	σ_u^I	0.030100786
λ_s^I	−1.868477669	λ_u^I	−1.190989999

Table 3.31. Kalman filter maximum likelihood parameter estimates for Greece: Part I. Sample period: 150 days from September 30th, 1999, until May 30th, 2000.

Parameter	g_1^G	g_2^G	g_3^G
Estimation	0.000889889	0.000557789	0.000302059
g_4^G	g_5^G	g_6^G	g_7^G
0.000240028	0.000374741	0.000452236	0.000513706

Table 3.32. Kalman filter maximum likelihood parameter estimates for Greece. Part II: Parameters of the short rate credit spread and uncertainty index processes. Sample period: 150 days from September 30th, 1999, until May 30th, 2000.

Parameter	*Estimation*	*Parameter*	*Estimation*
b_s^G	0.373241211	θ_u^G	0.00041234
a_s^G	0.147542315	a_u^G	0.06342136
σ_s^G	0.456662213	σ_u^G	0.07121165
λ_s^G	−0.23211112	λ_u^G	−1.1235121

Table 3.33. Test for normal distribution of the Italian standardized Kalman filter residuals. Sample period: 150 days from September 30th, 1999, until May 30th, 2000.

Mat.	3 years	4 years	5 years	6 years	7 years	8 years	9 years
L	1.79604	1.9342	1.0273	0.86506	7.9013	12.113	10.911

years. In addition to 3, 4, 5, and 6 years, we don't reject the normal distribution hypothesis on a 1%−significance level for 7 years. We reject the hypothesis on the 1%−significance level for maturities of 8 and 9 years.

- For Greece: According to table 3.34 we don't reject the normal distribution hypothesis on the 5%−significance level for all maturities under consideration.

Table 3.34. Test for normal distribution of the Greek standardized Kalman filter residuals. Sample period: 150 days from September 30th, 1999, until May 30th, 2000.

Mat.	3 years	4 years	5 years	6 years	7 years	8 years	9 years
L	5.88917	3.16618	0.187345	4.91219	4.94	2.7143	1.0266

Table 3.35. Box-Ljung tests for Italian standardized Kalman filter residuals. Sample period: 150 days from September 30th, 1999, until May 30th, 2000.

Mat. (years)	3	4	5	6	7	8	9
$Q-statistic$ $_{(Box-Ljung)}$	21.52	14.95	15.96	18.38	21.16	14.24	13.88

To test the standardized residuals for serial correlation we apply the Box-Ljung test on 1% and 5%- significance levels to different maturities. Under the null hypothesis that the standardized Kalman filter residuals for the specific maturities are not correlated, the Box-Ljung $Q-$statistic $Q(L)$ is asymptotically χ^2-distributed with

$$L - number\ of\ estimated\ parameters$$

degrees of freedom. As it is necessary, that the lag L grows with the number of observations, we choose $L = 2\sqrt{n} = 2\sqrt{150} \approx 24$. We reject the null hypothesis on the 1% significance level only if the test statistic is greater than the 99%-quantile of 21.67, or on the 5% significance level if the test statistic is greater than the 95%-quantile of 16.92. Table 3.35 summarizes the results of the Italian $Q-$statistics for several maturities: for the maturities of 4, 5, 8, and 9 years we find that the correlation is not significantly different from zero on the 5%-significance level, and for the maturities of 3, 6, and 7 years the correlation of the residuals is not significantly different from zero on the 1%-significance level. Table 3.36 shows the results of the Greek $Q-$statistics for several maturities: for the maturities of 4, 5, 8, and 9 years we find that the correlation is not significantly different from zero on the 1%-significance level.

Finally, we use the test for homoscedasticity as described in Harvey (1981), page 157. The 1% and 5% critical values are given in table 3.23. According to table 3.37, for Italy we don't reject the hypothesis on the 5%$-$significance level for the maturities of 3, 6, 7, 8 and 9 years. In addition, we don't reject the hypothesis of homoscedasticity on the 1%$-$level for the maturity of 5 years. According to table 3.38, for Greece we don't reject the hypothesis on the 5%$-$significance level for the maturities of 3, 6, 7, 8 and 9 years. In

Table 3.36. Box-Ljung Tests for Greek standardized Kalman filter residuals. Sample period: 150 days from September 30th, 1999, until May 30th, 2000.

Mat. (years)	3	4	5	6	7	8	9
$Q-statistic$ $(Box-Ljung)$	26.93	20.79	18.96	29.95	21.87	18.12	18.95

Table 3.37. Test for homoscedasticity of the Italian standardized Kalman filter residuals. Sample period: 150 days from September 30th, 1999, until May 30th, 2000.

Maturity	$H-statistic : H(50)$
3 years	0.81934
4 years	0.459982
5 years	0.526177
6 years	0.611612
7 years	0.700424
8 years	0.791193
9 years	0.846494

Table 3.38. Test for homoscedasticity of the Greek standardized Kalman filter residuals. Sample period: 150 days from September 30th, 1999, until May 30th, 2000.

Maturity	$H-statistic : H(50)$
3 years	0.923415
4 years	0.489632
5 years	0.538179
6 years	0.937615
7 years	0.887592
8 years	1.191873
9 years	0.976572

addition, we don't reject the hypothesis of homoscedasticity on the 1%−level for the maturities of 4 and 5 years.

Conclusion 3.6.4
Overall, based on the various tests we can conclude that the assumptions on the Kalman filter algorithm are sufficiently satisfied by our Italian and Greek data sets.

Testing of the Model Performance Based on the Italian and Greek Spread Data. In the following, we test the model performance by applying a test, e.g., used by (Titman & Torous 1989). We test the power of the model to explain the changes of observed credit spreads. If the results are satisfactory we can conclude that the model can price defaultable bonds and credit spreads accurately. Let

$$\Delta S_k^j(\tau) = S^j(t_k, t_k + \tau) - S^j(t_{k-1}, t_{k-1} + \tau),\ 2 \leq k \leq 150,\ j \in \{I, G\},$$

denote the changes of the observed credit spreads with time to maturity τ, and let $\widehat{\Delta S_k^j}(\tau)$, $2 \leq k \leq 150$, $j \in \{I, G\}$ denote the changes of the corresponding fitted credit spreads. The test equation is given by the following linear regression:

$$\Delta S_k^j(\tau) = a^j + b^j \widehat{\Delta S_k^j}(\tau) + \varepsilon_k^{j,*},\ \text{where } \varepsilon_k^{j,*} \sim N\left(0, \left(h^{j,*}\right)^2\right),\ j \in \{I, G\}. \tag{3.119}$$

We apply the test to the maturities $\tau = 3, ..., 9$ (all in years). If $\widehat{\Delta S_k^j}(\tau)$ is an unbiased estimate for $\Delta S_k^j(\tau)$, then a^j and b^j should be close to 0 and 1, respectively. In addition, the adjusted $\overline{R}^2$ statistics are a measure for the quality of the model. Table 3.39 shows the results of the regression for the Italian data:

- The test of the hypothesis that $a^I = 0$ is not rejected for all maturities on a 5%−significance level.
- The parameter values for b^I are always close to 1.
- The test of the joint hypothesis that $a^I = 0$ and $b^I = 1$ is not rejected on a 5%−significance level for all maturities but 6 years. Hence, the model prices these zero coupon bonds with acceptable accuracy.
- The adjusted $\overline{R}^2$ values vary between 71.7 % and 97.3 %.

Table 3.40 shows the results of the regression for the Greek data:

- The test of the hypothesis that $a^G = 0$ is not rejected for all maturities on a 5%−significance level.
- The parameter values for b^G are not very close to 1. Besides for the 7 year credit spreads the distance of all b^G values from 1 is greater than 0.1.
- The test of the joint hypothesis that $a^G = 0$ and $b^G = 1$ is not rejected on a 5%−significance level for all maturities but 6 years. Hence, the model prices these zero coupon bonds with acceptable accuracy.

Conclusion 3.6.5

The out-of-sample behavior is very different for Italy and Greece. For Italy the model behaves very well. For Greece the joint hypothesis that $a^G = 0$ *and* $b^G = 1$ *is not rejected only for the* 7 *year credit spreads on a* 5%−*significance level. The reason is quite obvious: for Italy we use zero coupon bonds whereas for Greece we have only coupon bonds available which induces additional noise. Furthermore, the Greek bonds are far less liquid than the Italian bonds.*

Table 3.39. Test of in-sample model explanatory power for Italy: Linear regression results.

Maturity	a^I	b^I	$\overline{R}^2$	*p-Value* $(a^I = 0)$	*p-Value* $(a^I = 0, b^I = 1)$
3 years	$6.11333 \cdot 10^{-6}$	0.938757	0.71706	0.814845	0.440907
4 years	$7.63096 \cdot 10^{-6}$	1.03916	0.83112	0.713915	0.452307
5 years	$7.73356 \cdot 10^{-6}$	1.06541	0.90744	0.610017	0.055909
6 years	$6.96232 \cdot 10^{-6}$	1.05084	0.96796	0.414893	0.004006
7 years	$5.64142 \cdot 10^{-6}$	1.01643	0.97338	0.452594	0.355994
8 years	$3.9653 \cdot 10^{-6}$	0.975102	0.88281	0.80251	0.320922
9 years	$2.05174 \cdot 10^{-6}$	0.934458	0.71720	0.937439	0.396085

Table 3.40. Test of in-sample model explanatory power for Greece: Linear regression results.

Maturity	a^G	b^G	$\overline{R}^2$	*p-Value* $(a^G = 0)$	*p-Value* $(a^G = 0, b^G = 1)$
3 years	$2.4842 \cdot 10^{-6}$	0.73553	0.82381	0.980181	0
4 years	$2.1248 \cdot 10^{-6}$	0.89199	0.94441	0.960677	0.01273
5 years	$3.1223 \cdot 10^{-6}$	0.86653	0.99282	0.807109	0.01196
6 years	$4.8976 \cdot 10^{-6}$	0.89471	0.97768	0.805628	0.03453
7 years	$7.0636 \cdot 10^{-6}$	0.90389	0.93128	0.825408	0.05342
8 years	$9.3651 \cdot 10^{-6}$	0.86207	0.87587	0.818706	0.01627
9 years	0.0000116379	0.8776	0.81765	0.809207	0.02481

Out-of-Sample Testing Based on the Italian and Greek Spread Data. In the previous section we did some in-sample-testing to examine the performance of the defaultable term structure model. To complete the analysis of the model we add an out-of-sample-test. We analyze if we can apply the model with the estimated parameters to the pricing of credit spreads after May 30*th*, 2000. Therefore we consider 70 additional time steps $t_k^* = 1, ..., 70$, for $k = 1, ..., 70$, from May 30*th*, 2000, until October 23*rd*, 2000, and apply the Kalman filter to the observed credit spreads for this time period. Note, that we keep the parameters of tables 3.29, 3.30, 3.31, and 3.32 fixed, i.e. we filter the values for $s^j(t)$ and $u^j(t)$, $j \in \{I, G\}$, and determine the credit spread predictors with given values for the vectors $\Phi^j_{s,u}$, $\Psi^j_{s,u}$, $j \in \{I, G\}$. To test the performance of the out-of-sample model we apply the linear regression (3.119) to the new data. We test the maturities $\tau_i = i + 2$, $i = 1, ..., 7$ (expressed in years). Table 3.41 shows the results of the regression for Italy:

- The test of the hypothesis that $a^I = 0$ is not rejected for all maturities on a 5%-significance level.

Table 3.41. Test of out-of-sample model explanatory power for Italy: Linear regression results.

Maturity	a^I	b^I	$\overline{R}^2$	*p-Value* $(a^I = 0)$	*p-Value* $(a^I = 0, b^I = 1)$
3 years	0.0000150071	0.90796	0.689351	0.828829	0.471914
4 years	0.0000109933	1.03144	0.802159	0.852410	0.134735
5 years	0.0000104826	1.07602	0.888956	0.813476	0.265945
6 years	0.0000122546	1.07674	0.952238	0.667574	0.037469
7 years	0.0000153419	1.05566	0.951507	0.590850	0.145532
8 years	0.0000190276	1.02615	0.862036	0.701499	0.219308
9 years	0.000022813	0.995921	0.714741	0.766278	0.044077

- The test of the joint hypothesis that $a^I = 0$ and $b^I = 1$ is not rejected on a 1%−significance level for all maturities, on a 5%-significance level for all maturities but 6 and 9 years. Hence, the model prices these zero coupon bonds with acceptable accuracy.
- The adjusted $\overline{R}^2$ values vary between 68.9 % and 95.2 %.

Overall the test suggests that the out-of-sample behavior of the model is very encouraging for the Italian data set.
Table 3.42 shows the results of the regression for Greece:

- The test of the hypothesis that $a^G = 0$ is not rejected on a 5%-significance level for all maturities but the 5 year credit spreads.
- The test of the joint hypothesis that $a^G = 0$ and $b^G = 1$ is not rejected on a 1%−significance level for all maturities but the 5 year credit spreads, on a 5%-significance level for all maturities but 3, 4, and 5 years. Hence, the model prices these zero coupon bonds with acceptable accuracy.
- The adjusted $\overline{R}^2$ values vary between 78.4 % and 99.3 %.

Conclusion 3.6.6
As with the in-sample tests, the model behaves better for the Italian than for the Greek data. But overall we find that the three-factor defaultable term structure model is able to describe real world credit spreads realistically.

Table 3.42. Test of out-of-sample model explanatory power for Greece: Linear regression results.

Maturity	a^G	b^G	$\overline{R}^2$	*p-Value* $(a^G = 0)$	*p-Value* $(a^G = 0, b^G = 1)$
3 years	0.000038583	0.89947	0.899371	0.546014	0.028564
4 years	0.000031957	0.89833	0.969776	0.283150	0.015647
5 years	0.000029042	0.90245	0.992684	0.027074	0.009645
6 years	0.000028369	0.91061	0.987908	0.064070	0.054732
7 years	0.000028880	0.92303	0.953614	0.303275	0.214875
8 years	0.000029837	0.94031	0.883109	0.493757	0.382732
9 years	0.000030760	0.96279	0.783838	0.610533	0.198473

3.7 Portfolio Optimization under Credit Risk

3.7.1 Introduction

The process of performing an optimal asset allocation basically deals with the problem of finding a portfolio that maximizes the expected utility of the portfolio manager. As long as it is supposed that the returns of the portfolio assets follow a normal distribution, the return distribution of any portfolio will be normal, too. In this case, as it is done throughout the traditional portfolio theory introduced by Markowitz (1952) and Sharpe (1964), the problem of finding an expected utility maximizing portfolio for a risk averse portfolio manager, represented by a concave utility function, can be restricted to finding an optimal combination of the two parameters mean and variance. This dramatically simplifies the whole asset allocation process and is known as mean-variance analysis. It is the aim of the portfolio manager to find a portfolio that maximizes the expected return given a specific risk level or a portfolio that minimizes the risk given a specific return level. In this case risk is measured by the variance of the portfolio return. Unfortunately, selection rules based on the two parameters mean and variance are of limited generality. They are optimal only if the utility function is quadratic or the return distribution is normal. Furthermore, the use of variance as a measure of risk for asymmetric return distributions has already been questioned by financial theorists like, e.g., Markowitz (1991), pages 188-201. He states that portfolio analyses based on semi-variance tend to produce better portfolios than those based on variance. Unfortunately, the computing cost involved with the use of semi-variance is much higher than with the use of variance. We need the entire joint distribution for the first technique while we only need the covariance matrix for the latter.

Extensive research has been done to derive concepts for ordering uncertain prospects resulting in principles like the stochastic dominance of order 1,

2 or 3 (see, e.g., Bawa (1975) or Martin, Cox & MacMinn (1988)). Bawa argues that it is quite reasonable to assume that the average investor decides consistent with a finite, increasing and concave utility function with decreasing absolute risk aversion, and that there is a strong rationale for using mean-lower partial variance rules as an approximation for the portfolio selection of this kind of investor. Under this rule one portfolio is better than the other if its mean is not lower and its lower partial variance is not higher than that of the other portfolio at every possible benchmark. As the lower partial variance is a generalization of the semi-variance, this follows the suggestion of Markowitz, still leaving the computational problems, because we have to calculate the lower partial variances for each distribution at every possible benchmark. If we can not assume special distributions to simplify that problem, the solution is often approximated by optimizing with a finite set of representative benchmarks. The so-called lower partial moments can be considered as a generalization of the lower partial variance (see, e.g., Harlow & Rao (1989) or Harlow (1991)). Therefore, they are consistent with the previous concept. Because they measure the risk of falling below a given benchmark, they have become very popular measures for the risk of a portfolio, especially when the return distribution is asymmetric. Consequently, we will use lower partial moments to control the downside risk of the portfolio exposure. Because we do not have any information on the distribution of the possible or optimal portfolios we approximate the distribution function based on a simulation model. The asset universe in our sample are sovereign bonds with different times to maturity and qualities of the issuers. Some of these bonds may default and thus stop paying interest. Or the value of a bond may fall only due to a downgrading of the issuing country.

We use our three-factor defaultable term structure model with $\beta = 0$ introduced in section 3.2 for pricing sovereign bonds. Based on parameter estimates, determined by Kalman filter techniques, we simulate the prices of the bonds for a future time horizon. For each future time step and for each given portfolio composition these scenarios yield distributions of future cash flows and portfolio values. In section 3.7.2 we show how the portfolio composition can be optimized by maximizing the expected final value or return of the portfolio under a set of constraints. One set of restrictions is due to a minimum required cash flow per period to cover the liabilities of a company. The second set limits the tolerated risk. As discussed above, both risks are measured by lower partial moments to account for the downside potential we have to consider. To visualize our methodology, in section 3.7.3 we present a case study for a portfolio consisting of various German, Italian, and Greek sovereign bonds.

3.7.2 Optimization

This section describes the problem of maximizing the final value of a portfolio under limited risk. We assume that there is a planning horizon $T \in [0, T^*]$. The universe of assets consists of n different types of sovereign bonds $i \in \{1, ..., n\}$ from Germany, Italy (I), and Greece (G) with maturities $0 \leq T_1, ..., T_n \leq T^*$. The prices of the bonds at any time $t \in [0, T]$ are given by $P_1(t), ..., P_n(t)$. Note, that in this context $P_i(t)$ is a general notation for the price of a bond - not a priori distinguishing between defaultable and non-defaultable bonds, or zero coupon and coupon bonds, i.e. $P_i(t) \in \{P(t, T_i), P^{d,I}(t, T_i), P^{d,G}(t, T_i), P_c(t, T_i), P_c^{d,I}(t, T_i), P_c^{d,G}(t, T_i)\}$. $\varphi = (\varphi_1, ..., \varphi_n)$ denotes the vector of the portfolio weights. In addition to the bond positions there is a cash account whose value at time $t \in [0, T]$ is denoted by $C_0(\varphi, t)$.

We consider three sources of risk:

- Market Risk caused by changing German interest rates over time.
- Spread Risk caused by the possibility of changes of the qualities of the Greece and Italian sovereign bonds.
- Default Risk caused by the possibility of default. As in the previous sections we assume Germany to be without any default risk. If we decide to invest in default risky sovereign bonds we may lack in coupon payments which we do not receive in case of default[75].

We want to find a portfolio allocation that satisfies certain limit conditions. More precisely, we set the following restrictions on our portfolio:

- A restriction on the portfolio value: We don't want the portfolio value fall below some given benchmark B at specific times $t \in \mathcal{T}_\mathsf{B} = \{T_1^\mathsf{B}, ..., T_{m_\mathsf{B}}^\mathsf{B}\} \subset [0, T]$, $m_\mathsf{B} \in \mathbb{N}$.
- A restriction on the cash flows: We assume a stream of liabilities $\mathsf{L}(t)$ at times $t \in \mathcal{T}_\mathsf{L} = \{T_1^\mathsf{L}, ..., T_{m_\mathsf{L}}^\mathsf{L}\} \subset [0, T]$, $m_\mathsf{L} \in \mathbb{N}$, which have to be covered by the coupon payments of the bond portfolio. Because these coupon payments are under default risk we also set a restriction on the cash flows. We don't want them fall below the corresponding liability.

In addition, to the definition of the risk sources and the limits we make the following assumptions:

Assumption 3.7.1

1. *All coupon payments, received between liability payment dates are given to a cash account earning continuous interest of R_{ca}, i.e. a cash flow $C_i(t)$*

[75] Although we have to admit that in practice the default risk of Italy and Greece is almost zero.

received from bond $i \in \{1, ..., n\}$ *at time* $t \in \left(T_{l-1}^{\mathsf{L}}, T_l^{\mathsf{L}}\right]$, $l \in \{1, ..., m_{\mathsf{L}}\}$, $T_0^{\mathsf{L}} = 0$, *will have a cash value of*

$$C_i\left(t, T_l^{\mathsf{L}}\right) = C_i(t) \cdot e^{R_{ca}\left(t, T_l^{\mathsf{L}}\right) \cdot \left(T_l^{\mathsf{L}} - t\right)}$$

on the cash account at time T_l^{L}.

2. *Country* $j \in \{I, G\}$ *defaults as soon as the corresponding uncertainty process* u^j *crosses some default boundary* $\xi^{d,j}$. *The default boundary is implicitly given and can be evaluated from the default probability of country* j. *Therefore, the time of the default event can be expressed as* $T^{d,j} = \inf\left\{t \in [0, T] : u^j(t) > \xi^{d,j}\right\}$. *As usual, we denote the default indicator function of country* $j \in \{I, G\}$ *by* H^j.
3. *In case of a default of a coupon bond* i *with price* $P_i(t) = P_c^{d,j}(t, T_i)$ *and maturity* $T_i \in \left[T^{d,j}, T^*\right]$ *before time* T *there are no more coupon payments, but a recovery payment of* $w \cdot P_c^{d,j}\left(T^{d,j}-, T_i\right)$ *fixed at time* $T^{d,j}$. *As usual,* $w \in [0,1]$ *denotes the recovery rate and* $P_c^{d,j}\left(T^{d,j}-, T_i\right)$ *is the price of the bond just before default.*
4. *The recovery payment is not available before the original maturity time* T_i *of the defaulted bond. Then the recovery payment causes a cash flow of*
$$Z\left(T^{d,j}, T_i\right) = e^{R_{ca}^{d,j}\left(T^{d,j}, T_i\right) \cdot \left(T_i - T^{d,j}\right)} \cdot w \cdot P_c^{d,j}\left(T^{d,j}-, T_i\right)$$
on the cash account. $R_{ca}^{d,j}\left(T^{d,j}, T_i\right)$ *denotes the interest rate earned on the recovery payment for the time period* $\left[T^{d,j}, T_i\right]$.

Hence, at each coupon payment date $0 \leq t_{i1} < \cdots < t_{in_i} = T_i$, if $j \in \{1, ..., n_i - 1\}$, the cash flow of a defaultable bond is

$$C_i^d(t_{ij}) = C_i(t_{ij}) \cdot \left(1 - H_{t_{ij}}^j\right)$$

and

$$C_i^d(T_i) = C_i(T_i) \cdot (1 - H_{T_i}) + H_{T_i} \cdot Z\left(T^{d,j}, T_i\right).$$

The cash flows within each liability period $\left(T_{l-1}^{\mathsf{L}}, T_l^{\mathsf{L}}\right]$, $l \in \{1, ..., m_{\mathsf{L}}\}$, are then put on the cash account accruing to a cash value of

$$C_{i0}\left(T_{l-1}^{\mathsf{L}}, T_l^{\mathsf{L}}\right) = \sum_{\substack{j \in \{1, ..., n_i\} \\ t_{ij} \in \left(T_{l-1}^{\mathsf{L}}, T_l^{\mathsf{L}}\right]}} C_i^d(t_{ij}) \cdot e^{R_{ca}\left(t_{ij}, T_l^{\mathsf{L}}\right) \cdot \left(T_l^{\mathsf{L}} - t_{ij}\right)}$$

at the liability payment dates $T_l^{\mathsf{L}} \in \mathcal{T}_{\mathsf{L}}$. In case of a non-defaultable bond this value is simply

$$C_{i0}\left(T_{l-1}^{\mathsf{L}}, T_l^{\mathsf{L}}\right) = \sum_{\substack{j \in \{1, ..., n_i\} \\ t_{ij} \in \left(T_{l-1}^{\mathsf{L}}, T_l^{\mathsf{L}}\right]}} C_i(t_{ij}) \cdot e^{R_{ca}\left(t_{ij}, T_l^{\mathsf{L}}\right) \cdot \left(T_l^{\mathsf{L}} - t_{ij}\right)}.$$

Hence, the time $T_l^{\mathsf{L}} \in \mathcal{T}_{\mathsf{L}}$ cash value of the portfolio cash flows within period $\left(T_{l-1}^{\mathsf{L}}, T_l^{\mathsf{L}}\right]$, $l \in \{1, ..., m_{\mathsf{L}}\}$, is given by

$$C_0\left(\varphi, T_{l-1}^{\mathsf{L}}, T_l^{\mathsf{L}}\right) = \sum_{i=1}^{n} \varphi_i \cdot C_{i0}\left(T_{l-1}^{\mathsf{L}}, T_l^{\mathsf{L}}\right)$$

leading to a total value of the cash account at time T_l^{L} of

$$C_0\left(\varphi, T_l^{\mathsf{L}}\right) = C_0\left(\varphi, T_{l-1}^{\mathsf{L}}\right) \cdot e^{R_{ca}\left(T_{l-1}^{\mathsf{L}}, T_l^{\mathsf{L}}\right)\cdot\left(T_l^{\mathsf{L}} - T_{l-1}^{\mathsf{L}}\right)} + C_0\left(\varphi, T_{l-1}^{\mathsf{L}}, T_l^{\mathsf{L}}\right) - L\left(T_l^{L}\right)$$

for all $l \in \{1, ..., m_{\mathsf{L}}\}$. We set

$$C_0\left(\varphi, 0\right) = \varphi_0\left(0\right) = C_0 - \sum_{i=1}^{n} \varphi_i \cdot P_i\left(0\right)$$

with C_0 denoting the initial budget to be invested at time $t = 0$.

Having estimated the parameters of the stochastic processes r, s^I, u^I, s^G, and u^G we now consider the vector of risk factors

$$\mathsf{F} = \left(\mathsf{F}_1, ..., \mathsf{F}_5\right) = \left(r, s^I, u^I, s^G, u^G\right).$$

The optimization problem is based on a simulation of the vector F over time. For this simulation, let $V_i\left(0\right)$ and $V_i\left(t\right)$ denote the value of a given stochastic variable V_i at times 0 and t, respectively. In our case, this may be either the cash account ($i = 0$) or the dirty price of bond i ($i = 1, ..., n$) plus potential coupon payments between times 0 and t, everything seen from time 0. According to our model we know that the values $V_i\left(t\right)$ are dependent on the vector F of risk factors and that the functional relation between the risk vector and the future value of V_i is known, i.e.

$$V_i\left(t\right) = V_i\left(\mathsf{F}, t\right), \; i = 1, ..., n.$$

Under this assumption we simulate the risk vector F and get values

$$\mathsf{F}^k = \left(\mathsf{F}_1^k, ..., \mathsf{F}_5^k\right)$$

with probabilities $p_k > 0$, $k = 1, ..., K$. Dependent on these simulated values of risk factors we get values

$$V_i^k\left(t\right) = V_i\left(\mathsf{F}^k, t\right), \; k = 1, ..., K,$$

for each $i = 1, .., n$. For each possible bond portfolio $\varphi = \left(\varphi_1, \cdots, \varphi_n\right)$, which we consider to be fixed from time 0 until the end of the planning horizon T, the future time t portfolio value $V\left(\varphi, t\right)$ is given by the random variable

$$V\left(\varphi, t\right) = \sum_{i=1}^{n} \varphi_i \cdot V_i\left(t\right)$$

with $V(\varphi, 0)$ denoting the portfolio value at time 0. The simulated portfolio value $V^k(\varphi, t)$ based on the values $V_i^k(t)$ is given by

$$V^k(\varphi, t) = \sum_{i=1}^{n} \varphi_i \cdot V_i^k(t), \; k = 1, ..., K.$$

To restrict the downside risk of the future portfolio value at time $t \in \mathcal{T}_{\mathsf{B}}$ we consider the discrete version of the lower partial moment of order $l \in \mathbb{N}$. Hereby, the investor specific benchmark $\mathsf{B}(\mathsf{t}) \in \mathbb{R}$ is defined by

$$LPM_l(\varphi, V, \mathsf{B}, t) = \sum_{\substack{k=1,...,K \\ V^k(\varphi,t) < \mathsf{B}(\mathsf{t})}} p_k \cdot \left(\mathsf{B}(\mathsf{t}) - V^k(\varphi, t)\right)^l. \tag{3.120}$$

The lower partial moment only considers realizations of the future value of V below the investor specific benchmark measured to a power of l. For $l = 0$ this is the probability that the random future value falls below the given benchmark, which is referred to as shortfall probability. Setting the benchmark equal to 0 this is the probability of loss. For $l = 1$, the lower partial moment is the expected deviation of the future values below the benchmark, sometimes called (expected) regret. For $l = 2$, the lower partial moment is weighting the squared deviations below the benchmark and thus is the semi-variance if the benchmark is set equal to the expected future value. For the ease of exposition we assume that the simulated lower partial moment is equal to the real one. If this is not the case the equality has to be interpreted as an approximation where we suppose that the number and quality of the simulations is sufficiently high. For a more detailed discussion of lower partial moments see, e.g., Harlow (1991) or Zagst (2001).

A portfolio manager or trader may be restricted to specific trading limits. Therefore, we introduce absolute lower (s_i) and upper bounds (S_i) for the amount φ_i of security $i = 1, ..., n$ in the portfolio and claim that

$$s_i \leq \varphi_i \leq S_i, \; i = 1, ..., n.$$

For $A^l_{\mathsf{B}}(t), A^l_{\mathsf{L}}(t) \in \mathbb{R}$ and $l \in \{0, 1, 2\}$, let us consider the following optimization problem

$$
(P)\begin{cases}
\sum_{i=1}^{n} \varphi_i \cdot E^{\mathbf{P}}\left[V_i(T)\right] \rightarrow \max \\
LPM_l(\varphi, V, \mathsf{B}, t) \leq A_{\mathsf{B}}^l(t), \ l \in \{0,1,2\}, t \in T_{\mathsf{B}} \\
LPM_l(\varphi, C_0, 0, t) \leq A_{\mathsf{L}}^l(t), \ l \in \{0,1,2\}, t \in T_{\mathsf{L}} \\
s_i \leq \varphi_i \leq S_i, \ i = 0, ..., n \\
C_0\left(\varphi, T_l^{\mathsf{L}}\right) = C_0\left(\varphi, T_{l-1}^{\mathsf{L}}\right) \cdot e^{R_{ca} \cdot \left(T_l^{\mathsf{L}} - T_{l-1}^{\mathsf{L}}\right)} + \\
\qquad + C_0\left(\varphi, T_{l-1}^{\mathsf{L}}, T_l^{\mathsf{L}}\right) - L\left(T_l^{\mathsf{L}}\right), \ l = 1, ..., m_{\mathsf{L}} \\
C_0(\varphi, 0) = \varphi_0 = C_0 - \sum_{i=1}^{n} \varphi_i \cdot V_i(0).
\end{cases}
$$

Note, that we have set $R_{ca}\left(T_{l-1}^{\mathsf{L}}, T_l^{\mathsf{L}}\right) \equiv R_{ca}$ for the ease of exposition. To implement the optimization problem let us have a closer look at the general LPM constraint, i.e. the LPM restriction for the future value V. We choose the numbers $m_k < 0$ to be sufficiently small and the numbers $M_k > 0$, $m_k^l > 0$ and $M_k^l > 0$ to be sufficiently large and define the constraints

$$M_k \cdot y_k + V^k(\varphi, t) \geq \mathsf{B}(\mathsf{t}) \tag{A}$$

$$m_k \cdot (1 - y_k) + V^k(\varphi, t) < \mathsf{B}(\mathsf{t}) \tag{B}$$

$$0 \leq \left(V^k(\varphi, t) - \mathsf{B}(\mathsf{t})\right)^l + (-1)^{l-1} \cdot w_k^l \leq M_k^l \cdot (1 - y_k) \tag{C}$$

$$0 \leq w_k^l \leq m_k^l \cdot y_k \tag{D}$$

with $w_k^l \in \mathbb{R}$, $y_k \in \{0,1\}$ for all $k = 1, ..., K$, where we consider $l \in \{0,1,2\}$ to be arbitrary but fixed as well as $t \in (0, T]$. A proof of the following lemma can be found in Zagst (2001).

Theorem 3.7.1.
Let $t \in (0, T]$, and $l \in \{0,1,2\}$ be arbitrary but fixed and $y_k \in \{0,1\}$ for all $k = 1, ..., K$.

a) Let condition (A) be satisfied. If $V^k(\varphi, t) < \mathsf{B}(\mathsf{t})$, then $y_k = 1$ for all $k = 1, ..., K$.
b) Let condition (B) be satisfied. If $V^k(\varphi, t) \geq \mathsf{B}(\mathsf{t})$, then $y_k = 0$ for all $k = 1, ..., K$.
c) Let conditions (A) and (B) be satisfied. Then, for all $k = 1, ..., K$:

$$V^k(\varphi, t) < \mathsf{B}(\mathsf{t}) \quad \textit{if and only if } y_k = 1.$$

d) Let $l \in \{0, 2\}$. Under conditions (A), (C), and (D), we have:

$$LPM_l(\varphi, V, \mathsf{B}, t) \leq \sum_{k=1}^{K} p_k \cdot w_k^l.$$

e) Under conditions (A), (B), (C), and (D), we have:

$$LPM_l(\varphi, V, \mathsf{B}, t) = \sum_{k=1}^{K} p_k \cdot w_k^l.$$

Note, that for the special case of $l = 0$, we can conclude that $w_k^l = 1$ if $y_k = 1$ and that $w_k^l = 0$ if $y_k = 0$ under conditions (C) and (D). Hence,

$$LPM_0(\varphi, V, \mathsf{B}, t) = \sum_{k=1}^{K} p_k \cdot y_k \tag{3.121}$$

under the additional conditions (A) and (B), with "$\leq$" instead of "$=$" if only condition (A) is satisfied in addition to (C) and (D). Using theorem 3.7.1 we can replace the lower partial moment constraint

$$LPM_l(\varphi, V, \mathsf{B}, t) \leq A^l \tag{LPM}$$

by the constraint

$$\sum_{k=1}^{K} p_k \cdot w_k^l \leq A^l \tag{E}$$

for $A^l \in \mathbb{R}$ and $l \in \{0, 1, 2\}$, if conditions (A), (B), (C), and (D) are satisfied. Hence, instead of using constraint (LPM), we can use inequality (E) if we add conditions (A), (B), (C), and (D) to the optimization problem. Furthermore, we can omit condition (B) if $l \in \{0, 2\}$. For $l = 0$ condition (LPM) is called shortfall constraint and the corresponding A^0, in this case chosen to be an element of $(0, 1)$, is called shortfall probability. Usually all commercial optimization tools use inequalities of the form $\leq$ or $\geq$ and a precision expressed by the smallest absolute number that can be recognized numerically within the tool and which will be denoted by $\varepsilon > 0$ here. That's why we rewrite equation (B) in the following form:

$$m_k \cdot (1 - y_k) + V^k(\varphi, t) \leq \mathsf{B}(t) - \varepsilon. \tag{B'}$$

For $l \in \{0, 1, 2\}$ and $t \in (0, T]$ let us therefore denote the set of restrictions (A), (B'), (C), and (D) by

$$MIP_l\left(\varphi, y^k, w_k^l, V^k, \mathsf{B}, t\right),\ k = 1, ..., K.$$

This yields the following optimization problem (P_1) which is (approximately) equivalent to (P):

$$
(P_1)\left\{
\begin{array}{l}
\sum_{k=1}^{K} p_k \cdot V^k(\varphi, T) \to \max \\
\quad MIP_l\left(\varphi, y^k, w_k^l, V^k, \mathsf{B}, t\right), \; k=1,...,K, \; t \in T_{\mathsf{B}} \\
\quad MIP_l\left(\varphi, y_0^k, w_{0k}^l, C_0, 0, t\right), \; k=1,...,K, \; t \in T_{\mathsf{L}} \\
\quad y_k, y_0^k \in \{0,1\}, \; k=1,...,K \\
\quad w_k^l, w_{0k}^l \in \mathbb{R} \\
\quad \sum_{k=1}^{K} p_k \cdot w_k^l \leq A_B^l, \; l \in \{0,1,2\} \\
\quad \sum_{k=1}^{K} p_k \cdot w_{0k}^l \leq A_L^l, \; l \in \{0,1,2\} \\
\quad s_i \leq \varphi_i \leq S_i, \; i=1,...,n \\
\quad C_0\left(\varphi, T_l^{\mathsf{L}}\right) = C_0\left(\varphi, T_{l-1}^{\mathsf{L}}\right) \cdot e^{R_{ca}\cdot\left(T_l^{\mathsf{L}} - T_{l-1}^{\mathsf{L}}\right)} + \\
\qquad\qquad + C_0\left(\varphi, T_{l-1}^{\mathsf{L}}, T_l^{\mathsf{L}}\right) - L\left(T_l^{\mathsf{L}}\right), \; l=1,...,m_{\mathsf{L}} \\
\quad C_0(\varphi, 0) = \varphi_0 = C_0 - \sum_{i=1}^{n} \varphi_i \cdot V_i(0).
\end{array}
\right.
$$

The variables of (P_1) to be optimized are $\varphi_0, ..., \varphi_n$, $y_k, y_0^k \in \{0,1\}$, and $w_k^l, w_{0k}^l \in \mathbb{R}$, $k = 1, ..., K$. Hence, we have to solve a mixed-integer linear program which can be rather easily done by commercial optimization tools[76].

3.7.3 Case Study: Optimizing a Sovereign Bond Portfolio

Data and Estimated Parameters. For the following case study we use process parameters estimated from observed data of German zero rates and credit spreads between AAA–rated German and AA–rated Italian as well as AAA–rated German and $(A-)$– rated Greek government bonds. As in

[76] If we define

$$
a_{ik} := \begin{cases} S_i, & \text{if } V_i^k(t) < 0 \\ s_i, & \text{if } V_i^k(t) \geq 0 \end{cases} \quad \text{and} \quad b_{ik} := \begin{cases} s_i, & \text{if } V_i^k(t) < 0 \\ S_i, & \text{if } V_i^k(t) \geq 0 \end{cases}
$$

for $i = 1, ..., n$ and $k = 1, ..., K$, we can choose

$$
M_k = \mathsf{B} - \sum_{i=1}^{n} a_{ik} \cdot V_i^k(t), \; m_k = \mathsf{B} - \varepsilon - \sum_{i=1}^{n} b_{ik} \cdot V_i^k(t),
$$

$$
M_k^l = \left[\sum_{i=1}^{n} b_{ik} \cdot V_i^k(t) - \mathsf{B}\right]^l, \text{ and } m_k^l = \left[\mathsf{B} - \sum_{i=1}^{n} a_{ik} \cdot V_i^k(t)\right]^l,
$$

$k = 1, ..., K$, $l \in \{0,1,2\}$, for a practical application.

Table 3.43. Estimated parameters for the German bond market.

Parameter	*Estimation*
θ_r	0.014413
a_r	0.238205
σ_r	0.015581
λ_r	−0.086076
$r(0)$	0.042434

Table 3.44. Estimated parameters for the Italian bond market.

Parameter	*Estimation*	*Parameter*	*Estimation*
b_s^I	0.274800	θ_u^I	0.000031
a_s^I	0.047687	a_u^I	0.068696
σ_s^I	0.158324	σ_u^I	0.030482
λ_s^I	−1.898668	λ_u^I	−1.228143
$s^I(0)$	0.001296	$u^I(0)$	0.005112

section 3.6.3 we assume throughout that the German bonds are default risk free whereas the Italian and Greek bonds are defaultable. We consider a 12 months time series of daily bond prices from November $1st$, 1999, until October $23rd$, 2000, provided by Reuters Information Services. The data set is a subset of the data considered in section 3.6.3. Whereas in section 3.6.3 we wanted to demonstrate the in-sample and out-of-sample properties of our model, i.e. we used one part of the data for parameter estimation and the other part for out-of-sample model validation, we now estimate the parameters for the case study from the latest available data. In addition, this choice of the time frame ensures that we don't get too much noise in the data due to convergence effects of the yields of the members of the European Monetary Union. Therefore, we repeat the whole Kalman Filter estimation for this specific subset of data. The results of the Kalman filter estimation are summarized in tables 3.43-3.45. Note, that we make exactly the same theoretical assumptions on the model as in section 3.6.3, especially we consider the stochastic processes r, s^I, s^G, u^I, u^G, but for simplification of the case study simulation assume that the deterministic function $\theta_r(t)$ is constant, i.e. $\theta_r(t) = \theta_r$ for all $t \geq 0$. Hence, we have to estimate one additional parameter.

If the Kalman filter is set up correctly and the theoretical formulas based on the estimated parameters can explain the observed data well, the standardized residuals of the Kalman filter, i.e. the standardized difference between the new observations and the corresponding Kalman filter forecasts, should be standard normally distributed. One method that we have already applied in section 3.6.3 is to refer the test statistic

Table 3.45. Estimated parameters for the Greek bond market.

Parameter	*Estimation*	*Parameter*	*Estimation*
b_s^G	0.343225	θ_u^G	0.000392
a_s^G	0.167814	a_u^G	0.074952
σ_s^G	0.446885	σ_u^G	0.067231
λ_s^G	−0.215937	λ_u^G	−1.109091
$s^G(0)$	0.002325	$u^G(0)$	0.012704

Table 3.46. Statistics for testing the quality of the Kalman filter estimation for different maturities.

Maturity	*L (Ger)*	*L (I)*	*L (G)*
3 years	11.593	0.598	12.161
4 years	9.201	4.134	5.973
5 years	5.202	0.940	2.076
6 years	12.850	0.223	11.662
7 years	6.234	0.982	10.513
8 years	3.985	9.048	5.812
9 years	1.729	8.619	2.945

$$L = n \cdot \left(\frac{skewness^2}{6} + \frac{excess\ kurtosis^2}{24} \right)$$

to the chi-squared distribution with two degrees of freedom (see, e.g., Harvey (1989), page 260, for a similar test). The critical values for 5% and 1% are 5.99 and 9.21, respectively. The null hypothesis is rejected if L is greater than the corresponding critical value. According to table 3.46 we get the following results:

- Germany: For the maturities 5, 8, and 9 years the normal distribution hypothesis isn't rejected on a 5%-significance level, and for the maturities 4, 5, 7, 8, and 9 years it isn't rejected on a 1%−significance level. The normal distribution hypothesis is rejected on both significance levels for the maturities 3 and 6 years.
- Italy: The normal distribution hypothesis is not rejected on a 5% - significance level for the maturities 3, 4, 5, 6, and 7 years, and on a 1%− significance level for all maturities.
- Greece: The normal distribution hypothesis is not rejected on both, a 5%− and a 1%−significance level for the maturities 4, 5, 8, and 9 years. The normal distribution hypothesis is rejected on both significance levels for the maturities 3, 6, and 7 years.

One of the critical model assumptions is that there is no correlation between any of the standard Brownian motions driving the underlying processes. Be-

Table 3.47. Statistics for testing the correlation of the filtered residuals dW_r, dW_s^j, and dW_u^j, $j \in \{I, G\}$.

	dW_s^I	dW_s^G	dW_u^I	dW_u^G	dW_r
dW_s^I	1				
dW_s^G	1.279	1			
dW_u^I	−0.819	−1.122	1		
dW_u^G	0.501	−1.684	1.974	1	
dW_r	−0.945	−1.702	−0.114	0.472	1

lieving in the estimated parameters we now use the filtered values for r, s^j and u^j to test for this assumption. We therefore apply the test statistic

$$T_{n-2} = \frac{R \cdot \sqrt{n-2}}{\sqrt{1-R^2}}$$

with R denoting the well-known sample correlation coefficient of the corresponding filtered values for dW_r, dW_s^j and dW_u^j, $j \in \{I, G\}$. Larsen & Marx (2001), page 626, show that under the assumption (null hypothesis) that the residuals are uncorrelated, the test statistic follows a Student-t distribution with $n-2$ degrees of freedom. The critical values for 5% and 1% are 1.97 and 2.60, respectively. The null hypothesis is rejected if $|T_{n-2}|$ is greater than the corresponding critical value. According to table 3.47 the null hypothesis is only rejected on a 5%−significance level for dW_u^I and dW_u^G and is not rejected on a 1%−significance level for all residuals. In our simulations we therefore assume that dW_r, dW_s^j and dW_u^j, $j \in \{I, G\}$ are pairwise uncorrelated.

Monte Carlo Simulation and Optimization in Practice. For the case study we choose a planning horizon of $T = 2$ years and 5 sovereign bonds with annual coupon payments for each of the countries Germany, Italy, and Greece, i.e. $n = 15$. The specification and dirty prices of the bonds at time $t = 0$ with a notional of 100 *Euro* each are summarized in table 3.48.

Furthermore, we set $\mathcal{T}_{\mathsf{B}} = \mathcal{T}_{\mathsf{L}} = \{6M, 1Y, 1Y6M, 2Y\}$ with a liability stream of $(50{,}000; 100{,}000; 200{,}000; 400{,}000)$ *Euro*, $R_{ca} = R_{ca}^{d,I} = R_{ca}^{d,G} = 0$, and a budget of $C_0 = 1$ *Mio. Euro*. As mentioned above, $V_i(t)$ is considered to be the dirty price of bond $i \in \{1, ..., n\}$ plus accumulated cash flows over time accrued at an interest of R_{ca}. For the optimization we choose $K = 100$ simulations, absolute lower bounds of $s_i = 0$ and upper bounds of $S_i = +\infty$, $i \in \{1, ..., n\}$, a benchmark of $\mathsf{B}(\mathrm{t}) = C_0$ for all $t \in \mathcal{T}_{\mathsf{L}}$, $l = 0$, i.e. we are dealing with shortfall constraints, and $A_{\mathsf{B}}^0(t) = 1\% = A_{\mathsf{L}}^0(t)$. The probabilities of default and the resulting default boundaries $\xi^{d,I}$ and $\xi^{d,G}$ are given in table 3.49.

According to the rather low default probabilities, no default took place in our simulations. Therefore, the shortfall constraint for covering the liability

Table 3.48. Specification of the portfolio universe.

i	*Country*	*Maturity*	*Coupon*	*Dirty Price*
1	Germany	$1.0Y$	6%	101.40
2	Germany	$1.5Y$	6%	104.92
3	Germany	$2.0Y$	6%	102.42
4	Germany	$2.5Y$	6%	104.92
5	Germany	$3.0Y$	6%	103.17
6	Italy	$1.0Y$	7%	100.94
7	Italy	$1.5Y$	7%	104.88
8	Italy	$2.0Y$	7%	101.91
9	Italy	$2.5Y$	7%	104.80
10	Italy	$3.0Y$	7%	102.79
11	Greece	$1.0Y$	8%	101.96
12	Greece	$1.5Y$	8%	106.74
13	Greece	$2.0Y$	8%	103.54
14	Greece	$2.5Y$	8%	107.02
15	Greece	$3.0Y$	8%	104.79

Table 3.49. Default probabilities and default boundaries for Italy and Greece.

	Default probability	Default boundary
Italy	0.02%	0.014659
Greece	0.04%	0.047047

stream degenerates to an exact cash flow matching restriction as stated, e.g., in Elton & Gruber (1991), pages 565-566.

Example 3.7.1.
In the first example we do not consider any shortfall or liability constraints. Our aim is simply to maximize the expected final portfolio value, i.e. the dirty price of the portfolio plus the value of the cash account at time T, allowing for a budget of C_0. The optimal portfolio consists of 9,658 of the 2 year 8% Greek bonds, i.e. a cash value of 1 *Mio. Euro.* This portfolio has an expected final value (including previous coupon payments) of 1,120,337 *Euro* corresponding to an expected rate of return of 5.68%. The probabilities of falling below the benchmark C_0 at times $t \in \mathcal{T}_L$ are given by the vector $(5\%, 2\%, 1\%, 0\%)$. The liability stream is not covered by this portfolio. The value of the cash account compared to the liability stream is shown in figure 3.50.

Example 3.7.2.
For the second example we add shortfall constraints for the portfolio value at times $t \in \mathcal{T}_L$ to the budget constraint of example 3.7.1 and get an optimal portfolio consisting of

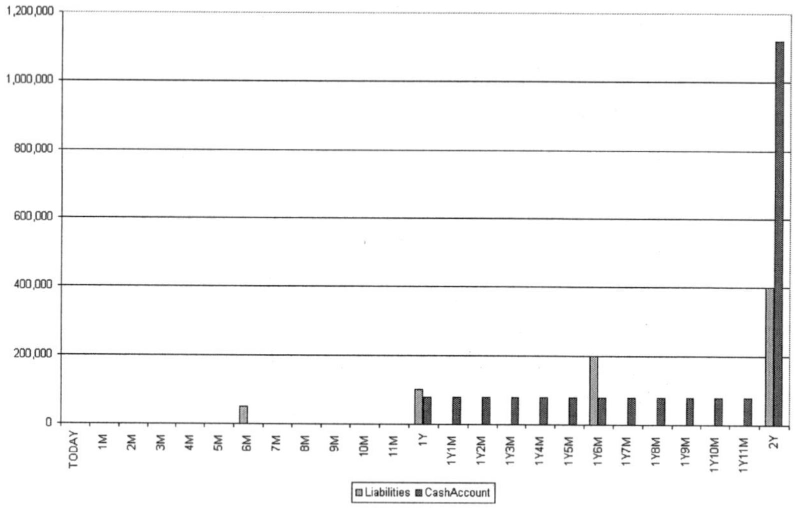

Fig. 3.50. Value of the cash account in example 3.7.1 over time compared to the liability stream.

3,008 (311,428 *Euro*)	of the 2 year 8% Greece bond
2,485 (253,287 *Euro*)	of the 2 year 7% Italian bond
3,604 (369,108 *Euro*)	of the 2 year 6% German bond
641 (66,177 *Euro*)	of the 3 year 6% German bond

This portfolio has an expected final value (including previous coupon payments) of 1,105,841 *Euro* corresponding to an expected rate of return of 5.03%. The probabilities of falling below the benchmark C_0 at times $t \in \mathcal{T}_L$ are given by the vector (1%, 1%, 0%, 1%). To satisfy the shortfall constraints, the investment into the Greek bond is reduced and shifted towards the less risky Italian and German bonds. Unfortunately, the liability stream is not covered by this portfolio. The optimal country allocation as well as the value of the cash account compared to the liability stream are shown in figures 3.51 and 3.52.

Example 3.7.3.
In this example we add the liability constraints (but not the shortfall constraints of example 3.7.2) at times $t \in \mathcal{T}_L$ to the budget constraint of example 3.7.1 and get an optimal portfolio which consists of

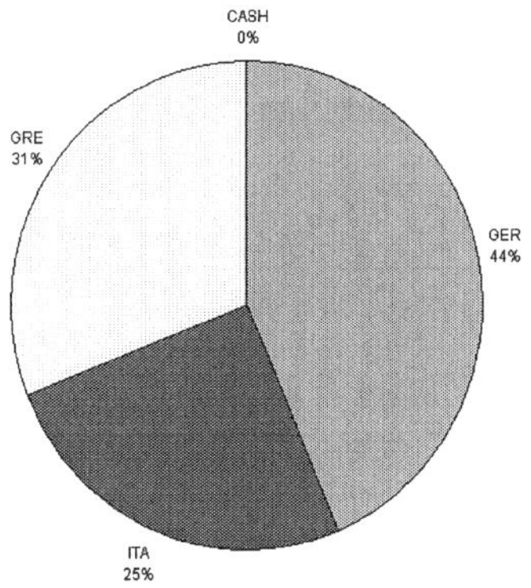

Fig. 3.51. Optimal country allocation in example 3.7.2.

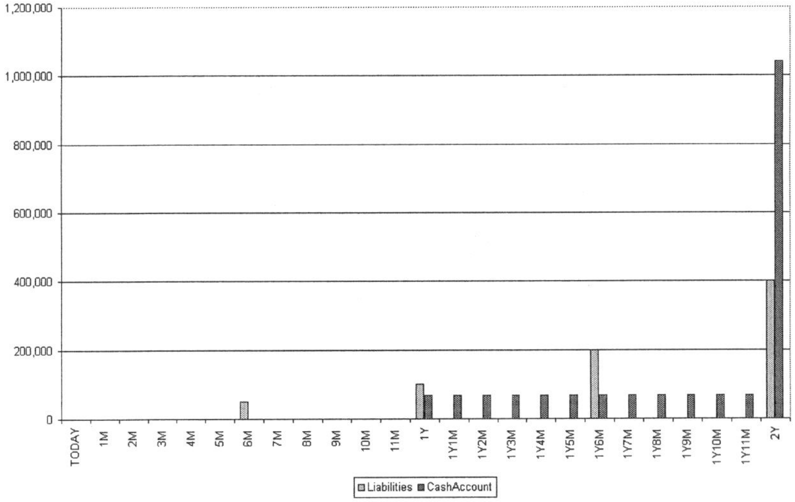

Fig. 3.52. Value of the cash account in example 3.7.2 over time compared to the liability stream.

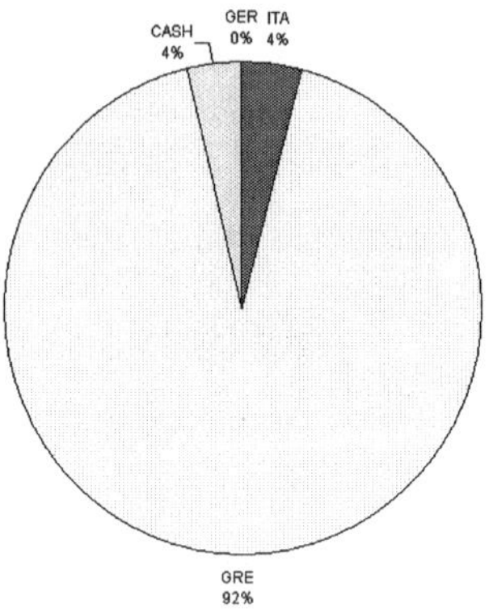

Fig. 3.53. Optimal country allocation in example 3.7.3.

7,009 (725,703 *Euro*)	of the 2 year 8% Greece bond
1,852 (197,672 *Euro*)	of the 1.5 year 8% Greece bond
411 (41,440 *Euro*)	of the 1 year 7% Italian bond
35,185 *Euro*	on the cash account.

This portfolio has an expected final value (including previous coupon payments) of 1,106,961 *Euro* corresponding to an expected rate of return of 5.08%. The maturities of the bonds are chosen according to the liability payment dates $t \in \mathcal{T}_L$. The probabilities of falling below the benchmark C_0 at times $t \in \mathcal{T}_L$ are given by the vector (5%, 2%, 0%, 0%). Unfortunately, the shortfall constraints are not met by this portfolio. The optimal country and maturity allocation as well as the value of the cash account compared to the liability stream are shown in figures 3.53, 3.54, and 3.55.

Example 3.7.4.
We add the shortfall and liability constraints at times $t \in \mathcal{T}_L$ to the budget constraint of example 3.7.1 and get an optimal portfolio which consists of

3,050 (315,815 *Euro*)	of the 2 year 8% Greece bond
2,133 (217,370 *Euro*)	of the 2 year 7% Italian bond
1,869 (196,040 *Euro*)	of the 1.5 year 7% Italian bond
465 (46,900 *Euro*)	of the 1 year 7% Italian bond
1,825 (186,959 *Euro*)	of the 2 year 6% German bond
36,916 *Euro*	on the cash account.

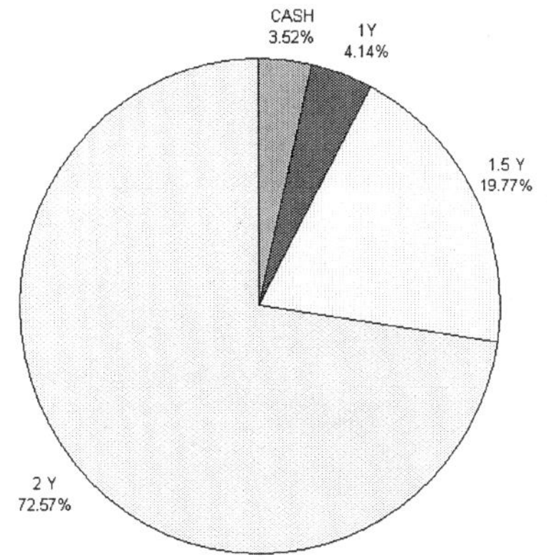

Fig. 3.54. Optimal maturity allocation in example 3.7.3.

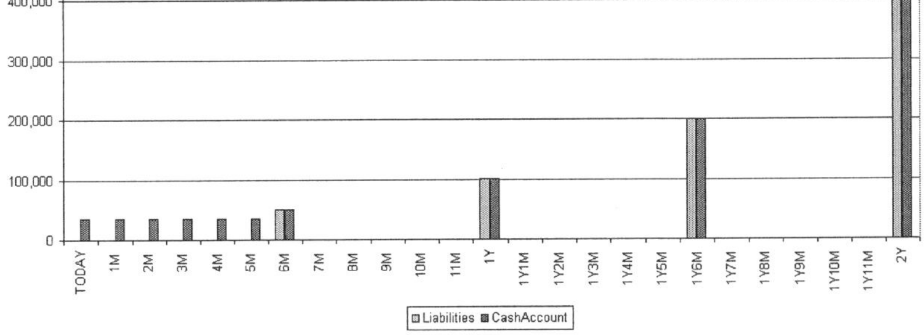

Fig. 3.55. Value of the cash account in example 3.7.3 over time compared to the liability stream.

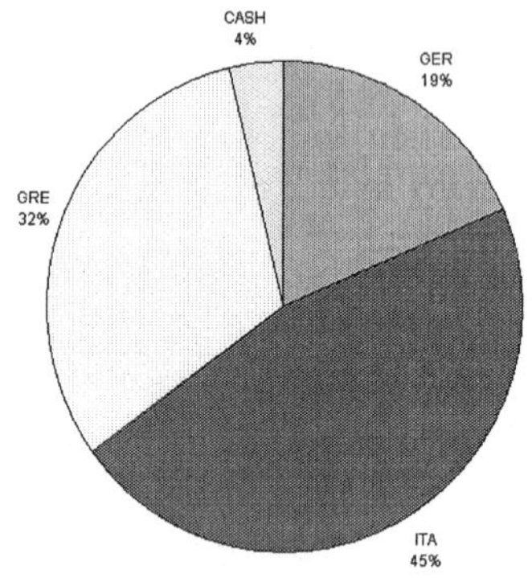

Fig. 3.56. Optimal country allocation in example 3.7.4.

This portfolio has an expected final value (including previous coupon payments) of 1,099,185 *Euro* corresponding to an expected rate of return of 4.73%. We now have a portfolio with maturity times according to the liability payment dates $t \in \mathcal{T}_\mathsf{L}$ and a country diversification including Italian and German bonds to increase the safety of the portfolio, i.e. to reduce the probability of falling below the given benchmark. The probabilities of falling below the benchmark C_0 at times $t \in \mathcal{T}_\mathsf{L}$ are given by the vector $(1\%, 1\%, 0\%, 0\%)$. The optimal country and maturity allocation as well as the value of the cash account compared to the liability stream are shown in figures 3.56, 3.57, and 3.58.

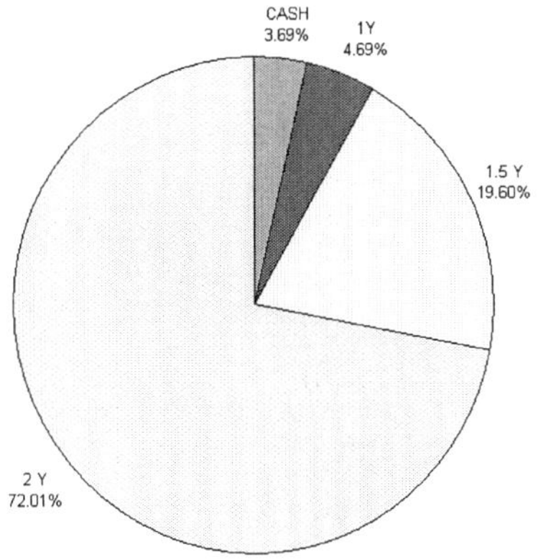

Fig. 3.57. Optimal maturity allocation in example 3.7.4.

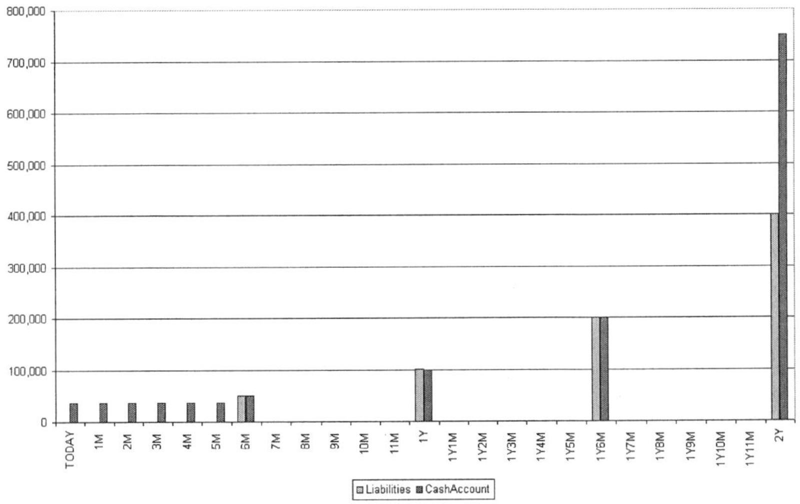

Fig. 3.58. Value of the cash account in example 3.7.4 over time compared to the liability stream.

A. S&P's Definition of Default

S&P's definition of corporate default :. "A default is recorded upon the first occurrence of a payment default on any financial obligation, rated or unrated, other than a financial obligation subject to a bona fide commercial dispute; an exception occurs when an interest payment missed on the due date is made within the grace period. Preferred stock is not considered a financial obligation; thus, a missed preferred stock dividend is not normally equated to a default. Distressed exchanges, on the other hand, are considered defaults whenever the debtholders are offered substitute instruments with lower coupons, longer maturities, or any other diminished financial terms."
- *Ratings Performance 1999: Stability & Transition* (2000)

S&P's definition of sovereign default :. "Sovereign debt is considered in default in any of the following circumstances:

- For local and foreign currency bonds, notes, and bills, when either scheduled debt service is not paid on the due date, or an exchange offer of new debt contains terms less favorable than the original issue.
- For central bank currency, when notes are converted into new currency of less than equivalent face value.
- For bank loans, when either scheduled debt service is not paid on the due date, or a rescheduling of principal and/or interest is agreed to by creditors at less favorable terms than the original loan. Such rescheduling agreements covering short- and long-term bank debt are considered defaults even when, for legal or regulatory reasons, creditors deem forced rollover of principal to be voluntary.

In addition, many rescheduled sovereign bank loans are ultimatively extinguished at a discount from their original face value. Typical deals have included exchange offers (such as for those linked to the issuance of Brady bonds), debt/equity swaps related to government privatization programs, and/or buybacks for cash. Standard & Poor's considers such transactions as defaults because they contain terms less favorable to creditors than the original obligation."
- *Ratings Performance 2000: Default, Transition, Recovery, and Spreads* (2001)

B. Technical Proofs

B.1 Proof of Lemma 3.2.1

Proof.
We want to find solutions of the SDE (3.4). First we show, that there exists a weak solution:
$\theta_r(t)$ is bounded on $[0, T^*]$, i.e. there exists a $\theta_r \geq 0$ such that $|\theta_r(t)| \leq \theta_r$ $\forall\, t \in [0, T^*]$. Because $b(.)$ and $\sigma(.)$ are continuous functions, we know that for every given initial distribution of (r_0, u_0, s_0) with compact support there exists a solution $X = (X_t)_{0 \leq t \leq T^*}$ which possibly blows up or explodes in finite time[1]. But since there exists a positive constant K, e.g.,

$$K = \max\left(a_r^2 + \sigma_r^2 + 2\theta_r a_r, a_u^2 + b_s^2 + \sigma_u^2 + 2\left(\theta_u a_u + b_s a_s\right),\right.$$
$$\left. a_s^2 + \sigma_s^2 + 2b_s a_s, \theta_r^2 + \theta_u^2 + \sigma_r^2 + \sigma_u^2 + \sigma_s^2 + 2\left(\theta_u a_u + \theta_r a_r\right)\right)$$

such that ($\|\cdot\|$ denotes the Euclidean norm)

$$\begin{aligned}
&\|\sigma(r_t, u_t, s_t)\|^2 + \|b(r_t, u_t, s_t)\|^2 \\
&= \sum_{j=1}^{3}\sum_{i=1}^{3} |\sigma_{ij}(r_t, u_t, s_t)|^2 + \sum_{i=1}^{3} |b_i(r_t, u_t, s_t)|^2 \\
&= \sigma_r^2 |r_t|^{2\beta} + \sigma_u^2 |u_t| + \sigma_s^2 |s_t| + |\theta_r(t) - a_r r_t|^2 + |\theta_u - a_u u_t|^2 + |b_s u_t - a_s s_t|^2 \\
&\leq \left(a_r^2 + \sigma_r^2 + 2\theta_r a_r\right) r_t^2 + \left(a_u^2 + b_s^2 + \sigma_u^2 + 2\left(\theta_u a_u + b_s a_s\right)\right) u_t^2 \\
&\quad + \left(a_s^2 + \sigma_s^2 + 2b_s a_s\right) s_t^2 + \left(\theta_r^2 + \theta_u^2 + \sigma_r^2 + \sigma_u^2 + \sigma_s^2 + 2\left(\theta_u a_u + \theta_r a_r\right)\right) \\
&\leq K\left(1 + r_t^2 + u_t^2 + s_t^2\right) = K(1 + \|(r_t, s_t, u_t)\|^2),
\end{aligned}$$

[1] Use theorem 2.3, p. 173, in Ikeda & Watanabe (1989b): Given continuous functions
$\sigma : \mathbb{R}^d \to \mathbb{R}^d \times \mathbb{R}^r$ and $b : \mathbb{R}^d \to \mathbb{R}^d$. Consider the stochastic differential equation

$$dX(t) = \sigma(X(t))\, dW(t) + b(X(t))\, dt.$$

Then for any probability μ on $\left(\mathbb{R}^d, \mathcal{B}\left(\mathbb{R}^d\right)\right)$ with compact support, there exists a solution
$X = (X(t))$ such that the law of $X(0)$ coincides with μ, i.e., a solution does exist locally but, in general, blows up (or explodes) in finite time. As always, $\mathcal{B}$ denotes the Borel σ–algebra.

we can conclude that the solution doesn't have any blow ups or explosions and therefore must coincide with an ordinary weak solution[2].
In the second part of the proof we show that a weak solution is pathwise unique[3]:
Let us suppose that there are two weak solutions X and $\widetilde{X}$ with $X_0 = \widetilde{X}_0$ a.s. We define their difference by

$$\begin{aligned}\Delta X_t &= \left(\Delta X_t^1, \Delta X_t^2, \Delta X_t^3\right)' = X_t - \widetilde{X}_t \\ &= \int_0^t \left\{b\left(X_l\right) - b\left(\widetilde{X}_l\right)\right\} dl + \int_0^t \left\{\sigma\left(X_l\right) - \sigma\left(\widetilde{X}_l\right)\right\} dW_l.\end{aligned}$$

For $x_j,\, y_j \in \mathbb{R},\, j = 1, 2, 3$,

$$|\sigma_{ii}(x_1, x_2, x_3) - \sigma_{ii}(y_1, y_2, y_3)| \le \max(\sigma_r, \sigma_u, \sigma_s)\sqrt{|x_i - y_i|} \tag{B.1}$$

and

$$|b_i\left(x_1, x_2, x_3\right) - b_i\left(y_1, y_2, y_3\right)| \le \max\left(a_r, a_u, a_s, b_s\right) \sum_{i=1}^{3} |x_i - y_i| \tag{B.2}$$

for $i = 1, 2, 3$. Let $h : [0, \infty) \to [0, \infty)$ with $h\left(x\right) = \max(\sigma_r, \sigma_u, \sigma_s)\sqrt{x}$. Then h has the following properties:

1. $h\left(0\right) = 0$.

[2] Use theorem 2.4, p. 177, in Ikeda & Watanabe (1989b): Given the continuous functions $\sigma : \mathbf{R}^{\mathrm{d}} \to \mathbf{R}^{\mathrm{d}} \times \mathbf{R}^{\mathrm{r}}$ and $b : \mathbf{R}^{\mathrm{d}} \to \mathbf{R}^{\mathrm{d}}$ satisfying the condition

$$\|\sigma\left(X\right)\|^2 + \|b\left(X\right)\|^2 \le K\left(1 + \|X\|^2\right)$$

for some positive constant K, then for any solution of equation (3.4) such that $E\left(\|X\left(0\right)\|^2\right) < \infty$, we have $E\left(\|X\left(t\right)\|^2\right) < \infty$ for all $t > 0$.

[3] There are two concepts of uniqueness that can be associated with weak solutions:

1. Suppose that whenever (X, W), $(\Omega, \mathcal{F}, \mathbf{P})$, $(\mathcal{F}_t)$ and $\left(\widetilde{X}, W\right)$, $(\Omega, \mathcal{F}, \mathbf{P})$, $\left(\widetilde{\mathcal{F}}_t\right)$ are weak solutions to (3.4) with common Brownian motion W (relative to possibly different filtrations) on a common probability space $(\Omega, \mathcal{F}, \mathbf{P})$ and with common initial value, i.e $\mathbf{P}\left[X_0 = \widetilde{X}_0\right] = 1$, the two processes X and $\widetilde{X}$ are indistinguishable: $\mathbf{P}\left[X_t = \widetilde{X}_t; \forall\, 0 \le t < \infty\right] = 1$. We say then that pathwise uniqueness holds for equation (3.4).
2. We say that uniqueness in the sense of probability law holds for equation (3.4) if, for any two weak solutions (X, W), $(\Omega, \mathcal{F}, \mathbf{P})$, $(\mathcal{F}_t)$ and $\left(\widetilde{X}, \widetilde{W}\right)$, $\left(\widetilde{\Omega}, \widetilde{\mathcal{F}}, \widetilde{\mathbf{P}}\right)$, $\left(\widetilde{\mathcal{F}}_t\right)$, with the same initial distribution, i.e., $\mathbf{P}\left[X_0 \in \Gamma\right] = \widetilde{\mathbf{P}}\left[\widetilde{X}_0 \in \Gamma\right]\ \forall\, \Gamma \in \mathcal{B}\left(\mathbf{R}^d\right)$, the two processes X and $\widetilde{X}$ have the same law.

Uniqueness in the sense of probability law does not imply pathwise uniqueness, but pathwise uniqueness does imply uniqueness in the sense of probability law.

2. h is strictly increasing.
3. $\int_{(0,\varepsilon)} h^{-2}(x)\,dx = \infty \ \forall\ \varepsilon > 0.$

Define a sequence $(a_n)_{n=0}^{\infty}$ such that

$$a_0 = 1,\ a_n = a_{n-1} \cdot \exp\left[-n \max^2(\sigma_r, \sigma_u, \sigma_s)\right],\ n \geq 1.$$

Then the following statements hold:

1. $(a_n)_{n=0}^{\infty} \subseteq (0,1]$.
2. $(a_n)_{n=0}^{\infty}$ is strictly decreasing with $\lim_{n\to\infty} a_n = 0$.
3. $\int_{a_n}^{a_{n-1}} h^{-2}(x)\,dx = \int_{a_n}^{a_{n-1}} \frac{1}{x \max^2(\sigma_r,\sigma_u,\sigma_s)}dx = \frac{1}{\max^2(\sigma_r,\sigma_u,\sigma_s)} \ln \frac{a_{n-1}}{a_n} = n.$

Define a function $\rho_n : \mathbb{R} \times [0,1] \times \left(0, \frac{a_{n-1}-a_n}{2}\right] \to \mathbb{R}$ such that

$$\rho_n(x,\delta,\varepsilon) = \begin{cases} \frac{1+\delta}{nh^2(a_n+\varepsilon)\varepsilon}(x-a_n) & ,\ \text{if } x \in (a_n, a_n+\varepsilon] \\ \frac{1+\delta}{nh^2(x)} & ,\ \text{if } x \in (a_n+\varepsilon, a_{n-1}-\varepsilon) \\ \frac{1+\delta}{nh^2(a_{n-1}-\varepsilon)\varepsilon}(a_{n-1}-x) & ,\ \text{if } x \in [a_{n-1}-\varepsilon, a_{n-1}) \\ 0 & ,\ \text{if } x \notin (a_n, a_{n-1}) \end{cases}.$$

Then the following statements hold:

1. ρ_n is a continuous function on each three-dimensional compact subinterval of $\mathbb{R} \times [0,1] \times \left(0, \frac{a_{n-1}-a_n}{2}\right]$.
2. $$0 \leq \rho_n(x,\delta,\varepsilon) \leq \frac{2}{nh^2(x)} \tag{B.3}$$
   on $\mathbb{R} \times [0,1] \times \left(0, \frac{a_{n-1}-a_n}{2}\right]$.
3. $\int_{a_n}^{a_{n-1}} \rho_n(x,\delta,\varepsilon)\,dx$ is continuous on each two-dimensional compact subinterval of $[0,1] \times \left(0, \frac{a_{n-1}-a_n}{2}\right]$.
4. There exists a pair $(\delta^*, \varepsilon^*) \in [0,1] \times \left(0, \frac{a_{n-1}-a_n}{2}\right]$ such that $\int_{a_n}^{a_{n-1}} \rho_n(x,\delta^*,\varepsilon^*)\,dx = 1$:
   $\lim_{\varepsilon\to 0,\varepsilon>0} \int_{a_n}^{a_{n-1}} \rho_n(x,1,\varepsilon)\,dx = \int_{a_n}^{a_{n-1}} \frac{2}{nh^2(x)}dx = 2$. Hence, there exists an $\varepsilon^* \in \left(0, \frac{a_{n-1}-a_n}{2}\right]$ such that $\int_{a_n}^{a_{n-1}} \rho_n(x,1,\varepsilon^*)\,dx > 1$. On the other hand, $\int_{a_n}^{a_{n-1}} \rho_n(x,0,\varepsilon^*)\,dx < 1$. Because of the continuity of $\int_{a_n}^{a_{n-1}} \rho_n(x,\delta,\varepsilon^*)\,dx$ in δ, there exists a $\delta^* \in [0,1]$ such that $\int_{a_n}^{a_{n-1}} \rho_n(x,\delta^*,\varepsilon^*)\,dx = 1$. We define $\rho_n^*(x) = \rho_n(x,\delta^*,\varepsilon^*)$.

For $k = 1,2,3$ we define approximation sequences $\Psi_n^{(k)} : \mathbb{R}^3 \to \mathbb{R}$ such that

$$\Psi_n^{(k)}(x_1,x_2,x_3) = \int_0^{|x_k|} \int_0^y \rho_n^*(u)\,du\,dy.$$

Then the following hold:

1. $\Psi_n^{(k)}$ is even and twice continuously differentiable.
2. $\frac{\partial \Psi_n^{(k)}}{\partial x_j} = 0 \; \forall \; j \neq k, \; \forall \; n.$
3. $\left| \frac{\partial \Psi_n^{(k)}}{\partial x_j} \right| \leq 1 \; \forall \; j, \; \forall \; n:$
   $\left| \frac{\partial \Psi_n^{(k)}}{\partial x_k} \right| = \left| \int_0^{|x_k|} \rho_n^* (u) \, du \right| \leq \int_{a_n}^{a_{n-1}} \rho_n^* (u) \, du = 1.$
4. For all k:
$$\Psi_n^{(k)}(x_1, x_2, x_3) \longrightarrow |x_k| \tag{B.4}$$
   for $n \to \infty$ and for all $x \in \mathbb{R}^3$:
   $\lim_{n\to\infty} \Psi_n^{(k)}(x_1, x_2, x_3) = \lim_{n\to\infty} \int_0^{|x_k|} \int_0^y \rho_n^* (u) \, du dy$
   $= \int_0^{|x_k|} \lim_{n\to\infty} \int_{a_n}^{a_{n-1}} \rho_n^* (u) \, du dy = |x_k| \, .$
5. $\left| \Psi_n^{(k)} (x_1, x_2, x_3) \right| \leq \int_0^{|x_k|} \int_0^y |\rho_n^* (u)| \, du dy \leq \int_0^{|x_k|} \int_{a_n}^{a_{n-1}} \rho_n^* (u) \, du dy$
   $\leq |x_k| \, .$ Then,
$$E \left[\left| \Psi_n^{(k)} (x_1, x_2, x_3) \right| \right] \leq E \left[|x_k| \right] < \infty, \tag{B.5}$$
   as $E \left[|x_k|^2 \right] < \infty$ by footnote 2.

If we apply Itô's formula (see footnote 3.110) to $\Psi_n^{(k)}$ and ΔX_t, we get

$$\begin{aligned}
&\Psi_n^{(k)} (\Delta X_t) \\
&= \sum_{i=1}^{3} \int_0^t \frac{\partial \Psi_n^{(k)}}{\partial x_i} (\Delta X_l) \, d\Delta X_i (l) + \frac{1}{2} \sum_{1 \leq i,j \leq 3} \int_0^t \frac{\partial \Psi_n^{(k)}}{\partial x_i \partial x_j} (\Delta X_l) \, d \left[\Delta X_i, \Delta X_j \right]_l \\
&= \int_0^t \frac{\partial \Psi_n^{(k)}}{\partial x_k} (\Delta X_l) \left\{ b_k (X_l) - b_k \left(\widetilde{X}_l \right) \right\} dl \\
&\quad + \frac{1}{2} \int_0^t \frac{\partial \Psi_n^{(k)}}{\partial^2 x_k} (\Delta X_l) \left\{ \sigma_{kk} (X_l) - \sigma_{kk} \left(\widetilde{X}_l \right) \right\}^2 dl \\
&\quad + \int_0^t \frac{\partial \Psi_n^{(k)}}{\partial x_k} (\Delta X_l) \left\{ \sigma_{kk} (X_l) - \sigma_{kk} \left(\widetilde{X}_l \right) \right\} dW_l.
\end{aligned}$$

Because $\left| \frac{\partial \Psi_n^{(k)}}{\partial x_k} (x) \right| \leq 1$ for $x \in \mathbb{R}^3$ and equation (B.1) holds,

$$\begin{aligned}
&E \left[\int_0^t \left| \frac{\partial \Psi_n^{(k)}}{\partial x_k} (\Delta X_l) \left\{ \sigma_{kk} (X_l) - \sigma_{kk} \left(\widetilde{X}_l \right) \right\} \right|^2 dl \right] \\
&\leq E \left[\int_0^t \left| \sigma_{kk} (X_l) - \sigma_{kk} \left(\widetilde{X}_l \right) \right|^2 dl \right] \\
&\leq \max(\sigma_r, \sigma_u, \sigma_s)^2 E \left[\int_0^t \left| \Delta X_l^k \right| dl \right] \\
&\leq t \cdot \max(\sigma_r, \sigma_u, \sigma_s)^2 \max_{0 \leq l \leq t} E \left| \Delta X_l^k \right| \\
&< \infty \; \forall \; 0 \leq t < \infty, \; \forall \; k.
\end{aligned}$$

The last inequality holds by theorem 2.4, page 177, in Ikeda & Watanabe (1989b)[4]. Hence, we can apply theorem 3.2.1 (iii) in Oksendal (1998)[5], page 30, and get

$$E\left[\int_0^t \frac{\partial \Psi_n^{(k)}}{\partial x_k}(\Delta X_l)\left\{\sigma_{kk}(X_l)-\sigma_{kk}\left(\widetilde{X}_l\right)\right\}dW_l\right]=0.$$

Using inequalities (B.1) and (B.3) we get

$$E\left[\frac{1}{2}\int_0^t \frac{\partial \Psi_n^{(k)}}{\partial^2 x_k}(\Delta X_l)\left\{\sigma_{kk}(X_l)-\sigma_{kk}\left(\widetilde{X}_l\right)\right\}^2 dl\right]\leq \frac{t}{n}.$$

Applying inequality (B.2) yields

$$E\left[\int_0^t \frac{\partial \Psi_n^{(k)}}{\partial x_k}(\Delta X_l)\left\{b_k(X_l)-b_k\left(\widetilde{X}_l\right)\right\}dl\right]$$
$$\leq \max(a_r,a_u,a_s,b_s)\sum_{k=1}^{3}\int_0^t E\left|\Delta X_l^k\right| dl.$$

Hence, we find that

$$E\Psi_n^{(i)}(\Delta X_t)\leq \frac{t}{n}+\max(a_r,a_u,a_s,b_s)\sum_{k=1}^{3}\int_0^t E\left|\Delta X_l^k\right| dl,\ \forall\ 0\leq t,\forall\ k.$$

For

$$\Psi_n=\sum_{k=1}^{3}\Psi_n^{(k)}$$

we get

$$E\Psi_n(\Delta X_t)\leq \frac{3t}{n}+3\cdot\max(a_r,a_u,a_s,b_s)\sum_{k=1}^{3}\int_0^t E\left|\Delta X_l^k\right| dl.$$

Hence by using properties (B.4), (B.5) and the dominated convergence theorem, as $n\to\infty$, we finally find that

$$E\sum_{k=1}^{3}\left|\Delta X_t^k\right|\leq 3\cdot\max(a_r,a_u,a_s,b_s)\int_0^t E\sum_{k=1}^{3}\left|\Delta X_l^k\right| dl,\ \forall\ 0\leq t,\forall\ k.$$

By applying Gronwall's lemma[6] and sample path continuity, we get

$$E\sum_{k=1}^{3}\left|\Delta X_t^k\right|=0,\ \forall\ 0\leq t,\ \text{and therefore}\ \left|\Delta X_t^k\right|=0\ \mathbf{P}\text{-}a.s.\ \forall\ k.$$

---

[4] See footnote 2.

[5] This is a basic property of Itó integrals.

[6] See, e.g., Karatzas & Shreve (1988), pp. 287-288: Suppose that the continuous function $g(t)$ satisfies

B.2 Proof of Theorem 3.3.1 for $\beta = \frac{1}{2}$

Proof.
If $\beta = \frac{1}{2}$, plugging in the partial derivatives of P^d yields the following system of ODEs

$$\frac{1}{2}\sigma_r^2 \left(B^d\right)^2 + \hat{a}_r B^d - B_t^d - 1 = 0 \tag{B.6}$$

$$\frac{1}{2}\sigma_s^2 \left(C^d\right)^2 + \hat{a}_s C^d - C_t^d - 1 = 0$$

$$\frac{1}{2}\sigma_u^2 \left(D^d\right)^2 + \hat{a}_u D^d - D_t^d - b_s C^d = 0$$

$$A^d \left(\theta_r B^d + \theta_u D^d\right) - A_t^d = 0 \tag{B.7}$$

The solutions for C^d and D^d are the same as in the case $\beta = 0$. As in equation (3.27), the solution to equation (B.6) that satisfies the boundary condition $B^d(T,T) = 0$ is

$$B^d(t,T) = \frac{1 - e^{-\delta_r (T-t)}}{\kappa_1^{(r)} - \kappa_2^{(r)} e^{-\delta_r (T-t)}},$$

where $\kappa_{1/2}^{(r)}$ is defined as in equation (3.25) and δ_r is given by equation (3.28). By direct substitution, the solution to equation (B.7) for A^d that satisfies the boundary condition $A^d(T,T) = 1$ is

$$A^d(t,T) = A^d(0,T) \exp\left[\int_0^t \theta_r(\tau) B^d(\tau,T) + \theta_u D^d(\tau,T)\, d\tau\right].$$

B.3 Proofs of Lemma 3.3.1 and Lemma 3.4.2

Proof.
As usual let $y = (y_r, y_s, y_u)$, $z = (r, s, u)$, and $x = (x_1, x_2, x_3)$. Let $\alpha > 0$ be a constant and $G^{(\alpha)}\left(y, \check{t}, z, t\right)$ the solution of the PDE

$$\begin{aligned} 0 = &\frac{1}{2}\sigma_r^2 r^{2\beta} G_{rr}^{(\alpha)} + \frac{1}{2}\sigma_s^2 s G_{ss}^{(\alpha)} + \frac{1}{2}\sigma_u^2 u G_{uu}^{(\alpha)} \\ &+ \left[\theta_r(t) - \hat{a}_r r\right] G_r^{(\alpha)} + \left[b_s u - \hat{a}_s s\right] G_s^{(\alpha)} \\ &+ \left[\theta_u - \hat{a}_u u\right] G_u^{(\alpha)} + G_t^{(\alpha)} - (r + \alpha \cdot s)\, G^{(\alpha)}, \end{aligned}$$

$$0 \le g(t) \le \alpha(t) + \beta \int_0^t g(s)\, ds, \; 0 \le t \le T,$$

with $\beta \ge 0$ and $\alpha : [0,T] \to \mathbb{R}$ integrable. Then

$$g(t) \le \alpha(t) + \beta \int_0^t \alpha(s)\, e^{\beta(t-s)} ds, 0 \le t \le T.$$

with boundary condition

$$G^{(\alpha)}\left(y,\check{t},z,\check{t}\right)=\delta\left(r-y_r\right)\delta\left(s-y_s\right)\delta\left(u-y_u\right).$$

The Fourier transformation of $G^{(\alpha)}\left(y,\check{t},z,t\right)$,

$$\widetilde{G}^{(\alpha)}\left(x,\check{t},z,t\right)=\frac{1}{(2\pi)^{3/2}}\iiint\limits_{\mathbf{R}^3}e^{ixy'}\widetilde{G}^{(\alpha)}\left(y,\check{t},z,t\right)dy,$$

is the solution of the PDE,

$$\begin{aligned}0=&\frac{1}{2}\sigma_r^2r^{2\beta}\widetilde{G}^{(\alpha)}_{rr}+\frac{1}{2}\sigma_s^2s\widetilde{G}^{(\alpha)}_{ss}+\frac{1}{2}\sigma_u^2u\widetilde{G}^{(\alpha)}_{uu}\\&+\left[\theta_r(t)-\hat{a}_rr\right]\widetilde{G}^{(\alpha)}_r+\left[b_su-\hat{a}_ss\right]\widetilde{G}^{(\alpha)}_s\\&+\left[\theta_u-\hat{a}_uu\right]\widetilde{G}^{(\alpha)}_u+\widetilde{G}^{(\alpha)}_t-(r+\alpha\cdot s)\,\widetilde{G}^{(\alpha)},\end{aligned}\tag{B.8}$$

with boundary condition

$$\widetilde{G}^{(\alpha)}\left(x,\check{t},z,\check{t}\right)=e^{izx'}.$$

Assume that $\widetilde{G}^{(\alpha)}\left(x,\check{t},z,t\right)$ is given by

$$\widetilde{G}^{(\alpha)}\left(x,\check{t},z,t\right)=A^{\widetilde{G}^{(\alpha)}}\left(x,\check{t},t\right)e^{-B^{\widetilde{G}^{(\alpha)}}\left(x,\check{t},t\right)r-C^{\widetilde{G}^{(\alpha)}}\left(x,\check{t},t\right)s-D^{\widetilde{G}^{(\alpha)}}\left(x,\check{t},t\right)u}.$$

Then solving the PDE (B.8) is equivalent to solving the following system of ODE's:
If $\beta=0$,

$$\hat{a}_rB^{\widetilde{G}^{(\alpha)}}-B^{\widetilde{G}^{(\alpha)}}_t-1=0,\tag{B.9}$$

$$\frac{1}{2}\sigma^2\left(C^{\widetilde{G}^{(\alpha)}}\right)^2+\hat{a}_sC^{\widetilde{G}^{(\alpha)}}-C^{\widetilde{G}^{(\alpha)}}_t-\alpha=0,\tag{B.10}$$

$$\frac{1}{2}\sigma_u^2\left(D^{\widetilde{G}^{(\alpha)}}\right)^2+\hat{a}_uD^{\widetilde{G}^{(\alpha)}}-D^{\widetilde{G}^{(\alpha)}}_t-b_sC^{\widetilde{G}^{(\alpha)}}=0,\tag{B.11}$$

$$A^{\widetilde{G}^{(\alpha)}}\left(\theta_rB^{\widetilde{G}^{(\alpha)}}+\theta_uD^{\widetilde{G}^{(\alpha)}}-\frac{1}{2}\sigma_r^2\left(B^{\widetilde{G}^{(\alpha)}}\right)^2\right)-A^{\widetilde{G}^{(\alpha)}}_t=0,\tag{B.12}$$

and if $\beta=\frac{1}{2}$,

$$\frac{1}{2}\sigma_r^2\left(B^{\widetilde{G}^{(\alpha)}}\right)^2+\hat{a}_rB^{\widetilde{G}^{(\alpha)}}-B^{\widetilde{G}^{(\alpha)}}_t-1=0,\tag{B.13}$$

$$\frac{1}{2}\sigma_s^2\left(C^{\widetilde{G}^{(\alpha)}}\right)^2+\hat{a}_sC^{\widetilde{G}^{(\alpha)}}-C^{\widetilde{G}^{(\alpha)}}_t-\alpha=0,$$

$$\frac{1}{2}\sigma_u^2\left(D^{\widetilde{G}^{(\alpha)}}\right)^2+\hat{a}_uD^{\widetilde{G}^{(\alpha)}}-D^{\widetilde{G}^{(\alpha)}}_t-b_sC^{\widetilde{G}^{(\alpha)}}=0,$$

$$A^{\widetilde{G}^{(\alpha)}}\left(\theta_rB^{\widetilde{G}^{(\alpha)}}+\theta_uD^{\widetilde{G}^{(\alpha)}}\right)-A^{\widetilde{G}^{(\alpha)}}_t=0,\tag{B.14}$$

in both cases with boundary conditions

$$A^{\widetilde{G}^{(\alpha)}}\left(x,\check{t},\check{t}\right)=1, \tag{B.15}$$

$$B^{\widetilde{G}^{(\alpha)}}\left(x,\check{t},\check{t}\right)=-ix_1, \tag{B.16}$$

$$C^{\widetilde{G}^{(\alpha)}}\left(x,\check{t},\check{t}\right)=-ix_2, \tag{B.17}$$

$$D^{\widetilde{G}^{(\alpha)}}\left(x,\check{t},\check{t}\right)=-ix_3. \tag{B.18}$$

Consider the case $\beta=0$:
The solution of equation (B.9) that satisfies the boundary condition (B.16) is

$$B^{\widetilde{G}^{(\alpha)}}\left(x,t,\check{t}\right)=-ix_1e^{-\hat{a}_r\left(\check{t}-t\right)}+\frac{1}{\hat{a}_r}\left(1-e^{-\hat{a}_r\left(\check{t}-t\right)}\right).$$

Consider the case $\beta=\frac{1}{2}$:
Equation (B.13) is the same as equation (B.6) in the bond pricing section and can be solved in the same way. All solutions are given by

$$B^{\widetilde{G}^{(\alpha)}}\left(x,t,\check{t}\right)=-\frac{2}{\sigma_r^2}\frac{\alpha_1\kappa_1^{(r)}e^{\kappa_1^{(r)}t}+\alpha_2\kappa_2^{(r)}e^{\kappa_2^{(r)}t}}{\alpha_1e^{\kappa_1^{(r)}t}+\alpha_2e^{\kappa_2^{(r)}t}}, \tag{B.19}$$

where α_1 and α_2 are some constants and $\kappa_{1/2}^{(r)}$ is defined as in equation (3.25). In order to satisfy the boundary condition (B.16),

$$\alpha_1=\alpha_2e^{\left(\kappa_2^{(r)}-\kappa_1^{(r)}\right)\check{t}}\varpi\left(x_1\right), \tag{B.20}$$

with

$$\varpi\left(j\right)=\frac{ij\sigma_r^2-2\kappa_2^{(r)}}{2\kappa_1^{(r)}-ij\sigma_r^2}. \tag{B.21}$$

Then, $B^{\widetilde{G}^{(\alpha)}}\left(x,t,\check{t}\right)$ can be determined from equations (B.19) and (B.20). By applying the same methods as in the proof of theorem 3.3.1, the solution to equation (B.10) with boundary condition (B.17) is given by

$$C^{\widetilde{G}^{(\alpha)}}\left(x,t,\check{t}\right)=\frac{\kappa_3^{(s,\alpha)}\left(x\right)-e^{-\delta_s^{(\alpha)}\left(\check{t}-t\right)}}{\kappa_4^{(s,\alpha)}\left(x\right)-\kappa_5^{(s,\alpha)}\left(x\right)e^{-\delta_s^{(\alpha)}\left(\check{t}-t\right)}},$$

where

$$\delta_x^{(\alpha)}=\sqrt{\hat{a}_x^2+2\alpha\sigma_x^2}, \tag{B.22}$$

$$\kappa_3^{(s,\alpha)}\left(x\right)=\frac{1+ix_2\kappa_2^{(s,\alpha)}}{1+ix_2\kappa_1^{(s,\alpha)}}, \tag{B.23}$$

$$\kappa_4^{(s,\alpha)}\left(x\right)=\frac{\kappa_1^{(s,\alpha)}-\frac{1}{2}ix_2\sigma_s^2}{1+ix_2\kappa_1^{(s,\alpha)}}, \tag{B.24}$$

$$\kappa_5^{(s,\alpha)}\left(x\right)=\frac{\kappa_2^{(s,\alpha)}-\frac{1}{2}ix_2\sigma_s^2}{1+ix_2\kappa_1^{(s,\alpha)}}, \tag{B.25}$$

with

$$\kappa_{1/2}^{(x,\alpha)} = \frac{\hat{a}_x}{2} \pm \frac{1}{2}\sqrt{\hat{a}_x^2 + 2\alpha\sigma_x^2}.$$

The solution to equation (B.11) with boundary condition (B.18) is given by

$$D^{\widetilde{G}^{(\alpha)}}\left(x,t,\check{t}\right) = \frac{-2\left(v^{\widetilde{G}^{(\alpha)}}\right)'\left(x,t,\check{t}\right)}{\sigma_u^2 v^{\widetilde{G}^{(\alpha)}}\left(x,t,\check{t}\right)},$$

where

$$\begin{aligned} & v^{\widetilde{G}^{(\alpha)}}\left(x,t,\check{t}\right) \qquad\qquad (B.26)\\ &= \vartheta_1\left(\sigma_u^2 e^{-\delta_s^{(\alpha)}\left(\check{t}-t\right)}\right)^{\frac{\hat{a}_u}{2\delta_s^{(\alpha)}}-\phi\left(\kappa_4^{(s,\alpha)}(x),\kappa_3^{(s,\alpha)}(x)\right)} F_1^{\widetilde{G}^{(\alpha)}}\left(x,t,\check{t}\right)\\ &+\vartheta_2\left(\sigma_u^2 e^{-\delta_s^{(\alpha)}\left(\check{t}-t\right)}\right)^{\frac{\hat{a}_u}{2\delta_s^{(\alpha)}}+\phi\left(\kappa_4^{(s,\alpha)}(x),\kappa_3^{(s,\alpha)}(x)\right)} F_3^{\widetilde{G}^{(\alpha)}}\left(x,t,\check{t}\right), \end{aligned}$$

where ϑ_1 and ϑ_2 are some constants and

$$\begin{aligned} F_1^{\widetilde{G}^{(\alpha)}}\left(x,t,\check{t}\right) = F\Big(&-\phi^{(\alpha)}\left(\kappa_5^{(s,\alpha)}(x)\right) - \phi^{(\alpha)}\left(\kappa_4^{(s,\alpha)}(x),\kappa_3^{(s,\alpha)}(x)\right),\\ &\phi^{(\alpha)}\left(\kappa_5^{(s,\alpha)}(x)\right) - \phi^{(\alpha)}\left(\kappa_4^{(s,\alpha)}(x),\kappa_3^{(s,\alpha)}(x)\right),\\ &1-2\phi^{(\alpha)}\left(\kappa_4^{(s,\alpha)}(x),\kappa_3^{(s,\alpha)}(x)\right),\\ &\kappa_5^{(s,\alpha)}(x)/\kappa_4^{(s,\alpha)}(x)\, e^{-\delta_s^{(\alpha)}\left(\check{t}-t\right)}\Big), \end{aligned}$$

$$\begin{aligned} F_3^{\widetilde{G}^{(\alpha)}}\left(x,t,\check{t}\right) = F\Big(&-\phi^{(\alpha)}\left(\kappa_5^{(s,\alpha)}(x)\right) + \phi^{(\alpha)}\left(\kappa_4^{(s,\alpha)}(x),\kappa_3^{(s,\alpha)}(x)\right),\\ &\phi^{(\alpha)}\left(\kappa_5^{(s,\alpha)}(x)\right) + \phi^{(\alpha)}\left(\kappa_4^{(s,\alpha)}(x),\kappa_3^{(s,\alpha)}(x)\right),\\ &1+2\phi^{(\alpha)}\left(\kappa_4^{(s,\alpha)}(x),\kappa_3^{(s,\alpha)}(x)\right),\\ &\kappa_5^{(s,\alpha)}(x)/\kappa_4^{(s,\alpha)}(x)\, e^{-\delta_s^{(\alpha)}\left(\check{t}-t\right)}\Big), \end{aligned}$$

with

$$\phi^{(\alpha)}(g,h) = \frac{1}{2\delta_s^{(\alpha)}}\sqrt{\frac{\hat{a}_u^2 g + 2b_s\sigma_u^2 h}{g}} \text{ and } \phi^{(\alpha)}(g) = \phi^{(\alpha)}(g,1),$$

and - as usual - $F(a,b,c,z)$ is the hypergeometric function. Differentiation of $v^{\widetilde{G}^{(\alpha)}}\left(x,t,\check{t}\right)$ yields

$$\left(v^{\widetilde{G}^{(\alpha)}}\right)'\left(x,t,\check{t}\right) = y_1^{\widetilde{G}^{(\alpha)}}\left(x,t,\check{t}\right) + y_2^{\widetilde{G}^{(\alpha)}}\left(x,t,\check{t}\right), \qquad (B.27)$$

where

$$y_1^{\widetilde{G}^{(\alpha)}}\left(x,t,\check{t}\right) = \vartheta_1 \left(\sigma_u^2 e^{-\delta_s^{(\alpha)}\left(\check{t}-t\right)}\right)^{\frac{\hat{a}_u}{2\delta_s^{(\alpha)}} - \phi^{(\alpha)}\left(\kappa_4^{(s,\alpha)}(x),\kappa_3^{(s,\alpha)}(x)\right)} \varphi_2^{(\alpha)}\left(x,t,\check{t}\right),$$

$$y_2^{\widetilde{G}^{(\alpha)}}\left(x,t,\check{t}\right) = -\vartheta_2 \left(\sigma_u^2 e^{-\delta_s^{(\alpha)}\left(\check{t}-t\right)}\right)^{\frac{\hat{a}_u}{2\delta_s^{(\alpha)}} + \phi^{(\alpha)}\left(\kappa_4^{(s,\alpha)}(x),\kappa_3^{(s)}(x)\right)} \varphi_1^{(\alpha)}\left(x,t,\check{t}\right),$$

with

$$\varphi_1^{(\alpha)}\left(x,t,\check{t}\right) = \zeta_2^{(\alpha)}\left(x\right) e^{-\delta_s^{(\alpha)}\left(\check{t}-t\right)} F_4^{\widetilde{G}^{(\alpha)}}\left(x,t,\check{t}\right) - \xi_1^{(\alpha)}\left(x\right) F_3^{\widetilde{G}^{(\alpha)}}\left(x,t,\check{t}\right),$$

$$\varphi_2^{(\alpha)}\left(x,t,\check{t}\right) = \xi_2^{(\alpha)}\left(x\right) F_1^{\widetilde{G}^{(\alpha)}}\left(x,t,\check{t}\right) - \zeta_1^{(\alpha)}\left(x\right) e^{-\delta_s^{(\alpha)}\left(\check{t}-t\right)} F_2^{\widetilde{G}^{(\alpha)}}\left(x,t,\check{t}\right),$$

where

$$\begin{aligned} F_2^{\widetilde{G}^{(\alpha)}}\left(x,t,\check{t}\right) = F\Big(&1 - \phi^{(\alpha)}\left(\kappa_5^{(s,\alpha)}\left(x\right)\right) - \phi^{(\alpha)}\left(\kappa_4^{(s,\alpha)}\left(x\right), \kappa_3^{(s,\alpha)}\left(x\right)\right), \\ &1 + \phi^{(\alpha)}\left(\kappa_5^{(s,\alpha)}\left(x\right)\right) - \phi^{(\alpha)}\left(\kappa_4^{(s,\alpha)}\left(x\right), \kappa_3^{(s,\alpha)}\left(x\right)\right), \\ &2 - 2\phi^{(\alpha)}\left(\kappa_4^{(s,\alpha)}\left(x\right), \kappa_3^{(s,\alpha)}\left(x\right)\right), \\ &\kappa_5^{(s,\alpha)}\left(x\right)/\kappa_4^{(s,\alpha)}\left(x\right) e^{-\delta_s^{(\alpha)}\left(\check{t}-t\right)}\Big), \end{aligned}$$

$$\begin{aligned} F_4^{\widetilde{G}^{(\alpha)}}\left(x,t,\check{t}\right) = F\Big(&1 - \phi^{(\alpha)}\left(\kappa_5^{(s,\alpha)}\left(x\right)\right) + \phi^{(\alpha)}\left(\kappa_4^{(s,\alpha)}\left(x\right), \kappa_3^{(s,\alpha)}\left(x\right)\right), \\ &1 + \phi^{(\alpha)}\left(\kappa_5^{(s,\alpha)}\left(x\right)\right) + \phi^{(\alpha)}\left(\kappa_4^{(s,\alpha)}\left(x\right), \kappa_3^{(s,\alpha)}\left(x\right)\right), \\ &2 + 2\phi^{(\alpha)}\left(\kappa_4^{(s,\alpha)}\left(x\right), \kappa_3^{(s,\alpha)}\left(x\right)\right), \\ &\kappa_5^{(s,\alpha)}\left(x\right)/\kappa_4^{(s,\alpha)}\left(x\right) e^{-\delta_s^{(\alpha)}\left(\check{t}-t\right)}\Big), \end{aligned}$$

and

$$\xi_{1/2}^{(\alpha)}\left(x\right) = \frac{\hat{a}_u}{2} \pm \delta_s^{(\alpha)} \phi^{(\alpha)}\left(\kappa_4^{(s,\alpha)}\left(x\right), \kappa_3^{(s,\alpha)}\left(x\right)\right),$$

$$\zeta_{1/2}^{(\alpha)}\left(x\right) = \delta_s^{(\alpha)} \frac{\kappa_5^{(s,\alpha)}\left(x\right)}{\kappa_4^{(s,\alpha)}\left(x\right)} \frac{\left(\phi^{(\alpha)}\right)^2\left(\kappa_5^{(s,\alpha)}\left(x\right)\right) - \left(\phi^{(\alpha)}\right)^2\left(\kappa_4^{(s,\alpha)}\left(x\right), \kappa_3^{(s,\alpha)}\left(x\right)\right)}{1 \mp 2\phi^{(\alpha)}\left(\kappa_4^{(s,\alpha)}\left(x\right), \kappa_3^{(s,\alpha)}\left(x\right)\right)}.$$

In order to satisfy the boundary condition $D^{\widetilde{G}^{(\alpha)}}\left(x,\check{t},\check{t}\right) = -ix_3$, ϑ_1 equals

$$\vartheta_1 = \vartheta_2 \left(\sigma_u^2\right)^{2\phi^{(\alpha)}\left(\kappa_4^{(s,\alpha)}(x),\kappa_3^{(s,\alpha)}(x)\right)} \frac{\pi_1^{(\alpha)}\left(x\right)}{\pi_2^{(\alpha)}\left(x\right)}, \tag{B.28}$$

where

$$\pi_1^{(\alpha)}\left(x\right) = 2\varphi_1^{(\alpha)}\left(x,\check{t},\check{t}\right) + ix_3\sigma_u^2 F_3^{\widetilde{G}^{(\alpha)}}\left(x,\check{t},\check{t}\right),$$

and

$$\pi_2^{(\alpha)}(x) = 2\varphi_2^{(\alpha)}\left(x, \check{t}, \check{t}\right) - ix_3\sigma_u^2 F_1^{\widetilde{G}^{(\alpha)}}\left(x, \check{t}, \check{t}\right).$$

Then $D^{\widetilde{G}^{(\alpha)}}\left(x, t, \check{t}\right)$ can be easily determined as

$$\begin{aligned}
&D^{\widetilde{G}^{(\alpha)}}\left(x, t, \check{t}\right)\\
&= \frac{-2}{\sigma_u^2}\Big(\pi_1^{(\alpha)}(x)\,\varphi_2^{(\alpha)}\left(x, t, \check{t}\right)\\
&\quad -e^{-2\delta_s^{(\alpha)}\phi^{(\alpha)}\left(\kappa_4^{(s,\alpha)}(x),\kappa_3^{(s,\alpha)}(x)\right)\left(\check{t}-t\right)}\pi_2^{(\alpha)}(x)\,\varphi_1^{(\alpha)}\left(x, t, \check{t}\right)\Big) /\\
&\Big(\pi_1^{(\alpha)}(x)\,F_1^{\widetilde{G}^{(\alpha)}}\left(x, t, \check{t}\right)\\
&\quad +e^{-2\delta_s^{(\alpha)}\phi^{(\alpha)}\left(\kappa_4^{(s,\alpha)}(x),\kappa_3^{(s,\alpha)}(x)\right)\left(\check{t}-t\right)}\pi_2^{(\alpha)}(x)\,F_3^{\widetilde{G}^{(\alpha)}}\left(x, t, \check{t}\right)\Big).
\end{aligned}$$

The equations for $A^{\widetilde{G}^{(\alpha)}}\left(x, \check{t}, t\right)$ follow directly from equations (B.12), (B.14), and (B.15):
If $\beta = 0$, by direct substitution, the solution of equation (B.12) for $A^{\widetilde{G}^{(\alpha)}}$ that satisfies the boundary condition (B.15) is

$$\begin{aligned}
&A^{\widetilde{G}^{(\alpha)}}\left(x, t, \check{t}\right)\\
&= e^{-\int_{\check{t}}^{t}\left(\frac{1}{2}\sigma_r^2\left(B^{\widetilde{G}^{(\alpha)}}\left(x,\tau,\check{t}\right)\right)^2 - \theta_r(\tau)B^{\widetilde{G}^{(\alpha)}}\left(x,\tau,\check{t}\right) - \theta_u D^{\widetilde{G}^{(\alpha)}}\left(x,\tau,\check{t}\right)\right)d\tau}.
\end{aligned}$$

If $\beta = \frac{1}{2}$, by direct substitution, the solution to equation (B.14) for $A^{\widetilde{G}^{(\alpha)}}$ that satisfies the boundary condition (B.15) is

$$A^{\widetilde{G}^{(\alpha)}}\left(x, t, \check{t}\right) = \exp\left[\int_{\check{t}}^{t}\left(\theta_r(\tau)\,B^{\widetilde{G}^{(\alpha)}}\left(x, \tau, \check{t}\right) + \theta_u D^{\widetilde{G}^{(\alpha)}}\left(x, \tau, \check{t}\right)\right)d\tau\right].$$

B.4 Proof of Lemma 3.4.3

Proof.
We substitute

$$\widetilde{y}_r = \frac{c_1 y_r}{c_0},\ \widetilde{y}_s = \frac{c_2 y_s}{c_0},\ \text{and}\ \widetilde{y}_u = \frac{c_1 y_u}{c_0},$$

and

$$\widetilde{a}_i = \frac{c_0 a_i}{c_i}\ \text{for}\ i = 1, 2, 3.$$

Then, we get

$$
\begin{aligned}
&\Lambda^C(a_1,a_2,a_3,c_0,c_1,c_2,c_3)\\
&= \frac{c_0^3}{c_1c_2c_3}\iiint_{\mathbf{R}^3} e^{-i\widetilde{a}_1\widetilde{y}_r-i\widetilde{a}_2\widetilde{y}_s-i\widetilde{a}_3\widetilde{y}_u}1_{\{\widetilde{y}_r+\widetilde{y}_s+\widetilde{y}_u\le 1\}}d\widetilde{y}_rd\widetilde{y}_sd\widetilde{y}_u\\
&= \frac{c_0^3}{c_1c_2c_3}\int_0^1\int_0^{1-\widetilde{y}_u}\int_0^{1-\widetilde{y}_s-\widetilde{y}_u} e^{-i\widetilde{a}_1\widetilde{y}_r-i\widetilde{a}_2\widetilde{y}_s-i\widetilde{a}_3\widetilde{y}_u}d\widetilde{y}_rd\widetilde{y}_sd\widetilde{y}_u\\
&= \frac{ic_0^3}{c_1c_2c_3\widetilde{a}_1}\left(e^{-i\widetilde{a}_1}\int_0^1 e^{-i(\widetilde{a}_3-\widetilde{a}_1)\widetilde{y}_u}\int_0^{1-\widetilde{y}_u} e^{-i(\widetilde{a}_2-\widetilde{a}_1)\widetilde{y}_s}d\widetilde{y}_sd\widetilde{y}_u\right.\\
&\quad\left.-\int_0^1 e^{-i\widetilde{a}_3\widetilde{y}_u}\int_0^{1-\widetilde{y}_u} e^{-i\widetilde{a}_2\widetilde{y}_s}d\widetilde{y}_sd\widetilde{y}_u\right)\\
&= -\frac{c_0^3}{c_1c_2c_3\widetilde{a}_1}\cdot\\
&\quad\left(\frac{e^{-i\widetilde{a}_1}}{\widetilde{a}_2-\widetilde{a}_1}\left(e^{-i(\widetilde{a}_2-\widetilde{a}_1)}\int_0^1 e^{-i(\widetilde{a}_3-\widetilde{a}_2)\widetilde{y}_u}d\widetilde{y}_u-\int_0^1 e^{-i(\widetilde{a}_3-\widetilde{a}_1)\widetilde{y}_u}d\widetilde{y}_u\right)\right.\\
&\quad\left.-\frac{1}{\widetilde{a}_2}\left(e^{-i\widetilde{a}_2}\int_0^1 e^{-i(\widetilde{a}_3-\widetilde{a}_2)\widetilde{y}_u}d\widetilde{y}_u-\int_0^1 e^{-i\widetilde{a}_3\widetilde{y}_u}d\widetilde{y}_u\right)\right)\\
&= -\frac{ic_0^3}{c_1c_2c_3\widetilde{a}_1}\cdot\\
&\quad\left(\frac{e^{-i\widetilde{a}_3}-e^{-i\widetilde{a}_2}}{(\widetilde{a}_3-\widetilde{a}_2)(\widetilde{a}_2-\widetilde{a}_1)}-\frac{e^{-i\widetilde{a}_3}-e^{-i\widetilde{a}_1}}{(\widetilde{a}_3-\widetilde{a}_1)(\widetilde{a}_2-\widetilde{a}_1)}+\frac{e^{-i\widetilde{a}_3}-1}{\widetilde{a}_2\widetilde{a}_3}-\frac{e^{-i\widetilde{a}_3}-e^{-i\widetilde{a}_2}}{\widetilde{a}_2(\widetilde{a}_3-\widetilde{a}_2)}\right).
\end{aligned}
$$

The proof for Λ^P works similarly.

B.5 Tools for Pricing Non-Defaultable Contingent Claims

Lemma B.5.1.
The solution to the PDE

$$
\begin{aligned}
0 &= \frac{1}{2}\sigma_r^2 r^{2\beta}\overline{G}_{rr}+\frac{1}{2}\sigma_s^2 s\overline{G}_{ss}+\frac{1}{2}\sigma_u^2 u\overline{G}_{uu}\\
&\quad+[\theta_r(t)-\hat{a}_r r]\overline{G}_r+[b_s u-\hat{a}_s s]\overline{G}_s\\
&\quad+[\theta_u-\hat{a}_u u]\overline{G}_u+\overline{G}_t-r\overline{G},
\end{aligned}
$$

with boundary condition

$$
\overline{G}(y,\check{t},z,\check{t})=\delta(r-y_r)\,\delta(s-y_s)\,\delta(u-y_u),
$$

is given by

$$
\overline{G}(y,\check{t},z,t)=\frac{1}{(2\pi)^{3/2}}\iiint_{\mathbf{R}^3} e^{-ixy'}\underline{G}(x,\check{t},z,t)\,dx \qquad \text{(B.29)}
$$

where

$$\underline{G}\left(x,\check{t},z,t\right)=A^{\underline{G}}\left(x,t,\check{t}\right)e^{-B^{\tilde{G}}\left(x,t,\check{t}\right)r-C^{\underline{G}}\left(x,t,\check{t}\right)s-D^{\underline{G}}\left(x,t,\check{t}\right)u}$$

with

$$C^{\underline{G}}\left(x,t,\check{t}\right)=\frac{2\hat{a}_s x_2}{\left(\sigma_s^2 x_2+2i\hat{a}_s\right)e^{-\hat{a}_s\left(t-\check{t}\right)}-\sigma_s^2 x_2},$$

$$D^{\underline{G}}\left(x,t,\check{t}\right)=\frac{-2\left(v^{\underline{G}}\right)'\left(x,t,\check{t}\right)}{\sigma_u^2 v^{\underline{G}}\left(x,t,\check{t}\right)},$$

and if $\beta=0:$

$$A^{\underline{G}}\left(x,t,\check{t}\right)=e^{-\int_t^{\check{t}}\left(-\frac{1}{2}\sigma_r^2\left(B^{\tilde{G}}\right)^2\left(x,\tau,\check{t}\right)+\theta_r(\tau)B^{\tilde{G}}\left(x,\tau,\check{t}\right)+\theta_u D^{\underline{G}}\left(x,\tau,\check{t}\right)\right)d\tau},$$

if $\beta=\frac{1}{2}:$

$$A^{\underline{G}}\left(x,t,\check{t}\right)=e^{-\int_t^{\check{t}}\left(\theta_r(\tau)B^{\tilde{G}}\left(x,\tau,\check{t}\right)+\theta_u D^{\underline{G}}\left(x,\tau,\check{t}\right)\right)d\tau}.$$

$v^{\underline{G}}\left(x,\check{t},t\right)$ *and* $\left(v^{\underline{G}}\right)'\left(x,\check{t},t\right)$ *are defined as in equations (B.44), (B.45) and (B.46) below.* $B^{\tilde{G}}\left(x,\check{t},t\right)$ *is given by equation (3.52).*

Proof.
The Fourier transformation of $\overline{G}\left(y,\check{t},z,t\right)$,

$$\underline{G}\left(x,\check{t},z,t\right)=\frac{1}{\left(2\pi\right)^{3/2}}\iiint_{\mathbf{R}^3}e^{ixy'}\overline{G}\left(y,\check{t},z,t\right)dy,$$

is the solution of the PDE

$$\begin{aligned}0=&\frac{1}{2}\sigma_r^2 r^{2\beta}\underline{G}_{rr}+\frac{1}{2}\sigma_s^2 s\underline{G}_{ss}+\frac{1}{2}\sigma_u^2 u\underline{G}_{uu}\\&+\left[\theta_r(t)-\hat{a}_r r\right]\underline{G}_r+\left[b_s u-\hat{a}_s s\right]\underline{G}_s\\&+\left[\theta_u-\hat{a}_u u\right]\underline{G}_u+\underline{G}_t-r\underline{G},\end{aligned}\qquad\text{(B.30)}$$

with boundary condition

$$\underline{G}\left(x,\check{t},z,\check{t}\right)=e^{izx'}.$$

Assume that $\underline{G}\left(x,\check{t},z,t\right)$ is given by

$$\underline{G}\left(x,\check{t},z,t\right)=A^{\underline{G}}\left(x,t,\check{t}\right)e^{-B^{\underline{G}}\left(x,t,\check{t}\right)r-C^{\underline{G}}\left(x,t,\check{t}\right)s-D^{\underline{G}}\left(x,t,\check{t}\right)u}.$$

Then solving the PDE B.30 is equivalent to solving the following system of ODE's:

If $\beta = 0$,

$$\hat{a}_r B^{\underline{G}} - B_t^{\underline{G}} - 1 = 0, \tag{B.31}$$

$$\frac{1}{2}\sigma^2 \left(C^{\underline{G}}\right)^2 + \hat{a}_s C^{\underline{G}} - C_t^{\underline{G}} = 0, \tag{B.32}$$

$$\frac{1}{2}\sigma_u^2 \left(D^{\underline{G}}\right)^2 + \hat{a}_u D^{\underline{G}} - D_t^{\underline{G}} - b_s C^{\underline{G}} = 0, \tag{B.33}$$

$$A^{\underline{G}} \left(\theta_r B^{\underline{G}} + \theta_u D^{\underline{G}} - \frac{1}{2}\sigma_r^2 \left(B^{\underline{G}}\right)^2\right) - A_t^{\underline{G}} = 0, \tag{B.34}$$

and if $\beta = \frac{1}{2}$,

$$\frac{1}{2}\sigma_r^2 \left(B^{\underline{G}}\right)^2 + \hat{a}_r B^{\underline{G}} - B_t^{\underline{G}} - 1 = 0, \tag{B.35}$$

$$\frac{1}{2}\sigma_s^2 \left(C^{\underline{G}}\right)^2 + \hat{a}_s C^{\underline{G}} - C_t^{\underline{G}} = 0,$$

$$\frac{1}{2}\sigma_u^2 \left(D^{\underline{G}}\right)^2 + \hat{a}_u D^{\underline{G}} - D_t^{\underline{G}} - b_s C^{\underline{G}} = 0,$$

$$A^{\underline{G}} \left(\theta_r B^{\underline{G}} + \theta_u D^{\underline{G}}\right) - A_t^{\underline{G}} = 0, \tag{B.36}$$

in both cases with boundary conditions

$$A^{\underline{G}}\left(x, \check{t}, \check{t}\right) = 1, \tag{B.37}$$

$$B^{\underline{G}}\left(x, \check{t}, \check{t}\right) = -ix_1, \tag{B.38}$$

$$C^{\underline{G}}\left(x, \check{t}, \check{t}\right) = -ix_2, \tag{B.39}$$

$$D^{\underline{G}}\left(x, \check{t}, \check{t}\right) = -ix_3. \tag{B.40}$$

Equations (B.31), (B.35), and (B.38) are the same as equations (B.9), (B.13), and (B.16). Therefore,

$$B^{\underline{G}}\left(x, t, \check{t}\right) = B^{\widetilde{G}}\left(x, t, \check{t}\right).$$

where $B^{\widetilde{G}}$ is defined by equation (3.52). Equation (B.32) has Bernoulli form

$$C_t^{\underline{G}} = \hat{a}_s C^{\underline{G}} + \frac{1}{2}\sigma^2 \left(C^{\underline{G}}\right)^2.$$

The solution is

$$C^{\underline{G}}\left(x, t, \check{t}\right) = \frac{1}{w^{\underline{G}}\left(x, t, \check{t}\right)},$$

where $w^{\underline{G}}\left(\check{t}, t\right)$ satisfies

$$\left(w^{\underline{G}}\right)' = -\hat{a}_s w^{\underline{G}} - \frac{1}{2}\sigma_s^2. \tag{B.41}$$

All solutions of ODE (B.41) are given by

$$w^{\underline{G}} = -\frac{\sigma_s^2}{2\hat{a}_s} + \alpha e^{-\hat{a}_s t},$$

where α is some constant. Then all solutions of equation (B.32) are given by

$$C^{\underline{G}}(x,t,\check{t}) = \frac{2\hat{a}_s}{2\hat{a}_s \alpha e^{-\hat{a}_s t} - \sigma_s^2}.$$

In order to satisfy the boundary condition (B.39),

$$\alpha = \frac{x_2\sigma_s^2 + 2i\hat{a}_s}{2x_2\hat{a}_s} e^{\hat{a}_s \check{t}},$$

and therefore

$$C^{\underline{G}}(x,t,\check{t}) = \frac{2\hat{a}_s x_2}{\left(\sigma_s^2 x_2 + 2i\hat{a}_s\right) e^{-\hat{a}_s\left(t-\check{t}\right)} - \sigma_s^2 x_2}.$$

Equation (B.33) has Ricatti form

$$D_t^{\underline{G}} = \frac{1}{2}\sigma_u^2 \left(D^{\underline{G}}\right)^2 + \hat{a}_u D^{\underline{G}} - b_s C^{\underline{G}}.$$

The solution is

$$D^{\underline{G}}(x,t,\check{t}) = \frac{-2\left(v^{\underline{G}}\right)'(x,t,\check{t})}{\sigma_u^2 v^{\underline{G}}(x,t,\check{t})}, \tag{B.42}$$

where $v^{\underline{G}}(\check{t},t)$ satisfies

$$\left(v^{\underline{G}}\right)'' - \hat{a}_u \left(v^{\underline{G}}\right)' - \frac{1}{2} C^{\underline{G}} b_s \sigma_u^2 v^{\underline{G}} = 0. \tag{B.43}$$

The solutions of equation (B.43) are given by

$$v^{\underline{G}}(x,t,\check{t}) = \vartheta_1 F_1^{\underline{G}}(x,t,\check{t}) + \vartheta_2 \left(e^{\hat{a}_s t} b_s \sigma_u^2 x_2\right)^{\frac{\hat{a}_u}{\hat{a}_s}} F_3^{\underline{G}}(x,t,\check{t}), \tag{B.44}$$

where ϑ_1 and ϑ_2 are some constants and

$$F_1^{\underline{G}}(x,t,\check{t}) = F\left(-\varrho_1, -\varrho_2, 1 - \frac{\hat{a}_u}{\hat{a}_s}, e^{-\hat{a}_s\left(\check{t}-t\right)}\eta(x)\right),$$

$$F_3^{\underline{G}}(x,t,\check{t}) = F\left(\varrho_2, \varrho_1, 1 + \frac{\hat{a}_u}{\hat{a}_s}, e^{-\hat{a}_s\left(\check{t}-t\right)}\eta(x)\right),$$

with

$$\varrho_{1/2} = \frac{\hat{a}_u\sigma_s \pm \sqrt{-4b_s\hat{a}_s\sigma_u^2 + \hat{a}_u^2\sigma_s^2}}{2\hat{a}_s\sigma_s} \text{ and } \eta(x) = \frac{x_2\sigma_s^2}{2i\hat{a}_s + x_2\sigma_s^2}.$$

Differentiation of $v^{\underline{G}}(x,t,\check{t})$ yields

$$\left(v^{\underline{G}}\right)'\left(x,t,\check{t}\right) = y_1^{\underline{G}}\left(x,t,\check{t}\right) + y_2^{\underline{G}}\left(x,t,\check{t}\right), \tag{B.45}$$

where

$$y_1^{\underline{G}}\left(x,t,\check{t}\right) = \vartheta_1 e^{-\hat{a}_s\left(\check{t}-t\right)}\eta\left(x\right)\iota_2 F_2^{\underline{G}}\left(x,t,\check{t}\right),$$
$$y_2^{\underline{G}}\left(x,t,\check{t}\right) = \vartheta_2\left(e^{\hat{a}_s t}b_s\sigma_u^2 x_2\right)^{\frac{\hat{a}_u}{\hat{a}_s}}\left(\hat{a}_u F_3^{\underline{G}}\left(x,t,\check{t}\right) - e^{-\hat{a}_s\left(\check{t}-t\right)}\eta\left(x\right)\iota_1 F_4^{\underline{G}}\left(x,t,\check{t}\right)\right),$$

with

$$\iota_{1/2} = \frac{b_s\hat{a}_s\sigma_u^2}{\sigma_s^2\left(\hat{a}_s \pm \hat{a}_u\right)}$$

and

$$F_2^{\underline{G}}\left(x,t,\check{t}\right) = F\left(1-\varrho_1, 1-\varrho_2, 2-\frac{\hat{a}_u}{\hat{a}_s}, e^{-\hat{a}_s\left(\check{t}-t\right)}\eta\left(x\right)\right),$$
$$F_4^{\underline{G}}\left(x,t,\check{t}\right) = F\left(1+\varrho_2, 1+\varrho_1, 2+\frac{\hat{a}_u}{\hat{a}_s}, e^{-\hat{a}_s\left(\check{t}-t\right)}\eta\left(x\right)\right).$$

In order to satisfy the boundary condition (B.40),

$$\vartheta_1 = \vartheta_2\left(e^{\hat{a}_s\check{t}}b_s\sigma_u^2 x_2\right)^{\frac{\hat{a}_u}{\hat{a}_s}}\mu\left(x\right), \tag{B.46}$$

with

$$\mu\left(x\right) = \frac{\left(2\hat{a}_u - ix_3\sigma_u^2\right)F_3^{\underline{G}}\left(x,t,\check{t}\right) - 2e^{-\hat{a}_s\left(\check{t}-t\right)}\eta\left(x\right)\iota_1 F_4^{\underline{G}}\left(x,t,\check{t}\right)}{ix_3\sigma_u^2 F_1^{\underline{G}}\left(x,t,\check{t}\right) - 2e^{-\hat{a}_s\left(\check{t}-t\right)}\eta\left(x\right)\iota_2 F_2^{\underline{G}}\left(x,t,\check{t}\right)}.$$

Then $D^{\underline{G}}\left(x,\check{t},t\right)$ can be determined from equations (B.42), (B.44), (B.45) and (B.46).
Consider the case $\beta = 0$:
The solution of equation (B.34) for $A^{\underline{G}}$ that satisfies the boundary condition (B.37) is

$$A^{\underline{G}}\left(x,t,\check{t}\right) = e^{-\int_t^{\check{t}}\left(-\frac{1}{2}\sigma_r^2\left(B^{\tilde{G}}\right)^2\left(x,\tau,\check{t}\right)+\theta_r(\tau)B^{\tilde{G}}\left(x,\tau,\check{t}\right)+\theta_u D^{\underline{G}}\left(x,\tau,\check{t}\right)\right)d\tau}.$$

Consider the case $\beta = \frac{1}{2}$:
The solution of equation (B.36) for $A^{\underline{G}}$ that satisfies the boundary condition (B.37) is

$$A^{\underline{G}}\left(x,t,\check{t}\right) = e^{-\int_t^{\check{t}}\left(\theta_r(\tau)B^{\tilde{G}}\left(x,\tau,\check{t}\right)+\theta_u D^{\underline{G}}\left(x,\tau,\check{t}\right)\right)d\tau}.$$

C. Pricing of Credit Derivatives: Extensions

If we let $\beta = 0$, we must take into account that r may become negative. Therefore, instead of considering the sets $\mathcal{B}_1$, $\mathcal{B}_2$, $\mathcal{B}_3$, and $\mathcal{B}_4$, we have to work with

$$\widetilde{\mathcal{B}}_1 = \left\{ r \in \mathbb{R},\ (s,u) \in \mathbb{R}_+^2 | B(T_O,T)\, r + C^d(T_O,T)\, s + D^d(T_O,T)\, u \le K^* \right\},$$

$$\widetilde{\mathcal{B}}_2 = \left\{ r \in \mathbb{R},\ (s,u) \in \mathbb{R}_+^2 | K^* \le B(T_O,T)\, r + C^d(T_O,T)\, s + D^d(T_O,T)\, u \right\},$$

and

$$\begin{aligned}
&\widetilde{\mathcal{B}}_3 = \left\{ r \in \mathbb{R},\ (s,u) \in \mathbb{R}_+^2 | \right. \\
&\left. C^d(T_O,T)\, s + D^d(T_O,T)\, u \le (T - T_O)\, K + \ln\left(A^d(T_O,T)/A(T_O,T)\right) \right\}, \\
&\widetilde{\mathcal{B}}_4 = \left\{ r \in \mathbb{R},\ (s,u) \in \mathbb{R}_+^2 | \right. \\
&\left. (T - T_O)\, K + \ln\left(A^d(T_O,T)/A(T_O,T)\right) \le C^d(T_O,T)\, s + D^d(T_O,T)\, u \right\}.
\end{aligned}$$

The only consequences are more complicated calculations of Λ^C and Λ^P. Everything else works like in the case $\beta = \frac{1}{2}$ which we presented in section 3.4. In the following we show the result for Λ^C, the calculation of Λ^P works identically:

$$\begin{aligned}
&\Lambda^C(a_1, a_2, a_3, c_0, c_1, c_2, c_3) \\
&= \frac{c_0^3}{c_1 c_2 c_3} \iiint\limits_{\mathbb{R}^3} e^{-i\widetilde{a}_1 \widetilde{y}_r - i\widetilde{a}_2 \widetilde{y}_s - i\widetilde{a}_3 \widetilde{y}_u} 1_{\{\widetilde{y}_r + \widetilde{y}_s + \widetilde{y}_u \le 1\}} d\widetilde{y}_r d\widetilde{y}_s d\widetilde{y}_u \\
&= \frac{c_0^3}{c_1 c_2 c_3} \int_0^1 e^{-i\widetilde{a}_3 \widetilde{y}_u} \int_0^{1-\widetilde{y}_u} e^{-i\widetilde{a}_2 \widetilde{y}_s} \int_{-\infty}^{1-\widetilde{y}_s-\widetilde{y}_u} e^{-i\widetilde{a}_1 \widetilde{y}_r} d\widetilde{y}_r d\widetilde{y}_s d\widetilde{y}_u,
\end{aligned}$$

where $\widetilde{y}_r$, $\widetilde{y}_s$, $\widetilde{y}_u$, and $\widetilde{a}_i$, $i = 1,2,3$, are defined as in section B.4. Because

$$\int_{-\infty}^{1-\widetilde{y}_s-\widetilde{y}_u} e^{-i\widetilde{a}_1 \widetilde{y}_r} d\widetilde{y}_r = \int_{-\infty}^{0} e^{-i\widetilde{a}_1 \widetilde{y}_r} d\widetilde{y}_r + \int_0^{1-\widetilde{y}_s-\widetilde{y}_u} e^{-i\widetilde{a}_1 \widetilde{y}_r} d\widetilde{y}_r,$$

we can concentrate on the calculation of

$$\begin{aligned}
\int_{-\infty}^{0} e^{-i\widetilde{a}_1 \widetilde{y}_r} d\widetilde{y}_r &= \int_0^{\infty} e^{i\widetilde{a}_1 \widetilde{y}_r} d\widetilde{y}_r \\
&= \int_{-\infty}^{\infty} H(\widetilde{y}_r)\, e^{i\widetilde{a}_1 \widetilde{y}_r} d\widetilde{y}_r,
\end{aligned}$$

where $H(\widetilde{y}_r)$ is the Heaviside step function[1]. According to Evans, Blackledge & Yardley (2000), page 43, the Fourier transform of $H(\widetilde{y}_r)$ is given by

$$\frac{1}{\sqrt{2\pi}}\left(\pi\delta(\widetilde{a}_1)-\frac{1}{i\widetilde{a}_1}\right),$$

where δ is the Dirac delta function[2]. Hence,

$$\int_{-\infty}^{0} e^{-i\widetilde{a}_1\widetilde{y}_r}d\widetilde{y}_r=\pi\delta(\widetilde{a}_1)-\frac{1}{i\widetilde{a}_1}.$$

Therefore,

$$\begin{aligned}
&\Lambda^C(a_1,a_2,a_3,c_0,c_1,c_2,c_3)\\
&=-\frac{ic_0^3}{c_1c_2c_3\widetilde{a}_1}\cdot\\
&\left(\frac{e^{-i\widetilde{a}_3}-e^{-i\widetilde{a}_2}}{(\widetilde{a}_3-\widetilde{a}_2)(\widetilde{a}_2-\widetilde{a}_1)}-\frac{e^{-i\widetilde{a}_3}-e^{-i\widetilde{a}_1}}{(\widetilde{a}_3-\widetilde{a}_1)(\widetilde{a}_2-\widetilde{a}_1)}+\frac{e^{-i\widetilde{a}_3}-1}{\widetilde{a}_2\widetilde{a}_3}-\frac{e^{-i\widetilde{a}_3}}{\widetilde{a}_2(\widetilde{a}_3-\widetilde{a}_2)}\right)\\
&+\frac{c_0^3}{c_1c_2c_3}\left(\pi\delta(\widetilde{a}_1)+\frac{i}{\widetilde{a}_1}\right)\int_0^1 e^{-i\widetilde{a}_3\widetilde{y}_u}\int_0^{1-\widetilde{y}_u} e^{-i\widetilde{a}_2\widetilde{y}_s}d\widetilde{y}_s d\widetilde{y}_u\\
&=-\frac{ic_0^3}{c_1c_2c_3}\left(\frac{e^{-i\widetilde{a}_3}-e^{-i\widetilde{a}_2}}{\widetilde{a}_1(\widetilde{a}_3-\widetilde{a}_2)(\widetilde{a}_2-\widetilde{a}_1)}-\frac{e^{-i\widetilde{a}_3}-e^{-i\widetilde{a}_1}}{\widetilde{a}_1(\widetilde{a}_3-\widetilde{a}_1)(\widetilde{a}_2-\widetilde{a}_1)}+\frac{e^{-i\widetilde{a}_3}-1}{\widetilde{a}_1\widetilde{a}_2\widetilde{a}_3}\right.\\
&\left.-\frac{e^{-i\widetilde{a}_3}-e^{-i\widetilde{a}_2}}{\widetilde{a}_1\widetilde{a}_2(\widetilde{a}_3-\widetilde{a}_2)}+\frac{e^{-i\widetilde{a}_3}-e^{-i\widetilde{a}_2}}{\widetilde{a}_1\widetilde{a}_2(\widetilde{a}_3-\widetilde{a}_2)}-\frac{e^{-i\widetilde{a}_3}-1}{\widetilde{a}_1\widetilde{a}_2\widetilde{a}_3}\right)\\
&-\frac{c_0^3}{c_1c_2c_3}\pi\delta(\widetilde{a}_1)\left(\frac{e^{-i\widetilde{a}_3}-e^{-i\widetilde{a}_2}}{\widetilde{a}_2(\widetilde{a}_3-\widetilde{a}_2)}-\frac{e^{-i\widetilde{a}_3}-1}{\widetilde{a}_2\widetilde{a}_3}\right)\\
&=\frac{c_0^3}{c_1c_2c_3}\left(\frac{e^{-i\widetilde{a}_3}-e^{-i\widetilde{a}_2}}{i\widetilde{a}_1(\widetilde{a}_3-\widetilde{a}_2)(\widetilde{a}_2-\widetilde{a}_1)}-\frac{e^{-i\widetilde{a}_3}-e^{-i\widetilde{a}_1}}{i\widetilde{a}_1(\widetilde{a}_3-\widetilde{a}_1)(\widetilde{a}_2-\widetilde{a}_1)}\right.\\
&\left.-\pi\delta(\widetilde{a}_1)\left(\frac{e^{-i\widetilde{a}_3}-e^{-i\widetilde{a}_2}}{\widetilde{a}_2(\widetilde{a}_3-\widetilde{a}_2)}-\frac{e^{-i\widetilde{a}_3}-1}{\widetilde{a}_2\widetilde{a}_3}\right)\right).
\end{aligned}$$

---

[1] For a definition of the Heaviside step function, see, e.g., section 3.3.5.
[2] For a definition of the Dirac delta function, see, e.g., section 3.3.5.

List of Figures

List of Tables

References

Abrahams, J. (1986). *A Survey of Recent Progress on Level Crossing Problems*, Springer.

Altman, E. I. (1997). Rating migration of corporate bonds - comparative results and investor/lender implications. Mimeo, Salomon Brothers.

Altman, E. I. & Eberhart, A. C. (1994). Do seniority provisions protect bondholders' investments, *Journal of Portfolio Management* **20**: 67–75.

Altman, E. I. & Kao, D. L. (1992a). The implications of corporate bond ratings drift, *Financial Analysts Journal* pp. 64–75.

Altman, E. I. & Kao, D. L. (1992b). The implications of corporate bond ratings drift, *Financial Analysts Journal* pp. 64– 75.

Altman, E. I. & Kishore, V. M. (1996). Almost everything you wanted to know about recoveries on defaulted bonds, *Financial Analysts Journal* pp. 57–63.

Altman, E. & Kishore, V. M. (1997). Defaults and returns on high yield bonds: Analysis through 1996. Special Report, New York University Salomon Center, New York.

Amin, K. (1995). Option pricing trees, *The Journal of Derivatives* pp. 34–46.

A New Capital Adequacy Framework (1999). Consultative paper issued by the Basel Committee on Banking Supervision, Basel.

Artzner, P. & Delbaen, F. (1992). Credit risk and prepayment option, *ASTIN Bulletin* **22**: 81–96.

Asarnow, E. & Edwards, D. (1995). Measuring loss on defaulted bank loans: A 24-year study, *The Journal of Commercial Lending* pp. 11–23.

Babbs, S. H. & Nowman, K. B. (1999). Kalman filtering of generalized Vasicek term structure models, *Journal of Financial and Quantitative Analysis* **34**(1): 115–130.

Baldwin, D. (1999). Business is booming, *RISK: Credit Risk Special Report* p. 8.

Barrett, B., Gosnell, T. & Heuson, A. (1995). Yield curve shifts and the selection of immunization strategies, *The Journal of Fixed Income* pp. 53–64.

Basin, V. (1996). On the credit risk of OTC derivative users. Discussion Paper, Board of Governors of the Federal Reserve System.

Bawa, V. (1975). Optimal rules for ordering uncertain prospects, *Journal of Financial Economics* **2**: 95–121.

BBA Credit Derivatives Report 1999/2000 (2000). British Bankers' Association.

Best Practices for Credit Risk Disclosure (2000). Basel Committee on Banking Supervision, Basel.

Bicksler, J. & Chen, A. (1986). An economic analysis of interest rate swaps, *Journal of Finance* **41**: 645–656.

Bingham, N. H. & Kiesel, R. (1998). *Risk-Neutral Valuation: Pricing and Hedging of Financial Derivatives*, first edn, Springer.

Black, F. & Cox, J. (1976). Valuing corporate securities: Some effects of bond indenture provisions, *Journal of Finance* **31**: 351–367.

Boyle, P. P. (1988). A lattice framework for option pricing with two state variables, *Journal of Financial and Quantitative Analysis* **23**(1): 1–12.

Brémaud, P. (1981). *Point Processes and Queues*, Springer Series in Statistics, Springer, New York.

Brennan, M. & Schwartz, E. (1980). Analysing convertible bonds, *Journal of Financial and Quantitative Analysis* **15**: 907–929.

Briys, E. & de Varenne, F. (1997). Valuing risky fixed rate debt: An extension, *Journal of Financial and Quantitative Analysis* **32**(2): 239–248.

Bronstein, I. N. & Semendjajew, K. A. (1991). *Taschenbuch der Mathematik*, 25th edn, Verlag Nauka, Moskau.

Brooks, R. & Yan, D. Y. (1999). London inter-bank offer rate (LIBOR) versus treasury rate: Evidence from the parsimonious term structure model, *The Journal of Fixed Income* pp. 71–83.

Caouette, D. J., Altman, F. & Narayanan, V. (1998). *Managing Credit Risk: The Next Great Financial Challenge*, John Wiley & Sons, Inc., New York.

Carty, L. & Lieberman, D. (1996). Defaulted bank loan recoveries. Moody's Special Report.

Carty, L. V. (1997). Moody's rating migration and credit quality correlation, 1920 - 1996. Special Comment, Moody's Investors Service.

Carty, L. V. (1998). *Moody's Rating Migration and Credit Quality Correlation, 1920-1996*, John Wiley & Sons (Asia) Pte Ltd, Singapore, chapter 10, pp. 349–384.

Carty, L. V. & Fons, J. (1993). Measuring changes in credit quality. Moody's Special Report, Moody's Investors Service.

Carty, L. V. & Lieberman, D. (1998). *Historical Default Rates of Corporate Bond Issuers, 1920 - 1996*, John Wiley & Sons (Asia) Pte Ltd, Singapore, chapter 9, pp. 317–348.

Cathcart, L. & El-Jahel, L. (1998). Valuation of defaultable bonds, *The Journal of Fixed Income* pp. 65–78.

Chen, L. (1996). *Interest Rate Dynamics, Derivatives Pricing, and Risk Management*, number 435 in *Lecture Notes in Economics and Mathematical Systems*, first edn, Springer.

Chen, R. & Scott, L. (1995). Multi-factor Cox-Ingersoll-Ross models of the term structure: Estimates and tests from a Kalman filter model. Unpublished Paper, Rutgers University.

Cooper, I. & Mello, A. (1991). The default risk of swaps, *Journal of Finance* **46**(2): 597–620.

Cox, J., Ingersoll, J. & Ross, S. (1980). An analysis of variable rate loan contracts, *Journal of Finance* **15**: 389–403.

Cox, J., Ingersoll, J. & Ross, S. (1985). A theory of the term structure of interest rates, *Econometrica* **36**(4): 385–407.

CreditMetrics - Technical Document (1997). J.P. Morgan, New York.

CreditRisk+ A Credit Risk Management Framework (1997). Credit Suisse Financial Products.

Crouhy, M. & Mark, R. (1998). A comparative analysis of current credit risk models. Working Paper, Canadian Imperial Bank of Commerce.

Dai, Q. & Singleton, K. J. (1998). Specification analysis of affine term structure models. Working Paper, Graduate School of Business, Stanford University.

Das, S. R. (1995). Credit risk derivatives, *The Journal of Derivatives* pp. 7–23.

Das, S. R. (1997). Pricing credit derivatives. Working Paper, Harvard Business School & NBER.

Das, S. R. & Tufano, P. (1996). Pricing credit-sensitive debt when interest rates, credit ratings and credit spreads are stochastic, *The Journal of Financial Engineering* **5**(2): 161–198.

Demchak, B. (2000). Modelling credit migration, *RISK* pp. 99–103.

Dickey, R. & Fuller, W. (1981). Likelihood ratio tests for autoregressive time series with a unit root, *Econometrica* **49**: 1057–1072.

Duffee, G. R. (1996a). Estimating the price of default risk. Working Paper, Federal Reserve Board, Washington.

Duffee, G. R. (1996b). The relation between treasury yields and corporate bond yield spreads. Working Paper, Federal Reserve Board, Washington.

Duffie, D. (1992). *Dynamic Asset Pricing Theory*, Princeton University Press, Princeton.

Duffie, D. (1998a). Credit swap valuation. Working Paper, Graduate School of Business, Stanford University, Forthcoming: Financial Analyst's Journal.

Duffie, D. (1998b). Defaultable term structure models with fractional recovery of par. Working Paper, Graduate School of Business, Stanford University.

Duffie, D. (1998c). First-to-default valuation. Working Paper, Graduate School of Business, Stanford University.

Duffie, D. & Huang, M. (1996). Swap rates and credit quality, *The Journal of Finance* **51**(3): 921–949.

Duffie, D. & Kan, R. (1996). A yield-factor model of interest rates, *Mathematical Finance* **6**(4): 379–406.

Duffie, D. & Lando, D. (1997). Term structures of credit spreads with incomplete accounting information. Working Paper, Graduate School of Business, Stanford University.

Duffie, D. & Pan, J. (1997). An overview of value at risk, *Journal of Derivatives* **4**(3): 7–49.

Duffie, D., Pan, J. & Singleton, K. (1998). Transform analysis and option pricing for affine jump-diffusions. Working Paper, Graduate School of Business, Stanford University.

Duffie, D., Schroder, M. & Skiadas, C. (1996). Recursive valuation of defaultable securities and the timing of resolution of uncertainty, *The Annals of Applied Probability* **6**(4): 1075–1090.

Duffie, D. & Singleton, K. J. (1997). Modeling term structures of defaultable bonds. Working Paper, Graduate School of Business, Stanford University.

Duffie, D. & Singleton, K. J. (1998). Credit risk for financial institutions: Management and pricing.

Düllmann, K. & Windfuhr, M. (2000). Credit spreads between German and Italian Sovereign bonds - do affine models work ?

Elsas, R., Ewert, R., Krahnen, J., Rudolph, B. & Weber, M. (1999). Risikoorientiertes Kreditmanagement Deutscher Banken, *Die Bank* **3**: 190–199.

Elton, E. J. & Gruber, M. J. (1991). *Modern Portfolio Theory and Investment Analysis*, John Wiley & Sons.

Estimating the Term Structure of Interest Rates (1997). *Monthly report*, Bundesbank.

Evans, G., Blackledge, J. & Yardley, P. (2000). *Analytic Methods for Partial Differential Equations*, Springer Undergraduate Mathematics Series, Springer, London.

Fons, J. S. (1994). Using default rates to model the term structure of credit risk, *Financial Analysts Journal* **50**(5): 25–32.

Franks, J. & Torous, W. (1994). A comparison of financial recontracting in distressed exchanges and chapter 11 reorganizations, *Journal of Financial Economics* **35**: 349–370.

Gastineau, G. (1996). *Dicitionary of Financial Risk Management*, Frank J. Fabozzi Associates, New York.

Geske, R. (1977). The valuation of corporate liabilities as compound options, *Journal of Financial and Quantitative Analysis* pp. 541–552.

Geyer, A. L. J. & Pichler, S. (1996). A state-space approach to estimate and test multi-factor Cox-Ingersoll-Ross models of the term structure.

Gihman, I. & Skorohod, A. (1980). *Introduction à la Théorie des Processus Aléatoires*, Mir.

Gordy, M. B. (1998). A comparative anatomy of credit risk models. Working Paper, Board of Governors of the Federal Reserve System, Washington.

Green, J., Locke, J. & Paul-Choudhury, S. (1998). Strength through adversity, *CreditRisk - A Risk Special Report* pp. 6–9.

Greene, W. H. (2000). *Econometric Analysis*, fourth edn, Prentice Hall International, Inc., New Jersey.

Hargreaves, T. (2000). Default swaps drive growth, *CreditRisk - A Risk Special Report* pp. 2–3.

Harlow, W. (1991). Asset allocation in a downside-risk framework, *Financial Analysts Journal* **47**(5): 28–40.

Harlow, W. & Rao, K. (1989). Asset pricing in a generalized mean-lower partial moment framework: Theory and evidence, *Journal of Financial and Quantitative Analysis* **24**: 285–311.

Harvey, A. C. (1981). *The Econometric Analysis of Time Series*, Philip Allan Publishers Limited.

Harvey, A. C. (1989). *Forecasting, Structural Time Series Models and the Kalman Filter*, Cambridge University Press, Cambridge.

Heath, D., Jarrow, R. & Morton, A. (1992). Bond pricing and the term structure of interest rates: A new methodology for contingent claims valuation, *Econometrica* **60**: 77–105.

Historical Default Rates of Corporate Bond Issuers, 1920-1999 (2000a). Special Comment, Moody's Investors Services, Global Credit Research.

Historical Default Rates of Corporate Bond Issuers, 1920-1999 (2000b). Special Comment, Moody's Investors Service, Global Credit Research.

Ho, T. & Singer, R. (1982). Bond indenture provisions and the risk of corporate debt, *Journal of Financial Economics* (10): 375–406.

Hull, J. (1997). *Options, Futures, and Other Derivatives*, Prentice-Hall International, Inc., London.

Hull, J. C. & White, A. (2000). Valuing credit default swaps I: No counterparty default risk, *The Journal of Derivatives* pp. 29–40.

Hull, J. & White, A. (1990). Pricing interest-rate-derivative securities, *The Review of Financial Studies* **3**(4): 573–592.

Hull, J. & White, A. (1994). Numerical procedures for implementing term structure models II: Two-factor models, *The Journal of Derivatives* pp. 37–48.

Ikeda, N. & Watanabe, S. (1989a). *Stochastic Differential Equations and Diffusion Processes*, 1st edn, North-Holland.

Ikeda, N. & Watanabe, S. (1989b). *Stochastic Differential Equations and Diffusion Processes*, 2nd edn, North-Holland.

Ingersoll, J. E. (1987). *Theory of Financial Decision Making*, Studies in Financial Economics, Rowman & Littlefield Publishers.

Jacod, J. & Shiryaev, A. (1987). *Limit Theorems for Stochastic Processes*, A Series of Comprehensive Studies in Mathematics, Springer, Berlin.

James, J. (1999). How much should they cost, *CreditRisk - A Risk Special Report* pp. 8–10.

Jarrow, R. A., Lando, D. & Turnbull, S. M. (1997). A markov model for the term structure of credit risk spreads, *The Review of Financial Studies* **10**(2): 481–523.

Jarrow, R. & Turnbull, S. (1995). Pricing options on financial securities subject to default risk, *Journal of Finance* **50**: 53–86.

Jarrow, R. & Turnbull, S. (1998). The intersection of market and credit risk. Working Paper.

Jones, E., Mason, S. & Rosenfeld, E. (1984). Contingent claim analysis of corporate capital structures: An empirical investigation, *Journal of Finance* **39**: 611–625.

Jones, F. (1991). Yield curve strategies, *Journal of Fixed Income* pp. 43–51.

Jordan, J. & Mansi, S. (2000). Estimation of the term structure from on-the-run treasuries. Working Paper, National Economic Research Associates, and George Washington University.

Karatzas, I. (1988). On the pricing of american options, *Applied Mathematics and Optimization* **17**: 37–60.

Karatzas, I. & Shreve, S. (1988). *Brownian Motion and Stochastic Calculus*, Springer.

Kealhofer, S. (1998). Portfolio management of default risk, *Net Exposure* **1**(2).

Keenan, S. & Sobehart, J. (2000). A credit risk catwalk, *RISK* pp. 84–88.

Kiesel, R. & Schmid, B. (2000). Aspekte der stochastischen Modellierung von Ausfallwahrscheinlichkeiten in Kreditportfoliomodellen, *in* A. Oehler (ed.), *Kreditrisikomanagement - Portfoliomodelle und Derivate*, Schäffer Poeschel, Stuttgart.

Kim, J., Ramaswamy, K. & Sundaresan, S. (1992). The valuation of corporate fixed income securities.

Kim, J., Ramaswamy, K. & Sundaresan, S. (Autumn 1993). Does default risk in coupons affect the valuation of corporate bonds ? A contingent claims model, *Financial Management* pp. 117–131.

Korn, R. & Korn, E. (1999). *Optionsbewertung und Portfolio-Optimierung*, first edn, Vieweg, Braunschweig/Wiesbaden.

Koyluoglu, H. U. & Hickman, A. (1998). A generalized framework for credit risk portfolio models. Working Paper, Oliver Wyman and Company and CSFP Capital, Inc., New York.

Lamberton, D. & Lapeyre, B. (1996). *Introduction to Stochastic Calculus Applied to Finance*, Chapman & Hall.

Lando, D. (1994). *Three Essays on Contingent Claims Pricing*, PhD thesis, Cornell University.

Lando, D. (1995). On jump-diffusion option pricing from the viewpoint of semimartingale characteristics, *Surveys in Applied and Industrial Mathematics* **2**(4): 605–625.

Lando, D. (1996). Modelling bonds and derivatives with default risk. Working Paper, Department of Operations Research, University of Copenhagen.

Lando, D. (1998). On Cox processes and credit risky securities. Working Paper, Department of Operations Research, University of Copenhagen.

Larsen, R. J. & Marx, M. L. (2001). *An Introduction to Mathematical Statistics and Its Applications*, third edn, Prentice Hall, New Jersey.

Leland, H. E. (1994). Corporate debt value, bond covenants, and optimal capital structure, *The Journal of Finance* **49**(4): 1213–1252.

Litterman, R. & Scheinkman, J. (1991). Common factors affecting bond returns, *The Journal of Fixed Income* pp. 54–61.

Longstaff, F. A. (1990). The valuation of options on yields, *Journal of Financial Economics* **26**: 97–121.

Longstaff, F. A. & Schwartz, E. S. (1995a). Valuing credit derivatives, *The Journal of Fixed Income* pp. 6–12.

Longstaff, F. & Schwartz, E. (1995b). A simple approach to valuing risky fixed and floating rate debt, *The Journal of Finance* **50**(3): 789–819.

Lopez, J. A. & Saidenberg, M. R. (1998). Evaluating credit risk models. Working Paper, Federal Reserve Bank of San Francisco and Federal Reserve Bank of New York.

Lucas, D. J. & Lonski, J. G. (1992). Changes in corporate credit quality 1970 - 1990, *Journal of Fixed Income* pp. 7–14.

Madan, D. B. & Unal, H. (1994). Pricing the risks of default. The Wharton School, University of Pennsylvania.

Madan, D. & Unal, H. (1998). Pricing the risks of default, *Review of Derivatives Research* **2**(2/3): 121–160.

Mansi, J. V. J. A. S. A. (2000). How well do constant-maturity treasuries approximate the on-the-run term structure, *The Journal of Fixed Income* **10**(2): 35–62.

Markowitz, H. (1952). Portfolio selection, *Journal of Finance* **7**: 77–91.

Markowitz, H. (1991). *Portfolio Selection*, Blackwell.

Martin, J., Cox, S. & MacMinn, R. (1988). *The Theory of Finance, Evidence and Applications*, Dryden.

Mason, S. & Bhattacharya, S. (1981). Risky debt, jump processes, and safety covenants, *Journal of Financial Economics* **9**: 281–307.

Masters, B. (1998). Credit derivatives and the management of credit risk, *Net Exposure* **1**(2).

McLeish, N. (2000). European credit markets: The case for growth, *CreditRisk: A Risk Special Report* pp. 4–6.

Merton, R. (1974). On the pricing of corporate debt: The risk structure of interest rates, *Journal of Finance* **29**: 449–470.

Musiela, M. & Rutkowski, M. (1997). *Martingale Methods in Financial Modelling*, Springer.

Nelder, J. A. & Mead, R. (1965). A simplex method for function minimization, *The Computer Journal* **7**: 308–313.

Nelson, C. & Siegel, A. (1987). Parsimonious modeling of yield curves, *Journal of Business* **60**: 473–489.

Nickell, P., Perraudin, W. & Varotto, S. (1998). Stability of rating transitions. Working Paper, Bank of England.

Nielsen, L., Saà-Requejo, J. & Santa-Clara, P. (1993). Default risk and interest rate risk: The term structure of default spreads. Working Paper, INSEAD.

Oksendal, B. (1998). *Stochastic Differential Equations - An Introduction with Applications*, Universitext, 5th edn, Springer.

Ong, M. K. (1999). *Internal Credit Risk Models: Capital Allocation and Performance Measurement*, Risk Books, London.

Overview of the New Basel Capital Accord (2001). Consultative Document, Basel Committee on Banking Supervision, Basel.

Patel, N. (2001). Credit derivatives: Vanilla volumes challenged, *RISK* pp. 32–34.

Pedrosa, M. & Roll, R. (1998). Systematic risk in corporate bond credit spreads, *The Journal of Fixed Income* **8**(3): 7–26.

Protter, P. (1992). *Stochastic Integration and Differential Equations*, Springer, Berlin.

Ratings Performance 1996: Stability & Transition (1997). New York.

Ratings Performance 1997: Stability & Transition (1998). New York.

Ratings Performance 1998: Stability & Transition (1999). New York.

Ratings Performance 1999: Stability & Transition (2000). New York.

Ratings Performance 2000: Default, Transition, Recovery, and Spreads (2001). New York.

Rendleman, R. J. (1992). How risks are shared in interest rate swaps, *Journal of Financial Services Research* pp. 5–34.

Ross, S. M. (1996). *Stochastic Processes*, Wiley Series in Probability and Mathematical Statistics, second edn, John Wiley & Sons, Inc., New York.

Saá-Requejo, J. & Santa-Clara, P. (1997). Bond pricing with default risk.

Sandmann, K. & Sondermann, D. (1997). A note on the stability of lognormal interest rate models and pricing of eurodollar futures, *Mathematical Finance* **7**(2): 119–126.

Sarig, O. & Warga, A. (1989). Some empirical estimates of the term structure of interest rates, *Journal of Finance* **44**(5): 1351–1360.

Schmid, B. (1997). CreditMetrics - setting a benchmark, *Solutions* **1**(3-4): 35–53.

Schmid, B. (1998a). Credit Risk - Verschiedene Methoden zur Berechnung von Kreditrisiken. RiskLab Research Paper No. 9807.

Schmid, B. (1998b). Kreditderivate - Neue Instrumente zur Steuerung des Kreditrisikos, *Solutions* **2**(4): 7–16.

Schmid, B. (1998c). Quantifizierung von Ausfallrisiken - Alternativen zu CreditMetrics, *Solutions* **2**(1).

Schmid, B. (2000). Das RiskLab Kreditrisiko Modell, *Solutions* **3**(3/4): 39–54.

Schmid, B. (2001a). *Pricing Credit Linked Financial Instruments - Theory and Empirical Evidence*, PhD thesis, Europe University Viadrina, Frankfurt/Oder.

Schmid, B. (2001b). The pricing of defaultable fixed and floating rate debt - closed form solutions for the Schmid and Zagst model, *in* M. Bellalah, M. Triki, A. Ghorbel, F. Abid & S. B. Hamad (eds), *Financial Markets, Risk Management and Corporate Governance*, pp. 388–408. Proceedings, International Finance Conference, Tunisia 2001, and accepted for publication in the Journal of International Finance.

Schmid, B. & Kalemanova, A. (2001). Credit spreads between German and Italian zero coupon government bonds - empirical assessment of a three-factor defaultable term structure model. Research Paper 0101, Risklab Germany, and accepted for publication in the Research in International Business and Finance (volume 16, publication 2002).

Schmid, B. & Zagst, R. (2000). A three-factor defaultable term structure model, *The Journal of Fixed Income* **10**(2): 63–79.

Schönbucher, P. J. (1996). The term structure of defaultable bond prices. Discussion Paper B-384, University of Bonn, Department of Statistics.

Schönbucher, P. J. (2000). *Credit Risk Modelling and Credit Derivatives*, PhD thesis, Rheinische Friedrich-Wilhelms-Universität Bonn.

Sharpe, W. (1964). Capital asset prices: A theory of market equilibrium under conditions of risk, *Journal of Finance* **29**: 425–442.

Shimko, D., Tejima, N. & Deventer, D. V. (1993). The pricing of risky debt when interest rates are stochastic, *The Journal of Fixed Income* pp. 58–65.

Sorensen, E. & Bollier, T. (1994). Pricing swap default risk, *Financial Analysts Journal* **50**(3): 23–33.

Structured Products/ ABS Market Monthly (1999). J. P. Morgan Securities Inc., SP/ABS Credit Research, New York.

Sundaresan, S. (1991). *Valuation of Swaps*, Elsevier (North-Holland), chapter 12.

Taurén, M. (1999). A comparison of bond pricing models in the pricing of credit risk. Working Paper, Indiana University, Bloomington.

The Internal Ratings-Based Approach (2001). Consultative Document, Supporting Document to the New Basel Capital Accord, Basel Committee on Banking Supervision, Basel.

The New Basel Capital Accord (2001). Consultative Document, Basel Committee on Banking Supervision, Basel.

The Standardised Approach to Credit Risk (2001). Consultative Document, Supporting Document to the New Basel Capital Accord, Basel Committee on Banking Supervision, Basel.

Titman, S. & Torous, W. (1989). Valuing commercial mortgages: An empirical investigation of the contingent-claim approach to pricing risky debt, *Journal of Finance* **44**: 345–373.

Update on Work on a New Capital Adequacy Framework (1999). Basel Committee on Banking Supervision, Basel.

Vasicek, O. (1977). An equilibrium characterization of the term structure, *Journal of Financial Economics* **7**: 117–161.

Vasicek, O. A. (1997). Credit valuation, *Net Exposure* **1**: 1–12.

Wei, D. G. & Guo, D. (1997). Pricing risky debt: An empirical comparison of the Longstaff and Schwartz and Merton models, *The Journal of Fixed Income* pp. 8–28.

Willner, R. (1996). A new tool for portfolio managers: Level, slope, and curvature durations, *The Journal of Fixed Income* pp. 48–59.

Wilmott, P., Dewynne, J. & Howison, S. (1993). *Option Pricing - Mathematical Models and Computation*, first edn, Oxford Financial Press.

Wilson, T. (1997a). Measuring and managing credit portfolio risk: Part I: Modelling systematic default risk, *The Journal of Lending and Credit Risk Management* pp. 61–72.

Wilson, T. (1997b). Measuring and managing credit portfolio risk: Part II: Portfolio loss distributions, *The Journal of Lending and Credit Risk Management* pp. 67–78.

Wilson, T. (1997c). Portfolio credit risk (I), *RISK* **10**(9).

Wilson, T. (1997d). Portfolio credit risk (II), *RISK* **10**(10).

Wilson, T. (1998). Trends in credit risk management, *The Journal of Financial Engineering* **7**(3/4): 217–240.

Young, G. & Bhagat, C. (2000). Credit risk's softer side, *Asia Risk* pp. 30–32.

Zagst, R. (2001). *Interest Rate Management*, Springer.

Zhou, C. (1997). A jump-diffusion approach to modeling credit risk and valuing defaultable securities. Working Paper, Federal Reserve Board, Washington.

Index

Druck: Strauss Offsetdruck, Mörlenbach
Verarbeitung: Schäffer, Grünstadt

Lecture Notes in Economics and Mathematical Systems

For information about Vols. 1–320
please contact your bookseller or Springer-Verlag

Vol. 325: P. Ferri, E. Greenberg, The Labor Market and Business Cycle Theories. X, 183 pages. 1989.

Vol. 326: Ch. Sauer, Alternative Theories of Output, Unemployment, and Inflation in Germany: 1960–1985. XIII, 206 pages. 1989.

Vol. 327: M. Tawada, Production Structure and International Trade. V, 132 pages. 1989.

Vol. 328: W. Güth, B. Kalkofen, Unique Solutions for Strategic Games. VII, 200 pages. 1989.

Vol. 329: G. Tillmann, Equity, Incentives, and Taxation. VI, 132 pages. 1989.

Vol. 330: P.M. Kort, Optimal Dynamic Investment Policies of a Value Maximizing Firm. VII, 185 pages. 1989.

Vol. 331: A. Lewandowski, A.P. Wierzbicki (Eds.), Aspiration Based Decision Support Systems. X, 400 pages. 1989.

Vol. 332: T.R. Gulledge, Jr., L.A. Litteral (Eds.), Cost Analysis Applications of Economics and Operations Research. Proceedings. VII, 422 pages. 1989.

Vol. 333: N. Dellaert, Production to Order. VII, 158 pages. 1989.

Vol. 334: H.-W. Lorenz, Nonlinear Dynamical Economics and Chaotic Motion. XI, 248 pages. 1989.

Vol. 335: A.G. Lockett, G. Islei (Eds.), Improving Decision Making in Organisations. Proceedings. IX, 606 pages. 1989.

Vol. 336: T. Puu, Nonlinear Economic Dynamics. VII, 119 pages. 1989.

Vol. 337: A. Lewandowski, I. Stanchev (Eds.), Methodology and Software for Interactive Decision Support. VIII, 309 pages. 1989.

Vol. 338: J.K. Ho, R.P. Sundarraj, DECOMP: An Implementation of Dantzig-Wolfe Decomposition for Linear Programming. VI, 206 pages.

Vol. 339: J. Terceiro Lomba, Estimation of Dynamic Econometric Models with Errors in Variables. VIII, 116 pages. 1990.

Vol. 340: T. Vasko, R. Ayres, L. Fontvieille (Eds.), Life Cycles and Long Waves. XIV, 293 pages. 1990.

Vol. 341: G.R. Uhlich, Descriptive Theories of Bargaining. IX, 165 pages. 1990.

Vol. 342: K. Okuguchi, F. Szidarovszky, The Theory of Oligopoly with Multi-Product Firms. V, 167 pages. 1990.

Vol. 343: C. Chiarella, The Elements of a Nonlinear Theory of Economic Dynamics. IX, 149 pages. 1990.

Vol. 344: K. Neumann, Stochastic Project Networks. XI, 237 pages. 1990.

Vol. 345: A. Cambini, E. Castagnoli, L. Martein, P Mazzoleni, S. Schaible (Eds.), Generalized Convexity and Fractional Programming with Economic Applications. Proceedings, 1988. VII, 361 pages. 1990.

Vol. 346: R. von Randow (Ed.), Integer Programming and Related Areas. A Classified Bibliography 1984–1987. XIII, 514 pages. 1990.

Vol. 347: D. Ríos Insua, Sensitivity Analysis in Multi-objective Decision Making. XI, 193 pages. 1990.

Vol. 348: H. Störmer, Binary Functions and their Applications. VIII, 151 pages. 1990.

Vol. 349: G.A. Pfann, Dynamic Modelling of Stochastic Demand for Manufacturing Employment. VI, 158 pages. 1990.

Vol. 350: W.-B. Zhang, Economic Dynamics. X, 232 pages. 1990.

Vol. 351: A. Lewandowski, V. Volkovich (Eds.), Multiobjective Problems of Mathematical Programming. Proceedings, 1988. VII, 315 pages. 1991.

Vol. 352: O. van Hilten, Optimal Firm Behaviour in the Context of Technological Progress and a Business Cycle. XII, 229 pages. 1991.

Vol. 353: G. Ricci (Ed.), Decision Processes in Economics. Proceedings, 1989. III, 209 pages 1991.

Vol. 354: M. Ivaldi, A Structural Analysis of Expectation Formation. XII, 230 pages. 1991.

Vol. 355: M. Salomon. Deterministic Lotsizing Models for Production Planning. VII, 158 pages. 1991.

Vol. 356: P. Korhonen, A. Lewandowski, J . Wallenius (Eds.), Multiple Criteria Decision Support. Proceedings, 1989. XII, 393 pages. 1991.

Vol. 357: P. Zörnig, Degeneracy Graphs and Simplex Cycling. XV, 194 pages. 1991.

Vol. 358: P. Knottnerus, Linear Models with Correlated Disturbances. VIII, 196 pages. 1991.

Vol. 359: E. de Jong, Exchange Rate Determination and Optimal Economic Policy Under Various Exchange Rate Regimes. VII, 270 pages. 1991.

Vol. 360: P. Stalder, Regime Translations, Spillovers and Buffer Stocks. VI, 193 pages . 1991.

Vol. 361: C. F. Daganzo, Logistics Systems Analysis. X, 321 pages. 1991.

Vol. 362: F. Gehrels, Essays in Macroeconomics of an Open Economy. VII, 183 pages. 1991.

Vol. 363: C. Puppe, Distorted Probabilities and Choice under Risk. VIII, 100 pages . 1991

Vol. 364: B. Horvath, Are Policy Variables Exogenous? XII, 162 pages. 1991.

Vol. 365: G. A. Heuer, U. Leopold-Wildburger. Balanced Silverman Games on General Discrete Sets. V, 140 pages. 1991.

Vol. 366: J. Gruber (Ed.), Econometric Decision Models. Proceedings, 1989. VIII, 636 pages. 1991.

Vol. 367: M. Grauer, D. B. Pressmar (Eds.), Parallel Computing and Mathematical Optimization. Proceedings. V, 208 pages. 1991.

Vol. 368: M. Fedrizzi, J. Kacprzyk, M. Roubens (Eds.), Interactive Fuzzy Optimization. VII, 216 pages. 1991.

Vol. 369: R. Koblo, The Visible Hand. VIII, 131 pages.1991.

Vol. 370: M. J. Beckmann, M. N. Gopalan, R. Subramanian (Eds.), Stochastic Processes and their Applications. Proceedings, 1990. XLI, 292 pages. 1991.

Vol. 371: A. Schmutzler, Flexibility and Adjustment to Information in Sequential Decision Problems. VIII, 198 pages. 1991.

Vol. 372: J. Esteban, The Social Viability of Money. X, 202 pages. 1991.

Vol. 373: A. Billot, Economic Theory of Fuzzy Equilibria. XIII, 164 pages. 1992.

Vol. 374: G. Pflug, U. Dieter (Eds.), Simulation and Optimization. Proceedings, 1990. X, 162 pages. 1992.

Vol. 375: S.-J. Chen, Ch.-L. Hwang, Fuzzy Multiple Attribute Decision Making. XII, 536 pages. 1992.

Vol. 376: K.-H. Jöckel, G. Rothe, W. Sendler (Eds.), Bootstrapping and Related Techniques. Proceedings, 1990. VIII, 247 pages. 1992.

Vol. 377: A. Villar, Operator Theorems with Applications to Distributive Problems and Equilibrium Models. XVI, 160 pages. 1992.

Vol. 378: W. Krabs, J. Zowe (Eds.), Modern Methods of Optimization. Proceedings, 1990. VIII, 348 pages. 1992.

Vol. 379: K. Marti (Ed.), Stochastic Optimization. Proceedings, 1990. VII, 182 pages. 1992.

Vol. 380: J. Odelstad, Invariance and Structural Dependence. XII, 245 pages. 1992.

Vol. 381: C. Giannini, Topics in Structural VAR Econometrics. XI, 131 pages. 1992.

Vol. 382: W. Oettli, D. Pallaschke (Eds.), Advances in Optimization. Proceedings, 1991. X, 527 pages. 1992.

Vol. 383: J. Vartiainen, Capital Accumulation in a Corporatist Economy. VII, 177 pages. 1992.

Vol. 384: A. Martina, Lectures on the Economic Theory of Taxation. XII, 313 pages. 1992.

Vol. 385: J. Gardeazabal, M. Regúlez, The Monetary Model of Exchange Rates and Cointegration. X, 194 pages. 1992.

Vol. 386: M. Desrochers, J.-M. Rousseau (Eds.), Computer-Aided Transit Scheduling. Proceedings, 1990. XIII, 432 pages. 1992.

Vol. 387: W. Gaertner, M. Klemisch-Ahlert, Social Choice and Bargaining Perspectives on Distributive Justice. VIII, 131 pages. 1992.

Vol. 388: D. Bartmann, M. J. Beckmann, Inventory Control. XV, 252 pages. 1992.

Vol. 389: B. Dutta, D. Mookherjee, T. Parthasarathy, T. Raghavan, D. Ray, S. Tijs (Eds.), Game Theory and Economic Applications. Proceedings, 1990. IX, 454 pages. 1992.

Vol. 390: G. Sorger, Minimum Impatience Theorem for Recursive Economic Models. X, 162 pages. 1992.

Vol. 391: C. Keser, Experimental Duopoly Markets with Demand Inertia. X, 150 pages. 1992.

Vol. 392: K. Frauendorfer, Stochastic Two-Stage Programming. VIII, 228 pages. 1992.

Vol. 393: B. Lucke, Price Stabilization on World Agricultural Markets. XI, 274 pages. 1992.

Vol. 394: Y.-J. Lai, C.-L. Hwang, Fuzzy Mathematical Programming. XIII, 301 pages. 1992.

Vol. 395: G. Haag, U. Mueller, K. G. Troitzsch (Eds.), Economic Evolution and Demographic Change. XVI, 409 pages. 1992.

Vol. 396: R. V. V. Vidal (Ed.), Applied Simulated Annealing. VIII, 358 pages. 1992.

Vol. 397: J. Wessels, A. P. Wierzbicki (Eds.), User-Oriented Methodology and Techniques of Decision Analysis and Support. Proceedings, 1991. XII, 295 pages. 1993.

Vol. 398: J.-P. Urbain, Exogeneity in Error Correction Models. XI, 189 pages. 1993.

Vol. 399: F. Gori, L. Geronazzo, M. Galeotti (Eds.), Nonlinear Dynamics in Economics and Social Sciences. Proceedings, 1991. VIII, 367 pages. 1993.

Vol. 400: H. Tanizaki, Nonlinear Filters. XII, 203 pages. 1993.

Vol. 401: K. Mosler, M. Scarsini, Stochastic Orders and Applications. V, 379 pages. 1993.

Vol. 402: A. van den Elzen, Adjustment Processes for Exchange Economies and Noncooperative Games. VII, 146 pages. 1993.

Vol. 403: G. Brennscheidt, Predictive Behavior. VI, 227 pages. 1993.

Vol. 404: Y.-J. Lai, Ch.-L. Hwang, Fuzzy Multiple Objective Decision Making. XIV, 475 pages. 1994.

Vol. 405: S. Komlósi, T. Rapcsák, S. Schaible (Eds.), Generalized Convexity. Proceedings, 1992. VIII, 404 pages. 1994.

Vol. 406: N. M. Hung, N. V. Quyen, Dynamic Timing Decisions Under Uncertainty. X, 194 pages. 1994.

Vol. 407: M. Ooms, Empirical Vector Autoregressive Modeling. XIII, 380 pages. 1994.

Vol. 408: K. Haase, Lotsizing and Scheduling for Production Planning. VIII, 118 pages. 1994.

Vol. 409: A. Sprecher, Resource-Constrained Project Scheduling. XII, 142 pages. 1994.

Vol. 410: R. Winkelmann, Count Data Models. XI, 213 pages. 1994.

Vol. 411: S. Dauzère-Péres, J.-B. Lasserre, An Integrated Approach in Production Planning and Scheduling. XVI, 137 pages. 1994.

Vol. 412: B. Kuon, Two-Person Bargaining Experiments with Incomplete Information. IX, 293 pages. 1994.

Vol. 413: R. Fiorito (Ed.), Inventory, Business Cycles and Monetary Transmission. VI, 287 pages. 1994.

Vol. 414: Y. Crama, A. Oerlemans, F. Spieksma, Production Planning in Automated Manufacturing. X, 210 pages. 1994.

Vol. 415: P. C. Nicola, Imperfect General Equilibrium. XI, 167 pages. 1994.

Vol. 416: H. S. J. Cesar, Control and Game Models of the Greenhouse Effect. XI, 225 pages. 1994.

Vol. 417: B. Ran, D. E. Boyce, Dynamic Urban Transportation Network Models. XV, 391 pages. 1994.

Vol. 418: P. Bogetoft, Non-Cooperative Planning Theory. XI, 309 pages. 1994.

Vol. 419: T. Maruyama, W. Takahashi (Eds.), Nonlinear and Convex Analysis in Economic Theory. VIII, 306 pages. 1995.

Vol. 420: M. Peeters, Time-To-Build. Interrelated Investment and Labour Demand Modelling. With Applications to Six OECD Countries. IX, 204 pages. 1995.

Vol. 421: C. Dang, Triangulations and Simplicial Methods. IX, 196 pages. 1995.

Vol. 422: D. S. Bridges, G. B. Mehta, Representations of Preference Orderings. X, 165 pages. 1995.

Vol. 423: K. Marti, P. Kall (Eds.), Stochastic Programming. Numerical Techniques and Engineering Applications. VIII, 351 pages. 1995.

Vol. 424: G. A. Heuer, U. Leopold-Wildburger, Silverman's Game. X, 283 pages. 1995.

Vol. 425: J. Kohlas, P.-A. Monney, A Mathematical Theory of Hints. XIII, 419 pages, 1995.

Vol. 426: B. Finkenstädt, Nonlinear Dynamics in Economics. IX, 156 pages. 1995.

Vol. 427: F. W. van Tongeren, Microsimulation Modelling of the Corporate Firm. XVII, 275 pages. 1995.

Vol. 428: A. A. Powell, Ch. W. Murphy, Inside a Modern Macroeconometric Model. XVIII, 424 pages. 1995.

Vol. 429: R. Durier, C. Michelot, Recent Developments in Optimization. VIII, 356 pages. 1995.

Vol. 430: J. R. Daduna, I. Branco, J. M. Pinto Paixão (Eds.), Computer-Aided Transit Scheduling. XIV, 374 pages. 1995.

Vol. 431: A. Aulin, Causal and Stochastic Elements in Business Cycles. XI, 116 pages. 1996.

Vol. 432: M. Tamiz (Ed.), Multi-Objective Programming and Goal Programming. VI, 359 pages. 1996.

Vol. 433: J. Menon, Exchange Rates and Prices. XIV, 313 pages. 1996.

Vol. 434: M. W. J. Blok, Dynamic Models of the Firm. VII, 193 pages. 1996.

Vol. 435: L. Chen, Interest Rate Dynamics, Derivatives Pricing, and Risk Management. XII, 149 pages. 1996.

Vol. 436: M. Klemisch-Ahlert, Bargaining in Economic and Ethical Environments. IX, 155 pages. 1996.

Vol. 437: C. Jordan, Batching and Scheduling. IX, 178 pages. 1996.

Vol. 438: A. Villar, General Equilibrium with Increasing Returns. XIII, 164 pages. 1996.

Vol. 439: M. Zenner, Learning to Become Rational. VII, 201 pages. 1996.

Vol. 440: W. Ryll, Litigation and Settlement in a Game with Incomplete Information. VIII, 174 pages. 1996.

Vol. 441: H. Dawid, Adaptive Learning by Genetic Algorithms. IX, 166 pages.1996.

Vol. 442: L. Corchón, Theories of Imperfectly Competitive Markets. XIII, 163 pages. 1996.

Vol. 443: G. Lang, On Overlapping Generations Models with Productive Capital. X, 98 pages. 1996.

Vol. 444: S. Jørgensen, G. Zaccour (Eds.), Dynamic Competitive Analysis in Marketing. X, 285 pages. 1996.

Vol. 445: A. H. Christer, S. Osaki, L. C. Thomas (Eds.), Stochastic Modelling in Innovative Manufactoring. X, 361 pages. 1997.

Vol. 446: G. Dhaene, Encompassing. X, 160 pages. 1997.

Vol. 447: A. Artale, Rings in Auctions. X, 172 pages. 1997.

Vol. 448: G. Fandel, T. Gal (Eds.), Multiple Criteria Decision Making. XII, 678 pages. 1997.

Vol. 449: F. Fang, M. Sanglier (Eds.), Complexity and Self-Organization in Social and Economic Systems. IX, 317 pages, 1997.

Vol. 450: P. M. Pardalos, D. W. Hearn, W. W. Hager, (Eds.), Network Optimization. VIII, 485 pages, 1997.

Vol. 451: M. Salge, Rational Bubbles. Theoretical Basis, Economic Relevance, and Empirical Evidence with a Special Emphasis on the German Stock Market.IX, 265 pages. 1997.

Vol. 452: P. Gritzmann, R. Horst, E. Sachs, R. Tichatschke (Eds.), Recent Advances in Optimization. VIII, 379 pages. 1997.

Vol. 453: A. S. Tangian, J. Gruber (Eds.), Constructing Scalar-Valued Objective Functions. VIII, 298 pages. 1997.

Vol. 454: H.-M. Krolzig, Markov-Switching Vector Autoregressions. XIV, 358 pages. 1997.

Vol. 455: R. Caballero, F. Ruiz, R. E. Steuer (Eds.), Advances in Multiple Objective and Goal Programming. VIII, 391 pages. 1997.

Vol. 456: R. Conte, R. Hegselmann, P. Terna (Eds.), Simulating Social Phenomena. VIII, 536 pages. 1997.

Vol. 457: C. Hsu, Volume and the Nonlinear Dynamics of Stock Returns. VIII, 133 pages. 1998.

Vol. 458: K. Marti, P. Kall (Eds.), Stochastic Programming Methods and Technical Applications. X, 437 pages. 1998.

Vol. 459: H. K. Ryu, D. J. Slottje, Measuring Trends in U.S. Income Inequality. XI, 195 pages. 1998.

Vol. 460: B. Fleischmann, J. A. E. E. van Nunen, M. G. Speranza, P. Stähly, Advances in Distribution Logistic. XI, 535 pages. 1998.

Vol. 461: U. Schmidt, Axiomatic Utility Theory under Risk. XV, 201 pages. 1998.

Vol. 462: L. von Auer, Dynamic Preferences, Choice Mechanisms, and Welfare. XII, 226 pages. 1998.

Vol. 463: G. Abraham-Frois (Ed.), Non-Linear Dynamics and Endogenous Cycles. VI, 204 pages. 1998.

Vol. 464: A. Aulin, The Impact of Science on Economic Growth and its Cycles. IX, 204 pages. 1998.

Vol. 465: T. J. Stewart, R. C. van den Honert (Eds.), Trends in Multicriteria Decision Making. X, 448 pages. 1998.

Vol. 466: A. Sadrieh, The Alternating Double Auction Market. VII, 350 pages. 1998.

Vol. 467: H. Hennig-Schmidt, Bargaining in a Video Experiment. Determinants of Boundedly Rational Behavior. XII, 221 pages. 1999.

Vol. 468: A. Ziegler, A Game Theory Analysis of Options. XIV, 145 pages. 1999.

Vol. 469: M. P. Vogel, Environmental Kuznets Curves. XIII, 197 pages. 1999.

Vol. 470: M. Ammann, Pricing Derivative Credit Risk. XII, 228 pages. 1999.

Vol. 471: N. H. M. Wilson (Ed.), Computer-Aided Transit Scheduling. XI, 444 pages. 1999.

Vol. 472: J.-R. Tyran, Money Illusion and Strategic Complementarity as Causes of Monetary Non-Neutrality. X, 228 pages. 1999.

Vol. 473: S. Helber, Performance Analysis of Flow Lines with Non-Linear Flow of Material. IX, 280 pages. 1999.

Vol. 474: U. Schwalbe, The Core of Economies with Asymmetric Information. IX, 141 pages. 1999.

Vol. 475: L. Kaas, Dynamic Macroeconomics with Imperfect Competition. XI, 155 pages. 1999.

Vol. 476: R. Demel, Fiscal Policy, Public Debt and the Term Structure of Interest Rates. X, 279 pages. 1999.

Vol. 477: M. Théra, R. Tichatschke (Eds.), Ill-posed Variational Problems and Regularization Techniques. VIII, 274 pages. 1999.

Vol. 478: S. Hartmann, Project Scheduling under Limited Resources. XII, 221 pages. 1999.

Vol. 479: L. v. Thadden, Money, Inflation, and Capital Formation. IX, 192 pages. 1999.

Vol. 480: M. Grazia Speranza, P. Stähly (Eds.), New Trends in Distribution Logistics. X, 336 pages. 1999.

Vol. 481: V. H. Nguyen, J. J. Strodiot, P. Tossings (Eds.). Optimation. IX, 498 pages. 2000.

Vol. 482: W. B. Zhang, A Theory of International Trade. XI, 192 pages. 2000.

Vol. 483: M. Königstein, Equity, Efficiency and Evolutionary Stability in Bargaining Games with Joint Production. XII, 197 pages. 2000.

Vol. 484: D. D. Gatti, M. Gallegati, A. Kirman, Interaction and Market Structure. VI, 298 pages. 2000.

Vol. 485: A. Garnaev, Search Games and Other Applications of Game Theory. VIII, 145 pages. 2000.

Vol. 486: M. Neugart, Nonlinear Labor Market Dynamics. X, 175 pages. 2000.

Vol. 487: Y. Y. Haimes, R. E. Steuer (Eds.), Research and Practice in Multiple Criteria Decision Making. XVII, 553 pages. 2000.

Vol. 488: B. Schmolck, Ommitted Variable Tests and Dynamic Specification. X, 144 pages. 2000.

Vol. 489: T. Steger, Transitional Dynamics and Economic Growth in Developing Countries. VIII, 151 pages. 2000.

Vol. 490: S. Minner, Strategic Safety Stocks in Supply Chains. XI, 214 pages. 2000.

Vol. 491: M. Ehrgott, Multicriteria Optimization. VIII, 242 pages. 2000.

Vol. 492: T. Phan Huy, Constraint Propagation in Flexible Manufacturing. IX, 258 pages. 2000.

Vol. 493: J. Zhu, Modular Pricing of Options. X, 170 pages. 2000.

Vol. 494: D. Franzen, Design of Master Agreements for OTC Derivatives. VIII, 175 pages. 2001.

Vol. 495: I Konnov, Combined Relaxation Methods for Variational Inequalities. XI, 181 pages. 2001.

Vol. 496: P. Weiß, Unemployment in Open Economies. XII, 226 pages. 2001.

Vol. 497: J. Inkmann, Conditional Moment Estimation of Nonlinear Equation Systems. VIII, 214 pages. 2001.

Vol. 498: M. Reutter, A Macroeconomic Model of West German Unemployment. X, 125 pages. 2001.

Vol. 499: A. Casajus, Focal Points in Framed Games. XI, 131 pages. 2001.

Vol. 500: F. Nardini, Technical Progress and Economic Growth. XVII, 191 pages. 2001.

Vol. 501: M. Fleischmann, Quantitative Models for Reverse Logistics. XI, 181 pages. 2001.

Vol. 502: N. Hadjisavvas, J. E. Martínez-Legaz, J.-P. Penot (Eds.), Generalized Convexity and Generalized Monotonicity. IX, 410 pages. 2001.

Vol. 503: A. Kirman, J.-B. Zimmermann (Eds.), Economics with Heterogenous Interacting Agents. VII, 343 pages. 2001.

Vol. 504: P.-Y. Moix (Ed.),The Measurement of Market Risk. XI, 272 pages. 2001.

Vol. 505: S. Voß, J. R. Daduna (Eds.), Computer-Aided Scheduling of Public Transport. XI, 466 pages. 2001.

Vol. 506: B. P. Kellerhals, Financial Pricing Models in Continuous Time and Kalman Filtering. XIV, 247 pages. 2001.

Vol. 507: M. Koksalan, S. Zionts, Multiple Criteria Decision Making in the New Millenium. XII, 481 pages. 2001.

Vol. 508: K. Neumann, C. Schwindt, J. Zimmermann, Project Scheduling with Time Windows and Scarce Resources. XI, 335 pages. 2002.

Vol. 509: D. Hornung, Investment, R&D, and Long-Run Growth. XVI, 194 pages. 2002.

Vol. 510: A. S. Tangian, Constructing and Applying Objective Functions. XII, 582 pages. 2002.

Vol. 511: M. Külpmann, Stock Market Overreaction and Fundamental Valuation. IX, 198 pages. 2002.

Vol. 512: W.-B. Zhang, An Economic Theory of Cities.XI, 220 pages. 2002.

Vol. 513: K. Marti, Stochastic Optimization Techniques. VIII, 364 pages. 2002.

Vol. 514: S. Wang, Y. Xia, Portfolio and Asset Pricing. XII, 200 pages. 2002.

Vol. 515: G. Heisig, Planning Stability in Material Requirements Planning System. XII, 264 pages. 2002.

Vol. 516: B. Schmid, Pricing Credit Linked Financial Instruments. X, 246 pages. 2002.